"My father, Maurice "Mice" Balma (RIP), retired in the early '80s after working 47 years for the Southern Pacific Railroad. I kept Mice busy in his golden years packaging Tracker Copers, Lappers and hardware. Three days a week, he would drive his 1964 El Camino up to Los Angeles, California to pick up and deliver Tracker castings at our foundry and polisher. As you can see, Mice had a little accident as he rolled some Tracker Sixtrack hangers up to the front door of our shop in Oceanside, circa mid 1980s."—Larry Balma

Built by John S. Morra in his high school woodshop class in June 1978, this yellow pine woodcut, based on William Sharp's photo of Jay Adams below, meaures 19" tall x 31 3/16" wide x 3/4" thick. Larry Balma bought it at the Del Mar Fair right after it was made.

Jay Adams, circa 1977. Photo: William Sharp

TRACKER

Forty Years *of* Skateboard History

By Larry Balma

FOUNDRY PRESS

Larry Balma

Publisher, Author: Larry Balma
Editor, Writer, Art Director, Photoshop Artist: Garry Davis
Associate Publisher, Project Manager, Curator: Louise Balma
Photo Editor, Studio Photographer: Lance Smith
Historical Consultant, Writer: Bryan Ridgeway
Photoshop Artist: Evan Shoman
Copy Editors: Peggy Cozens, Steve Vosseller
Videographer, Video Editor: Cameron Wetzler
Digital Media, Interviewer: Jake Stewart
Consultant, Writer: David Hackett
Consultant, Writer: Tony Magnusson
Special Contributors: Gary Dodds, Dave Dominy
Sales, Distribution: Max Dufour

Photographers: Grant Brittain (jgrantbrittainphotos.com), James Cassimus (cassimusfotos@cox.net), Glen E. Friedman (burningflags.com), Jim Goodrich (facebook.com/jimgoodrich214), Darryl Grogan (groganfilm@yahoo.com), Glenn Miyoda (gmiyoda@hotmail.com), Lance Smith (lancesmithphotography@gmail.com), CR Stecyk III

Contributing Photographers: Attila Aszodi, Mike Ballard, Larry Balma, Louise Balma, Maurice "Mice" Balma (RIP), Bob Ballou, Mike Baltes, David Barranco, Otis "O" Barthoulameu, Battipaglia, Don Baumea, Tim Bee, Bill Billing, Mike Bing (RIP), Mike Blake, Neil Blender, Warren Bolster (RIP), Sutherland Boswell, Dan Bourqui, Brans, Art Brewer, Brider, Jay Bridges, Neil Britt, Dobie Campbell, Marfa Capadanno, Maria Carrasco, Jeff Cole, Bruce Cooley, Peggy Cozens, Garry Davis, Joe D'Elia, Michelle D'Elia, Jesse de Martino, Marshall Denton, Depth Leviathan Dweller, Pete Diantoni, Ed Dominck, Di Dootson, Peder Draxton, Ed Economy, Chuck Edwall, Dan Estabrook, Frank Fahey, Craig Fineman (RIP), Brian Fink, Joel Freeman, Steve Gaidini, M Goldman, Larry Gordon Archives, James Gregory, Lucia Griggi, John Grigley, Erik Gross, David Hackett Archives, Boyd Harnell, Rusty Harris, Frank Hawk (RIP), Bruce Hazelton, Ed Hickey, Roger Hickey, Bruce Hitchcock, Per Holknekt, Chris Hooten, Marc Hostetter, Brad Jackman, Atiba Jefferson, Spencer Johnson, Thomas Kalak, Bryce Kanights, Billy Keiper, Peter Kiss, Kuda, Bucky Lasek, Johnny Law, Butch Lawson, Dominic Leonard, Stevan Levas, Lloyd, Patrick Malpass, Jon Malvino, Dan Mathieu, Matt Mecaro, Gary Medeiros (RIP), George Medino, Cheri Melville (RIP), Sonny Miller (RIP), Wynn Miller, Bill Minadio, Bev Morgan, Chip Morton, Guy Motil, Lance Mountain, Jeffery Moustache, Jeff Newton, Uli Niehwohner, Judah Oakes, Craig "Hector" Ogata, Chris Ortiz, Harold Osborne, Britt Parrot, Doug Pensinger, Sean Peterson, Joe Picciolo, William Pickett, Matt Pingel, Woody Porter, Linda Prettyman, Bob Pribble, Kevin Reed, Bryan Ridgeway, Rogers, Billy Ruff, Chuck Saccio, Davo Scheich, Shapiro, Stan Sharp (RIP), William Sharp, Steve Sherman, Adam Small, Kimathi Smith, Ralph Starkweather, Scott Starr, Dan Sturt, Sean Sullivan, Paul Sunman, Todd Swank, Eric Swanson, Dave Swift, Ted Terrebonne, Kevin Thatcher, Dean Tirkot, Seu Trinh, Mark Underwood, Val Valentine, Robert Vente, Miki Vuckovich, Mark Waters, Kris White, Steve Wilkings, Shelby Woods, Xeno, Chris Yandall (RIP), Tobin Yelland, John Yunker, Mark Zemnick

Acknowledgements: Michael Brooke, Monica Campana, Duncan Campbell, Buddy Carr, Steve Cathey, Adam Cozens, Dawn Dominy, Peter Ducommun, Mackenzie Eisenhour, Bob Feigel, Liam Ferguson, Jim Fitzpatrick, Norb Garrett, Daniel Gesmer, Larry Gordon, Keith Hamm, Jonathan Harms, Louie Hayward, Mike Horelick, Marc Hostetter, Russ Howell, Darren "Cookie" Jenkins, Paul Kobriger, David LeMothe, Keith Lenharr, Gordy, Lienemann, Monty Little, Monica Lucas, Ben Marcus, Dave McIntyre, John S. Morra, Jim O'Mahoney, John O'Malley, Stacy Peralta, Eric Schlitz, Laurie Balma Shoman, Chuck Silva, Dale Smith, Jack Smith, Craig Snyder, Jamey Stone, Dave Swift, Steve Van Doren, Miki Vuckovich, Mike Williams, Woody Woodward, John Wright, Tim Wrisley

Interviews: Jay Adams, Tony Alva, Gregg Ayres, Larry Balma, Sal Barbier, Bill Billing, Neil Blender, Beau Brown, Steve Caballero, Buddy Carr, David Carrasco, Rene Carrasco, Richy Carrasco, Kim Cespedes, Ron Chatman, Peggy Cozens, Bill Danforth, Garry Davis, Adrian Demain, Gary Dodds, Dave Dominy, Craig Dootson, Di Dootson, Max Dufour, Jason Ellis, Murray Estes, Steve Evans, Alan Gelfand, John Gibson, Jim Goodrich, Russ Gosnell, Jim Gray, David Hackett, Omar Hassan, Gunnar Haugo, Tony Hawk, Henry Hester, Paul Hoffman, Christian Hosoi, John Hughes, Kyle Jensen, Tony Jetton, Marty Jimenez, Hunter Joslin, Tom Karre, Lester Kasai, Jeremy Klein, Bucky Lasek, Brad Logan, Brian Logan, Bruce Logan, Robin Logan, Allen Losi, Chuy Madrigal, Tony Magnusson, Mike McGill, Patrick Melcher, Sonny Miller (RIP), David Paul, Bryan Pennington, Stacy Peralta, Laban Pheidias, Linda Prettyman, John Reeves, Bryan Ridgeway, Dan Rogers, Tommy Ryan, Willy Santos, Yo-Yo Schulz, Bob Skoldberg, Dale Smith, Lance Smith, Kevin Staab, CR Stecyk III, Kenneth Stelmasky, Michael Stelmasky, Chris Strople, Laura Thornhill, Jerry Valdez, Miki Vuckovich, Gregg Weaver, Dan Wilkes, Chris Yandall (RIP)

Magazines, Publications, Zines and Ads: *Action Now*, *Air*, Alva Skates, Bahne, *Bail*, Bennett, *Big Brother*, *Concrete Wave*, *Death Zone*, *DogTown - The Legend of the Z-Boys* (Glen E. Friedman and CR Stecyk III photographs printed with permission from the book *DogTown - The Legend of the Z-Boys* courtesy of Burning Flags Press), G&S Skateboards, *Good Grief*, *Juice*, *Kamikaze*, Kronik, Lip Slider, Logan Earth Ski, Lotus, *Monster Magazine*, John S. Morra, *Ollie Magazine*, San Diego Union Tribune, SBC, Sims, *Skate*, *Skate Attack*, *Skateboard!*, *Skateboarder*, *The Skateboard Mag*, *Skateboard Plus*, *Skateboard World*, *Skate Fate*, *Skateline*, *Skate Punk*, Skull Skates, *Speeed Zine*, *Thrasher*, *TransWorld Business*, *TransWorld Skateboarding*, Tunnel, World Industries

TRACKER – Forty Years of Skateboard History is distributed through
Pure Distribution 3820 Oceanic Drive #311, Oceanside, California 92056 USA (760) 722-1455 trackertrucks.com
Publisher: Foundry Press 517 Seagaze Drive Unit 88, Oceanside, California 92049 USA

Library of Congress control cataloging in publication data is available.
ISBN 978-0-692-34073-8

Printed in PRC • Designed in USA • First Edition

TRACKER TRUCKS™

being there

"Madman" Balma, still in the garage. A.S.R. Trade Show, San Diego, January '91.

BACK TO ROOTS

I've always believed the garage is a special place. It's not where we park our cars, it's where we invent our dreams. As a sacred place, the garage rates right up there with the local church—and for some of us, it's an even more useful sanctuary.

In the garage, you can play music as loud as you want. Get your hands dirty. Let your body relax. Set your mind free.

Ever since I was a kid, the garage was where I dreamed, tinkered and created. I'd build go carts, motor scooters, or whatever—discovering the rush of engineering things that work. When you find something that is designed just right, you know it. You feel the fit, the function, the finesse. Like the '56 pickup I drove out of the showroom with my dad. I raced it, hauled fish in it, showed off to the girls in it. And I spent a lot of hours under the hood.

I went from working on my pickup, to making surfboards, to designing skateboards—but the whole point has always been to build something that goes fast, looks good, and is capable of putting you in places that scare the hell out of you.

By 1975, I was manufacturing skateboard trucks in the garage with my partners, Dave Dominy and Gary Dodds, and continuing research and development that would revolutionize the skateboard in the coming years. A few other skateboarders, inventors, and entrepreneurs were busy in their garages at the same time. Together, we created a whole new industry.

That's another great use the garage has: it's a place to start a new business. The U.S. Department of Commerce says 80% of all the new jobs created during the last decade were in small companies of less than 50 people. It wasn't the corporate gi-

ants who were putting people to work in this country; it was the guy making speaker cabinets, silk-screen prints, or urethane wheels in his garage.

My garage has served as assembly plant, warehouse, office, design lab, and local gathering spot. Any skateboard company worth its salt can probably say the same. It's where the kids hang, where the juice flows, where stuff happens; it's my roots.

Larry

LARRY BALMA

PUBLISHER
MANUFACTURER
MASTER DISTRIBUTOR

Being There, *TransWorld Skateboarding Business*, May 1991, Volume 2 Number 5.

4

CONTENT

Left: **Marty Grimes** busts a stylish high-speed backside carve grind at Oxnard skatepark in Oxnard, California, December 1977. Photo: Jim Goodrich
Front cover: **The quintessential Tracker pro, Tony Hawk,** lifts a table top lien air out of the keyhole and in your face at Del Mar Skate Ranch in Del Mar, California, circa 1987. Del Mar is in North San Diego County, which is home turf to both Tony and Tracker. Photo: Grant Brittain
Back cover: **Jay Adams (RIP)** slashes Gonzo's pool in Los Angeles, California, circa 1977. Photo: William Sharp

INTRODUCTION

A Permanent Part of the American Landscape

Skateboarding is a funny thing. To some, it's a competitive sport. To others, it's a lifestyle and an art form. Some simply use it as a convenient means of transportation. Skateboarding has been a saving grace to so many who would have otherwise drowned in life; many found skateboarding a way to identify themselves, and it gave them a sense of purpose. Others have come into skateboarding, enjoyed it for a while and then moved on. A few found fame and fortune. To some who don't skate, it's a nuisance. Most who ride are hooked for life. Skateboarding is really one of the most versatile and innovative activities of modern life.

But before it became so, a few things had to happen: for one, youth culture needed to arrive at a point where individual achievement was celebrated and doing your own thing became the cool thing, which started to happen in the early 1960s. Skateboarding rose and fell quickly then. It didn't last because the crude equipment just couldn't accommodate what skateboarding was destined to be. The steel and clay wheels just didn't work well enough for skateboarding to flourish, and the technology for trucks that existed then wasn't designed to be any better than the wheels. So, the whole experience was quite lackluster and non-functional.

If you don't skate, it's hard to imagine just how crude the skateboards of the '60s were and the incredible advancement made in skateboard technology just a few years later—after the invention of the urethane wheel in the early '70s. A good comparison would be an old rotary telephone compared to a modern iPhone or a wooden wagon wheel to a modern car wheel; it really was that much of a difference. Urethane is an incredibly resilient and wear-resistant plastic-like material that seemed like it was specifically invented for skateboarding. Although it was derived from the space program and first applied to roller skating rinks, millions of kids seeking a new alternative lifestyle didn't care where it came from, just that it was perfect for skateboarding.

But then there was a problem: urethane wheels allowed skaters to really push the limits of what skateboards could do, but the other two components, the trucks and the boards, weren't quite ready for prime time. This inspired a few passionate designers to scramble to produce parts that could keep up. Building strong and lightweight skateboard decks wasn't exactly rocket science, but strong and lightweight trucks were another story. Trucks are like the suspension on a car, they determine your ability to turn and how fast that can happen. Strength is critical, as urethane wheels allowed skaters to bomb hills at over 50 mph. At those speeds, you can't afford to have trucks fail in any way. Even at lower speeds, when a rider is in the middle of a critical move, truck failures are perilous. Skateboarding relies a lot on "board feel" and most of that comes from the trucks. Most professional riders deplore changing old and worn-

in trucks for new ones. Board feel is essential and is only acquired over time using the best trucks.

In 1975, Southern California surfers and skateboarders Larry Balma, Dave Dominy and Gary Dodds found themselves right in the middle of this skateboard revolution. They saw a need for trucks that skaters could really trust to deliver a matching performance to the urethane wheel and the newer boards that were coming onto the market with ferocious speed. Tracker Trucks was born in Southern California, which would become the center of the universe for skateboarding. In 1976, the area experienced a major drought and people had to empty their swimming pools. With urethane wheels, Tracker Trucks and modern laminated maple board designs, skateboarders found what would be a lifelong passion: riding these brand new and improved skateboards that had the quality and strength to withstand the intense pressure of pool riding.

Getting vertical was the new mantra, and it wasn't

long before these pool warriors invented a new move that would require the trucks to withstand a whole new assault on its properties: the frontside grind. Riders would smash their rear truck into the concrete coping, which was designed for swimmers to grab, making it one of the most important elements of modern pool skating. The coping was there to grind on, to use as a takeoff point for riders to fly into the air high above the edge of the pool and then land back on the vertical surface to continue the ride of a lifetime. With each new move invented, further demands were placed on the equipment—especially the trucks—and Tracker was not only busy making them for millions of skaters, but also heavily involved in making sure that the trucks progressed in strength and performance to accommodate a seemingly endless demand on them to perform.

If a truck failed when a rider landed a six-foot air, a major slam was the usual aftermath. Tracker Trucks quickly became the "trucks you can trust" and the choice for most of the original professional skateboarders: guys like Jay Adams, Stacy Peralta, David Hackett and many others. By 1978, concrete skateparks were built for skateboarding, all with the swimming pool concept as the center of the design. However, the skatepark pools were much bigger than your average backyard swimming pool, which allowed for even more radical maneuvers. By this time, punk rock and other revolutionary music movements converged with skateboarding, and a whole new attitude toward what it meant being young in America was in full swing. Not everyone was all that happy with skateboarders or the new youth culture being built by the pioneers of skateboarding as a lifestyle and youth movement. With their freewheeling attitude toward life, skateboarders engaged in what seemed like a tough and dangerous activity, which had a way of offending the sensibilities of most average people.

Ten years later, circa 1988, skateboarding had grown into a worldwide phenomenon and a new form of skateboarding was about to take shape: street skating. A whole generation of younger riders discovered that a lot of modern architecture in the urban landscape was perfectly suitable for this new style of skateboarding. It was also a declaration of war of sorts with local communities, who now saw skateboarders in front of the grocery store and other highly public locations instead of just being limited to backyard ramps and skateparks. The modern street skaters had the benefit of riding equipment that had gone through 15 years of torturous testing by vert and pool skaters, so they could trust the modern boards—especially the trucks—to allow them to essentially jump off of buildings with their skateboards and live to tell about it.

Tracker Trucks played a huge role in supporting the entire modern skateboarding movement, and more tricks were invented on Trackers than any other. Through the years, hundreds of professional riders have trusted the most important component of their skateboard, Tracker Trucks, including the most notable skateboarder of all time, Tony Hawk. Thanks to Tracker and all of the other quality skateboard brands of the 1970s and '80s, the lifestyle, maneuvers and general philosophy of skateboarding have grown to become a permanent part of the American landscape.—**Tony Magnusson**

Skateboarding's
BIG BANG
The Urethane Wheel Revolution

Frank Nasworthy did not invent urethane wheels, but he was the first to slap a set on a skateboard. In 1970, this Navy brat was just out of high school and living in Virginia when he visited Creative Urethane, a company that made urethane wheels for roller skate rinks. As soon as he glanced at a large barrel of the magical cylinders in their warehouse, a light bulb went off in his head: "Those would be perfect for my skateboard!" Soon after, Frank and his friends became the first people in the world to ride skateboards with urethane wheels, at least three years before anyone else! Inspired by the smooth, grippy ride the wheels provided, Frank eventually started Cadillac Wheels, and by 1973, found himself driving all over Southern California to sell them to surf shops. Frank had no idea then that his application of this miracle compound would go on to provide creative fun for millions of people. Just think about it. Without the urethane wheel, there would be no Bert, no Ollie, no McTwist, no Gonz, no handrails, no loop, no mega ramp, no way! Simply put, the Cadillac wheel was the Big Bang of modern skateboarding that directly inspired all subsequent skateboard companies to set up shop, including Tracker. Our story starts here.—**GSD**

Thanes: Stacy Peralta Waxes Poetic on the Wheel

I had heard about these mysterious Cadillac wheels; that they were supposedly coming out and they were made of urethane. I had no idea what urethane was, but I knew it was made from petroleum. I flipped when I saw how expensive they were. I couldn't believe they were selling individual skateboard wheels for 50 cents each, a set costing two dollars. That was a ton of money considering the minimum wage was 65 cents per hour at that time, and all of the previous skateboard wheels we had ridden cost us pennies from thrift stores. So, due to the price, I was not the first kid on my block to have them, and I didn't trust they were going to live up to their building reputation.

Finally, one of my best friends from down the block, Kevin Farlee, was the first skater I knew who bought a set of Cadillac wheels. He was the very first, and I'd been skating with him since I was 12. He came up to my house one day after school to show them to me, we were both 15 years old. I looked them over and found them fascinating. I'd never seen skateboard wheels that glowed, that were semi-transparent. My reaction was probably similar to that of a primitive man seeing fire for the first time. It just didn't seem possible. Kevin then told me he was now able to do hard turns on a skateboard and not slide out, which we always did with hard clay wheels. (When you turned hard on clay wheels, your board just slid out as if you were riding on ice.) It all sounded good, but I still found it so difficult to believe, primarily because it was too good to be true. We had ridden wheels made of Flintstones technology for so long.

So, I got on his board, pushed out of my driveway and did a leaning hard left turn onto the sidewalk and the wheels gripped. They didn't slide out; they gripped like nothing I'd ever ridden. I simply couldn't believe how revolutionary they were. They were super smooth in a way I had never experienced while skating: they rode over cracks, they rode over dreaded pebbles and they rode over bad concrete. The leverage we now had was so profound; we could begin to skate the way we used to dream about. The Cadillac wheel liberated us, freed us. We could do anything now—and thus the real revolution began.—**Stacy Peralta**

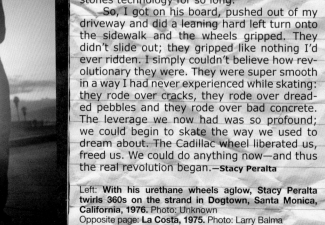

Left: **With his urethane wheels aglow, Stacy Peralta twirls 360s on the strand in Dogtown, Santa Monica, California, 1976.** Photo: Unknown
Opposite page: **La Costa, 1975.** Photo: Larry Balma

7

Riding for Alva Skates and Tracker Trucks, David Hackett blasts a huge frontside air in his final run at the Marina Dog Bowl Pro, landing in third place (the highest placing Dogtown local), April 29, 1979. Photo: Craig Fineman

FOREWORD
Trucks You Can Trust

I broke my arm skateboarding when the pivot busted off of my little Chicago trucks as I blazed down the big hill at Paul Revere Jr. High School in 1975. I was 15. My dad was so pissed, he sawed my skateboard in half, said I could never ride one again, and that skateboarders were "outlaws, losers and drug addicts who would never amount to anything in this world." Just a little before that, Cadillac urethane wheels had literally revolutionized skateboarding overnight by allowing riders the ability to take their bodies and boards past the limits of what was previously thought possible. At that point, they were pushing the limits on all terrain: pools, parks, pipes, bowls, ditches, banks, streets and more. With urethane wheels in place, we needed some solid trucks we could trust that would match their performance. At the time, skateboards contained trucks that were designed for roller skates with narrow, archaic, un-heat treated, pressed steel hangers that were dangerous and performance-limiting, to say the least.

1975 was the same year I won the junior men's slalom event at the Hang Ten World Pro-Am Championships on September 20 at the Los Angeles Sports Arena. (Jay Adams won the junior men's freestyle and obstacle course race.) After that win, I started getting free equipment and sponsorship offers, so I had the opportunity to test and / or ride almost any combination of trucks, wheels and decks that I wanted, which was every young skater's dream! The first three trucks I knew of that were specifically designed for skateboarding and met the performance level of the new urethane wheels were Bahne, Bennett and Tracker. I had already bent the Bahne trucks jumping off of a loading dock behind the Mayfair Market in Malibu. With its all-steel stamped and welded construction, Bahne boasted "safety and high performance," as well as a metal-to-metal pivot pin, which they claimed would eliminate breakage and wheel wobble.

I can't count how many of Bennett's plastic baseplates I broke. This was also around the time we started to grind our back axles on the coping of ditches and makeshift ramps complete with broomstick coping! Even though the Bennett truck turned better than the Bahne, it just wasn't a good truck for grinding with its square axle hanger. Enter the Tracker Fultrack, which was more than twice as wide as a roller skate truck, and beefy! I will never forget the first time I laid my eyes on a set: they were mounted on a G&S Fibreflex slalom board, set up with OJ wheels and precision bearings. Remember, I had just won the slalom title on a deck I made in woodshop class set up with Sure Grip trucks and Roller Sports urethane loose ball bearing wheels, so I was starting to take racing slalom seriously.

I practiced running cones in the upper parking lot at Pacific Palisades High School, which contained a hill that was smooth, fast and perfect. I heard there were fast guys racing and practicing there, so I hitched a ride up, and to my surprise, there were some of the guys who had been coming up to bomb the hills in my Malibu neighborhood of Sunset Mesa! I'm talking about famous local Topanga / Malibu surfers and skaters I had seen in *Surfer* and *Skateboarder* magazines, like Torger Johnson, Woody Woodward, Danny Bearer, Craig Collidge, George Trafton, Craig Halley and Robbie Dick, along with a few San Diego cats like Gary "King Fish" Coccaro, Joe Roper and others. Most of them were riding Logan Earth Ski decks with Tracker Trucks.

These men showed me how to log my times and push my limits to go faster and turn quicker than ever before—all because one of them showed up with a G&S slalom board mounted with Tracker Fultracks and OJ wheels. When he let me try it through the cones, it was like I was racing a brand-new Porsche compared to my old board, which was a beat up VW bus. Holy shit! I was blown away. In that one instant, I realized that everything was coming together at the same time in perfect unison: a symbiotic performance relationship that was beyond what I thought was ever possible. I was now riding a deck that could maximize the torque of each turn into a faster and more efficient forward thrust with wheels that had superior grip, rebound and speed—all held together with the most precise turning high-tech performance steering system ever developed specifically for skateboarding. My very next run through those cones was almost two seconds faster! It was incredible. I had to have that skateboard!

Unfortunately, that guy would not sell it or let me have it, but he did show up at most of our weekly practice sessions, so I got to ride it as much as I wanted until I convinced him to let me ride it in my first real pro contest against some real pro racers at the 1976 Magic Mountain Masters. There, I placed second in the men's pro slalom behind Tony Alva and second in the men's pro obstacle course behind Bob Skoldberg. And I was only 16 years old! I realized it was the combination of components on this magic board—specifically the Tracker Trucks—that also played a big role in Alva and Skoldberg's win, as I noticed that both of them were also running Trackers. Thanks to Trackers, I had proven myself against some of the heaviest racers of the time. I started to get invited on skate trips all over California by older guys who took me under their wing. One of the first journeys was down south to San Diego to ride and race on the perfect blacktop hills of La Costa, which was the holy Mecca of slalom and downhill racing in skateboarding. Man, was I stoked!

When I got there, it was surreal. Skateboarders everywhere: young and old, girls and boys, freestylers doing nose wheelies, other riders bombing the hill, and of course, a loosely organized dual slalom course where the heavies raced for cash. All of the dudes I had seen

in the magazines were there! Denis Shufeldt, Chris Yandall, Bob Skoldberg, Danny Trailer, Vince Turner, the whole Logan family—Brian, Bruce, Brad and Robin—Laura Thornhill, Di Dootson, Steve Sherman, Lance Smith, Tom Padaka, Mike Williams, Skip Frye, Dale Dobson, and of course the King of the Hill, Henry Hester. Most of them were riding and racing on Tracker Trucks with a few Gullwings mixed in. I realized then that Tracker was dominating the slalom and skateboard racing scene, which I was now a part of.

Between 1975 and 1977, skateboarding changed rapidly on all fronts, including the technological breakthroughs of equipment, discovery of new terrain, regional and world contests, team formation and most importantly, the advancement of state-of-the-art, high-performance maneuvers. Back in the '70s, skateboarders rode all terrain and pursued all disciplines, including pools, parks, banks, schools, streets, freestyle, slalom, downhill and also stand alone events such as barrel jump and high jump, consecutive 360s, one wheelers or highest air. If you were a skateboarder, that's just what you did, you rode it all. At the time, Tracker was clearly the dominant truck brand among almost every champion pro skateboarder and young gun coming up who were looking to make a name for themselves. That included me.

Once I established myself as a fast racer, and since I was already riding a G&S Fibreflex, I was asked if I wanted to become part of the G&S team. On paper, it looked like a good fit: I was a young surfer / skateboarder and I was clean cut...or so they thought. I didn't have a car or even a license to drive yet, so I had to get a ride down to the G&S factory to talk to the team manager, Dave "Fibrefats" McIntyre, to close the deal. When I got there, he asked me if I wanted to be on the team. I said, "Yes." He asked, "What do you want?" I said, "To start, I need a box of 27", 29" and 30" Stacy Peralta Warptails, a box of Road Rider 2s and 4s, a box of precision German bearings, a whole roll of grip tape and a box of Tracker Trucks!" He was stunned. No one had ever asked for so much equipment. I told him that I probably wouldn't be able to get down to San Diego for another six months and I'd break all of this stuff by then anyway, except for the Tracker Trucks. In his toughest voice, Dave said, "Oh, okay, David! Take whatever you need. Welcome to the team." I replied with, "Oh, and I need a new surfboard, too!" So, I grabbed one at the G&S shop next door as I made my way out to the car!

A few weeks after I got on the G&S team, I received in the mail a super light 29" G&S Fibreflex Bowlrider deck with a note that said, "Please test." It arrived at the exact time I received another new product called Suspenders, which were Velcro straps that attached your feet to your skateboard, allowing you to fly off of the riding surface. At that time in skateboarding history, the very first airs on vertical were already being done by Tony Alva, Tom Inouye, Jay Adams and George Orton—all at about the same time and all on Trackers! But, no one had done a hand held air higher than maybe two feet. Orton blasted the highest frontside stinkbugs at the time in the two or maybe two-and-a-half foot range, and Inouye and Adams were doing tail tap-style backside airs out of the second bowl at the new Reseda skatepark. Alva blasted some of the first—if not *the* first—and for sure the most stylish tuck knee frontside airs in the Dog Bowl.

As corny as it sounds now, back then everything was wide open to experimentation in an effort to push the limits of realistic possibility. So, in my mind, I wasn't just a slalom racer, I was an all-around skater just like my mentors Torger Johnson, Tony Alva and Stacy Peralta. So, I set my sights on being the first to do the highest airs ever out of a pool or bowled riding surface. I immediately set up this new, light Fibreflex Bowlrider with the strongest trucks, Trackers, and softest wheels, red Kryptonics, and took it to Reseda skatepark. I knew the G&S deck was strong enough and light enough to take to the air with the Velcro bindings, the soft red Kryptonics wheels would provide somewhat of a cushion for landing high airs on concrete, and that the Trackers were the only trucks I could trust not to break or bend during any harsh landings. Believe me, I already had more bad landings than I'd like to remember. The end result was that the combination of these components all working in unison allowed me to realize my goal of blasting the first backside airs in the three to three-and-a-half foot range—some of them even higher. When those photos came out in *Skateboarder* magazine, I had finally arrived. People, and most importantly, other skateboarders took note. Assisted with Velcro or not, those airs were higher than anything before and put me on the map in the skateboard world.

Trackers were the trucks I trusted to make it happen and save me from getting seriously injured while trying crazy things like strapping my feet to a skateboard and catching big air in 1977 and pulling off the loop in 2006 at age 46. Woo-hoo! Likewise, Trackers are the trucks most skateboarders have trusted to not only improve their own performance, but also invent many of the basic tricks all modern day skateboarding maneuvers are based upon. Early freestyle tricks, countless slalom and downhill race championships, the first airs on vertical, the Ollie, the Boneless One, the McTwist—the list goes on and on. Roger Hickey won 314 races and 20 World Championships on Trackers, and during his reign as the most winning and famous professional skateboarder in history, Tony Hawk won more contests and invented more tricks on Trackers than I have the space to list!

In my 35-plus years of professional skateboarding, I've ridden for quite a few other truck companies including Gullwing, Independent, Thunder, Randal, and Radi-

kal. However, I have always felt proud and honored to be one of the original members of the Tracker family. So, now that you've finished reading this foreword, sit down and get comfortable, because you're in for a long journey and a real trip down skateboarding's memory lane. Enjoy reading the behind-the-scenes stories of the men and women who formed Tracker's rich legacy, and looking at all of the amazing photos of the many skateboarders sponsored by the brand that has solidly woven itself into the fabric of the history of skateboarding like no other. Forty years of skateboard evolution—full of integrity, dignity, class and style—with respect for all skateboarders, worldwide, who are all part of the family. Tracker: Trucks You Can Trust Since 1975. Enjoy the ride.—**David "HACKMAN!" Hackett**

Above: **Ageless and shirtless, David Hackett puts his new Tracker Axis Jay Adams trucks to the test on a stylish and mean layback in Oceanside, California, 2014.** Photo: Lance Smith
Opposite page: **A hungry Alva-esque Hackett shocks the skateboard racing world at the 1976 Magic Mountain Masters by capturing two third places and a second place behind Tracker riders Tony Alva and Bob Skoldberg.** Photo: Hackett Archives

1900s-1970s
Skateboarding Timeline

1760-1862 · A crude form of roller skates gets the ball rolling.

1863 · Designed by James Plimpton, the modern four-wheel roller skate contains the first real trucks with rubber cushions that turn via a pivoting action. In the future, these trucks will prove to be perfect for skateboards.

Early 1900s · Inspired by motorcycles, kids make wood crate scooters using 2" x 4"s with a roller skate truck nailed on each end and a wood fruit crate nailed to the front with a wood handlebar. The kids make motorcycle sounds as they ecstatically race through their neighborhoods.

1922 · Sitting on a board on top of a large clamp-on steel wheel roller skate, Clarence Sherrill rides downhill luge-style.

1925 · The first known production street luge, the Kne Koster, is built with trucks that turn by leaning like roller skates. The board is ridden on your knees, lying down face first like a sled, or sitting luge-style while grabbing the side rails. Measuring 9" x 35 ½", the Kne Koster features 5 ½" diameter wagon wheels with

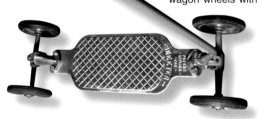

rubber tires, 6" wide steel axles and a wood deck with grab rails.

1940 · Chicago Roller Skate Co. offers the first inner cone for solid wood roller skate wheels and cone nuts using replaceable loose ball bearings.

1945-1951 · The Skeeter Skate debuts as the first scooter with aluminum roller skate-style trucks, which measure 7" wide. It also includes four 6" wagon wheels with rubber tires and an aluminum deck measuring 7 ½" x 16" with a very low roll center. With the handle removed, the Skeeter Skate can be ridden like a skateboard. The second generation introduces a streamlined steel deck with a slightly higher roll center and a slower turning angle.

1947 · Windansea surfer Peter Parkin of La Jolla, California nails roller skates to a 2" x 4" with no handle and invents the first documented stand-up skateboard. While riding his board down to the beach, he unknowingly starts a whole new sport. Surfers begin to experience the feeling of surfing on asphalt and concrete.

1956 · Chicago Roller Skate Co. is the first to

produce clay composition rubber roller skate wheels. Mixed with rubber, then compressed and vulcanized, clay results in a hard wheel that rolls fast on smooth surfaces.

1960 · Tresco debuts the plywood Skee-Skate with steel wheels, which is arguably the first commercial skateboard. Although Humco is granted a patent for the Humco Surfer skateboard in 1958, the company doesn't actually produce it until 1963, when Roller Derby, Nash, Sidewalk Surfer and others enter the scene. These skateboards sell at toy and department stores and some pharmacies.

1962 · Kids begin referring to skateboarding as sidewalk surfing. The strong connection with surfing gives skateboarding a direction that influences everything to come, from maneuvers and style to fashion and attitude.
· Southern California surf shop Val Surf begins making its own skateboards. Owner Bill Richards makes a deal with the Chicago Roller Skate Company to produce sets of skate wheels, attaching them to squared-off wooden boards. Val Surf is the first known surf shop to sell skateboards.

1963 · After watching surfers ride skateboards when the waves are flat, Larry Stevenson designs and manufactures Makaha skateboards out of sturdy oak with two revolutionary components: clay composite roller rink wheels and the first double-action adjustable trucks, made by Chicago.
· The first known organized skateboard contest, sponsored by Makaha, is held at the Pier Avenue Junior High School in Hermosa, California.

1964 · Hansen surfboards produce the first pro model skateboard decks for world champion surfers L.J. Richards and Linda Benson. Makaha produces the Phil Edwards pro model for Hobie one month later, and sponsors the first skateboard team.
· Working with Bill Richards at Val Surf, surfing legend Hobie Alter introduces the Hobie Super Surfer skateboard. Hobie later teams up with Baron Hilton and the Vita Pakt juice company to create Hobie Skateboards.
· Larry Gordon and Floyd Smith, co-founders of Gordon & Smith Surfboards, develop a revolutionary new manufacturing process that combines fiberglass-reinforced epoxy Bo-Tuff with a maple wood core to create the G&S Fibreflex skateboard. This is the first laminated deck created for the skateboard market.
· Larry Stevenson from Makaha buys some urethane wheels from Chicago Roller Works to test on his skateboard. They work well, but the price is too exorbitant. Nearly 10 years will pass before urethane is finally used for skateboard wheels.
· Surfer Publications debuts *The Quarterly Skateboarder* magazine.

· The musical group Jan and Dean appear on Dick Clark's *American Bandstand* to sing "Sidewalk Surfin'." Dean performs a few tricks and rides a board across the stage.
· Makaha team member, Jim Fitzpatrick, goes on a two-month, 14-country tour to promote Makaha and introduce skateboarding to countries all over Europe and the UK.
· Upcoming talent includes Danny Bearer, Joey Cabell, Jim Fitzpatrick, John Freis, Skip Frye, Davey Hilton, Stevie Hilton, Skitch Hitchcock, Mike Hynson, Torger Johnson, Bruce Logan, Pat McGee, Tommy Ryan, Joey Saenz, Danny Schaefer, Denis Shufeldt, Bob Skoldberg, George Trafton and Woody Woodward.

1965 · While most skateboarders take to the streets or sidewalks, some begin to explore riding more radical terrain like banks and swimming pools. The first documented backyard pool sessions occur in Menlo Park near San Francisco, California, as shown in the debut issue of *The Quarterly Skateboarder*, and Foxtail Park near Santa Monica.
· The world's first known skatepark, Surf City, opens in Tucson, Arizona, consisting of nothing more than flowing sidewalks.
· Skateboard companies struggle to keep up with demand as skateboarding becomes very popular and widespread.
· A year after Larry Stevenson, Hobie Alter also looks into using urethane for skateboard wheels, but is turned down by Vita-Pakt executives because the price is too high.
· Randolph Mfg. Co. debuts the world's first skate-

board shoe, the Randy 720.
• San Diego skateboarder, Pat Mc-Gee, is featured on the covers of *Life* and *Skateboarder* magazines.
• After publishing two issues, *The Quarterly Skateboarder* shortens its name to *Skateboarder Magazine*, which runs for two more issues before calling it quits.
• The first skateboard movie, *Skater Dater*, is released and later wins an Academy Award for Best Movie Short.
• The first skateboard organization, the National Skateboard Championships Association is formed in Anaheim, California.
• On May 22-23, the International Skateboard Championships are held in Anaheim, California, and are shown on ABC's *Wide World of Sports*. John Freis wins the Overall title.
• Many public officials and safety organizations begin condemning skateboarding as unsafe, urging stores not to sell skateboards and parents not to buy them. Many cities start banning skateboarding on public streets. The fad thus dies quickly, primarily due to inferior product (steel and clay wheels), too much inventory and a public upset by reckless riding.

Tom Calvin gets edgy in the shallow end of the Kona Bowl in Escondido, California, circa 1977. Photo: Lance Smith
Below: **The premiere issue of *The Quarterly Skateboarder*, Winter 1964.** Photo: Bev Morgan
Opposite page, left to right: **Skeeter Skate, 1945. Style master Danny Bearer hangs 10, 1965.** Photo: James Gregory
Roller Derby ad, 1964.

1966 • Surfer's World, the world's second known skatepark, opens in Anaheim, California. Hobie and Vita Pakt sponsor a contest at the newly-opened park. Other skateparks are built in Orange County, California and Kelso, Washington. All of these parks consist of simple sidewalk-inspired designs.
• Vans shoes get their start in the surf and skateboard scene after brothers Jim and Paul Van Doren build a shoe factory in Anaheim, later opening a chain of stores in California.
• The National Film Board of Canada releases *The Devil's Toy*, a documentary movie about the skateboarding craze in Montreal.

1968 • Skip Engblom, Jeff Ho and CR Stecyk III co-found Zephyr Surfboards in Santa Monica, California. Zephyr will go on to play a profound role in skateboarding in the 1970s.

1969 • Larry Stevenson invents and patents the kicktail. Though not accepted at first, other manufacturers eventually copy the idea. Most skateboard brands balk at paying a royalty to Stevenson and he eventually loses his patent rights in court. Gordon & Smith, Hobie, Sure Grip, and Logan Earth Ski are the only brands who agree to pay a royalty on Stevenson's design.

1970 • Frank Nasworthy visits Creative Urethane in Virginia and grabs some urethane roller skate wheels to put on his skateboard. Blown away by the smooth, grippy ride, he works on bringing them to market.

1973 • La Costa in northern San Diego County becomes the most popular local skateboard spot in history. The hillside streets and sidewalks, which have been built in preparation for a new housing tract (the construction of which is delayed for

years), become a Mecca for skateboarders from all over southern California.
• Frank Nasworthy teams up with Bahne to debut Cadillac wheels, the first urethane wheels made exclusively for skateboarding. Offering a vastly superior ride to clay or steel, Cadillac wheels single-handedly kickstart the rebirth of skateboarding.
• Inspired by Cadillac, board manufacturers spring up everywhere; the industry is booming with new products and ideas.
• Northern California surfing buddies, Rich Novak, Doug Haut and Jay Shuirman, join forces to form NHS, the powerhouse behind Santa Cruz Skateboards.

1974 • In their January issue, *Surfer* magazine publishes an article on the resurgence of skateboarding.
• Larry Balma, Dave Dominy and Gary Dodds work on developing the Tracker Fultrack, a wider, more stable truck for use in the slalom races at La Costa in North San Diego County. Trackers are the first truck that can handle the more aggressive skateboarding that is developing at the time.
• After a 10-year hiatus, Gordon & Smith resumes production on its popular Fibreflex skateboard line.

1975 • Kent Sherwood (Jay Adams' stepfather) is approached by Jeff Ho, Skip Engblom and CR Stecyk III of Zephyr Surf Shop to create a fiberglass Zephyr skateboard. The Zephyr skateboard team is formed, with Jay Adams, Tony Alva, Bob Biniak, Shogo Kubo, Jim Muir, Nathan Pratt, Stacy Peralta, and Wentzle Ruml IV as the original members. Paul Constantineau and Peggy Oki join later.
• Tom Sims begins manufacturing the first Sims skateboards.
• Tracker, Bennett and Bahne debut the first trucks ever designed specifically for skateboarding.

• The first reverse kingpin trucks, Speed Springs, debut to marginal success because of their metal spring cushioning and slow turning angle. In 1976, they replace the spring with skateboarding's first urethane cushion, but the slow-turning trucks never really catch on.
• Mike Rector and Bob Wolfe create the first safety gear designed specifically for skateboarders.
• Jessup markets the first grip tape for skateboards.
• *Skateboard Handbook* magazine is published by James O'Mahoney.
• After producing four issues in 1964-'65, *Skateboarder* magazine resumes publishing bi-monthly.
• The movie *Spinnin' Wheels* is released, featuring the talents of Larry Bertleman, Henry Hester, Skitch Hitchcock, Torger Johnson, the Logans, Ty Page, Mike Weed and others. The film opens with the first skateboarding animation clip by John Lamb.
• The Bahne-Cadillac National Championships lead to the creation of the first skateboarding celebrities, who are heavily featured in the magazines. The appearance of the Z-Boys, with their unique, low-slung, aggressive surf-skate style, causes a major sensation and controversy at the competition, which mostly consists of stick man gymnastic moves.
• USSA President Jim O' Mahoney produces the first World Skateboard Championships at Jack Murphy Stadium in San Diego, California, including freestyle, slalom, high jump, barrel jump, etc. Jim also holds a downhill race at Signal Hill, California for *The Guinness Book of World Records* TV show. Most experts claim this event is the first true, sanctioned downhill skateboard race. Guy Grundy clocks in at 50.2 miles per hour, which nets him a trophy and entry into the *Guinness Book*.
• Upcoming talent includes Tony Alva, Steve Cathey, Russ Howell, Stacy Peralta, Tom Sims, Bruce Walker, Greg Weaver and Chris Yandall.

1976 • The Zephyr team begins breaking up. Kent Sherwood starts making his own boards called Z-Flex, taking Jay Adams, Tony Alva and Jim Muir with him. Adams, Alva and Bob Biniak later switch to Logan Earth Ski, and Stacy Peralta moves over to Gordon & Smith. Shogo Kubo is the only one who

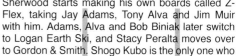

Alan Gelfand pops an early Ollie on one of the first halfpipe ramps anywhere to sport flat bottom, Hollywood, Florida, circa 1979. Photo: Glen E. Friedman
Below: **Gregg Weaver scores the first cover of the re-launched** *Skateboarder,* **Winter 1975.** Photo: Warren Bolster

clocks in at 54 mph while riding luge-style.
• Upcoming talent includes Jay Adams, Kevin Anderson, Waldo Autry, Paul Constantineau, Guy Grundy, Henry Hester, Paul Hoffman, Doug Saladino, Laura Thornhill and Mike Weed.

1977 • From the summer of 1976 through 1978, many new skateparks begin construction around the United States, especially in southern California. Some of the most popular parks in the Los Angeles area are Big O, Concrete Wave, Lakewood, Oxnard, Pipeline, Reseda, Skatopia and Whittier. The main San Diego skateparks are Carlsbad, Del Mar, El Cajon, La Mesa, Movin' On, Oasis and Vista. The main skateparks in the San Francisco Bay Area are Campbell, Milpitas, Newark and Winchester. Some of the best parks across the rest of the country are Cherry Hill (New Jersey), Clearwater (Florida), Kona (Jacksonville, Florida), Rainbow Wave (Tampa, Florida), Sensation Basin (Gainesville, Florida) and Solid Surf (Fort Lauderdale, Florida). Wally Hollyday, Jack Graham and John O'Malley are the main skatepark designers and builders at the time.
• Top pros from California session the massive 22-foot diameter concrete Desert Pipes in Arizona.
• Tom Stewart builds the world's first halfpipe out of plywood in the front yard at his house in Encinitas, California.
• Gil Losi and Ray Losi release the Variflex Connection reverse kingpin truck, along with decks and wheels, to both the core and mass markets. Their pro team riders are nicknamed the Varibots because of their technical trick-oriented style.
• *Skateboarder* magazine goes monthly with their July issue. *Wide World of Skateboarding* magazine debuts, soon joined by *Skateboard World.*
• Russ Howell and Stacy Peralta do a six-month tour of Australia to promote provincial skateboard contests for apparel company Golden Breed.
• Vertical, slalom, downhill and freestyle skateboarding all progress at an incredible rate and are included in an increasing number of contests.
• The Pacific Skateboard Association changes its name to the International Skateboard Association to better represent skaters worldwide, and hires Sally Ann Miller as director.
• The Third Annual Signal Hill Speed Run heralds the birth of skate cars, which are enclosed skateboards steered by leaning and slowed down by a variety of braking systems, including parachutes.
• Peter Camann organizes Another Roadside Attraction, a successful pro and amateur downhill and slalom skateboard race series held in Colorado.
• Upcoming talent includes Gregg Ayres, Rick Blackhart, Kim Cespedes, Chris Chaput, Eric Dressen, Russ Gosnell, Tay Hunt, John Hutson, Tom Inouye, Rodney Jesse, Shogo Kubo, Arthur Lake, Dennis Martinez, Ellen Oneal, Bobby Piercy, Doug Schneider, Chris Strople and Lonnie Toft.

1978 • At the first annual *Skateboarder* magazine poll banquet, Tony Alva wins the men's division while Laura Thornhill snags first in women's. Tony forms Alva Skates, the first eponymous skateboarder-owned brand.
• The average width of skateboards increases from seven or eight inches to more than nine or 10 inches. These super wide decks become known as pigs.
• Stacy Peralta leaves G&S to start Powell-Peralta with George Powell. Their first board is the Beamer, a wood laminate with aerospace beams for reinforcement. Stacy is responsible for creating one

stays with Z-Flex up until the company folds. Wes Humpston and Jim Muir trademark the Dogtown name and start Dogtown Skates. Wes begins creating the first real graphics for skateboard decks.
• In early March, Skateboard City skatepark, built by Joe Quinn, opens in Port Orange, Florida. In mid-March, Carlsbad Skatepark, designed and built by Jack Graham and John O'Malley, opens in North San Diego County, California. Graham and O'Malley also consult on and design a dozen skatepark projects, including Concrete Wave in Anaheim and Shady Acres in Long Beach. This is the beginning of the construction of skateparks with banks and bowls all over Southern California, the United States, and eventually worldwide.
• Rockit Skateboards by Tracker pioneers the first stiff hardwood laminated skateboard decks. Soon after, the Logan Earth Ski Duralite and G&S Warptail II explode on the market. Wee Willie Winkels builds similar decks up in Canada for himself and many prominent American brands.
• Two brothers, Rick and Peter Ducommun, found Great North Country Skateboards in Saskatchewan, Canada. In 1978, they change the name to Skull Skates. In the early '80s, they move operations to Vancouver. Skull Skates is one of the few Canadian skateboard companies to gain widespread popularity worldwide. Over the years, top riders Bill Danforth, David Hackett, Christian Hosoi, Steve Olson and Duane Peters ride for Skull Skates.
• George Powell teams up with Tom Sims to produce the Quicksilver Pro Slalom deck, constructed of aircraft-grade aluminum skins around a maple core. Shortly afterward, the company produces the Quicktail to appeal to the growing freestyle/vertical market. Powell also introduces Bones, the first double-radius wheel.
• Banzai markets the first skateboard with a kicktail

and a kick nose, which is promptly ignored. (The fact that the deck is made out of aluminum with a three-inch long tail and nose probably doesn't help.) The double kick concept finally catches on in the early '90s.
• Lonnie Toft pioneers the Outrageous Eight Wheeler skateboard.
• Surfer and slalom skateboarder, Mike Williams, and San Diego aerospace tooling company, High Precision Grinding, release the Gullwing, a reverse kingpin split-axle slalom truck.
• Road Riders debut as the first skateboard wheels to use precision bearings, ending decades of loose ball bearings spitting out all over the ground. Road Riders soon bring an end to the very popular Cadillacs, which still use loose ball bearings.
• The first skateboard wheels with rounded outer edges, Yo-Yos, are released by Gordon & Smith.
• Vans launches Off the Wall shoes, which many consider *the* skateboard shoe to this day.
• Di Dootson publishes the *National Skateboard Review,* a newsprint tabloid that covers grass roots demos, contests and skatepark openings.
• Produced by Scott Dittrich, the skateboard movie *Freewheelin'* is released, starring Stacy Peralta and Russ Howell.
• G&S with Dave MacIntyre spearheads the Pacific Skateboard Association and hires Di Dootson as executive secretary. Pro skateboard equipment manufacturers join forces to promote safety, and to promote skateboard events in a cost effective and cohesive way to help the sport advance.
• Noted promoter Don E. Branker holds the World Skateboarding Championships at a series of giant arena rock concerts with the Beach Boys, Jethro Tull, Peter Frampton, Santana and Rick Derringer.
• The $1000 first prize at the second annual Signal Hill Speed Run is claimed by Sam Puccio, Jr., who

A SURFER PUBLICATION
SkateBoarder
Hot Action
High Speed
Radical Runs
Slalom, Tricks
Freestyle
Equipment Info
8

of the all-time most successful skateboard teams, the Bones Brigade. Steve Caballero, Alan Gelfand, Mike McGill and Ray "Bones" Rodriguez are the original members. Tommy Guerrero, Tony Hawk, Lance Mountain and Rodney Mullen join later.

• Tracker unleashes another round of startling innovations in the skateboard market with the first magnesium trucks, the first Gnarly trucks, the first Copers and the first portable halfpipe.

• Fausto Vitello and Eric Swenson, with input from Jay Shuirman, Rick Blackhart and Kevin Thatcher, creates the Independent truck, which combines the best design features of both Tracker and Bennett, and takes the skateboard world by storm with its quick-action geometry.

• The movie *Skateboard* is released, starring teen heartthrob Leif Garrett and skateboarders Tony Alva and Ellen Oneal.

• The *Skateboard Mania* stage show premieres at the Forum in Los Angeles, California. The plot has hero skateboarders decked out in glittery costumes battling against the Evil Emperor.

• Duane Peters claims to complete a successful ride through a plexiglass loop, but no film exists.

• The first organized professional skateboard contest series, and the first held in a vertical pool, the Hester Series founded by Henry Hester, goes down at Skateboard Heaven in Spring Valley, California. Steve Alba earns fist place. The Hester Series continues at Pipeline Skatepark in Upland, Ride-On Skatepark in Newark and the Big O Skatepark in Orange. Steve Olson wins overall.

• The California Free Former team performs the largest skateboard demo in front an estimated

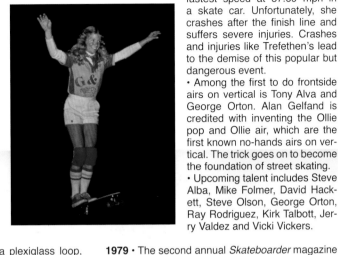

400,000 people at a huge rock concert called Cal Jam II.

• The fourth and final Signal Hill Speed Run goes down. With his revolutionary "arms back" position, John Hutson wins the stand-up division with a speed of 53.45 mph. Roger Williams takes the skate car class with a speed of 59.92 mph. Tina Trefethen claims the women's division with the fastest speed at 57.69 mph in a skate car. Unfortunately, she crashes after the finish line and suffers severe injuries. Crashes and injuries like Trefethen's lead to the demise of this popular but dangerous event.

• Among the first to do frontside airs on vertical is Tony Alva and George Orton. Alan Gelfand is credited with inventing the Ollie pop and Ollie air, which are the first known no-hands airs on vertical. The trick goes on to become the foundation of street skating.

• Upcoming talent includes Steve Alba, Mike Folmer, David Hackett, Steve Olson, George Orton, Ray Rodriguez, Kirk Talbott, Jerry Valdez and Vicki Vickers.

1979 • The second annual *Skateboarder* magazine poll banquet goes down, with Steve Olson grabbing the top spot.

• To offer more set-up time between tricks, flat bottom starts to appear on halfpipe ramps, copying the cross section of wide keyhole pools like Winchester.

• The first (and only) transparent full-pipe with a capsule end, the Turning Point ramp is attached to

a trailer equipped with hydraulics to offer an adjustable angle of attack.

• Street skating as it is known today—skateboarding on obstacles—gets a humble start on curbs.

• Vision begins manufacturing skateboards and goes on to become one of the biggest brands of the '80s.

• Conical skateboard wheels become all the rage, with Alva, Hobie, Kryptonics, Sims and Yo-Yo leading the way. G&S takes the conical concept to its logical conclusion with the Rollerball, a completely sphere-shaped wheel.

• The Hester Series returns for a second and final go-around at Winchester in San Jose, California, High-Roller in Boulder, Colorado, and back to California at Del Mar, Whittier, and Upland. Micke Alba is the overall series winner.

• The Action Sports Retailer trade show launches.

• Spiraling insurance rates and declining skatepark attendance begins forcing all but a few skateparks out of business. The punk movement infiltrates the skateboard scene, promptly alienating many riders and commercial sponsors. Throughout 1979, interest in skateboarding declines, and the industry is all but commercially dead by the end of the year. The majority of skateboarders move on to other things.

• Upcoming talent includes Micke Alba, David Andrecht, Brad Bowman, Eddie Elguera, Alan Gelfand, Peter Gifford, Eric Grisham, Lonnie Hiramoto, Steve Hirsch, Tony Jetton, Bert Lamar, Mike McGill, Darrell Miller and Doug de Montmorency.

La Costa overview, San Diego, California, 1975. Photo: Larry Balma
Above: **Ellen Oneal brushes up on her freestyle, 1976.** Photo: Warren Bolster

DEDICATION

Larry Balma and his wife, Louise, in the mix at a contest in Carson, California, circa 1987. Photo: Peter Kiss
Below: In 2015, Tracker was honored by the International Association of Skateboard Companies with an Icon Award in the Skateboarding Hall of Fame. The Icon Awards celebrate industry pioneers and cultural icons who have left a permanent imprint on the history and culture of skateboarding.

My name is Larry Balma. After spending over half of my life at Tracker, I've finally decided to take a look back at all of the wonderful people I've shared exceptional experiences with over the years. The skateboard world is a dynamic, action-packed arena full of interesting characters. The following pages will roll you through the history of Tracker and chronicle many of the characters and products that helped put the brand on the map. I figured out early in life that we spend more of our waking hours at work than with our families, so I decided to surround myself with people who I wanted to be around, and work at something I enjoyed. From the very beginning, I've considered Tracker to be my extended family. But, instead of bickering at the dinner table, we build skateboards and distribute fun all around the world.

Thanks to my wife, Louise, who enjoyed both the good times and endured the hard times in the skateboard industry over the years, and for her extraordinary dedication to and passion for the Tracker book. Louise worked three years organizing the Tracker collection in preparation for this project. Thanks to my Tracker co-founders, Dave Dominy and Gary Dodds, who had the vision, passion and guts to launch the Tracker adventure. Thanks to all Tracker team riders, who offered their valuable design input and promotional abilities. Thanks to all of our employees, who shared their lives with Tracker and worked hard to make it successful. Thanks to all of the photojournalists who helped promote Tracker along the way. A huge thanks is due to everyone who helped to bring the Tracker book itself to life. A tremendous thanks to everyone who spent countless hours to mold and shape this book in order to showcase our illustrious history. Tracker team rider Garry Davis (GSD) served as art director, editor, writer, Photoshop artist and historian, getting the project back on track after it had stalled. Former Tracker team manager Lance Smith photographed all of our products, some even more than once, all while researching and chasing down photos and photographers, and proofing historical content. Tracker team riders David Hackett, Tony Magnusson and Max Dufour all gave me a big shove of inspiration at the right time. Finally, a special thanks goes out to every skateboarder who laid down hard cash to ride Trackers and support the growth of our company, which would not otherwise have been possible.

—**Larry Maurice Balma**

16

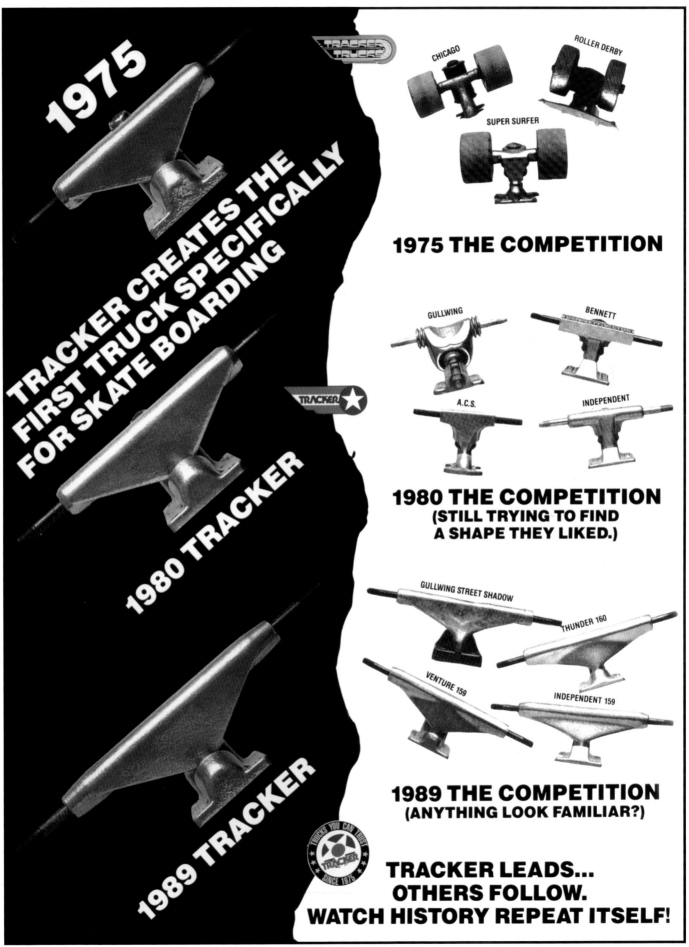

1975

TRACKER CREATES THE FIRST TRUCK SPECIFICALLY FOR SKATE BOARDING

1980 TRACKER

1989 TRACKER

1975 THE COMPETITION

CHICAGO

ROLLER DERBY

SUPER SURFER

1980 THE COMPETITION
(STILL TRYING TO FIND A SHAPE THEY LIKED.)

GULLWING

BENNETT

A.C.S.

INDEPENDENT

1989 THE COMPETITION
(ANYTHING LOOK FAMILIAR?)

GULLWING STREET SHADOW

THUNDER 160

VENTURE 159

INDEPENDENT 159

TRACKER LEADS...
OTHERS FOLLOW.
WATCH HISTORY REPEAT ITSELF!

Tracker Leads, March 1990.

Above: **Larry Balma** with the second surfboard he shaped after a shaping lesson from Dewey Weber in Venice Beach, California in 1960. Gary Dodds was with Larry that day, and they both made 8' 4" boards that were unusually short for the time. Larry built surfboards for a local boat shop in 1961. Photo: Maurice Balma
Above right: **Larry's first skateboard**, which measures 2" x 8" x 18". Larry started stand-up surfing in 1958 at T Street in San Clemente, California. He went home after that weekend and ripped apart an old pair of clamp-on skates with steel wheels and nailed them to this redwood 2" x 8". The extra width added stability.
Opposite page, top to bottom: **Larry** takes

the drop at Haleiwa, Hawaii, winter 1971. Photo: Woody Porter
Larry's second skateboard, a 1" x 6" x 11" job.
After watching Ed "Big Daddy" Roth airbrush sweatshirts at a Los Angeles car show in 1959, 15-year-old Larry started his first business; he got ahold of an airbrush, went down to the garment district to purchase sweatshirts, and painted them all through high school.
Photo: Maurice Balma
Larry's 10-ton Kettenburg fishing boat, the Kitty Lee, circa 1972. Photo: Unknown
Larry catches a white sea bass in Baja California, circa 1968. Photo: Bill Keiper

LARRY
BALMA

When I was a kid, my dad Maurice and I built wonderful things together out of scraps. One that immediately springs to mind was an orange crate scooter with split steel wheel roller skates that I covered with bottle caps and raced with the neighborhood kids on the sidewalks. Maurice, also known as Mice, was a finish carpenter with the Southern Pacific Railroad, as well as a mechanic and fabricator. My grandpa Balma, who grew up in France near the border of Italy, was a writer and a musician. My grandpa Claus, who was from Germany, was a very successful entrepreneur, tinkerer and inventor. All three of them inspired me to be creative, too.

The Balma name is Italian. I was born on 11-22-44, and grew up in Alhambra, California, which is in the San Gabriel Valley in the Los Angeles basin. My cousin, Ron Baker, lived right on the beach at Hermosa, which was a short drive from my house, thus we bodysurfed and belly boarded there all the time. The first time I saw stand-up surfers, I knew that's what I wanted to do. I started stand-up surfing in 1958 with a friend, Paul Jessup, whose family had a home in San Clemente that included an 8' 6" Velzy pig.

I came home and built a skateboard that week, so I could practice surfing when I couldn't get to the beach. Skateboarding was also an easy way to enjoy the feel of surfing when the waves were flat. I took a 2" x 8" piece of old growth redwood, split apart a clamp-on steel wheel roller skate, and nailed it to the redwood deck. The 2" x 8" width added more stability; unlike most people, I never had an actual 2" x 4" skateboard. My second skateboard was made out of a 1" x 6" plank, which offered a lower center of gravity.

I built all kinds of skateboards, from a one foot long 1" x 6" with no cushions, to eight foot long planks with four trucks. I even had a 16" wide board on which I could do knee paddle take-offs! The skates I used had steel wheels, which I could wear through in one day while riding long asphalt hills. I would go door-to-door in my neighborhood and ask the ladies if I could clean out their garages for them for $5.00. When I finished, I'd have a bunch of trash for them to look at before I tossed it. Next to the trash, I'd have a pile of old roller skates,

19

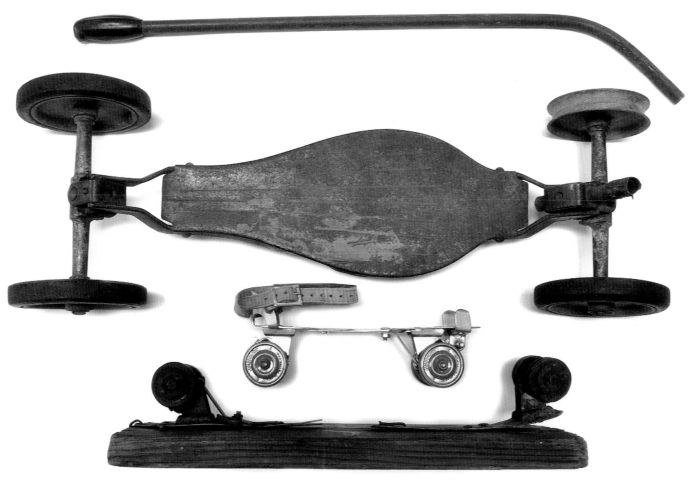

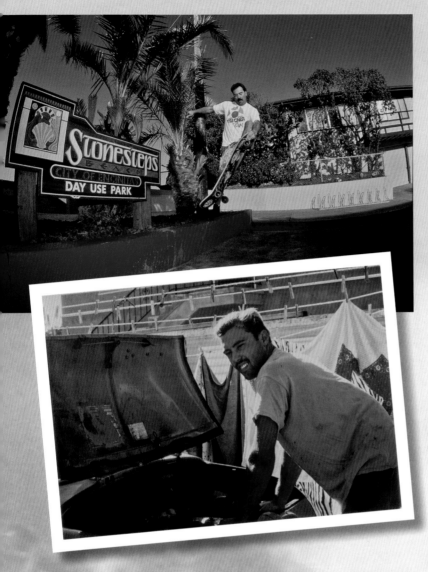

One night, back when we used to sneak into high school dances at the YMCA, Gary Dodds, Joe D'Elia and I climbed through an upstairs window into the sports equipment room, where all of these roller skates with composite clay wheels were hanging up on the wall. We'd never seen anything like it before. "Look at these wheels!" The clay wheels were more than twice as wide as the steel wheels. Even though they would still screech to a halt when they hit a large grain of sand, they worked 1000 times better than the steel wheels and were the first real advancement to the skateboard.

My first commercial skateboard was a Hobie Super Surfer. I bought both sizes—a 22" and a 28"—at a Thrifty drug store in 1964. The decks were 3/4" thick oak and mahogany, 6" wide, with 1 7/8" wide roller skate trucks and clay wheels. Gary, Joe and I, along with our posse, would skate the glassy smooth concrete surface of a strip mall in Monterey Park for hours late at night. These were the days before security guards were everywhere, so we never even got hassled! In 1966, I moved to Pacific Beach, San Diego, where, although I skated a little bit, I went surfing most of the time. I was a telephone lineman for a couple of years, and then quit to become a commercial fisherman for white sea bass and albacore, and I also trapped lobster.

By early 1973, I had moved to Leucadia in North San Diego County. I was still a commercial fisherman patching lobster traps at my house, when my friends came by and shouted, "Come on, we're going skateboarding!" I said, "Skateboarding? What are you talking about? I haven't skateboarded in years." And they said, "No, we've got these new wheels!" They were talking about the new polyurethane Cadillac wheels that had just been introduced to skateboarding by Frank Nasworthy. We went up to skate on the hills of La Costa, and the Cadillacs were awesome. Compared to the advancement from steel wheels to clay, the progression from clay to urethane was momentous. Insanely smooth and fast, urethane could even roll over a rock without screeching to a halt. I was so stoked, I immediately wanted a skateboard, so I bought some Sure Grip roller skate trucks, built one, and started riding again. The urethane wheel was nothing less than the Big Bang that set Tracker and all other modern skateboard companies in motion.—LMB

about which I'd ask, "Do you still want these old things?" They would always say no, which resulted in a never-ending supply of steel skateboard wheels.

I had a steel scooter from the late 1940s called a Skeeter Skate with aluminum trucks that were built with a roller skate-type action. These trucks were 7" wide with 6" tall wheels that were made out of aluminum

with rubber tires! When we started skateboarding and building our quivers, I got out my old Skeeter, cut off the handle and rode it like a skateboard. The deck was very low, right at the roll center of the trucks, which accentuated the caster effect (speed wobbles). The wide trucks worked well at slower speeds, but at high speeds, I would develop uncontrollable wobbles and get pitched off onto the ground.

This page, top to bottom: **Larry offers up a curb sweeper at Stone Steps in Encinitas, California, circa late 1980s.** Photo: Louise Balma
Larry wrenches on the family car, circa 1964. Photo: Sheri Melville
Larry's 1971 Lamborghini Muira S. Photo: Larry Balma
Larry's Super Surfer skateboard from the mid 1960s.
Opposite page, top to bottom: **The first wide aluminum trucks were built for the Skeeter Skate scooter in the late 1940s. In the late 1950s, Larry Balma cut off the handle and rode it like a skateboard. A metal roller skate and Larry's first skateboard are shown for a size comparison.**
The Skeeter Skate and a first production run Tracker Fultrack from 1975 are shown together for an axle width comparison.

Above: **Dave Dominy cruises through a shady spot in the Escondido reservoir in Escondido, California, circa 1976.** Photo: Lance Smith

Right: **Laura Thornhill, Sam Durick, Gary "King Fish" Coccaro and Dave Dominy relax in the shade at the VC Bowl in Valley Center, California, circa 1977.** Photo: Lance Smith

Opposite page, top row, left to right: **Dave Dominy's personal Skateboards Hawaii deck that he built in 1964. It was glued up out of pine and mahogany, and backed with 1/4" thick plywood for strength. The deck has a resin pigment design panel and gloss coat similar to the surfboard designs of 1964. An experimental Bonneville race car-like skateboard designed by Dave Dominy in 1974. It measures 2" thick x 7 1/2" wide x 29" long with raised deep wheel wells and a built-in kicktail with prototype Tracker Fultrack hangers with 3/8" axles and Stoker wheels. The latter were machined by Larry Balma to accept R8 precision ball bearings, which was unheard of at the time. These bearings helped the Tracker team roll fast! Some of Dave's downhill testing of prototype Tracker Fultracks was performed on this lightweight pine skateboard, which gave the skater an extremely low center of gravity. The low roll center resulted in a very smooth and stable ride.**
Dave Dominy on the cover of an early Tracker brochure, circa 1975.
Opposite page, bottom: **Skateboards Hawaii order form, August 14, 1964.**

DAVE DOMINY

Born in 1950, Dave Dominy grew up as a Navy brat, moving from town to town along the East Coast, West Coast and Hawaii. When Dave began skateboarding in 1958, he was living in Vista, California. Like many other people during this time, he took steel wheel roller skates and nailed them onto a 2" x 4". Dave's family later moved to Clairemont, which is just a little bit East of the beach in San Diego, where he would go mat surfing and bodysurfing with his older brothers. In 1962, Dave's dad, who was a chaplain in the Navy, got transferred to Hawaii, where Dave learned to stand-up surf at Waikiki beach. He spent his high school years there skateboarding and surfing.

In the mid '60s, an older skateboard friend of Dave actually pressed out the axle of a roller skate truck and inserted a bolt using washers to make the truck wider. He took off the wheels, took out the axle and bought bolts that were 1" longer than the axles. Then he put washers in between the truck and the wheels to space them out 1/2" on each side of the casting, resulting in trucks that were almost three inches wide. This was Dave's first experience with wide trucks, and although they only had steel wheels at the time, Dave was so impressed at how well the wide trucks worked that he never forgot them. In the '60s, Makaha was one of the first commercial skateboards advertised and sold. Balking at the slightly hefty price, Dave couldn't believe any-

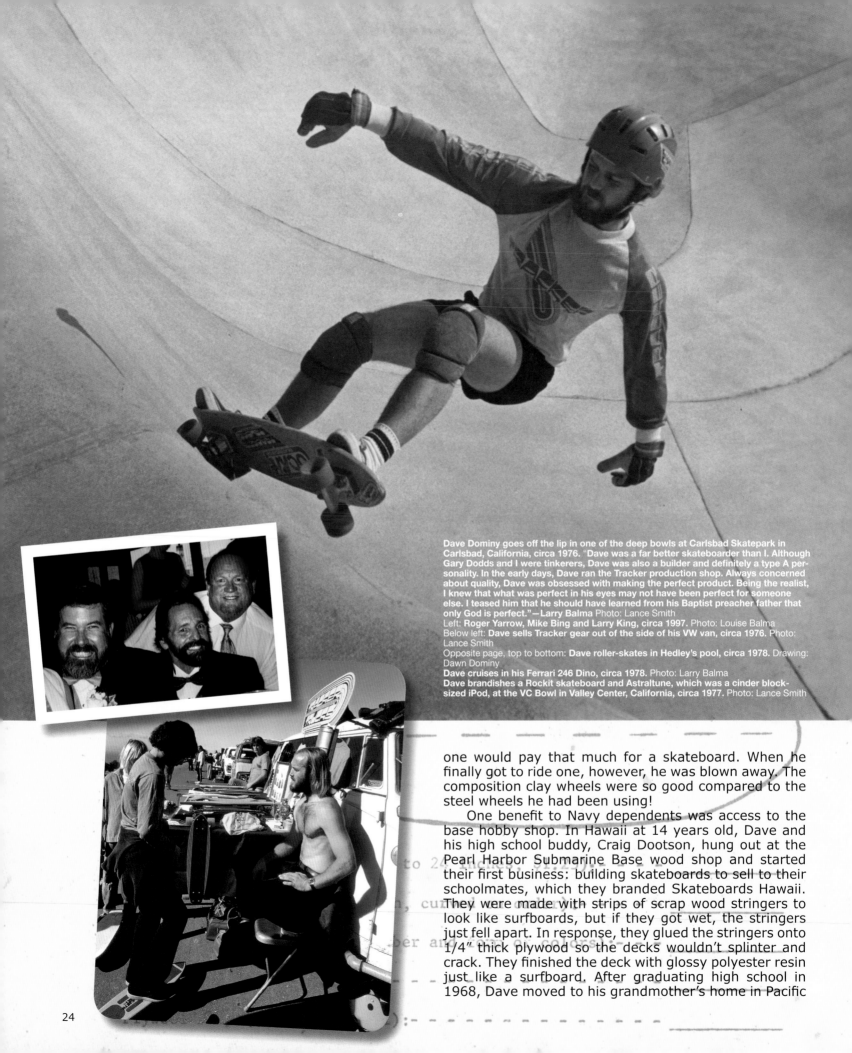

Dave Dominy goes off the lip in one of the deep bowls at Carlsbad Skatepark in Carlsbad, California, circa 1976. "Dave was a far better skateboarder than I. Although Gary Dodds and I were tinkerers, Dave was also a builder and definitely a type A personality. In the early days, Dave ran the Tracker production shop. Always concerned about quality, Dave was obsessed with making the perfect product. Being the realist, I knew that what was perfect in his eyes may not have been perfect for someone else. I teased him that he should have learned from his Baptist preacher father that only God is perfect."—Larry Balma Photo: Lance Smith

Left: Roger Yarrow, Mike Bing and Larry King, circa 1997. Photo: Louise Balma
Below left: Dave sells Tracker gear out of the side of his VW van, circa 1976. Photo: Lance Smith
Opposite page, top to bottom: Dave roller-skates in Hedley's pool, circa 1978. Drawing: Dawn Dominy
Dave cruises in his Ferrari 246 Dino, circa 1978. Photo: Larry Balma
Dave brandishes a Rockit skateboard and Astraltune, which was a cinder block-sized iPod, at the VC Bowl in Valley Center, California, circa 1977. Photo: Lance Smith

one would pay that much for a skateboard. When he finally got to ride one, however, he was blown away. The composition clay wheels were so good compared to the steel wheels he had been using!

One benefit to Navy dependents was access to the base hobby shop. In Hawaii at 14 years old, Dave and his high school buddy, Craig Dootson, hung out at the Pearl Harbor Submarine Base wood shop and started their first business: building skateboards to sell to their schoolmates, which they branded Skateboards Hawaii. They were made with strips of scrap wood stringers to look like surfboards, but if they got wet, the stringers just fell apart. In response, they glued the stringers onto 1/4" thick plywood so the decks wouldn't splinter and crack. They finished the deck with glossy polyester resin just like a surfboard. After graduating high school in 1968, Dave moved to his grandmother's home in Pacific

DAVID AT HEDLEYS   5/24   PAWN

Beach, San Diego, California. Dave's old school chums Mike Bing, Dominic Leonard and Craig Dootson were also living close by at that time. Mike and Dominic were also surf buddies of mine. Mike brought Dave and Craig over to my workshop, where I made auto and marine systems under the name Balma Engineering. That was the first time we met. Around 1970, Dave had a girlfriend who rode a Humco Surfer skateboard, which was a toy made out of thin plywood with weak 6" wide bent metal trucks with springs for cushioning. Dave liked the width of the trucks, but didn't ride them much, as he didn't want to trash her board. This was his second experience with wide trucks.

Mike Bing's friend, surfer, skateboarder and moto-cross racer, Larry King, grew up in the North San Diego county beach town of Encinitas. Larry King, his younger brother Gary, best friend Roger Yarrow and Bing skated the hills of a new housing tract called La Costa right after it got paved. Larry purchased some well-used leather boot skates from a roller rink in Solana Beach, sawed the plates in half and mounted them on a deck that he cut out of a water ski with a slight upturned nose. He shaped it to look like the new short, wide surfboards of 1972. Although the wheels were a high-quality composite, the 1 3/4" wide trucks were absolutely dinky under the 7" wide deck. Larry's metal shop teacher at San Dieguito high school, Mr. Walton, coached him to punch out the existing axles and machine new longer ones. Larry had to thread the axles all the way to the casting in order to spin on the cone nuts that seated the loose bearing clay wheels. He installed the wheels in their original position next to the casting, inserted the loose ball bearings, and adjusted the outer bearing cone nut. Then he slipped on a spacer, locked it using another cone nut, and installed a second wheel. The result was a truck with two wheels on each side! This effectively widened the space between the outside wheels to 4 1/4". Dave skated Larry's double wheel skate trucks, which was his third experience with wide trucks, and he was stoked! The problem with these double wheel trucks was that when the loose ball bearings wore down, it was next to impossible to adjust the bearing cones. The inner wheel bearings would wear and spit out, and the inner wheel would lock up. They worked great when adjusted correctly until the axles bent, rendering them useless.

After Frank Nasworthy and Bill Bahne teamed up to launch the Cadillac urethane wheel upon the skateboarding world in 1973, Mike Bing was the one who got us all into skateboarding again. Mike brought his childhood friends Dave, Craig and Dominic into the La Costa skateboard group. La Costa was where Dave first tried the Cadillac urethane wheels. As Dave recalls, "They were insanely smooth and quiet—like skating on black powder snow." Next, Mike Bing brought Jon Hall and me into the La Costa group to ride the new urethane wheels on the glassy smooth asphalt. Dave and I had met years before, but it was on the hills of La Costa that we forged our friendship that led to a partnership. I had ridden the Skeeter Skate with the ultra-wide trucks years before, and Dave now had three experiences riding widened skateboard trucks. The stage was set for us to experiment together and ultimately create the modern skateboard truck, the Tracker.—**LMB**

Above: **Just like a band posing for an album cover photo, Larry Balma, Gary Dodds and Dave Dominy hang out in front of a sweet 1978 Jaguar, circa 1978. These three made a great R&D team. Dave was a good test pilot, draftsman and dreamer. He called Larry his "brother curve." Gary was a fabricator, machinist and pattern maker. He knew the molding and casting process inside and out. Larry was a dreamer, fabricator and engineer, but also a realist. They were all skateboarders and surfers.** Photo: Frank Fahey
Opposite page, top to bottom: **Gary Dodds on his Bultaco Pursang motorcycle, circa 1975.**
Photo: Butch Lawson
Gary with his 1948 Ford woody wagon, circa 1965.
Photo: Joe D'Elia.

2.50

TRACKER DESIGNS LTD.

MATERIAL	SCALE	DRAWN BY
CAST IRON	FULL	G. DODDS

SHELL CORE BOX
18 CAVITY EXTRACK

DATE		
2-6-79		

1.06
(2 PL)

GARY DODDS

Gary Dodds grew up in Monterey Park in the San Gabriel valley of Los Angeles, California. He lost his father at a young age, entered the Boy Scout program and adopted many surrogate dads. Our Scout troop had a great program with many dads sharing their trades and stimulating our quest for the American dream. Gary and I built surfboards and skateboards together. We also skated and surfed together and wrenched on our cars, hot-rodding and creating our own identities. During and after World War II, aircraft plants constantly developed and tested new materials, fueling a manufacturing and hard goods technology advancement right in our backyards. Aircraft companies used different alloys of aluminum and magnesium, along with fiberglass and nylon cloths with polyester and epoxy resins, all in their quest for strength and light weight. Gary and I often shopped the surplus yards to find new strong and lightweight materials to use on all of our projects.

In 1964, Gary, Joe D'Elia and I all bought the new Hobie Super Surfer skateboards with clay wheels. Late night sessions at the shopping mall honed our skills with the new wheels. Gary's uncle had a machine shop, where Gary learned machining at a young age. After graduating from high school, Gary enrolled at Santa Monica City College and graduated as a pattern maker. A master pattern is the first step to molding any product. His first job after school was working for Industrial Design Affiliates in Beverly Hills. IDA had a contract with Mattel to build the master patterns used to create the molds for Hot Wheels toy cars! Gary was living his dream already.

Ultimately, Gary took a job with Swickard Pattern Shop that offered a bigger paycheck and was closer to home. His years at Swickard allowed Gary the chance to develop relationships at foundries that turned out to be golden when we started to cast Tracker Trucks. Just like I tried to run Tracker at first while still commercial fishing for a living, Gary continued to build patterns at Swickard until Tracker got going. It's a hard decision to leave a steady job to try something as crazy as launching a skateboard company. Back in the early 1970s, very few people had ever seen a skateboard, and those who had, regarded it as a toy and most likely a nuisance. Gary also had a wife and two children to support, but hey, we were surfers, and when the big one peaks, you don't jump off of your board, you go for it!

Gary moved from Rancho Cucamonga down to Leucadia in North County San Diego so he could work at Tracker on a daily basis. Tracker had just moved manufacturing from Dave Dominy's house in Cardiff to Sor-

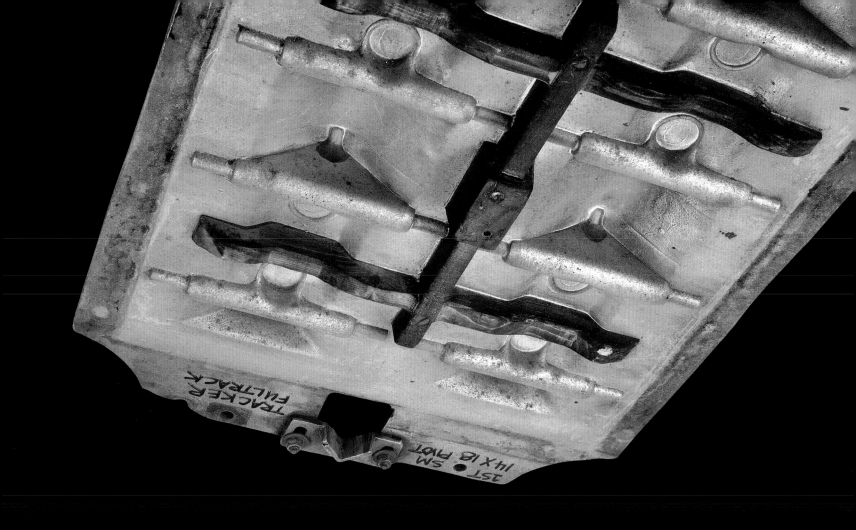

rento Valley in San Diego. Ron Taylor and Rob Dykema were looking for a place to set up a wood shop, and Gary needed a prototype shop that was not a part of the Tracker production area. We set up Gary's shop in a building shared with Ron Taylor and Rob Dykema in Rose Canyon, down the street from G&S. Eventually, it also ended up in its own building in Sorrento Valley.

Although Gary did not work with Dave and I on the prototype engineering for the original Tracker Fultrack, he made necessary molding changes. Another one of his major contributions was the axle hole. Gary asked how we expected to make the axle hole, and I said we would drill it. Even though he didn't think we could do it, he cast the first few prototype hangers with no axle hole anyway. I quickly found out that it was very time-consuming and next to impossible to drill a perfect hole through the axle hanger. Gary made another mold for a core box that would cast a resin-bonded sand axle. This sand core was placed into the proper slots in the hanger casting sand mold. The aluminum flowed into the mold around the core and formed the axle hole. A

minor reaming operation then resulted in a perfect hole. Gary took the axle hole core one design step further that resulted in hollowing out parts of the axle casting at the same time it created the axle hole. This improvement helped lighten Tracker axle hangers considerably.

By 1978, Tracker was booming; we had 45 employees and there was a lot of pressure. Gary wanted to have his kids grow up in a more rural environment, so Dave and I bought out Gary's shares of Tracker in October 1979. After working with thermoset plastics and elastomers with our job shops, Gary ultimately moved to Grass Valley, which is North of Sacramento on the way to Tahoe, to establish an injection-molding company, partnering with two mold makers who had been building Tracker molds. Naming the new company Tri-Industries, they purchased a 50-ton injection-molding Boy press and began molding parts for Tracker and other clients. After purchasing Tri-Industries from his partners in 1981, Gary expanded to four Arburg 80-ton presses. He continues to mold parts for Tracker to this day.—**LMB**

Opposite page: **Tracker Fultrack match plates designed by Gary Dodds, circa 1975. The match plates are used to form the sand molds, which the 1525º F molten aluminum is poured into.**
This page, left column top to bottom: **Gary Dodds business cards.**
Gary designed the first Tracker baseplate master pattern and the mold it created that was used to make the match plate on the opposite page, circa 1975.
Gary also designed this first sample core box mold, a sand core that created the axle hole in the Tracker Fultrack. Note the hollow cavities added in to lighten the hanger. See the drawing on page 27.
Above: **Gary's 427 Ford Cobra from 1967, circa late 1980s.** Photo: Larry Balma

An early shot of Dave Dominy skating slalom at La Costa, California, circa 1975. Photo: Larry Balma
Below: **Dave Dominy (far left, sitting on top of Larry Balma's truck) and friends at La Costa, circa 1974.** Photo: Mike Bing
Opposite page: **Larry Balma and Woody Porter, circa 1974.** Photo: Dominic Leonard

TRACKER
GENESIS Birth of
the Modern Skateboard Truck

In early 1973, we hit the super smooth hills full of brand new asphalt in La Costa, California with our new polyurethane Cadillac skateboard wheels. The Teamsters Union Pension Fund had invested and developed the roads of La Costa, which would one day become an upscale housing tract suburb of North San Diego County. Little did they know that they had provided the first free downhill skatepark that would be ridden by hundreds over the next few years. Thanks to Di Dootson, we held loosely organized skateboard contests every weekend. As the main hills we skated were unused dead-end streets, security guards were non-existent. Although one of the skaters always had a pick-up truck to act as our skate lift on free ride days, during slalom contests in which head-to-head courses took up the whole width of the street, everyone just walked back up the hill.

Our early skate crew, which consisted of Dave Dominy, Dominic Leonard, Jon Hall, Mike Bing and I, met at my home office after a skate session one day to discuss the great invention of the Cadillac wheels and how much the loose ball bearing cone nut set-up sucked. As you were flying down the hill, the bearings would wear down and spit out. If you lost too many bearings, the wheel would seize, fling you onto the asphalt and turn you into ground beef. I got out my industrial catalogs, looked up sealed precision ball bearings and prices and said, "If we had real bearings, we should have wider trucks, too." Dave had been thinking the same thing since back in high school, when his friend had drilled out the axle of a roller skate truck, replaced it with a longer bolt and used washers to space out the wheels. More recently, Dave had ridden Larry King's double-wheel wide truck at La Costa. Back in the late '50s, I had ridden the wide trucks on my Skeeter Skate. We both agreed that the wide trucks were inherently more stable.

We talked about making trucks and wheels. I could set up the machining, because I was a mechanic and an engineer on my fishing boats, and a journeyman machinist. I looked up the price of bearings. I guessed at how much it would cost to make an axle and other parts, and figured that a skateboard would have to retail for $30. I said, "Thirty dollars? Nobody would ever pay $30 for a skateboard!" The meeting ended and the idea went dormant. Dave pestered me to build him some wide trucks, but I always had too many projects stacked up, and the economic feasibility of a skateboard truck or precision bearing wheels dropped low on my list of priorities.

Almost a year later, after a skate session on the Black Hill at La Costa, I got the same group of guys back together and said, "Hey guys, Bill Bahne sold 100,000 skateboards for $30 a piece last year. Maybe we should take another look at this." None of the other guys wanted to commit to a project, but Dave Dominy was all over it. We started our partnership then and there. Dave was working as a finish carpenter for Ron Taylor and Rob Dykema, who built restaurants and remodeled houses. With access to their woodshop, Dave cut out skateboard decks using Finnish birch plywood and also custom-shaped an ultra-low center of gravity board with deep, car-like wheel wells (see pages 22-23).

After riding all of the current roller skate and skateboard trucks, we evaluated what we liked and disliked about each. One thing we noticed is they all had 1 7/8" wide hangers, and that some were cast with aluminum and others steel. With full use of a machine shop that I had worked at—plus a workbench with tools, a drill press and welders at my home—I machined spacers, drilled out some roller skate trucks and experimented

with different width trucks. I moved around the axle geometry a little and began to figure out what made the truck work. The roller skate trucks had 7 mm case hardened axles. Case hardening means that the surface of the axle is very hard but the center core is soft. Wider width added more leverage on the axles, and the skateboard produced higher shock loads than any of those ever experienced on roller skates. I tried 3/8" cold rolled steel axles on the first widened test trucks, but they began to bend. Although we used grade five 3/8" axles in subsequent tests, we chose 5/16" diameter (8 mm) axles for our production truck. Employing chrome molybdenum solid heat-treated steel alloy, which was used in automobile axles, for strength, we finished off our 5/16" axles with 24 fine threads and aircraft locknuts, which was unheard of on skateboard trucks then.

At the same time, I was machining out Stoker urethane wheels and pressing in R8 sealed ball bearings, center-set in the 2" wide wheels. They were quiet, smooth and fast! Using an 8" axle with these wheels

resulted in a hanger width of 4 1/4". We also wanted to develop a precision bearing wheel. As Dave pushed forward with urethane research, he coined the name Saturn Wheels. With no experience in plastics, I concentrated on prototyping and sourcing parts for the truck.

Bill Bahne heard about the truck we were working on from some of the skaters. I knew him from Mission Beach back in the 1960s. Bill and his brother Bob already had a surfboard factory that included skateboard production and distribution. The Bahnes wanted us to bring our truck to them so they could produce and market it. It would have been a good opportunity, but Dave and I wanted to try to do it on our own. If we had any idea of how much risk and work it would be to build a company, we probably would have chosen to throw in with Bahne.

After a year of testing, we figured out the right truck geometry. Then Dave and I met at his house in Cardiff. Using our sketches while surrounded with roller skate trucks and our prototypes, we used clay to sculpt the look of our new wide skateboard truck. Then we took all of our skateboards and prototype trucks up to Gary Dodds, a pattern maker friend of mine from as far back as Cub Scouts, who lived up in Cucamonga. We gave him our dog and pony show, hoping he would come on board (pun intended) to make the master patterns of the truck that would ultimately form the molds that the

The G&S trick team—Tommy Ryan, Denis Shufeldt, Sammy Jimenez, Sal Peluso and Ricky Ryan—take a run through the cones at the G&S factory in San Diego, California, circa 1965. Photo: *San Diego Tribune*, archived by the San Diego Historical Society
Below: **Dave Dominy and Larry Balma at a La Costa reunion, 2009.** Photo: L. Balma
Opposite page, top to bottom: **Back in the 1960s, Tracker attorney Steve Angus was a surfboard shaper on the North Shore of Hawaii. Here he drops in at Pupukea in 1964.** Photo: Val Valentine
The prototype shop in Dave Dominy's garage on Lake Drive in Cardiff, California, where Tracker got its humble start, circa 1974. Photo: Unknown
Having worked in some modern and fully equipped machine shops, Gary Dodds got us to upgrade our equipment to industrial strength machines early on. Gary built our prototype shop and hired another machinist named Pat "Doc" Doolin to keep our ideas moving forward. Gary spent most of his time in the prototype shop and sourcing suppliers and job shops. Photos: Lance Smith

aluminum was poured into at the foundry.

Our final prototype truck was made of aluminum and steel covered with clay for the aesthetic form. For the finishing touch, we painted it grey to look like aluminum. This was the look we wanted for our truck, and not only did it look beautiful, it was chock-full of innovation. We established the four-hole mounting pattern, spaced wide for the increased leverage of a skateboard deck with wider trucks. We designed the first fixed kingpin for double action trucks. The roller skate kingpins required two wrenches to adjust properly and, as most skaters didn't understand it, that rarely happened. When not adjusted properly, the roller skate kingpins would wobble until the threads were stripped and the truck base was ruined. We also designed the first baseplate in which the inner cushion boss was molded into the casting, which eliminated the need for an inner cushion washer. The cheap roller skate washers would always bend. Our axles were made of chrome moly heat-treated to spring temper, which made them hard all the way through, with nylon insert aircraft locknuts. Our prototype truck hanger was 4 1/4" wide, versus a roller skate truck, which was only 1 7/8" wide. As Gary was a gear head like me, he immediately

appreciated all of our innovations. He built racecars and boats in his spare time—vehicles that had to be constructed with the highest quality or they would break. Ditto our new truck, which was beefy and strong.

Gary asked what we were going to get out of all of this effort. I said there were a lot of guys out there skateboarding now with the new urethane wheels and that I didn't know where it would go. But, at the very least, we would end up with a bunch of cool skateboards. We sold Gary on the idea of building a skateboard company. Like Dave and I, Gary was a surfer, and he decided to go for it! We went to attorney Steve Angus, who was one of the original Waimea Bay big wave riders, and he formed a partnership we named Dodds, Dominy and Balma. Dave and I were a dynamite R&D team, and when Gary joined us with his expertise, we blossomed into a great design force. Had it not been for the unfortunate economic downturn of 1980-'81, we would probably still be together today. Gary went to work building the first master patterns. We had to make some subtle design changes as Gary schooled us in the art of mold-making, draft angles, parting lines, shrinkage and gating.

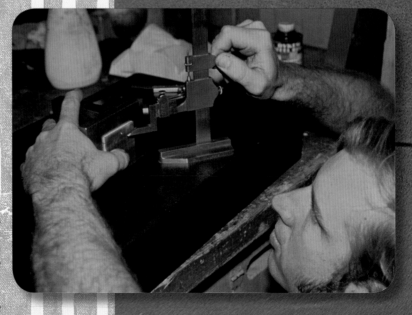

Back in the late 1960s, I was fabricating some of the first custom steel pipe bumpers for pick-up trucks under the name Balma Engineering. I also designed and built hydraulic winches and rigging for a commercial fishing fleet, and worked for Machinery Repair Company in San Diego, where I became a journeyman machinist. As it was not a production shop, every job was different, which allowed me to learn how to run every type of machine and make all kinds of set ups. I also learned about the properties in each alloy of all different metals. I honed my welding skills on ARC, TIG and oxy acetylene hardfacing. All of these skills would help me immensely in the coming years.

The task at hand was to set up machines and begin to form our production company. Dave Dominy found a new King drill press that was well-built, so I purchased four of them. Joe D'Elia discovered a Cosmo wheel grinding system and also the Burr King grinders that we still use today. I had full use of the Machinery Repair Company, which was equipped with Bridgeport mills, South Bend lathes and more, all at my disposal for tooling development. We began setting up in Dave's garage and shed, which was quite a humble beginning, indeed.

Gary took his first master casting patterns of our base and hanger to the aluminum foundry to pour one-off pre-production prototype trucks out of A356 aluminum. Our first sample castings came from the foundry with no name yet. Next, I began building jig fixtures designed to drill repeatable holes in our baseplates. Little did I know that I would be improving these jig fixtures for the rest of my life!—**LMB**

Conrad Miyoshi (RIP) navigates the slalom cones on the Black Hill at La Costa, California, circa 1975. Photo: Larry Balma
Opposite page, top to bottom: **A Tracker Fultrack pre-production run truck, circa 1975.** Photo: Larry Balma
Gary Dodds starts to build a baseplate pattern, circa 1976. Photo: Larry Balma

Left: "The very first-ever set of MAC trucks with the name ground off were assembled by Dominic Leonard, and he mounted them on a fish-shaped deck made of Finnish birch cut out by Dave Dominy. Dominic had the insight to sign and date it for posterity. He handed me the skateboard and made me promise to save it unused."—Larry Balma
Above: Two MAC baseplates, one intact, and one with the name ground off.

Opposite page, top to bottom: **Dominic Leonard cruises through the cones at La Costa, California, circa 1975.** Photo: Larry Balma
A sheet of ideas for MAC Trucks and Saturn Wheels. A MAC / Saturn combo logo drawn by Dave Dominy. **Chuck Edwall, Bruce Cooley and Steve Byron hang out in Chuck's offices in San Diego, where many of Tracker's product photos, logos and ad concepts were dreamed up.** Photo: Unknown.

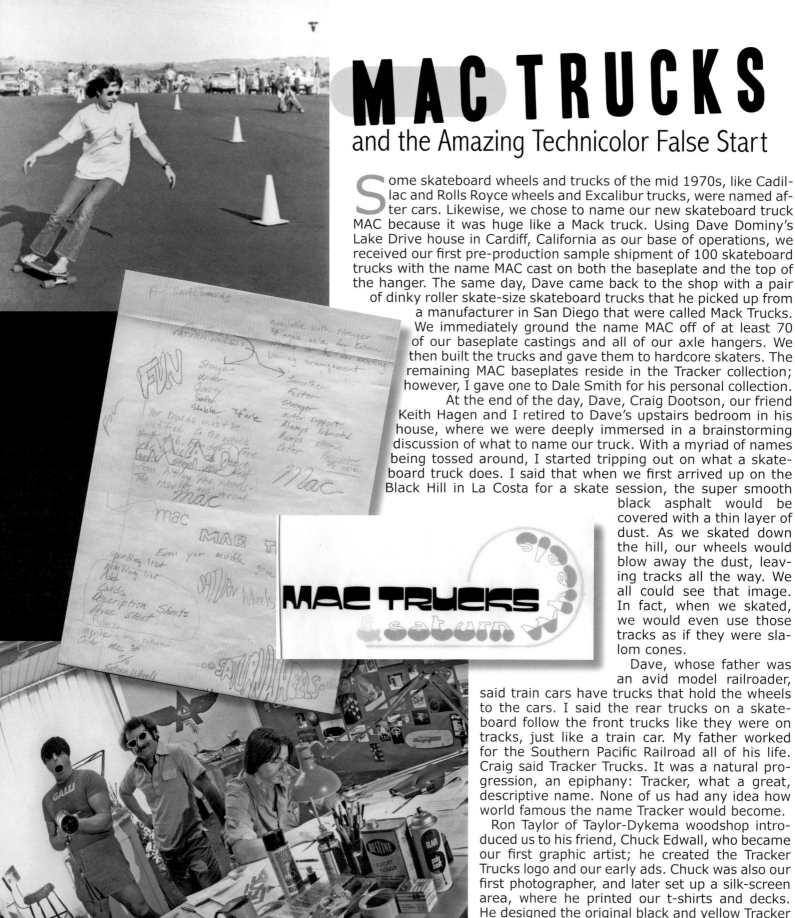

MAC TRUCKS
and the Amazing Technicolor False Start

Some skateboard wheels and trucks of the mid 1970s, like Cadillac and Rolls Royce wheels and Excalibur trucks, were named after cars. Likewise, we chose to name our new skateboard truck MAC because it was huge like a Mack truck. Using Dave Dominy's Lake Drive house in Cardiff, California as our base of operations, we received our first pre-production sample shipment of 100 skateboard trucks with the name MAC cast on both the baseplate and the top of the hanger. The same day, Dave came back to the shop with a pair of dinky roller skate-size skateboard trucks that he picked up from a manufacturer in San Diego that were called Mack Trucks. We immediately ground the name MAC off of at least 70 of our baseplate castings and all of our axle hangers. We then built the trucks and gave them to hardcore skaters. The remaining MAC baseplates reside in the Tracker collection; however, I gave one to Dale Smith for his personal collection.

At the end of the day, Dave, Craig Dootson, our friend Keith Hagen and I retired to Dave's upstairs bedroom in his house, where we were deeply immersed in a brainstorming discussion of what to name our truck. With a myriad of names being tossed around, I started tripping out on what a skateboard truck does. I said that when we first arrived up on the Black Hill in La Costa for a skate session, the super smooth black asphalt would be covered with a thin layer of dust. As we skated down the hill, our wheels would blow away the dust, leaving tracks all the way. We all could see that image. In fact, when we skated, we would even use those tracks as if they were slalom cones.

Dave, whose father was an avid model railroader, said train cars have trucks that hold the wheels to the cars. I said the rear trucks on a skateboard follow the front trucks like they were on tracks, just like a train car. My father worked for the Southern Pacific Railroad all of his life. Craig said Tracker Trucks. It was a natural progression, an epiphany: Tracker, what a great, descriptive name. None of us had any idea how world famous the name Tracker would become.

Ron Taylor of Taylor-Dykema woodshop introduced us to his friend, Chuck Edwall, who became our first graphic artist; he created the Tracker Trucks logo and our early ads. Chuck was also our first photographer, and later set up a silk-screen area, where he printed our t-shirts and decks. He designed the original black and yellow Tracker wing logo by hand, before desktop computers. If you look closely, you'll see the shape of a skateboard wheel with an axle nut in the center with speed lines flowing off. Finally, with our brand name in place, Tracker was ready to roll!—**LMB**

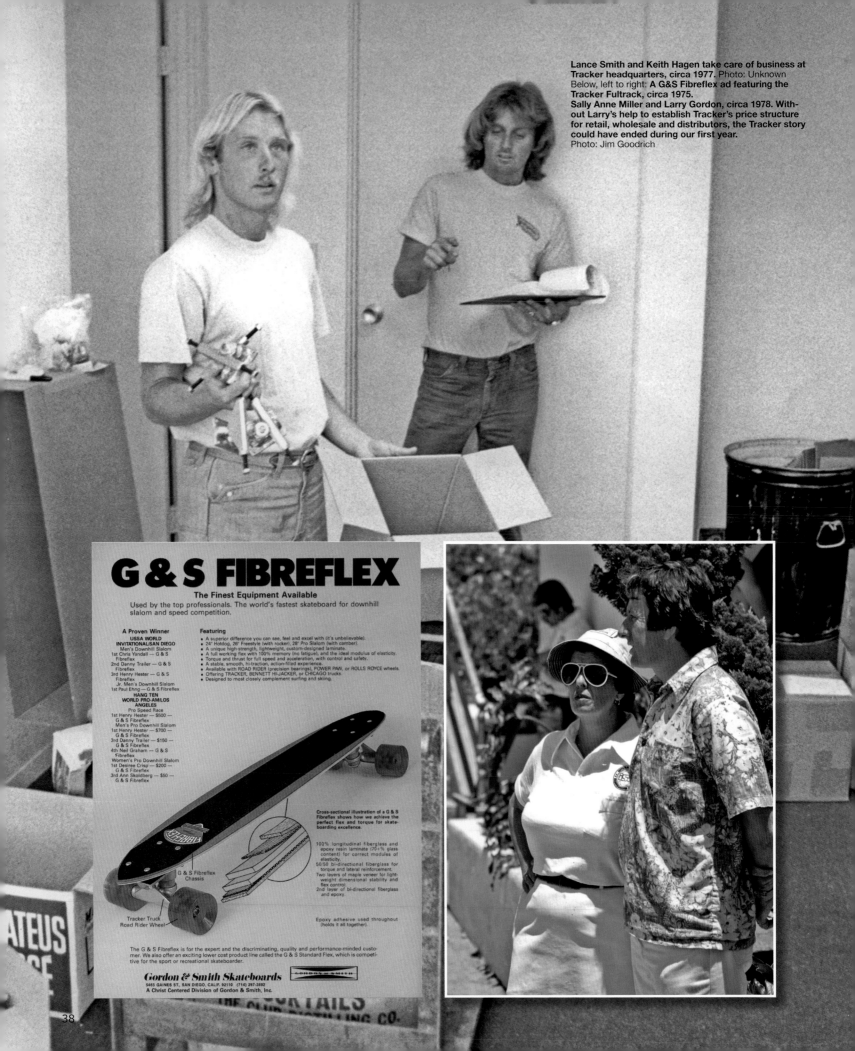

Lance Smith and Keith Hagen take care of business at Tracker headquarters, circa 1977. Photo: Unknown
Below, left to right: **A G&S Fibreflex ad featuring the Tracker Fultrack, circa 1975.**
Sally Anne Miller and Larry Gordon, circa 1978. Without Larry's help to establish Tracker's price structure for retail, wholesale and distributors, the Tracker story could have ended during our first year.
Photo: Jim Goodrich

START-UP
FINANCING
Rolling in the Bucks!

During the research and development phase of the Tracker Fultrack, I put in money as needed that added up to over $8,000. Likewise, Dave Dominy talked his brother Dan into loaning Tracker $5,000, while Gary Dodds dropped in his hard-earned savings, which caused his wife Judy to say, "Gary, you're going to lose your money." Gary replied, "No, our kids are just going to end up with some really expensive skateboards." Our outside salesman, Keith Hagen, sold his Porsche and gave us $5000 as pre-payment for 1000 trucks to help fund our first order. Keith had hung out with us from the beginning and wanted to be our salesman; he did indeed ultimately become a great salesman for Tracker.

In April 1975, I took our production prototype Tracker Fultrack to Larry Gordon to see if he would consider adding it to his line of G&S skateboard products. I first met Larry in the late '60s at his surfboard factory. G&S had become a major distributor in the surf and fledgling skateboard industry. Larry was impressed with the first modern skateboard truck by Tracker. G&S was using the current tiny roller skate trucks that were only 1 7/8" wide on their skateboards. In contrast, at 4 1/4" wide, the Tracker Fultrack was beefy! Larry imme-diately wanted to use Trackers on his G&S skateboards and also offer them for sale through his dealer network as components.

When I told Larry the Fultrack's price, it sounded too low to him. So, he asked me what our margin was, but I was clueless. Then he asked me how much it cost us to build each truck. I started to go through the cost of each part and Larry made a list. He asked me for our part numbers, but I had none. Larry, with his calm de-meanor, launched into business 101 and spent his pre-cious time schooling me while we established the Track-er parts numbering system that is still in use today. He showed me how to set a wholesale and retail price that would produce enough profit margin so Tracker Trucks could survive and be a successful company.

I walked out of Larry's office that afternoon with an education and a business plan that would ultimately help Tracker elevate to a multi-million dollar company. Oh, and by the way, without my asking, Larry, with his great business sense and gut feeling, handed me a check for $10,000 as a pre-payment for trucks to help finance our foundry order! Yes, there was a handshake, too, and G&S became the first and largest Tracker distributor for years to come.

At the same time, Keith Hagen met with Con Col-burn up in Santa Monica. I knew Con from the old surf days; G&S and Con Surfboards were two of the biggest distributors in the surf industry. Con Colburn gave us a pre-payment of $10,000 for a batch of Tracker Trucks. So, after investing $13,000 of our own money, we now had a total of $38,000 in hand. But, wait, there's more! Gary got the foundry to give us a credit line of $40,000! Tracker was finally off and rollin'!—**LMB**

A 22-year-old Larry Gordon gives the cones a go on his new G&S Fibreflex on Soledad Mountain Road in La Jolla, California, circa 1965. Photo: Larry Gordon Archives

the professional TRACKERS

chris yandell

© TRACKER DESIGNS, Ltd. 1976

FIBREFLEX
SKATEBOARD

Left: An early Tracker poster featuring Chris Yandall with his name misspelled Yandell. Unfortunately, that little typo spread to skateboard magazines, and went on to haunt Chris until the day he died, God rest his soul.
Below: A Tracker sales flyer featuring Kyle Jensen, circa 1978.
Bottom: A comparison of Chicago, Tracker Fultrack and Sure Grip hanger widths.
Opposite page, top to bottom: Lance Smith and Dawn Dominy in the Tracker booth at a trade show, circa 1977. Photo: Chuck Edwall
Tracker salesman Keith Hagen hard at work, 1976. Photo: Larry Balma

WHY TRACKER TRUCKS?

BECAUSE THEY SELL. We want to help you sell them. We believe an informed retail environment is the most likely to become and remain successful.

The successful seller is an informed seller. The satisfied buyer is an informed buyer. This is why we have prepared this brochure, with education in mind. This information will help you answer questions your customers may ask.

Skaters give many reasons for choosing Tracker Trucks. Our company's aim is incredibly single-minded. We aim to build safe, reliable, high-performance trucks.

- Our trucks offer the best strength-to-weight ratio available. This is provided by our attention to intelligent, careful engineering and choice of materials.

- Castings made of prime aircraft aluminum-magnesium alloy, heat treated to T-6 specs, or high-performance, light weight prime magnesium, heat treated to T-4 conditions, for your customers concerned with weight.

- Molybdenum (spring steel) axles and king pin studs with roll formed threads. Other truck companies won't use this material or technique because it is so expensive and hard to machine. There are no stronger or more durable axles or studs on the market.

- Improved, larger, super strong pivot. Designed for strength, these large pivots are complemented by our new large, durable, cushioned pivot bushings. This feature provides even more strength and durability to a Tracker Truck.

- Improved, gnarly base plate. Add this to our undisputedly lightest space pads, (included with every truck), and the Tracker system is not only high performance, but safer.

- Complete and versatile suspension grommet system for fine tuning. Adaptable to all Tracker Trucks, these grommets are not only new materials, but new shapes as well.

- Aircraft fiber lock nuts all around. These nuts, like every part of a Tracker Truck, are made entirely in the U.S.A.

But a Tracker Truck is more than a collection of strong parts. The true value of a Tracker Truck is its ride. The pivot angle and axle placement are very critical, and slight changes in steering geometry create radical differences in the way the board will ride. This is a point incredibly basic, but often overlooked by truck manufacturers making mindless changes in geometry in their attempts to solve other problems.

Chicago

Tracker Fultrack

HOW TO SELL
a New Wide Skateboard Truck

Most people resist change, because it's outside their comfort zone. Skateboarders, however, have always lived on the edge of mainstream society, eager to push the limits and try new things. Thus, every skater who saw Tracker Trucks for the first time was instantly psyched. In 1975, most of the surf shops, sporting goods and toy stores that sold skateboards did not have skateboarders working for them. Tracker co-founders Dave Dominy, Gary Dodds, myself and our sales staff—Keith Hagen, Ottis Tavlin and Joe D'Elia—were all going into shops showing off our Tracker Fultracks to make a sale, but the clueless shop buyers would say, "Oh, no. Those trucks are too wide. Your feet will hit the wheels." We replied, "Well, boards are going to get wider. Look at ours." They said, "No, they're too wide and they won't turn."

So we'd go out on the sidewalk, ride the skateboard around and turn it all over the place, but they still didn't get it. Wide trucks were too much of a shock, too much of a change. So, Dave, Keith and I had a meeting upstairs in Dave's house. I had an idea to create demand. We called all of our sales guys and got them to rip out pages from the phone books that had listings for sporting goods stores or surf shops, no matter which city they were in. The idea was that we would call up these shops and ask them, "Do you have Tracker Trucks?" Their answer would always be, "What are Tracker Trucks?" We would reply, "Tracker, the new wide skateboard trucks. You don't

have them?" They'd respond, "No, we have Excalibur, Bennett, etc." Then we'd cut off the call with, "Oh, you don't have any Tracker Trucks? Okay, thanks."

We made a list of all of the shops that we contacted and gave it to Keith. He would then load up the trunk of his VW Karman Ghia—remember he sold his Porsche to invest in Tracker—and he would drive out to the skate shops and sell them the Tracker Trucks that "everyone" was calling about! We created demand by putting Tracker in the minds of shop buyers, so when they would see our Tracker ad—or the G&S or Con ad—in *Skateboarder* magazine, they wouldn't want to miss out on

sales. Thus, they started ordering the Tracker Fultrack. Whenever skateboarders came in to a skate shop and saw Trackers, they bought them in a heartbeat. So, it was a win-win for everyone involved.—**LMB**

Sure Grip

BAHNE

introduces the 1st unitized ALL-STEEL skateboard running gear.

Bahne engineers have specifically designed this all-steel truck and hanger plate for safety and high performance. It is "the" running gear to withstand the extreme loads of this downhill motion sport.

The revolutionary Bahne truck features:
- Aerospace engineering for high-stress durability.
- All steel — stamped and welded.
- Larger diameter case-hardened steel axle — 5/16" O.D.
- Reinforced steel axle holder — 2-5/8" width between cone nuts (3/4" greater for optimum wide axle strength and support).
- Hardened steel pivot pin and hardened steel hanger base eliminate wear, breakage and wheel wobble.
- Greater ground clearance — designed to eliminate wheel rub on chassis.
- Gold zinc chromate plated truck — the ultimate corrosive resistant finish.
- Aerospace lock nuts provide vibration resistance.
- Fully guaranteed.

The all-new, ALL-STEEL Bahne truck makes everything else obsolete.

Available at finer surf shops, sporting goods and department stores everywhere. Or write or phone direct for information and prices.

Premium Made Professional Skateboard Equipment

BAHNE

P.O. Box 3368, Encinitas, Calif. 92024 (714) 753-0258

The first Bahne trucks ad, Fall 1975.

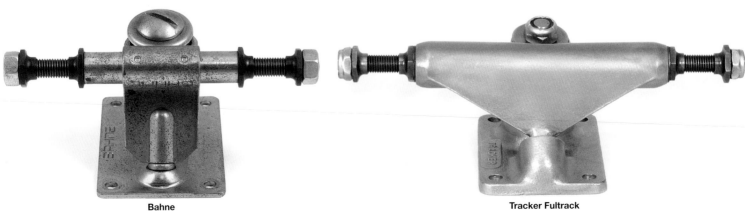

Bahne   **Tracker Fultrack**

A TALE OF THREE TRUCKS

The Debut of Bahne, Bennett and Tracker in 1975

The first-ever purpose-built skateboard trucks brought to market included the new Bahne all-steel truck that measured 2 1/2" between the wheels, and the new Bennett Hijacker truck, with an aluminum hanger and a plastic baseplate, that measured 2 1/4" between the wheels. Both trucks were just slightly wider than the tiny roller skate standard hanger width of 1 7/8". Measuring 4 1/4" between the wheels, our new all-aluminum Tracker Fultrack was wide, dwarfing all other trucks.

Skateboarders have long debated which real skateboard truck came out first. They usually think the first one that they saw at their local shop was the first. Bill Bahne developed his truck in private without showing it off in front of too many skateboarders. Having been a surfboard and fin manufacturer for years, he knew to hold his product development close to the vest. Ron Bennett developed his truck with his son and friends, also mostly excluding hardcore skateboarders. In contrast, we developed Tracker Trucks out in the wild at La Costa, the Escondido reservoir and the Kona bowl for all to see and take their turn riding; the point being that Tracker was never influenced by Bahne or Bennett.

Bahne Trucks

Bill Bahne was schooled to be an aeronautical engineer. Much to his parents' dismay, he quit school to build surfboards and ultimately design a removable fin and fin box system that became Fins Unlimited. After moving his factory to Encinitas, California, Bill met Frank Nasworthy, another aeronautical engineer, who was skateboarding and selling polyurethane wheels to local surfers and skaters. Already having manufacturing in place, Bill and his brother Bob brought in Frank and partnered to make Cadillac Wheels.

Soon, Bahne was producing pultruded fiberglass skateboards, purchasing Chicago plate trucks and adding Cadillac urethane wheels to offer completes. Surfer, skateboarder and yoga instructor, Denis Shufeldt, was their pro skater. Another local upstart, Gregg Weaver, became the Cadillac Wheels poster boy. By 1974, Bahne was producing 2000 skateboards per week, which meant they needed 4000 trucks per week! Skateboarding had entered a boom cycle, and the Chicago roller skate company had trouble producing enough trucks to satisfy the needs of all of the new

Denis Shufeldt takes a speed run on a Bahne complete, circa 1975. Photo: Warren Bolster
Bottom row: A comparison of Bahne, Tracker Fultrack and Bennett Hijacker hanger widths.

skateboard manufacturers. Bahne designed his skateboard truck based on the Chicago double action roller skate truck. Like Chicago, he used steel, but stamped and welded together the pieces, making the truck lighter than solid steel but heavier than aluminum. Bahne retained the low center of gravity like the Chicago truck and widened the axle a little. The width between the wheels was 2 1/2". The Bahne truck was manufactured in his existing factory and pushed by an established distribution network, making it the first modern skateboard truck seen by many.

Bennett Hijacker Trucks

Ron Bennett was an architect, never a skateboarder. He saw his son skateboarding with some new large diameter wheels, which would rub against the deck during turns and cause a fall. We called this wheel bite. Ron decided to design a skateboard truck that would hold the wheels away from the deck. He basically copied the Chicago roller skate truck geometry, but raised the axle drastically to give his Hijacker truck more wheel clearance. Measuring in at 2 1/4" between the wheels, the Bennett Hijacker was 3/8" wider than a roller skate truck. Not being a skateboarder or understanding the geometry of steering, Ron unwittingly gave the Hijacker truck an extremely tippy feel because of the much higher roll center, and increased caster or trail.

Of course, a skateboarder can adjust their type of

Bennett Hijacker

43

A slalom racer funks his way through the cones at the Bahne-Cadillac contest in Del Mar, California, 1975. Note the other racer's cartoon-like slam headfirst into the hay bale on the right. Photo: Lance Smith

Tony Alva cruises down a sun-blasted Squidley's ditch in Camp Pendleton, California, circa 1976. Photo: Lance Smith
Opposite page, right: **Back in the mid '70s, Tracker sales-man Keith Hagen slapped Mr. Bennett on the back at a contest and said hello. Mr. Bennett unwittingly wore that Tracker sticker all day!** Photo: Larry Balma

riding to any truck; it's all about balance and application of power. Ron Bennett went to an existing manufacturing company and paid them to develop tooling and produce the Bennett truck. With production capacity already in place, Bennett trucks flew out the door. The problem that plagued Bennett trucks from their inception was that the brittle plastic baseplates couldn't survive the heavy shock loads applied by skateboarding, thus they broke all the time. At the *Skateboarder* magazine awards ceremony in 1978, they "honored" Mr. Bennett for his truck design by handing him a trophy while holding it from the bottom. As Ron grasped the trophy, the base fell off and clanked on the floor, causing the crowd to erupt in laughter! A faulty trophy for a faulty truck!

Tracker Fultrack Trucks

The 1975 Bahne-Cadillac Skateboard Championships in Del Mar, California was the public soft debut of Tracker. Up until then, La Costa and the Escondido reservoir had been our proving grounds. Tracker co-founder Dave Dominy, salesman Keith Hagen and team manager Lance Smith interacted with all of the skateboarders, while Gary Dodds and I stayed in the background. Everyone was excited about our new wide truck. G&S, Logan Earth Ski and Turner Summer Ski were already informed and waiting for it to be produced. At this event, we made contact with Tom Sims, Skip Engblom and CR Stecyk III and locked in the beginning of our massive skateboard team. Now our work was cut out for us: just

produce Tracker Trucks in quantity! The next big contest was skater and promoter Jim O'Mahoney's first World Skateboard Championships at the Jack Murphy Stadium in San Diego. We had many skaters on Tracker Fultracks by then. Bahne and Bennett had skaters on their new trucks, too. Chris Yandall won the men's slalom on Tracker Fultracks riding my custom Stoker wheels with the large R8 sealed precision bearings. Tracker Trucks were King of the Hill!

In 1975, we were grinding, drilling and assembling our trucks in the Lake Street garage behind Dave Dominy and Keith Hagen's house in Cardiff. Di Dootson lived there for a while, but when we took over her kitchen with bulk hanger and baseplate storage, she was over it and moved out. Lance Smith took her room and joined our production team. I had set up the drill jigs, and put Dominic Leonard, Woody Porter and Harvey Porter to work with Lance. At the same time, Joe D'Elia was grinding castings in his garage in Los Angeles.

During this time period, I was still commercial fishing for rock cod on the Cortez and Tanner outer banks in the Pacific Ocean, about 100 miles West of San Diego. I would call Dave every day and ask how many trucks were built, if there were any problems, how our suppliers were delivering, etc. Anyone with a marine radio could listen in on my calls. "These guys built 170 trucks today? Just what are these Tracker Trucks? Have you seen one? Hello?" I thought I could set up Tracker to run and keep it as a side job, but by March 1976, I had to make a decision, fish or build Tracker. I turned over my 10-ton Kettenburg Monterey-style fishing boat to my fishing mentor, Romolo Ghio, and his son, Mark, along with the permit to fish Mexican waters for white sea bass. It was a big decision. Not only did I own one of only 12 remaining Mexican permits, but every adult who knew me thought I was crazy to give up my secure fishing livelihood to build skateboards. At the time, skateboards were still considered toys,

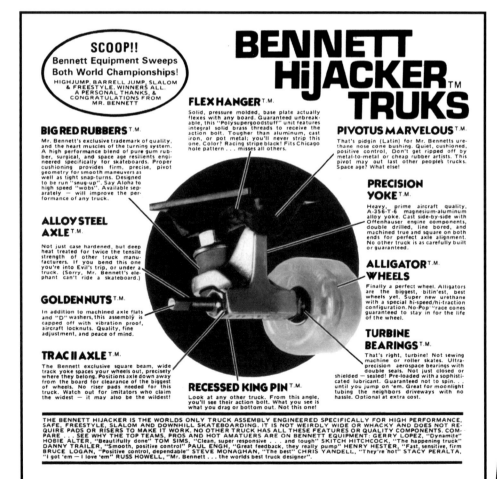

Bennett Hijacker Truks, Winter 1975.

The second Tracker ad: Proven Performance, Bob Skoldberg, Tommy Ryan, Vince Turner, Chris Yandall, April 1976.

part of a fad that had come and gone once already in the 1960s.

In 1976, skateboarding was booming for the second time in history, and this time it wasn't just a cheaply built toy. Well, there were plenty of cheaply built toy skateboards being produced, but Tracker and a group of dedicated hardcore companies were about to change all of that. The demand for our Tracker Fultrack was overwhelming. We could not produce enough trucks to fill the demand. I took a gamble and decided to work on land. We rented our first official industrial space down in Sorrento Valley near San Diego, where Dave and I set up a real production line and grinding stations. Gary found a used dust collection cyclone that we plumbed into our Burr King belt sanders and Cosmo grinding wheels. As our workbenches evolved for maximum efficiency, we learned how to produce a product quickly. In fact, our original assembly bench, coated with many new surface layers over the decades, is still in use today!

Our new lease required us to have an insurance policy for Tracker. We needed to be above board and part of the system with a business license, taxes, payroll, the whole bit. The insurance company sent out a man to inspect our factory. Although it was a surprise visit, it was okay, because Dominic Leonard kept the shop clean. The insurance inspector praised it. He was quite impressed that we were ahead of the curve at the time by having all of our grinders wear ear protection. Little did he know that they were actually headphones wired to a stereo system blasting 120 decibels of Ted Nugent into their ears!

Bahne, with his in–house manufacturing capability, and Bennett, who had another company build his trucks, shipped more product than Tracker during 1975 and the first half of 1976. By spring 1976, we had jobbed out drilling holes in the baseplates to a small machine shop while we concentrated on grinding, assembly and shipping. By the end of 1976, Tracker was the most popular truck, and would go on to maintain the highest production numbers and popularity for the next 15 years. Every day, our orders increased, our suppliers' shipments came on time, our efficiency bloomed, and we hired employees as needed. Our truck production grew to 20,000 trucks per month by 1977, and reached 40,000 per month in 1978 right up until late 1979, when the skateboard industry began to spiral down for the second time.—**LMB**

Left: **The first Tracker ad, featuring Chris Yandall, Winter 1975.**
Below: **Keith Hagen and Lance Smith with a delivery of Tracker parts, circa 1976. Note the custom pipe bumper built by Balma Engineering.**
Photo: Larry Balma
Right: **Larry Balma's fishing mentor, Romolo Ghio, circa 1975.**

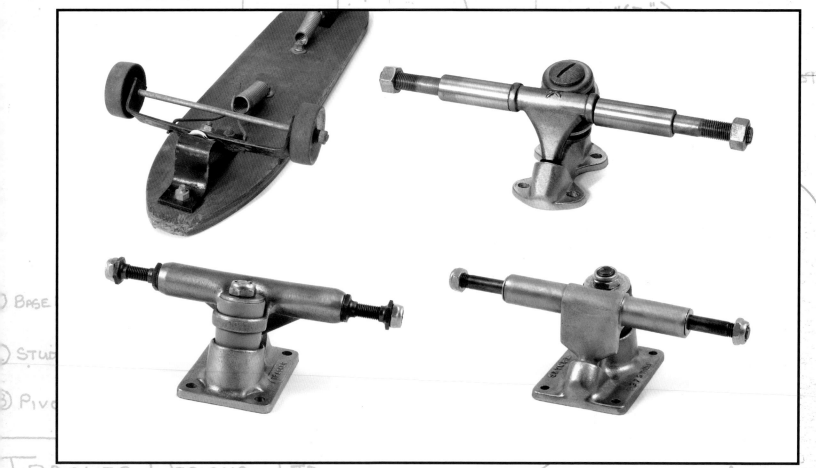

TRACKER DESIGNS LTD.

MAY 1, 1975

L.M. BALMA

TRACKER
FULTRACK

Our First Truck (1975)

In 1975, Tracker introduced the Fultrack, our first truck. With a 4 1/4" (106 mm) hanger width, it dwarfed the tiny roller skate trucks of the day, which were only 1 7/8" wide. Tracker originated the triangle-shaped truss on the face of the hanger that gave it a unique look unlike any other skateboard truck in 1975. This truss added superior strength to the hanger, which was necessary to support the width of the axle. By the late 1980s, every skateboard truck on the market copied Tracker's triangular truss.

Tracker aluminum castings were made of A356-T6 prime aircraft aluminum-magnesium alloy and heat treated to T-6 hardness. A356-T6 prime means that the aluminum was smelted from raw aluminum ore, never a remix of cheap aluminum cans and junk. Trackers were hand-cast in sand molds that allowed the gasses to escape and made solid aluminum alloy castings that could then be heat-treated. Sand casting is much more costly than die-casting. Many roller skate trucks were made of cheap, heavy zinc die-cast alloys that were weak and full of air bubbles that couldn't be heat-treated for strength.

Tracker established the four-hole mounting pattern spaced wide for the increased leverage of a skateboard deck and wider trucks. At the time, almost every roller skate truck had a different mounting pattern. Bahne and Bennett copied the Chicago truck's three-hole baseplate mounting pattern. Decks were sold without any truck mounting holes, as the roller skate trucks were mounted by the shops or by the skater, first using screws and, finally, bolts. Screws were no longer strong enough to hold the trucks to the deck, as the increased leverage of wider trucks caused the screws to pull out of the wood.

A company called Taylor Dykema, who built solid oak boards for G&S, Logan Earth Ski, Sims and others, drilled all of their blank decks with Tracker's new four-hole mounting pattern with 3/16" holes, which encour-

Skip Frye guns the cones at La Costa on a pair of early Tracker Fultracks, circa 1975. Photo: Larry Balma
Opposite page, top: **A Tracker Fultrack first production run truck from 1975.**
Opposite page, bottom photo, clockwise from top left: **A 1960s-era Humco skateboard with the first wide—yet frail—skateboard trucks. A Sure Grip baseplate with an Excalibur hanger and axle extensions built by Dave Dominy and Larry Balma in 1974 to test out axle widths and geometries for the upcoming Tracker Fultrack. A Tracker Fultrack with its triangular face narrowed for a stress test. A back view of a Tracker Fultrack first production run truck.**

49

② ③

TRACKER DESIGNS LTD.

MAY 1, 1975

L.M. BALMA

aged the use of #10 bolts and, of course, Tracker Trucks. Other deck manufacturers followed suit, and soon all of the other truck companies were forced to adopt the Tracker four-hole mounting pattern or be left in the aluminum dust.

The 6 7/8" wide axles on Tracker Fultracks were made of chrome molybdenum solid steel alloy, which is used in automobile axles, heat-treated clear through to spring temper for strength. We increased the Tracker axle diameter to 5 1/6" (8 mm) for strength, with 24 fine threads. The roller skate trucks had 7 mm case hardened axles. Case hardening means that the surface of the axle is very hard but the center core is soft, just like a Tootsie Pop, making the axles very brittle. Case hardened axles are much cheaper than chrome moly. Other manufacturers who later copied Tracker's wide trucks found out the hard way when their case hardened axles began to snap with the increased leverage applied by the wider trucks!

The kingpins on roller skate trucks required two wrenches to adjust properly, but, as most skaters didn't understand it, that rarely happened. When not adjusted properly, the roller skate kingpins would wobble until the threads were stripped and the truck base was ruined. Tracker kingpins were made of grade 8 quality chrome moly. Tracker's cushion adjustment was simply performed using one wrench by turning a 3/8" nylon insert aircraft locknut with 24 threads in or out on top of the fixed kingpin. Tracker also designed the first baseplate in which the inner cushion boss was molded into the casting, which eliminated the need for an inner cushion washer. All of these innovations were unheard of on skateboard trucks at the time. Needless to say, the Tracker Fultrack rocked the skateboard world, and demand went through the roof! No wonder that in the June 2000 issue of *TransWorld Skateboarding Business*, the Tracker Fultrack was named "Skateboarding's First Modern Truck," in an article of the same name by Miki Vuckovich.—**LMB**

Above right: **Jeff Tatum transfers from pipe to pipe at Nukéland in San Onofre, California, circa 1979.** Photo: Lance Smith
Right: **The inventor of the Jetton slide (frontside 360 slide, go up forward, come down backward), Tony Jetton takes the big drop at Del Mar Skate Ranch in Del Mar, California, March 1979. In the late '70s, Tony also had a pro deck on G&S and starred as Ghost Boy in the *Skateboard Mania* show.** Photo: Lance Smith
Opposite page, clockwise from top left: **In the 1980s, after the Tracker Sixtrack took over, the Fultrack was mostly used by freestylers like Rodney Mullen, who performs his magic, circa 1981.** Photo: Unknown
In the late '80s, Primo and Diane Desiderio had a paid gig putting on a daily freestyle show at Sea World in San Diego, California. Photo: Unknown
For a brief period of time during the wide deck explosion of late 1978, the Tracker Fultrack was the truck of choice for vertical skateboarding. Soon after, the Extrack and Sixtrack took over. Here, big boy Gregg Ayres grinds the coping on a pair of small pivot Fultracks at the Big O in Orange, California, 1978. Photo: Glenn Miyoda

Lonnie Toft, July 1978.
52

It's Tough Being Number One, August 1978.

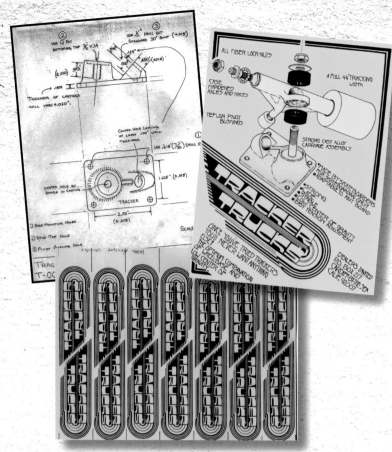

Above: An original baseplate drawing by Larry Balma dated May 1, 1975, an exploded view flyer, and a sheet of original Tracker stickers, which were Xeroxed on Avery label paper then dyed yellow. Larry Balma rattle canned them with clear lacquer and the crew cut them out with scissors in the evening while watching TV.

Torger Johnson, October 1976.

The Original Floating Power, June 1976.

Chris Yandall, classic cruise at La Costa, California, circa 1975. Photo: Larry Balma

54

A shoeless Samoan with hamburger feet, Chris Yandall was one of the top pro slalom racers of the mid 1970s. The first skateboarder to be sponsored by Tracker, he was also the fledgling brand's first shipper and driver, and starred in the debut Tracker ad! Always into computers, Chris left California in the late '70s for a programming job in Germany. Since computers were science fiction to us at the time, we could not understand that move. Chris was always ahead of the curve, moving at warp speed. In the '90s, he saved the trackertrucks.com domain name for us and hosted our web site because we were so clueless. Chris continued to skate slalom and free ride until he passed away on April 20, 2014 at 59 years old. He invented skogging, or skateboard jogging, which is free riding on the flats for exercise. He even marketed a line of decks suited to pushing using both feet, which was the perfect activity for Mr. Perpetual Motion. Rest in peace, Chris. You will be greatly missed, but never forgotten.
—LMB + GSD

Chris Yandall
INTERVIEW

When did you get your first Trackers?
I got my first set in late 1974 or early 1975. Basically, I got a call from my brother asking me if I knew who Dave Dominy was, assuming I knew everyone involved with skateboarding back then, as I was working at Pacific Beach Surf Shop as a skateboard sales guy. Well, my brother was wrong, I didn't know Dave. Anyway, some of my friends who did know Dave told him that I had just won the 1974 City Championships in San Diego and that he should meet me.

We made a plan and Dave drove down to meet up. Upon arriving, he pulled out what appeared to be a very oddly shaped skateboard and asked me what I thought. I looked at it and my first reaction was, "Whoa!" I rode it for a bit. It was a little stiff, but I was really taken aback by the trucks. So, I asked him point blank, "Can you take off the trucks?" I really wanted them. So, that is pretty much the first time I was introduced to Tracker Trucks.

So, you were approached after being somewhat established in the world of skateboarding?
I became engulfed in skateboarding after I graduated high school in Michigan. Right after that, I moved back in with my brother in California. He helped me get a skateboard at the San Diego Surf Shop, and it all started. I remember bombing Tourmaline hill barefoot with my surfboard under my arm every morning to go check the waves. People thought I was crazy, but to me it was no big deal. It was just another day. Looking back now, I guess it was pretty crazy, as it is a 30 mph hill.

Were you sponsored by G&S then?
I was actually working at PB Surf Shop, which was owned by Larry Gordon at the time. I wasn't on the team, so to speak, but the idea for the company was in Larry's back pocket. So, when it did materialize, I was in the mix.

Before skateboarding started to actually get branded, you were fully involved in the sport/activity?
Right! I was putting loose ball bearings in wheels.

So, it was a no-brainer for companies to approach you.
Yeah, basically, I was known as the crazy guy who bombed Tourmaline hill every morning barefoot. In the beginning, it was me and a couple of buddies, Danny Trailor and Neil Graham, who would tinker with the components and try to find the best possible set-ups to ride. Mixing and matching boards, just trying to find something that worked so we kicked ass when we got to the contest.

When you saw Tracker Fultracks for the first time, did you realize you were looking at the future of skateboard trucks?
Yes. Up until that point, I had been riding Chicago trucks and similar brands that would always break, and simply put, just felt weak! We were constantly seeing our trucks bend and fall apart. So, to see a casted truck was like, "Whoa!" It was like God just answered our prayer!

It's like Tracker was the first company to do research and development to figure out how to make a skateboard product better.
Exactly. It was the first casted truck that was made heavy duty to withstand heavy transitions.

Why was Tracker so important in the history of skateboarding?
Back in 1975, we were making the transition from composite wheels, loose ball bearings, plastic and solid oak decks to laminated decks, heavy-duty trucks and, most importantly, urethane wheels. All of this stuff came out together, and Tracker was the first company that made a truck you could trust. There were other truck companies out there, but Tracker was the only brand that didn't cut corners for cost. Basically, they came out with a solid truck that was hard to break.

How did the Tracker truck push the limits of what was possible?

Well, I was a racer back then, so, for racing, it was a great truck. To crank those high G turns through the cones at very high speeds, you needed a truck that was reliable, trustworthy and performed well; and Trackers had all of that.

It's interesting to look at the truck from a racer's standpoint. Having a solid truck was the difference between slamming and not. It was more of a safety issue.
Exactly, yes! You have to understand, I ate a lot of shit from trucks breaking. I mean, seriously: truck axles bending, cone nuts failing, the list goes on.

Who are your favorite Tracker riders?
Back then, for freestyle, there was Richy Carrasco. There were just so many. Looking at the later years, I always had a lot of respect for Christian Hosoi and Jay Smith.

To finish up this thing, is there anything Tracker related that stands out?
The 1975 World Championships in San Diego stand out to me. That was a pretty big deal. CBS covered the event, and there were competitors from all over the world. I ended up winning, with my good friend Danny Trailor taking second. I remember crossing the finish line and holding up my board with a big Tracker sticker on it in front of the cameras. Everyone watching that day was introduced to Tracker Trucks.

Above: **Hamburger feet, circa 1975.** Photo: Warren Bolster. Below: **Chris Yandall rips the Massage Pool in El Cajon, California, circa 1976.** Photo: Unknown

By Larry Balma

Robin Logan, circa 1977. Photo: Warren Bolster

A SURFER PUBLICATION

SkateBoarder

CDC 00142

Vol. 2, No. 2 $1.00

Vertical Slopes
New Terrains
Racing Coverage
How to Fall
The Hot Riders

Brad Logan, *Skateboarder*, Fall 1975. Photo: Warren Bolster

Brian Logan, circa 1975. Photo: Warren Bolster

TRACKER TRUCKS

Bruce Logan, circa 1976. Photo: Warren Bolster

In the mid 1970s, The Logans were the first family of skateboarding. At the time, you couldn't pick up a skateboard magazine without seeing a photo of Bruce, Brad, Brian or Robin. Raised in Hermosa Beach, California, they started skating in the late 1950s and early '60s and went on to influence the sport in myriad ways. Read on for a little peek into their life and times.—GSD

Logan Family
INTERVIEW

Did you guys have a team in the '60s?
Bruce: Yes, we did. It was called the South Bay Skateboard Club. My older brother and I started it. He was the team manager. Then we got familiar with Bing Surfboards on Pacific Coast Highway and they sponsored our skateboard team.

How did you get hooked up with Makaha?
Bruce: The Makaha team was doing a skateboard demo on the strand and some of the people from our team were skating there and the Makaha guys noticed me first. They gave me one of their boards. I really liked how it maneuvered; it worked well on tricks. I loved the board and liked everybody on the team, so they asked me if I would like to skate for Makaha, and I said sure. One of my dreams as a little boy was to ride for Makaha.

When did you move down to San Diego?
Brian: I moved down first in 1969. My siblings and mom moved down in 1973. I left skateboarding in '66, because it just went dead. Except for Bruce, I didn't know of anyone who really skated during a two or three-year period in there. There probably was, but very few.

So, Bruce, you stayed up there skating with the Makaha guys all the way into the early '70s.
Bruce: Yes, I did. It was fun. I couldn't give it up because I loved it so much.

You guys were skating La Costa when we were prototyping Tracker trucks. When did you get your first Trackers?
Bruce: In 1975, when Trackers first came out to La Costa, we were there first, so seniority counts. Dave Dominy gave me a set of Trackers for my board to bomb the Black Hill on a nose wheelie at 40 miles per hour.
Brian: I was the first one approached by Dave Dominy. Skateboarding had been back with the urethane wheels maybe a year. I was walking up the hill and this guy approached me from the side with a skateboard with these wide trucks. He said, "Mr. Logan, would you try out my skateboard with my new trucks?" They were the Tracker Fultracks. At the time, they were so wide, it was like you were standing on a train.
Brad: I remember Torger Johnson rode Dave Dominy's board and he loved it. He was doing all kinds of tricks like nose wheelies. The balance, stability and the safety of Trackers increased Torger's skating tenfold.
Brian: After that day, I tried Trackers. Other people noticed that they were bizarre-looking trucks, compared to what we were riding. Not too long after, Dave said, "These are getting ready to go into production." I said, "I want some of those trucks." Then I designed a skateboard with cut-out wheel wells. I think

it was probably the first one, because we didn't have trucks like this. With that board, I was ready for Trackers the day they came out.
Robin: That was our slalom board.
Brian: Yes. I think it was one of the very first, if not the first, cut-out skateboards, because we didn't have those in the '60s.

Which Tracker truck models did you end up riding the most?
Bruce: My favorite always was and always will be the Fultrack, even though I don't ride anymore. I had my place in the sun. I skated for 54 years, and I'd had enough. I accomplished everything I ever wanted to, and more than I ever imagined.
Brian: I liked the Fultrack, because I liked slalom back then. Then I really liked the Midtrack when it came out.
Robin: I was a Haftrack rider, I loved freestyle.

Did you ride that in slalom, too?
Brian: No, I stuck with the Fultrack. I had to keep up with Henry Hester and those guys. I was always two-tenths to three-tenths of a second behind him, but I was close. I was on a wood board; which wasn't fair, because they were pumping those flexible boards. But, it was all fun.
Brad: I had three boards set up. I had a 32" Torger Johnson with Fultracks for the Concourse. I used to go down there with Torger and Tony Alva and skate all night long. The trucks and the length of the board worked really great. You could just carve, go back and forth and go all the way down, then jump back on the elevator and go all the way back up. We never got hassled at all. I also had a 29" diamond tail with Haftracks and another 29" with Midtracks.

Did you guys invent any tricks on Trackers?
Bruce: Yes, I did. The nose to tail wheelie, and the forward high pirouette in the air. Everybody else did them backward, but I did them forward. A kickturn in the air. Torger Johnson called it the space walk. I don't want to take anything away from him, but I was the first one to do the kickturn in the air. That's what I called it. Torger got credit for the space walk. He and I did it all the way up the hill at a skateboard contest in Santa Barbara in 1975, swinging left to right on your dial.
Robin: My first kickflip and my two-boarded kickflip were on Trackers. I was supposedly the first girl to do a kickflip.

Who did the first nose wheelie?
Bruce: At the Santa Monica Sports and Arts Festival, my brother Brian did a nose wheelie the whole length of the concrete floor. But, John Freis invented the nose wheelie and I took it even further to 360s, 720s and 1080s. I would hold it all the way down to the bottom of the Black Hill at 40 mph.
Brian: In those early days, there was a time when I was doing longer nose wheelies than Bruce. But, then he took it over and became the king. Skateboarding has always gone to the next person and the next level.

Worst wipeout you ever saw?
Bruce: The worst wipeout by far scared the shit out of me. Steve Piccolo drove the Logan Earth Ski team station wagon up the hill at La Costa at 50 mph. My older brother Brian was

holding onto the door handle, wearing only shorts and tennis shoes. He got the high-speed wobbles and slid up the pavement on his stomach like a baseball player over home plate. He got road rash all over his body.

Why was Tracker so important in the history of skateboarding?
Brian: They changed the way skateboard trucks were made from day one. Nobody changed trucks like Tracker from the way they were in the '60s going into the next generation. They were so durable and they didn't break, unlike some of the other trucks.
Brad: They changed it in all terrain: flat, slalom, vertical and pipes. You could climb the side of pools much more efficiently with Trackers because of the way they pivoted.

Do you recall any memorable times with the Tracker team?
Brian: A lot of the Tracker team came around during the latter part of our involvement in the industry. I remember Russ Gosnell was one of the very early ones, but we were starting to fade out of the industry while you guys kept adding more people. The 1970s changed skateboarding forever. That was the generation who defined what skateboarding is now with the products. The trucks made now are still very similar to the original Trackers, and the wheels are still urethane—that hasn't changed.

Di Dootson refers to the '70s as the golden years of skateboarding.
Robin: These guys today wouldn't be who they are if it wasn't for what was done in the '70s. The Tony Hawks and the Rodney Mullens have taken it, launched it and grown from it. Rodney said he looked at the maga-

zines in the '70s and saw my brother Bruce do something, which inspired Rodney to do something else with it. Rodney took a nose wheelie and threw it into a heelflip, etc. and look what the guy does now. The '70s was the launching pad for skateboarding.
Bruce: Don't forget about us '60s guys, because skateboarding actually started through surfing. It was something we would do when the surf was flat so we could practice our style. Years later, you had surfers flying out of waves. They took that from skateboarding and added it into surfing. We kind of patted each other's backs from the '60s to now.

Read the full-length interview at trackertrucks.com

Above: **Brad, Robin, Bruce and Brian Logan, 2014.**
Photo: Lance Smith

By Larry Balma

Back in the 1970s, big guy Henry Hester was a top pro slalom racer for G&S and skate car driver who, oddly enough, founded the first-ever pool contest series, the Hester Series, in 1978. After spending the 1980s and '90s working in the snowboard industry, today Henry owns Swami's Cab in Encinitas and occasionally races slalom.—GSD

How did you hook up with G&S?

Well, G&S came about through my surf connections: Gary Keating and Bill Andrews, the guys who were working at Pacific Beach Surf Shop. But, before that, what really happened to get me back into skating was my friend Bob Skoldberg. He tells me that I got him into it, but, actually, it was him who got me into it. I was just coming back from doing a year in Sun Valley in the Watergate year, 1974. Bob called me up and said, "Hey, we're skating up in La Costa. This place is unreal! You've got to come on up." The first boards we rode were those little orange Bahnes with Chicago trucks and little clay wheels. We were riding on some pretty crude stuff. Those were the days of the cones with the square bottoms. You'd hit 'em and go flying.

I started skating the weekly races, and we'd all throw in three to five dollars. Bob and I would do well and take home 35 bucks. We thought we were pro skateboarders at the time. It was classic. I could never stand up going down hill past 35 mph. I have very weak ankles and I'd get the shakes. I don't care what truck set-up I had, I'd get the shakes and wobbles, so I wasn't able to do that. I weighed 205 pounds, but I could ride in the downhill skate car and do well.

Who gave you your first Trackers?

I think my first set of Trackers came from Dave Dominy. He was racing with us. He was a fidgety guy working on all of the mechanics of the trucks. We were riding the Bennett trucks, which led to the Indy geometry. They were quick turning. When the Trackers came out, they had the set back geometry, which was a little bit slower turning. So, Trackers were more stable at higher speeds, and were thus better for the pool guys, because they

weren't quite as fidgety and nervous. So, we were riding Bennetts with these really wide wheels; we were getting the length and the width, but we were trying to push around all of this urethane, and it just didn't work.

When the Trackers came out, we were able to use smaller wheels, and that was really good, because we had the width and we had more distance between the wheels, and, in slalom, the distance between the wheels was almost more critical than the distance on the outside. You know, it was like night and day riding down the hills. It was unbelievable! Our speeds went up, like, two seconds, which was a 20% increase on a 10-second course. Changing to Tracker Trucks was a 20% increase in speed. That's how revolutionary the trucks were at the time for slalom. What was cool about it is that the guys who rode the pools could ride the same trucks and get the same benefits. They could have more aluminum on the coping and were able to grind better, so it worked out for everybody.

Looking back, do you have any regrets?

I feel like it was a personal mistake not to have started a company like my friend Tom Sims. I probably could have started Hester Skateboards or some sort of company and done pretty well with it. I have a good business sense, but I just never really felt confident that I could do that, which was a giant mistake in my life. The message to anyone who reads this would be that if the doors open, go through them, because if you don't, you'll regret it for the rest of your life. Tom Sims went through the door, Stacy Peralta went through the door, Tony Alva went through the door. Other people took a chance at owning a business, but, at the time, I thought I just wasn't savvy enough. Now I realize I could have done that. What I did was give back to the sport. I did the Hester Series skateboard contests. Curtis Hesselgrave was the head judge of the Hester Series. He was in charge of the skaters, the banners, and keeping things going. Curtis stepped in as head judge, because we didn't want the judging to be subjective or unfair. It was really hard to be fair in judging, plus a lot of tricks happened in the Hester Series for the first time, like the first air, the first rock and roll. We saw history, when tricks were done the first time: they knew it, the crowd knew it, and the judges stood up and applauded. But, it was hard, because that was just one maneuver, and the judges still had to judge the whole run. That was where Curtis came in. He was able to look at the entire run.

We ran contests for the pool riders, who previously had no contests. They had no chance to be competitive. Back in those days, competition was a big thing. And pool riders would have to do flatland skating and go up against trick guys. I'm talking about the Dogtown and Upland guys. Warren Bolster didn't know them. So, I started a series of pool contests, and, all of a sudden, all of these no-name guys came to light: Steve Alba, Micke Alba, Steve Olson, Scott Dunlap. All of these guys came out of nowhere and, in one year, became skateboard stars, and rightfully so, because they ripped. We just didn't know it. Needless to say, Warren had to get a bigger phone book to handle the load, because there were a lot of new stars,

and I felt proud that I was able to introduce a lot of these guys to the industry. It was almost like the start of the X Games, but at a lower level.

So, you didn't start your own company, but you had a pro model with G&S.

Yeah, I had a pro slalom model with G&S. I had my signature right there on the Fibreflex logo. It was a cut-away model, because, back then, we rode with our feet parallel so we could turn the board faster.

You really used the flex. They made those boards for different weight people, so you could really spring like a ski.

Yeah, we would have it laminated with different levels of wood, some stiffer than others. Actually, the stock boards were really flexible. I couldn't ride the stock board. I had to ride one that was a little beefier. I was doing this at 25-26 years old; so I was big, I was a grown man. They were making boards for kids who weighed a buck twenty-five. They couldn't flex the boards I rode, they couldn't even turn them. But when they got on the stock boards, they could flex them and turn them. They were really springy. It's interesting to fast forward to 2006-'08, as flex boards don't exist anymore in slalom. They're all stiff—the flex comes from the truck system. The front truck moves, and the back truck follows the front truck. The whole pattern of skating has changed. There is no room or no time for flex anymore, the riders go too fast to have the board flex, flex, flex.

I went to a contest in Austin, Texas. I had a flex board, and these guys were all laughing at me. They had stiff wood boards: Pavells, Skate Kings, and all of that stuff with kicktails on them and the trucks mounted back. So, the back truck wouldn't turn and just followed the front truck. I wondered, "What's going on here?" I made the mistake of switching boards during a contest. So, there I was at 59 years old, trying to skate, and I did all right after I got loosened up with a little bit of aspirin. So, I went there with three flex boards, which was completely the wrong idea. I went into the contest with old school technology, and the guys got me on

By Larry Balma

Henry Hester
I N T E R V I E W

something more modern quickly.

Richy Carrasco, the king of knowing what to put a guy on, got me all set up on a concave kicktail. It looked like a regular pool board that was shaped narrower. It had what are called money bumps, so it wouldn't break in half, which they used as a toe accelerator pedal. So, all of the bumps and twists and curves you see on these modern slalom boards, plus the kicktail lift in the front, and the nose block to keep your foot from falling off the front of the board, all have a purpose, and it's all very technical. The trucks are all machined and cost $350 per set. But, it all came from Tracker, Chicago and Bennett.

Read the full-length interview at trackertrucks.com

Above: **Henry Hester engages the cones at La Costa, California, circa 1976.** Photo: Warren Bolster

THE SPIRIT OF COMPETITION

HENRY HESTER has the SPIRIT OF COMPETITION, it shows! Henry is one of the best professional slalom racers in skateboarding today and he heads up the Gordon and Smith FIBRE FLEX TEAM because he consistently wins slalom events around the country. Henry uses TRACKER TRUCKS in competition exclusively because Trackers have been engineered and refined to withstand the rigors of close competition.

Competition is the proving ground for all performance products and it is through competition that the Tracker engineers have developed TRACKER TRUCKS to such a high degree of precision and dependability that winning competitors like Henry Hester use TRACKERS exclusively. Henry's choice of wheels is important too, his choice is the precision bearing ROAD RIDER wheel.

TRACKER TRUCKS in the SPIRIT OF COMPETITION can offer the up and coming competitor a performance proven product that will carry him to the finals, if he has what it takes to get there himself.

Tracker Trucks (per pair) $20.00. T-Shirts $4.50. Stickers $ .25. Free Brochure. Postage paid within the U.S. California residents add 6%. Send cashiers check or money order ONLY to:
Tracker Trucks, P.O. Box 217, Cardiff-by-the-Sea, California 92007. Dealer enquiries **(714) 481-9551**
Distributor: Control Product Surfing Equipment

Henry Hester, August 1976.

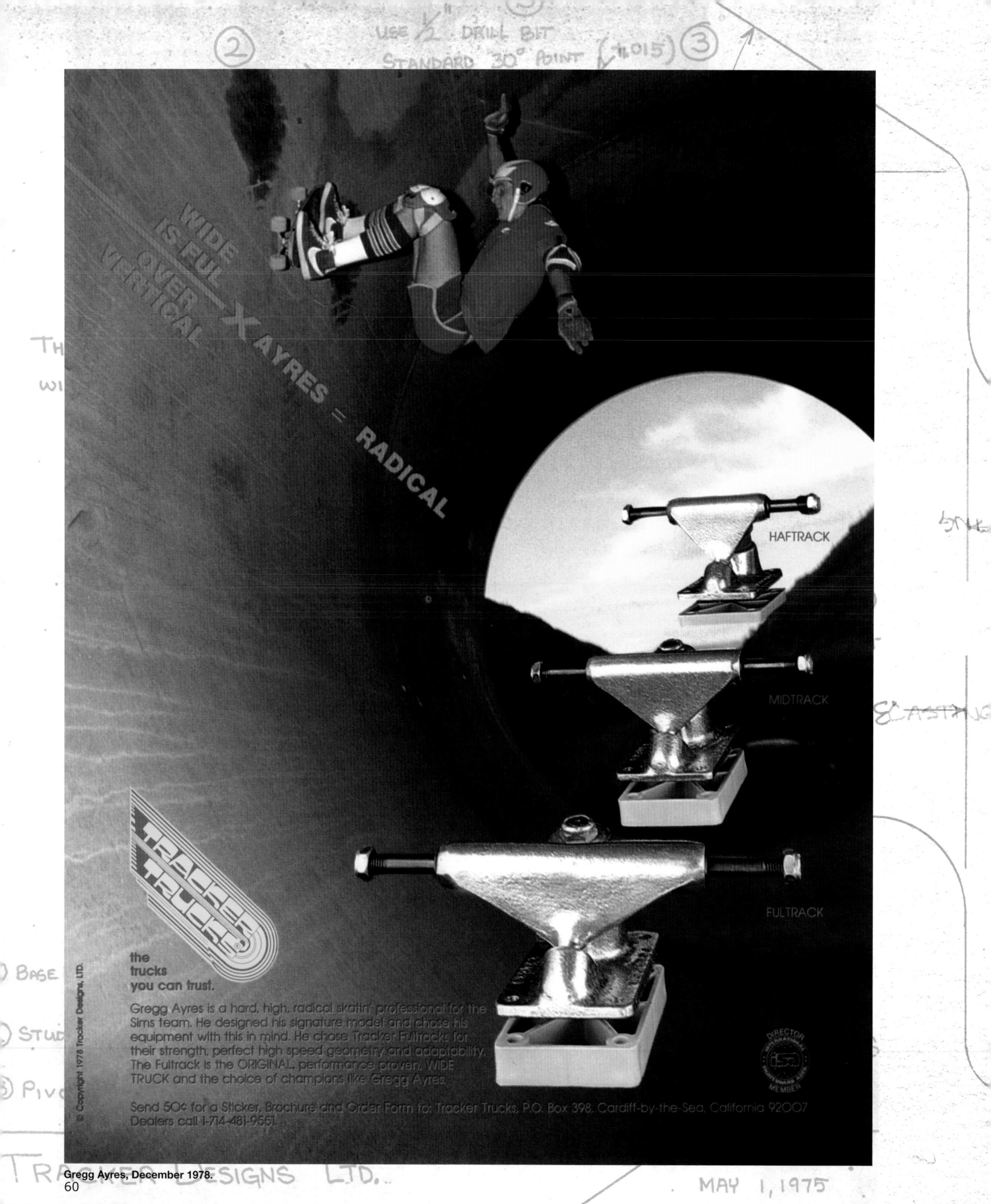
USE 1/2" DRILL BIT
STANDARD 30° POINT (±.015)
WIDE IS FUL OVER VERTICAL X AYRES = RADICAL
HAFTRACK
MIDTRACK
FULTRACK
TRACKER TRUCKS
the trucks you can trust.
Gregg Ayres is a hard, high, radical skatin' professional for the Sims team. He designed his signature model and chose his equipment with this in mind. He chose Tracker Fultracks for their strength, perfect high speed geometry and adaptability. The Fultrack is the ORIGINAL, performance proven, WIDE TRUCK and the choice of champions like Gregg Ayres.
Send 50¢ for a Sticker, Brochure and Order Form to: Tracker Trucks, P.O. Box 398, Cardiff-by-the-Sea, California 92007
Dealers call 1-714-481-9551.
© Copyright 1978 Tracker Designs, LTD.
DIRECTOR ISA MEMBER
TRACKER DESIGNS LTD.
MAY 1, 1975
L.M. BALMA

Gregg Ayres, December 1978.

Standing tall at six-foot-four, Gregg Ayres literally towered over his peers in the skateboard world of the mid to late 1970s (see page 109). Using his height as an asset rather than a hindrance, this human pendulum became a pipe and pool master, scoring three *Skateboarder* magazine covers in just one year! After famously flying a Tunnel jersey from 1976 to '78, Gregg went on to skate for Sims, who gave him a pro model deck (which now sells for crazy amounts of money on eBay), as well as Kryptonics and Pepsi. Born on April 15, 1959 in Red Bank, New Jersey, Gregg celebrates his birthday every year by filing tax returns, which kind of makes sense, since he earns his living as a math teacher.—GSD

SkateBoarder

DISCOVERY: GIANT PIPES
RADICAL SKATEPARK ACTION
22 HOT FREESTYLERS

When did you start skateboarding?
Probably around 1965 or '66, when my parents moved to Redondo Beach, California.
Describe your first good skateboard.
Back in the late '60s, we coveted a board that had the brick red Roller Derby wheels, which were not clay. Way before urethane, I think these wheels were rubber or rubberized somehow, which made them ride smoothly and grip well so they didn't come to a stop on little pebbles. The wheels were very slow and wore out quickly, but they were so much better than anything else from that era, that we hunted everywhere for them. We lived on a steep hill and we were always trying to slow down anyway, so the lack of speed wasn't an issue. In the mid '70s urethane era, I started to make my own Boats Boards out of plywood and fiberglass. We called them boats because they were long for the time—probably 32"-34"—when most boards were 22"-26". In the later '70s, I had my own model

boards and the Tunnel Rodriguez model with solid wood kicktails that worked really well. I always thought the laminates flexed too much and the kicktail flattened out too much while riding, but I had to switch when solid wood boards went totally out of favor.
How did you get on the Tracker team?
That is a very good question, and I can't say that I totally remember, but I think Stacy Peralta introduced me to David Dominy and put in a good word for me. I was thinking Mitch Haake of Tunnel was critical to getting me on the team, as he did take me to the Tracker factory several times. But, I was on the Tracker team while I still rode for ET Surfboards skate team of Hermosa Beach, prior to Tunnel. Stacy Peralta was always very helpful to my skateboarding career and he never expected anything in return. I passed a little of this spirit on later by giving Tony Jetton some of my Trackers when he rode for Magnum and helped get him on the team.
Which Tracker models did you ride?
To be honest, I tried the original Fultracks and didn't like them. They were primarily built for slalom, thus were too wide for our skinny boards of the time and too low to keep the wheels from rubbing on the board. But, when Haftracks came along, it was a perfect match for the boards of the day and my relatively wide Tunnel Rock wheels. Haftracks were also much higher, so they did not have the problems with wheels contacting the board. I rode this set-up for a long time. Extracks and Sixtracks were also perfect matches for the wider boards that came out later. Both Extracks and Sixtracks had the same great feel and performance of Haftracks, so it was easy to adjust to the wider wheelbases.
Tell us about your favorite Tracker ads.
I was lucky enough to be in three Tracker ads, but just one featured me by myself skating in the Arizona pipes in December 1978. That would have to be my favorite.
Did you invent any tricks on Trackers?
The switch-foot carve, the slide to get back to regular footed, and probably some others I can't remember. We spent a lot of time trying to think up new tricks, and in those days, it was easier to come up with them.
What stood out about the performance of Trackers Trucks'?
The geometry. Who knew whether it was brilliant design or luck, but I found the feel of the trucks better than the rest. I was always able to turn very sharply yet feel stable and never wobbly. An example of a maneuver like this would be a figure 8 carve in a pool, which took some very sharp turning, but also required a lot of stability to pull off. Many of the friends I rode with were Indy guys, like Rodd Saunders, Steve Olson, Rick Blackhart, etc. and they always had me try their new trucks, but I never thought they felt as good as Trackers.
Tell us about some memorable times with the Tracker team.
I don't know that I really travelled with the

official Tracker team much. I always considered that the San Diego Tracker crew. But, I do think that we frequently put together our own Tracker team North consisting of Stacy Peralta, Paul Hoffman, Rodd Saunders, Jerry Valdez, Kent Senatore, Mark Smith, David Ferry, Tony Jetton and myself. This was a great group to skate with. Everyone got along well, and yet we pushed each other pretty hard. Everyone had a pretty good sense of humor and no one took themselves too seriously.
Tell us a couple of crazy stories from road trips.
This one has been told many times, but the best was probably the Arizona trip with Rick Blackhart and Doug Schnieder with Blackhart midnight power-sliding Schnieder's old station wagon on gravel service roads for hours until a gas tank puncture stranded us in the middle of the night in the middle of nowhere.
Why was Tracker so important in the history of skateboarding?
They made a great truck that delivered performance and durability at a time when the sport needed a higher quality truck. I was constantly bending and replacing axles until Tracker came out with their spring steel axle. Even their risers were innovative. I still have a set of their yellow magnesium Extracks, the coolest truck ever?
Which skateboarders inspired you most?
Early on, Jay Adams' sequence in Hal Jepsen's *Super Session* was amazing. Later, Kevin Anderson, a fearless and very underappreciated skater, plus Stacy Peralta, Rodd Saunders, Tony Jetton and Steve Olson.
What have been the highlights of your time in skateboarding?
Without a doubt, being on the cover of *Skateboarder* magazine three times in 1977 and leading the very first pool contest in Spring Valley after day one. And, of course, being able to do what we loved to do around the clock for three or four years.
What are you up to today?
Today, I'm a math teacher in the San Fernando Valley. My students don't believe me when I say I used to skate. It's pretty funny to see their reactions when I get out the photos. As a long suffering LA Kings fan since 1969, when my mom took me to my first hockey game for my 10th birthday, no one could be more excited or shocked to see their success. I was in the 16,500 seat Forum many times with 2,000 other fans during the rough years. I still play, coach and watch hockey. I think that my hockey balance had a lot to do with my success at skateboarding. I still like to ski

Gregg Ayres
INTERVIEW

and watch Formula 1 and MotoGP.
Closing comments?
Thank you to Larry, Louise and David for their generosity, unwavering support, appreciation and positive encouragement. They hung in there through team changes, injuries and lots of ups and downs. Tracker was a constant in my skating and they were always a class operation.

Left: **Gregg Ayres tackles the legendary Desert Pipes in Arizona, April 1977.** Photo: James Cassimus

Around 1976-'77, a whole nation full of teenage boys had a crush on Laura Thornhill. I know, because I was one of them. With her long locks flowing, she watercolored the world under her wheels with such style and grace. Not only was Laura the first girl to be honored with a pro model deck in the '70s, she was also the first girl to score a Who's Hot and an interview in *Skateboarder* magazine. She was a big deal then, and despite several injuries that took her out of the limelight, she still rolls around today. So, let's play catch-up with Laura and reminisce upon those halcyon days of the mid 1970s, when skateboarding was beautiful.—GSD

LMB: Where were you born?
I was born in Dallas, Texas in 1961, where I grew up. I moved out to California on Super Bowl Sunday 1974. I had just started to skateboard a little bit before that, and realized that Palos Verdes was a great place to do it. All I wanted was a skateboard. I got a Black Knight with black wheels on it for my 13th birthday, which I rode every day after school. All I wanted to do was ride. I just wanted to start getting good. The first *Skateboarder* magazine came out with Gregg Weaver on the cover, and there were two or three pictures of girls in there riding. I saw that and said, "I want to be in this magazine." Like everybody else, when the magazine came out, I just devoured it cover to cover. What I wanted more than anything was to be really good at skateboarding and be in that mag. A contest happened at my school, I entered it, I was the only girl and I won. A month or so later, there was the Steve's South Bay contest and I won it, too. At that contest, Danny Bearer came up and asked me to be on Logan. He introduced me to Brian Logan, and the rest is history. I started with Logan and stayed with them for a long time.

LMB: What was your favorite terrain?
A little bit of everything. I loved La Costa and being out on the Black Hill. I loved doing freestyle and slalom, but the Escondido reservoir was my favorite intense terrain. Those weekends out at the Black Hill were special—learning tricks and skating with everyone.

GSD: Did you ever ride vert?
I rode a little bit of vert at a couple of empty pools by my house. We would sneak in the backyard of that house and a couple of other places. I went on one of the first trips with Warren Bolster out to the Arizona pipes. That

was my first experience in a serious back-to-back vert place. I had gone out to Mt. Baldy prior to that, but there was always water running down it. Back then, everyone was kind of an all-around skater: freestyle, downhill, slalom, vert—a little bit of everything.

LMB: Where did you get your Trackers?
I was given my first set of Trackers from my good friend Dave Dominy at La Costa out of the back of his Volvo station wagon.

LMB: Which model were they?
My first set was Fultracks. I wish I could say that I still have them.

LMB: Which model did you end up riding most of the time?
Mostly Fultracks, but I remember having some Haftracks, too. Looking at all of the photos I have, it seemed that I did everything on Fultracks. I had the Haftracks on my freestyle board.

LMB: Tell us about the Carlsbad sessions.
Just about every weekend, I was down here staying with the Logans. John O'Malley had just built the Carlsbad skatepark and we would go out there and skate until it got dark. We were also shooting some things for *Skateboarder* magazine at night, including my interview.

LMB: Why was Tracker so important in the history of skateboarding?
Just like when the Cadillac wheels came out, Tracker changed everything. It was a new sensation, a better application for riding, and it made everything smoother. Tracker was the new invention that everyone wanted. It was the latest, greatest new thing that came and stayed for a very long time—even to this day.

LMB: Which skaters inspired you?
I would say definitely the Logans and Torger Johnson. Torger had an amazing style and grace. He was a huge inspiration with his fluidity. I didn't invent the spacewalk—Torger and Bruce did that—but I definitely tried to emulate it. Bruce Logan invented the kickturn in the air, which Torger called the spacewalk. Torger was someone to admire, to watch him skate. Ty Page was also a huge inspiration, because he was an excellent all-around skater. At one point, we had the best skaters in the world on the Logan Team. After the Zephyr team fell apart, all of those guys came and rode for us: we had Tony Alva, Jay Adams and Bob Biniak, too. It was inspiring to have skaters like that around.

LMB: Do you recall any memorable times with the Tracker team?
When we—the Sims, Logan and G&S teams—all piled into an RV to go to the Cow Palace. It was like a traveling circus of people, different factions that made up a community of people. All of those trips and contests were always filled with antics, escapades and a wild cast of characters. They were all fun times.

LMB: Did your mom ever worry about you hanging out with a bunch of wild and crazy guys?
I'm sure she did, but Robin Logan, Kim Cespedes, Ellen Oneal and Desiree Von Essen were in the mix, so there were always women around. Although mom met the Logans and felt that I was safe enough and in the hands of a great group of people, I think she worried about me all the time.

LMB: Do you still skate?
I do still skate. I do a little freestyle and I cruise and carve. I'm not into getting hurt, which is what ultimately ended my skating career, when I dislocated my elbow. That was kind of the beginning of the end. I dislocated it two more times after that on a skateboard and a third time after that on skis. I'm just not into that kind of severe pain, so I backed off and segued into other things in life. But, I always continued skating, just not actively in parks and doing things that could seriously hurt me. I love riding my board and being part of the skating community.

GSD: When did that injury happen?
It happened at Skatepark Montebello in 1978. It was pre-opening day when they let all of the pros ride, so everyone was there. I borrowed Stacy Peralta's board, did the snake run, came back and did a kickturn to stop and give him his board. There was super slick polished concrete at the top of the run, so I slid out, fell back and caught myself with my arm and it dislocated.

LMB: When you got out of skating, what did you do?
I segued into the entertainment industry and worked for a record distribution company that imported records from all over the world. I started working as a production co-ordinator in a place called Studio Instrument Rentals in Hollywood in 1984, which was full of bands rehearsing, video shoots, etc. After getting married in 1987, I had my first child, a son named Sage, who was born in 1990, and my second child in 1993, a daughter named Kylie.

Shortly thereafter, my husband, his partner, and I started our own company that provided state of the art rehearsal studios, and musical equipment and gear for the top musical acts in the world of rock and roll. We also built a beautiful soundstage where many music videos and TV shows would take place. We provided musical production support for just about every award show and music special on the planet and everything in between. I am still involved in the entertainment industry and am currently working on the development of a couple of TV shows and other exciting projects.

LMB: Do you have any hobbies?
I'm totally into cycling and mountain biking. I

Laura Thornhill INTERVIEW

live in Valencia, so there's amazing riding up there. I love snowboarding, it's my favorite. I also love hiking, trail running, yoga and being healthy, trying to stay fit and still skating carefully and casually.

LMB: Closing comments?
It's an honor to be sitting here with you, Larry, being interviewed to be part of an amazing book. I'm honored to have some historical roots in skateboarding and to call the community of people that I've known for a really long time family.

Read the full-length interview at trackertrucks.com

Above left: **Laura Thornhill, night session at Carlsbad Skatepark in Carlsbad, California, circa 1976.** Photo: Warren Bolster

Laura Thornhill arcs another stylish frontside off the lip at a sun-splashed Carlsbad, circa 1976. Photo: Warren Bolster

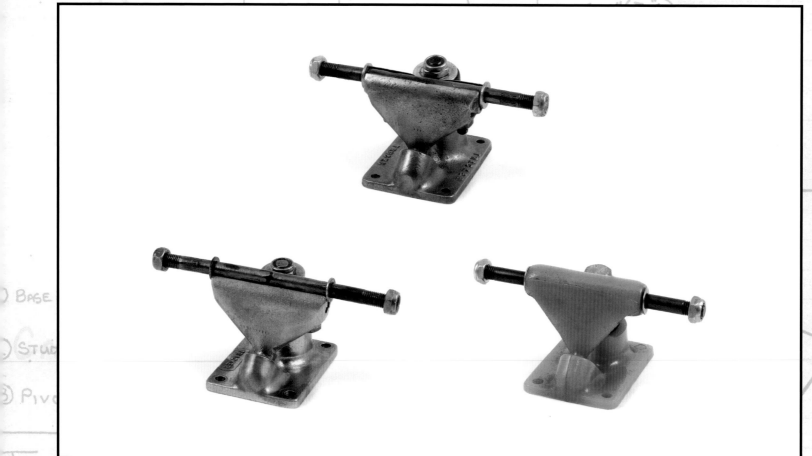

TRACKER DESIGNS LTD.

T-002 BASE HANGER

MAY 1, 1975

L.M. BALMA

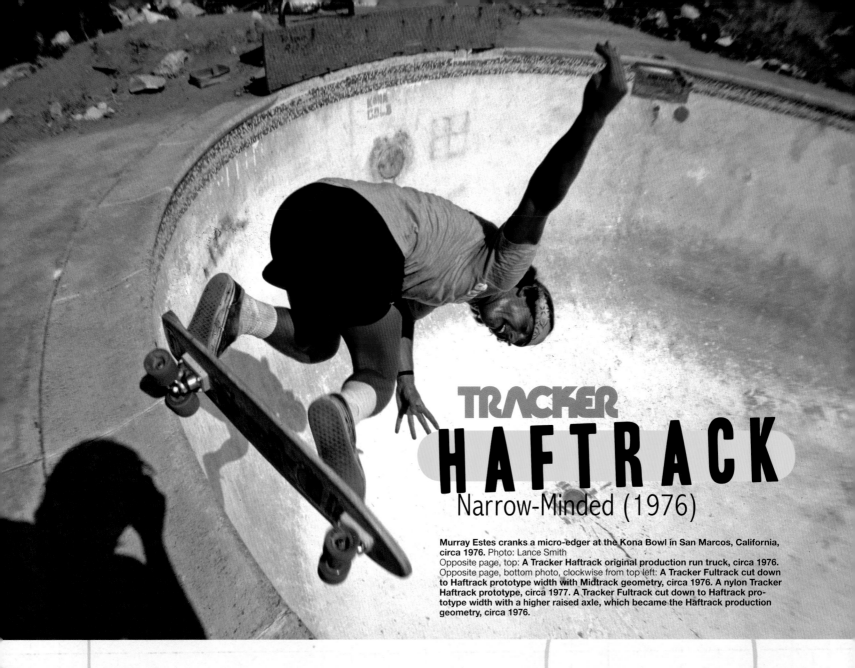

TRACKER
HAFTRACK
Narrow-Minded (1976)

Murray Estes cranks a micro-edger at the Kona Bowl in San Marcos, California, circa 1976. Photo: Lance Smith
Opposite page, top: **A Tracker Haftrack original production run truck, circa 1976.**
Opposite page, bottom photo, clockwise from top left: **A Tracker Fultrack cut down to Haftrack prototype width with Midtrack geometry, circa 1976. A nylon Tracker Haftrack prototype, circa 1977. A Tracker Fultrack cut down to Haftrack prototype width with a higher raised axle, which became the Haftrack production geometry, circa 1976.**

In 1976, many skaters weren't quite ready for the 4 1/4" width of the Tracker Fultrack truck. In fact, some were downright afraid of it! Most skateboard widths were still very narrow, clocking in at around 6" to 7". Even as boards began to widen, the wheels of the time were so wide that you could still ride a narrow truck. Tracker responded to the market with the Haftrack, a truck with a 2 5/8" (66 mm) hanger width. Tracker skaters now had a choice. The Haftrack was just slightly wider than the original Bahne and Bennett trucks that debuted along with the Fultrack; therefore they became popular among bowl skaters. Freestylers and even some slalom racers also preferred the narrower width.

During development of the Haftrack, we had our team experiment with many different hanger geometries and give us their feedback. We finally built the Haftrack axle hanger with a higher roll center by raising the axle, which also offered more kingpin nut clearance. The Haftrack baseplate was the same as the Fultrack, composed of all of the same strong and lightweight materials. Although at first we were still using cone nuts on Haftracks to accommodate loose ball bearing wheels, by late 1976, we eliminated them and built all of our trucks to accept precision bearings.

In 1978, we introduced all of our truck sizes with Gnarly pivots (see page 106). As decks grew dramatically wider in the second half of 1978—reaching 9" to 10" or more—sales of the Haftrack slowed down considerably. Since we had a huge stock of small pivot Haftracks, we never went into full production on the Gnarly Tracker Haftrack. Likewise, we also worked on a small pivot lightweight nylon Haftrack prototype developed by Gary Dodds that never went into production. (There are probably only two or three of those in existence!) In 1979, when we developed the Tracker roller skate plates and Trekker strap-on skates, we outfitted them with our overstock of small pivot Haftracks. In fact, I still have a few leftover boxes full of them to this day. In the '80s, sales of Haftracks never rebounded and, in fact, it's the only Tracker truck width that we no longer produce. Even modern day eight-wheelers, which used to sport Haftracks in the '70s, have switched over to Midtracks. So, let us all observe a moment of silence for the death of the Tracker Haftrack!—**LMB**

Flying harsh Dogtown colors in your face, **Paul Constantineau wheels it in Skatopia's famous halfpipe in Buena Park, California, circa 1977.** Photo: Jim Goodrich
Opposite page: **Desiree Von Essen flows a graceful one-foot wheelie, circa 1976.** Photo: Unknown

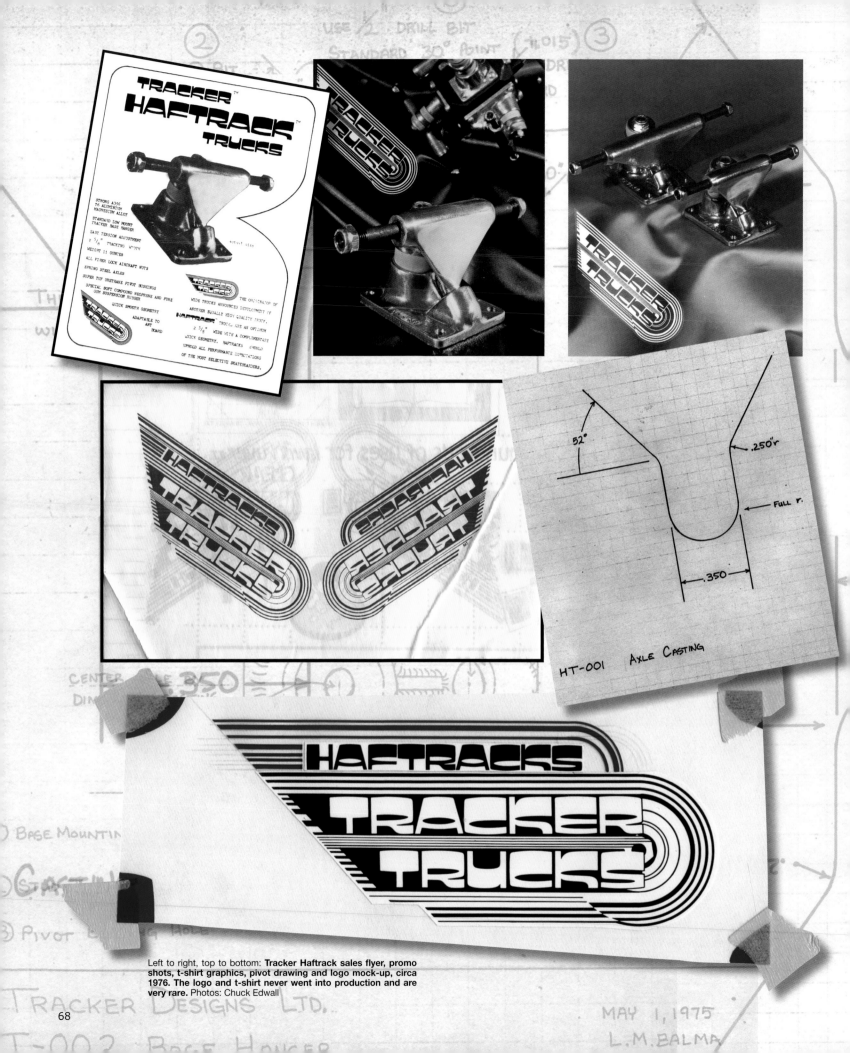

Left to right, top to bottom: **Tracker Haftrack sales flyer, promo shots, t-shirt graphics, pivot drawing and logo mock-up, circa 1976. The logo and t-shirt never went into production and are very rare.** Photos: Chuck Edwall

Dennis Martinez tail taps at Spring Valley skatepark in San Diego, California, circa 1978. Photo: Jim Goodrich

David Paul acid drops into the Kona Bowl in San Marcos, California, circa 1976. Photo: Lance Smith

RODNEY JESSE
on the edge
of a deep hole
on his favorite trucks.

HAFTRACKS

TRACKER TRUCKS
P.O. Box 217
Cardiff-By-The-Sea
California, 92007
photo: Lance Smith

Rodney Jesse, June 1977.

Gunnar Haugo, December 1977.

TRACKER TRUCKS

THE BEST YOU CAN GET

Gunnar Haugo finds TRACKER HAFTRACKS to be the perfect take-off gear for the Bozoz Bowl. TRACKER HAFTRACKS specially designed for bowls and freestyle.
P.O. Box 398 Cardiff-by-the-Sea, CA 92007

TRACKER TRUCKS

TRACKER
HAFTRACK
Trucks

RUSS GOSNELL
FLYING HIGH

PO Box 217 Cardiff by the Sea, Cal 92007 (714) 481-9551

Russ Gosnell, circa 1976.

IN THE
SPIRIT OF
COMPETITION

TRACKER
TRUCKS
Presents

THE
HAFTRACK

During the past year TRACKER TRUCKS has set the standards for performance, strength, and durability with the original wide truck design. Several other manufacturers have tried to imitate our original wide truck, but the serious skateboarder still recognizes the performance proven TRACKER.
Now TRACKER presents our new design. The HAFTRACK, every bit as STRONG, DURABLE and BEAUTIFUL as our original wide truck. We named it HAFTRACK because of its narrower tracking width, 2⅞ inches. The HAFTRACK is engineered to provide the SMOOTH and QUICK geometry demanded by today's aggressive skateboarder. HAFTRACKS are cast of the same prime A356 aluminum-magnesium alloy. They have the same hardened axle material and aircraft locknuts.

TRACKER is also proud to announce

The Tracker Guaranty

Tracker Designs, LTD. A California corporation, guarantees all metal assemblies of Tracker Trucks and Haftrack Trucks to be free of defects in materials and workmanship.
Should your Tracker Truck or Haftrack Truck fail in ordinary use, send the broken part, postage prepaid, to Tracker Designs, LTD. P.O. Box 217, Cardiff-by-the-Sea, California 92007
Please enclose a 3"x5" card with your name, address and zip code. A brief description of the circumstances surrounding the part failure would be appreciated.

TRACKER TRUCKS $22.00 per pair. HAFTRACK TRUCKS $21.00 per pair, T-shirts $4.50, Stickers 25¢, free brochure, (out of state) add $1.00 shipping. California residents add 6%, send cashiers check or money order ONLY to: Tracker Trucks, P.O. Box 217, Cardiff-by-the-Sea, California 92007. Dealer Inquiries (714) 481-9551.

Distributors: CONTROL PRODUCTS

Tracker Trucks presents the Haftrack, December 1976.

IN THE SPIRIT OF COMPETITION

Stacy and equally Radical Friends with the trucks that work

New from Tracker is the **Perfect Slalom Cone** , bright orange, unbreakable, **P.I.S.A.** approved size and weight $1.00 ea. Also new is the **Henry Hester Slalom Champion Poster** 2'x3' and full color $1.20 ea

Stacy Peralta, a ripping member of the Gordon & Smith skateboard team, prefers our new **Haftrack Trucks.** He never hesitates recommending Tracker Trucks to his friends, because Trackers consistently uphold a high level of **performance** and **excellent durability.**

Trackers come with the **finest guarantee** in the business on all the metal components under ordinary use. If you have a problem send the damaged part and a self addressed card with a brief description of how the part failed to Tracker Trucks and the part will be replaced. Tracker Trucks are the best thing you can do for your skateboard!

Ask for Trackers, always available with finer skateboards!

Tracker Trucks per pair $22.00, Haftracks per pair $21.00, T shirt $4.50, Sticker 25¢, Free Brochure, out of state add $1.00 shipping, California residents add 6%, send cashiers check or money order ONLY to: Tracker Trucks P.O. Box 217, Cardiff by the Sea, California 92007 Dealer Inquiries 1-714-481-9551

Stacy Peralta, June 1977.

Tony Hawk and Stacy Peralta shred the Hawk facility in Fallbrook, California, circa 1987. Photo: Grant Brittain

As one of the top pro skateboarders of the 1970s, Stacy Peralta's atoms were activated across a wide swath of reality: participating in a lion's share of contests, demos and tours, and appearing in a mammoth mound of magazines, movies and merchandise. After a lucrative career riding for G&S, Stacy joined forces with George Powell in 1978 to form Powell-Peralta and the Bones Brigade, which went on to become one of the top brands and teams of the '80s. After pioneering the first-ever skateboard video in 1984, *The Bones Brigade Video Show*, Stacy applied the lessons he learned to direct full-blown documentaries in subsequent decades like *Dogtown and Z-Boys*, *Riding Giants*, *Crips and Bloods: Made in America* and *Bones Brigade: An Autobiography*. Stacy still skates and films today.—GSD

Stacy Peralta
INTERVIEW

When did you first start skateboarding?
I believe I was four or five years old the first time I rode a box cart skateboard scooter. But, the first time I actually connected with skateboarding, I was seven years old, skating down the street from my house. There was a drugstore, Steve's Rexall Drugs, a block down with a very wide sidewalk around it with beautifully groomed concrete. I remember skating there for the first time on this concrete. I hadn't experienced anything like that feeling before. When you ride a bicycle, you sit down on a seat and you have handlebars to grip and hold onto—there's a security factor that bicycles provide. Skateboards offer no security. It's a completely insecure act. You're standing on this moving little magic carpet, you have nothing to grasp onto, no seat and no handlebars. You know that if you fall, you're going to face plant into concrete. And so, I was seven years old going down this sidewalk. I could feel the rumble of the concrete coming up through my feet and the wind on my face. And the whole time I was balancing: this way to the right, that way to the left, then a bit forward, then a bit back, constantly adjusting. I was searching or feeling for my equilibrium and my center. So, in the middle of all of this chaos, all of the noise and rumble and fear, I suddenly found my center, my equilibrium, and then this intense feeling and sense of stillness filled me. I was jamming down the sidewalk on this little board with all of this chaos swirling around me and I was totally at peace.

When did you get your first Trackers?
I distinctly remember seeing my first set of Tracker Trucks. I was skating La Costa sometime in the '70s, and Dave Dominy arrived on the hill with a set of Fultracks. I laid my eyes on those things and was completely knocked off my feet, absolutely flabbergasted at the sight of them. I couldn't believe what I was seeing. It was a complete and total Eureka moment! I remember thinking, "Of course, trucks should be wider! How did we not think of this earlier?" It was such a pure moment I'll never forget. From that point forward, there was no other truck for me.

Why was Tracker so important in the history of skateboarding?
The revolution and evolution of skateboard trucks began with Tracker. Tracker can take the credit for being the first truck designed specifically for skateboards that was not based on past roller skate truck designs, but based on what skateboarders demanded and needed. I'm quite sure it was the very first truck designed by people who actually rode skateboards. Very few remember that as skateboarders back then in the '60s and '70s, we had to rely on hand-me-down roller skate technology—nothing was built for us—we had to scrounge for roller skate parts and any and everything to build our own boards. For a company such as Tracker to suddenly appear and build something specifically designed for us skateboarders was simply overwhelming and amazing. It wasn't just the invention of the Tracker Truck that was so important to us, but the statement the invention made to us. The invention of the Tracker Truck was one of those pivotal moments in skateboarding when we could suddenly see that there was going to be a future for us as skateboarders.

Which tricks did you invent on Tracker Trucks?
360 torque spacewalk, reverse G-turn, banked 540 slide, vertical 540 slide, aerial bert-revert, etc.

You and Russ Gosnell were doing demos for bank openings on the Tracker Ramp. What do you remember about that?
How tight the ramp was—there was no flat bottom at all, it was just a tight U. So, pumping back and forth was like being a hamster on a wheel, forever spinning and going nowhere. We were so limited in so many ways back then.

Your G&S Warptail and Warptail II must have been the largest selling skateboard deck in the late '70s. How did you decide to step up to be a company owner with George Powell?
I wanted a future in skateboarding, and I realized I was not going to be able to make that happen at Gordon and Smith, unfortunately. Larry Gordon was very good to me; he changed my life by giving me the opportunity of riding for him. Many of my peers rode for companies that made big promises to them but failed to deliver. When Larry Gordon said to me, "We're going to make this many of your model boards per month, every month," he did. He built them, sold them and shipped them, and, as a result, I was paid quite a bit of money and was given so many life-changing opportunities to travel the world and introduce modern skateboarding to countries that had never seen it.

You and Craig Stecyk were an awesome marketing team. You brought him to Tracker to help us with our ad image.
That was during skateboarding's dark age in the early to mid '80s. George and I couldn't pay Stecyk enough money per month for what he was providing us, and I knew Stecyk needed more income, so I thought up the idea of hooking you up with him. I knew that you needed someone to conceive and carry out your advertising campaign. Craig didn't trust a lot of people back then, but he trusted people who had "put in the time," and who were there from the start, and you were one of those original guys, so he felt comfortable with you. Plus, you didn't talk a lot. You're a man of few words, and I think he respected you for that. I think Craig saw you as someone who gets things done but doesn't make a big deal about it. Plus, you like cars, which is always a big deal with Craig.

You introduced me to skate zines, GSD and Bryan Ridgeway at Del Mar in 1982. What do you remember about that?
I remember how fresh and experimental the time was. We all had nothing to lose, because we were all hanging by a thread to keep our businesses alive and to keep skateboarding alive, so we were essentially willing to try anything. Unusual people like GSD and the Ridge were part of skateboarding at that time because they were both great "outsider characters" who helped to provide definition to what skateboarding was and was becoming.

Do you recall any other memorable times with Tracker?
Being one of the voices who helped talk Peggy Cozens into appearing in the Tracker ad in which she is dressed up as an old lady with a walking cane getting run down by GSD on a skateboard. That was one of the boldest strokes of genius I've ever been party to. I also have very fond memories of helping to get the first issues of *TransWorld Skateboarding* up and running. I remember the meetings with you, myself, Neil Blender, GSD and Peggy. It was all such a "seat of our pants" type of thing.

Do you still skate today?
Yes, I still skate today. I do it for exercise and for spiritual reasons. Spiritual in that skateboarding is a part of who I am, it's something that helped shape me, and it also opened the world up to me, so I feel it's important that I remain connected to it by doing it.

Are you still riding Trackers?

One of my boards that I've been riding for decades and still ride today has one of my original sets of Haftracks bolted to it, if you can believe that. The trucks even have the original grey Tracker bushings. I ride that board with those trucks almost every day. What more can I say than that?

Read the full-length interview at trackertrucks.com

Above: **Stacy Peralta demonstrates his signature space walk dance in the late 1980s.** Photo: Tod Swank

By Larry Balma

73

On more than one occasion back in 1975, San Diego golden boy Gregg Weaver was in the right place at the right time! Cadillac urethane wheel developer Frank Nasworthy befriended Gregg, noticed his nascent four-wheeled talent, and featured him in the brand's first ad, dubbing him The Cadillac Kid in the process. Around the same time, *Skateboarder* magazine editor and head photographer Warren Bolster snapped a photo of Gregg soul-carving the San Marcos pool and ran it on the cover of the re-launched mag's first issue since the original skateboard boom back in 1965. On that day, Gregg became one of Warren's favorite subjects; in fact, from 1975 through '77, it was difficult to flick through a copy of *Skateboarder* without seeing Gregg's mug plastered somewhere.—GSD

LMB: When did you start skating?
In the sixth grade, my neighbor gave me a Black Knight clay wheel skateboard, and that became my transportation. It wasn't really a sport endeavor for me at first. I would go to Cardiff elementary, bomb the hill, hit a couple of pebbles and lose some skin. Clay wheels really sucked. Eventually, I got a Hobie, my first real board. It had clay wheels, too. Then I got a set of Cadillac wheels and I was stoked—no pebbles, no problem! When I was skateboarding to my sister's house down Neptune, I met Frank Nasworthy, who was the first to put urethane wheels on skateboards. When I was riding by his house, he stopped me and said he was supposed to go shoot his first Cadillac wheel ads with some other kid, but he couldn't find him. Frank said, "Well I can't find him, so do you want to go shoot some pictures?" and I replied, "Well, okay." He said, "I'll give you a wetsuit." I got a free ride to La Costa and I got a wetsuit. So, we went out and took some pictures, and to this day, I don't think Frank ever gave me that wetsuit. He's such a liar (laughs)! Those were the original Cadillac wheel ads, but I guess *Surfer* magazine lost the slides; so they sent Art Brewer down to re-shoot the ads. Art sat on the back of a pick-up and I followed him down the hill.

LMB: When did you get your first set of Tracker Trucks?
I know I bought them. Prior to Trackers, I rode Bennetts, but they just weren't dependable. I don't know how many Bennett trucks I broke. That was the best thing about Trackers, they were more durable than your board. You could count on them. I started riding the Midtrack, which was my favorite truck for pools and bowls. Fultracks were a little wide, but I loved Midtracks, and Haftracks were a little tippy for pools. Tracker is a great truck with great turning response, and the durability is unquestionable.

LMB: How did you get on the Hobie team?
I did those Cadillac ads and I loved that 30" stringer woody board, so I think they got ahold of me originally to be on the team. I went and met with Hobie Alter at his house on the beach in Dana Point—he was a really nice gentleman—and it just started slow like that. I think I signed a contract for, like, $500 per month, plus 50 cents per board. I liked that team. I loved everyone on it—Kim Cespedes, Mike Weed was a nice guy, Skitch Hitchcock. It was a really good assembly of characters.

LMB: Warren Bolster was kind of like your pocket photographer, wasn't he?
Yeah, Warren Bolster made my career. He took me under his wing. I was his partner to shoot with. I was the only one who would go with him, because his car was so filthy (laughs). It was like, "Did you did get a tetanus shot before you got into Bolster's Pinto (laughs)?" He and I became good friends. He would take me to Big Rock and go surfing. He was an awesome surf photographer. When he and his wife Susan were out of town, I'd watch his house with my girlfriend. He wasn't the easiest guy to click with. Warren was a complex character, but a great guy and photographer. The first cover of *Skateboarder*, where I was halfway up the pool, I said, "Really, Warren, I was hitting the tiles." But Warren replied, "This shot is aesthetically perfect," and I said, "Really? I'm just right above the shit line, below the light, and you had to use this?" He didn't care. It was all about the lighting and the angle.

LS: So, you were hitting tiles?
Oh, yeah. That was just a weak shot, it was embarrassing. It gave the Dogtown guys a bunch of fuel [to tease me]. "Look what's happening down South." I never lived down that one.

LMB: Who were Tracker's best riders?
Kim Cespedes. Rodney Jesse. He's by far the best in my opinion, as good or better than all of us. Rodney was the gnarliest, he had no fear. I've never seen anyone skate like that. There's super 8 film of him just blowing away Carlsbad skatepark. I'm embarrassed to be on the same film with him. Tony Alva is an all-time great.

LMB: Which Tracker ad is your favorite?
The one where I'm at El Cajon skatepark, doing a handplant, just because I remember Craig Stecyk saying, "Flush twice, it's a long way to El Cajon." He thought that would piss me off, but it just gave me a fire in my belly.

LMB: Why was Tracker so important in the history of skateboarding?
Because the trucks worked, they were functional and didn't break. You could count on Tracker, the most dependable truck I've seen. I don't know what you guys did with the radius, but they turned. Thanks for the trucks, they saved my ass.

LMB: Which was your favorite spot?
Escondido reservoir, I loved that place. The Valley Center pool was a bitchin' place. The Kona Bowl. The Fruit Bowl was cool. Mt Baldy. The Arizona pipes were awesome, like nothing you've ever skated before. We flew out there two or three times with Warren Bolster, Tom Inouye, Waldo Autry and Stacy Peralta. When we drove up the first time, there were these massive pipe sections sitting in the middle of nowhere, and we were all, "Really? Cha-ching!" They were perfectly smooth like silk. We found some that were already connected into a tunnel to bring Northern Arizona water to Phoenix. It was a monstrosity that descended into the darkness on a six percent grade. Before I knew it, I was dropping in and going side to side. There were two-inch wide gaps between the sections, but I didn't really think about that. So, I was going frontside, then came down and caught my wheel on a gap and...thud! I was just laying there, thinking, "Someone pull me out!" No one had on their safety gear. We were all so stoked to see the pipes, we just jumped on our boards. After that, it was like, "Okay, let's put on the gear."

LMB: You needed Alan Gelfand to show you the Ollie.
You couldn't see the gaps in the dark, though. It was brutal.

LMB: Anything else?
During my senior year, I was sent up to Los Angeles to live with my stepfather. I was the only surf kid at Burbank High School in North Hollywood. So, basically, I ended up ditching class every day to skate this pool in Barry White's guesthouse backyard. He had a kidney-shaped black pool with a cascading waterfall back there, which was so cool. We would sneak around back to get in. We skated it every day for probably two months. We even met his son, Barry Junior, who was an amateur photographer. He came out and shot pictures, and took us down into his parents' house, where we met his sister. We all become friends.

Gregg Weaver
INTERVIEW

I saw an interview with Bob Biniak, and he actually called me "The Great Gregg Weaver." It was complimentary, because I didn't think those Dogtown guys liked us. Bob was a really cool guy. One day, I ran into him in Venice while I was skating back and forth on the street, and I told him about the pool at Barry White's house. Soon after, in the middle of summer, when it was 105 degrees in the shade, Bob showed up there. While we were skating, Barry White walked up wearing an intimidating, full-length mink stole with a mink cap on, and said, "Mmm, I'm afraid you boys are going to have to leave!" We said, "Okay!" then ran and jumped over the fence. So, we got a little shakedown from Barry White. We never skated there again.

Read the full-length interview at trackertrucks.com

Above left: **Gregg Weaver, Massage Pool, San Diego, California, circa 1976.** Photo: Jim Goodrich

By Larry Balma + Lance Smith

Top: **Gregg Weaver samples a virgin snake run at the Concrete Wave in Anaheim, California, circa 1976.** Photo: Warren Bolster
Bottom: **Rodney Jesse and Gregg pause with their quivers in Rancho Santa Fe, California, early 1980.** Photo: Lance Smith

By Larry Balma

As a strong-willed tomboy, San Diego, California native Kim Cespedes was the gnarliest girl skateboarder of the 1970s, and a card-carrying member of the Hobie team. After living in Hawaii for years, she's now based back in San Diego, still cruising on her longboard. —GSD

Kim Cespedes
INTERVIEW

How old were you when you started skateboarding?

I want to say 14. The first time I got on a skateboard, I fell straight back on my rear end. I said, "I'll never do that again! That was stupid." I had been living in Hawaii and missed surfing a lot. My younger brother, who was my idol and taught me how to skateboard, was a great skater, and a great stylist. I watched him bombing the hills surf skating every day, and I just thought, "God, I've got to do that!" So, I slowly got into it with my brothers.

Was that with urethane wheels or clay?

No, my younger brother Travis came home with a Hobie wooden skateboard with stringers, white clay wheels and loose ball bearings. Then we got a white Hobie scooped board with a blue stripe down the middle and clay wheels, as well. So, when you bombed down the hill, your axle nuts flew off and the loose ball bearings went flying. We spent hours running around on the street, looking for the bearings, putting our wheels back together. But, it was such a rush. That was a big deal, because you could go fast down the hill on steel wheels, but you didn't have a lot of control, because they slid when you turned. So, when the clay wheels came out, some were a little wider, which offered better tracking. They were the bomb, because you could do longer and faster turns.

My brother started making skateboards in wood shop. They made 48" woody boards with a lot of flex that were really good for downhill. We mostly just bombed the hills, because they weren't designed for tight turns, but you could do big, sweeping turns. By the time of the 48" boards, the original Cadillac wheels came out. When we saw the first ads and photos of Gregg Weaver on Cadillac wheels, we were like, "That's what we've got to have," because that guy could skate. He was the guy; he was the stylist we all wanted to be. We all wanted to be like Gregg. It was ironic that I ended up riding for Hobie skateboards. I remember when I was asked, I was floored, I didn't know what to say, and all I could think of saying was, "You mean the team that Gregg Weaver is on?" I was like, "Wow!" With Skitch Hitchcock, Mike Weed and all of those guys, it was a really great team.

So, you were an all-around girl skater.

Yeah. Most of the women skaters were just freestylers, and they were phenomenal. That's one of the reasons why I didn't do freestyle. I saw Ellen Berryman do her gymnastics routine, and I went, "Nope, I don't think I'm doing that on a skateboard. They can have that." They were very good at it, it just wasn't my cup of tea. Being sponsored

by Hobie, they wanted their name out there, and wanted me out there. So, I either did freestyle or slalom. I never really raced slalom before contests, but that's where it was. If you were going to get a sponsor, then you had to participate in contests. I really liked the speed more than I liked doing tricks to music. I'm more of a free spirit, so it was just hard to contain that. I just wanted to surf skate anyway. The only time all of us girls would really get together was when we would get a hotel room. The guys would do their own thing and we'd do ours. During a Catalina race, I remember getting a hotel room with all of the girls, and Bobby Piercy knocked on the door, trying to get in to flirt. We were like, "No, don't let Bobby Piercy in here!" Robin Logan and I lived in the same town and we were great friends, but the rest of the girls were spread out. So, the only time I really saw the girls was at skate contests or maybe out at La Costa.

As far as riding parks, pools and ditches, you were the gnarliest girl skater then.

Thank you for that. A lot of people have told me that I was advanced before my time, and I take a lot of pride in that. I put a lot of time into it. If I wasn't surfing, I skated every night. I was always at the skatepark trying to get better in increments, like, "Oh, I'm going to learn this trick by that time." I was always trying to learn new tricks. It would take a while, but once I got it, I moved on to another trick. But mostly, I was in love with surf skating and just feeling like I was riding a surfboard. That was my main motivation. I just wanted to cut loose, carve big turns and do all of the surf maneuvers. I remember skating in the skatepark with Jerry Lopez and Larry Bertlemann. I was so thrilled. Jerry Lopez was my favorite surfer in *Surfer* magazine, and here I was skateboarding with him. He was a great man, and a really nice guy. It was super fun to surf skate with him. That's what they were doing: transferring their surfing onto the concrete. Larry was doing his Bertlemann slides and all of that stuff. That's what really motivated me, surf skating and developing myself, getting better every day. Equipment was slowly getting better and better, and so were we as skaters. In the '70s, we were doing things nobody did before. It was really fun to be at the forefront of that and to watch it play out.

In that process, you guys also had to learn how to fall and how to use pads.

In the old days, if you fell in giant slalom, the pads didn't really work. You had to learn how to fall even though you didn't have equipment. Nobody really taught you those things. We did have a man named Curtis Hesselgrave running around who knew aikido. I remember one day we were in a pool, and he said, "Okay, you guys, here's how you fall." He taught us the aikido way to fall: tuck your right shoulder and just flip into a summersault or just slide on your pads. Finally, at that time, we had pads with plastic covers, so you could literally slide on them when you fell. That was a huge breakthrough, because

you didn't just hit the concrete and bounce.

Did you ride ditches before skateparks?

I loved reservoirs for skating, because you could go around them and it seemed infinite. We used to go to the VC reservoir and get chased out by the cops. There was also a neighbor out there with a shotgun who would show up, and we'd all scatter. We were always looking for something to skate. I basically lived at Carlsbad skatepark, until Del Mar Skate Ranch eventually opened. I was actually a resident pro there. I taught skateboard classes on Saturday mornings. I loved the keyhole and the reservoir in front. It was such a fun park, I could ride it for hours.

When did you get your first Tracker?

That was around 1976. I had some Haftracks that I bought from a skateboard shop before I rode for Hobie. When Hobie signed me, I got a bunch of boards and all of them had Tracker Trucks on them. I had ridden them a few times before and was really thrilled because I liked them, and those were the trucks I wanted. We had to have Bennetts at first, because Tracker wasn't quite there yet. But when Tracker came out, Bennetts were such an obsolete truck in comparison, so it was a no-brainer to rider Tracker. Once I started riding Trackers, I always rode them, because they fit my style of skating.

The thing that was really neat about Tracker was that they had a really great team, so they got a lot of insight on design, and what people wanted and needed. The beauty of it was that the people who made Tracker Trucks could deliver that: they could sit down, draw it up on paper, develop it, create it and make it. The sport was advancing so quickly in the '70s, it really just escalated, and Tracker was right there innovating with the skaters. That era of skating was really quite fun to go through. Coming away from ball bearing wheels, and then getting

into Cadillacs and going from there. Every year, there was better and better equipment. Tracker Trucks was at the forefront of it and I always say they were a leader. There are other truck companies, and yes, some people like them, but Tracker was the original. It was a no-brainer to ride them.

Read the full-length interview at trackertrucks.com

Above: **Kim Cespedes goes off the lip on a Nor Cal deathbox, circa 1977.** Photo: Kevin Reed
Opposite page: **Kim grinds the keyhole at Del Mar Skate Ranch in Del Mar, California, circa 1976.** Photo: Chuck Edwall

DOGTOWN
The Legend of the Z-Boys

Even before he started surfing, Jeff Ho rode a skateboard at quite a young age. Always working with his hands, craftsmanship was in his bones from the very beginning. After nailing together his first skateboard in 1958, using a 2" x 4" Chicago clamp-on roller skate with steel wheels that he cut in half, Jeff went on to shape his first surfboard in 1965. Training with surfboard maker Dewey Weber in Venice Beach, Jeff produced lightweight, progressive longboards until the short board revolution hit in 1967. The following year, Jeff opened his Zephyr surf shop in Venice Beach, California, which soon became a local landmark and hangout spot for the hardcore surfers and skateboarders. With the gift of gab, his buddy Skip Engblom befriended the customers and ran the shop like a pro, while *Surfer* magazine photojournalist, eccentric artist and all-around counter culture misfit CR Stecyk III handled all things graphically artistic. With such a talented trio in place, the Zephyr shop was destined to become a legend in the worlds of water and concrete.

Whenever the waves were flat, and after sunset, the surf rats who hung out at the Zephyr shop turned to carving concrete on their skateboards. Knowing a good thing when he saw it, Jeff recognized an opportunity to equip the burgeoning land shark movement and quickly tooled up his shop to build solid oak skateboards. Soon after, the famous fiberglass Zephyr deck with a molded-in rocker and a center beam appeared on the scene. As the team riders—including Jay Adams, Tony Alva, Bob Biniak, Chris Cahill, Paul Constantineau, Shogo Kubo, Jim Muir, Peggy Oki, Stacy Peralta, Nathan Pratt, Wentzle Ruml and Allen Sarlo—advanced to shredding berts on banks and catching blue tile fever in backyard pools, the stage was set for them to change the skateboarding world.

The Zephyr team finally made their public debut in the wider world outside of Dogtown in April 1975, when Skip and Craig drove them down to Del Mar near San Diego to compete in the Bahne-Cadillac Skateboard Championships, the first big contest since the sport's original boom in 1965. Described as more of a street gang than a team, the boys launched an all-out attack on the stick man freestyle tricksters with an arsenal of low-slung, forceful, surf-influenced moves

Tony Alva pops the first aerials in skateboarding history with this full-on frontal assault at the Dog Bowl in Santa Monica, California, circa **1977.** Photo: Glen E. Friedman
Opposite page: **Chowing down on a mouth full of metal, Jim Muir stirs up a lil' rivalry with the Badlands, circa 1977.** Photo: CR Stecyk III

that stunned all onlookers. Nothing less than the public debut of modern skateboarding, history was made that fateful day.

Although other ripsters like Jerry Valdez and Kent Senatore in the San Fernando Valley; Steve Alba, Tay Hunt and Lee Gahimer in the Badlands; and Gunnar Haugo, Jeff Tatum and Gregg Weaver down south in San Diego (plus many more from all three areas we don't have the space to name) were also setting banks and bowls on fire, their rivals, the Z-Boys, as the Zephyr team came to be known, were the most mythologized and glorified. A series of cryptic articles ghost written by CR Stecyk III under the pseudonyms John Smythe and Carlos Izan for *Skateboarder* magazine delved into the outrageous exploits of the Z-Boys—both on and off the board—creating a larger than life mystique for them and, unwittingly, himself that went on to deeply influence a whole generation of hardcore skateboarders, musicians and artists. By dint of their raw ability and extensive documentation, Dogtown became the de facto architects of the modern aggressive skateboarder archetype.

Although Tracker is from down south, we backed the Dogtowners 100% from the beginning to the end and beyond. By 1978, the aura of the white-hot Z-Boys burned so brightly, it went supernova. As soon as suc-

In 1978, Wes Humpston (pictured) and Jim Muir started up Dogtown Skates. By boasting the first intricate and colorful skateboard deck graphics, Dogtown one-upped a whole graveyard full of dull, logo-driven designs, setting the stage for an explosion of creative deck art to come in the '80s. Photo: Glen E. Friedman

Top: **In this, the most iconic skateboarding photo of all time, Jay Adams punches through barriers, perfectly conveying the essence, style and attitude of skateboarding. Dogtown, Santa Monica, California, 1975.**
Above: **Jay Boy portrait, 1976.**
Right: **Nathan Pratt, thoroughly ensconced in Skate Town style, 1976. Spray-paint by Low Boy.** All photos this page: CR Stecyk III

Paul Constantineau styles a classic frontside grind on an original Dogtown deck at the Dog Bowl in Santa Monica, California, circa 1977. Photo: Glen E. Friedman
Opposite page, top: A classic Zephyr skateboard from 1975.
Oposite page, bottom: The original Zephyr team at the Bahne-Cadillac contest in Del Mar, California, 1975. Front row, left to right: Wentzle Ruml, Peggy Oki, Jay Adams, Paul Constantineau. Back row, left to right: Shogo Kubo, Bob Biniak, Nathan Pratt, Stacy Peralta, Jim Muir, Allen Sarlo, Chris Cahill, Tony Alva. Photo: CR Stecyk III

cess and money entered the picture, egos flared and the gang splintered apart. Tony Alva, who was the number one skateboarder in the world, created Alva Skates, the first eponymous skateboard brand. Jim Muir and Wes Humpston formed Dogtown Skates, which boasted ever-increasing deck widths along with the first substantial graphics. Stacy Peralta moved to G&S, and then joined forces with George Powell to incorporate Powell-Peralta, who went on to build the most successful and influential skateboard team of the 1980s, the Bones Brigade. Most of the other Dogtowners signed lucrative but short-lived deals with other established skateboard brands.

Fast-forward two decades. After publishing a collection of his *Skateboarder* stories and photos in the book *Dogtown – The Legend of the Z-Boys* with Glen E. Friedman in 2000, CR Stecyk III teamed up with Stacy Peralta to produce a documentary version called *Dogtown and Z-Boys*. Combining archival skating footage with contemporary team rider interviews, the film went on to garner wide critical acclaim, winning two awards at the Sundance Film Festival in 2001. Stacy followed it up in 2005 with a dramatic adaptation called *Lords of Dogtown*, starring Heath Ledger and Emile Hirsch; consulting with most of the major

Dogtown players for authenticity. In the decades since the 1970s, the heavy influence of Dogtown has continued to reverberate throughout the collective conscious of the hardcore—permeating everything from *Thrasher* magazine and skate zines to punk rock, skate rock, deck graphics, videos and incalculably more—most importantly, attitude. In fact, the debt runs so deep, it's not an exaggeration to say that whenever you slappy a curb, slash a pool, grind down a handrail or launch off of a Mega Ramp, you keep alive the spirit of Dogtown.—**LMB + GSD**

"We were not the valedictorians of the school; we were the guys who would have been chosen 'last to succeed.' And for some reason, by doing something everyone said was just a waste of time, we ended up influencing kids all around the world."—**Stacy Peralta, on the Z-Boys**

All photos in this chapter reprinted with permission from the book *Dogtown - The Legend of the Z-Boys* ©2000 by CR Stecyk III and Glen E. Friedman (Burning Flags Press). Also check out Glen's new and expanded coffee table book, *My Rules* (Rizzoli), featuring many of his iconic skateboarding and music photos from the 1970s and '80s.

84

TRACKER
RACETRACK
Slalom Prototypes (1976)

Some of our slalom racers liked the action of the Haftrack, but still preferred the width of the Fultrack. So, in 1976, I machined a batch of spacers that we welded to some Haftrack hangers, increasing the width to 4 1/4", which required Fultrack axles. We flowed these handcrafted custom trucks, which were affectionately called Racetracks, to many Tracker team slalom racers. Although slalom racing on skateboards began in the '60s, the clay wheels would slide out as soon as you leaned off center, thus races were usually run on a smooth surface without much slope. Back then, slalom was more of a balancing act than a race. When urethane wheels hit the scene in 1973, slalom racing blossomed into a real sport. The grip of the urethane allowed the racers to push hard into turns. If you pushed too hard past the limit of adhesion of the urethane, it offered a controlled slide, unlike clay wheels, which would skid out of control and slam you on the ground.

Slalom racing demands a technical application of skateboard gear. The first racer who negotiates his way to the bottom of the course is the winner, and goes on to race head-to-head with the next racer in eliminations. Flexible decks that enhanced loading and unloading power while pushing into the turns, similar to snow skiing, were popular in the '70s. Downhill courses could consist of tight slalom, giant slalom and hybrid or a combination of both. Racers would show up at the race with a duffel bag containing a couple of tight slalom decks and a couple of giant slalom decks, depending on how steep the hill was, and the layout of the cones. A wedge pad was placed under a truck on one end or the other to either increase or decrease the turning angle.

Another bag was stuffed full of truck axle hangers of various sizes and wheels of various durometers ready to mount depending on how steep, smooth or rough, and hot or cold the surface was. (The surface temperature would change significantly from morning to afternoon.) The racers were ready to adapt to any variables based on practice runs and racer experience. Because of our roots on the hills of La Costa, Tracker has always embraced slalom, which lost favor in the '80s, when it gave way to pure downhill speed and luge, and, of course, backyard vert ramps. Slalom racing survived in Europe due to the skier crossover and gained popularity again in the US by 2000. Of course, Tracker was still around, ready and willing to support the racers once again. (See page 320 for further evolution of the Tracker Racetrack.)—**LMB**

Tommy Ryan, April 1977.

Right: **Continental Surf Skater, circa 1965.** "The Continental Surf Skater was the first skateboard after the metal wheel and Chicago trucks era. Chicago had such a corner on the market. They sold trucks to Makaha and the red Roller Derby board. Later, when Chicago couldn't build enough trucks for every board company, we built the Continental trucks. I remember riding the Continental for the first time, and I said, 'Wow! The center of gravity is higher.' I think that was when it really hit me that skateboarding was going to start taking some different turns. The Continental was distributed to every Montgomery Ward store in the US, and I toured for maybe three years, going to every one of their stores across the US to promote that skateboard. Continental went as far as it could go, then G&S came out with the first Fibreflex. At that point, Continental pretty much folded. I was lucky to be involved with Tracker from the very beginning with Dave Dominy and Larry Balma. Larry handed me a pair of Tracker Fultrack prototypes. I rode them and could not believe—because they were so wide—the traction I got with those little Cadillac wheels. I could actually grip the urethane on the asphalt. I said, 'This is it. Skateboarding is going to change again.' Between the urethane wheels, the Tracker Trucks and the flex, a sport was all of a sudden created from our equipment. We always told people, 'Let's set up a course at La Costa—no money, no nothing. Just come up and race.' At first, everyone said no, then it turned into every Sunday. It was major. The hill was crammed packed. Tracker was there, and it was a cool thing, because we would give them input, and almost immediately, Larry would go back to the shop and shave down the truck a little bit. I think the Midtrack was developed because we wanted a little bit narrower track so we could do tighter cones. We were changing the equipment to meet the course. No one would show up there without five boards, 80 sets of wheels, 20 sets of trucks, changing this, changing that. Those were some good times and good days of racing. Tracker was a big part of changing the way skateboarding was going, because the trucks made before then were too narrow. Skateboarding would never be the same ever again from those days to now. You guys have been around for 40 years. Lance Smith and myself have been there since day one. We were the original guys. We owe Tracker a lot for what you've done for us."
—Excerpt from an interview with Tommy Ryan
Opposite page: **Tracker Racetrack prototypes made from extended Haftracks, circa 1976.**

ROCKIT SKATE BOARDS

Laminated Decks Blast Off! (1976)

Up until 1975, much of our skateboarding had been concentrated on the hills of La Costa. From that point on, Tracker co-founder Dave Dominy, salesman Keith Hagen and team manager Lance Smith also branched out to other terrain like the Escondido reservoir, as well as ditches, pipes and the Charcoal Bowl. Most skateboards that were ridden at these spots were made of 3/4" thick solid oak. Dave was riding his super thick skateboard with deep wheel wells when he got the idea to cut out decks using lightweight Finnish birch laminated cabinet grade plywood, which was only 1/2" thick, yet strong and lightweight. We never produced these decks for sale to the public, but everyone close to us who was not sponsored by a deck company rode one.

G&S first built Fibreflex slalom boards in the '60s by laminating maple with Gordon Plastics Bo-Tuff on the top and bottom. Most of these boards had a short wheelbase and did not have much flex. By the '70s, they had the process down to make flexible slalom decks, which were not suited to skating transitions. This fact became painfully obvious to me while I was skating a ditch at the boat launch ramp in Oxnard harbor, where I was docked while commercial fishing for rock cod outside the Santa Barbara Channel Islands. I was using the flex of my 28" G&S Fibreflex slalom board to pump up the harsh transition of the six-foot deep ditch and accelerate up the opposite bank. It felt great until I launched off the board and came down on the ball of my left foot, twisting my lower leg backward at the knee and snapping my ACL. Apparently, I needed a stiff deck.

I first met Charlie Watson in the '60s when my brother-in-law, Chuck Keiper, rented an apartment from Charlie's mom. By 1975, Charlie was trying to make flexible slalom skateboard decks by pressing wood and fiberglass laminations. He liked how Dave's deep wheel well deck rode with its low roll center, so he built a molded laminated deck featuring a dropped riding surface that curved upward over each truck. Tracker marketed these decks for Charlie as Archery Flex. Since the boards actually didn't have much flex, and most skaters did not appreciate the extra low roll center, Archery Flex had

Dave Dominy shows off yet another Rockit deck shape, circa 1977. Photo: Jim Goodrich
Opposite page, top row, left to right: **Two rare and unreleased Rockit slalom decks, one with Gullwing trucks, the other with Strokers. A Rockit prototype deck with Magnum trucks and wheels manufactured by Mattel, the maker of Hot Wheels. A Rockit prototype deck with hand airbrushed graphics and Tracker Fultracks.** Bottom row, left to right: **A Rockit prototype deck with the original hook tail. A Rockit production deck with a hook tail. Another Rockit production deck with a normal kicktail and wheel wells. The graphic on the latter two decks is actually just a huge sticker.**

limited success. The deck was way ahead of its time, though, as free ride longboards with drop-through truck mounts and a low center of gravity made a comeback in the 2000s, and are still in high demand today.

What piqued our interest in Archery Flex was the fact that Charlie was able to mold the curvature of the deck using the lamination method. Oak decks of the day had wedge kicktails that had to be cut out, glued on and sanded, which were all expensive operations. We immediately saw the potential to mold in kicktails at a much lower labor cost! Dave and I approached him and partnered to develop a stiff laminated skateboard deck. I had a 20-ton hydraulic jack and helped Charlie build a prototype press. Working in the Taylor Dykema shop, Dave helped cut out molds. Charlie experimented using

A studio shot of a Rockit deck, circa 1976.
Left: Dave Dominy's sketches of his first and second hippie skateboards with deep wheel wells that influenced Charlie Watson to design the Archery Flex deck.
Archery Flex ad, circa 1976.
Opposite page, bottom left to right: A close-up of the Rockit deck's hook tail.
A Rockit t-shirt, circa 1977.
Larry Balma poses with his own early personal skateboards and a Rockit, circa 1976.
Photo: Unknown

archeryflex

An innovative skateboard which meets and exceeds skateboarding's demand for excellence and advancement. Produced with precision craftsmanship and quality materials to create an effect never before achieved in skateboard control and maneuverability. FEATURES INCLUDE: Archery-grade maple, which affords superior strength, durability and flexibility. Extra wheel clearance for maximum turnability, stability and torque. Custom rubber cushions combined with the unique curved design and additional width (a full 8" wide!) provides ultimate traction and control. DEALERS CONTACT: Keith Hagen, 714-481-9551, P.O. Box 217, Cardiff-by-the-Sea, CA 92007 or Archeryflex, P.O. Box 99793, San Diego, CA 92109

myriad types of hardwood laminates of various thickness and glue types. We rejected the use of fiberglass after the first few runs, because of the process, plus the glass was highly abrasive on the milling head cutters. We experimented with different laminations of maple in both longitudinal and cross plies, some of which were prone to warping. Ultimately, we settled on alternating cross plies just like plywood; young and hard headed, we thought we could find a better way. Seven plies of 1/16" hard rock maple laminate turned out to work best.

Rich Novak and Jay Shuirman from NHS, which was one of Tracker's distributors, came down to Tracker and saw a prototype nine-ply Rockit skateboard deck on Dave Dominy's desk. They flipped out over it and asked Dave what we were planning to do with the board. Dave explained that we were just making prototypes, and that we didn't make decks, we made trucks. Rich and Jay realized that the laminated skateboard deck would soon become the industry standard. Dave gave them the board, which they took to a bent wood manufacturer in Wisconsin. Soon after, they began producing Santa Cruz five-ply laminated maple decks that were 1/2"

thick. Five-ply was cheaper to produce, but heavier and not as strong, so they soon moved to seven-ply maple.

We called our laminated decks Rockit skateboards, as in "rock it," not a rocket ship. Rockit decks were much lighter and stronger than the 3/4" thick oak decks that were standard at the time, and wouldn't split after they slammed into a curb. The real beauty of lamination is that the kicktail could be molded into the deck, as opposed to being cut out and glued to the top. Later, concave was added for even more strength. Taylor Dykema, who had tooled up to build solid oak skateboards, was producing thousands of them for Logan, G&S and others every week. Ron had been interested in curve-molded furniture and researched how the big guys did it. Then he invested in a couple of eight-foot wide hydraulic presses and set up for production. Since Tracker supplied trucks to all of the major skateboard deck companies, we thought it would be a bad idea to compete with them. So, we licensed our Rockit skateboard deck to G&S, who got Charlie Watson to produce them at his fledgling new company, Watson Laminates. The Rockit was the first modern custom-laminated stiff skateboard

Russ Gosnell, November 1977.

John Winchester, January 1978.

Dave Dominy, April 1978.

Radical Ripping, May 1978.

deck. Tracker set the bar for the strongest, most cost-effective deck production process, which is still in use to this day.

Next, Taylor Dykema laminated the Stacy Peralta Warptail II for G&S and the Logan Earth Ski Duralite, and went on to remain the largest deck manufacturing company for the next 20 years. Watson Laminates went on to become a huge manufacturing company and still exists today. As time moved on, various concaves were developed on skateboard decks based on each pro's preference. Double kicktails evolved on street decks in the late '80s, while noses grew on them and vert decks, as well. Although laminated skateboard deck evolution continues, space age materials like carbon graphite and foam have never replaced the durable and cost-effective hard rock maple laminates.—**LMB**

In the early days of Tracker, Russ Gosnell was one of the gnarliest pro skaters around. Particularly hard on equipment, Russ became our best truck test pilot, and miraculously transformed himself into the Rockit Man, who was responsible for promoting Rockit Skateboards, one of the first—if not the first—stiff laminated maple decks.—GSD

LS: Did you like the VC and Escondido bowls because they were so surf style?
Yeah, it was surf style, with the transitions and the speed, and it was way before we had skateparks. All we had was crusty concrete ditches alongside a freeway. It had a sidewalk around it so you could really push.

LS: Which trucks did you ride there?
I started out with Chicago Roller Derby trucks with clay loose ball bearing wheels, and then we made our own boards. My brother Steve

Russ Gosnell
INTERVIEW

grew up next door to Stacy Peralta, so when the Zephyr came out, Steve and I had the only two Zephyr skateboards in San Diego county, and we had clay wheels on those at first. Then Frank Nasworthy came out with the Cadillac wheels, and I got my first pair of loose ball bearing Cadillacs. The Cadillac urethane wheels, Tracker Trucks and Rockit laminated boards just changed the whole world, and made skateboarding a legitimate sport. Before that, it was just something we did to fool around when the surf was flat.

LMB: When did you get your first set of Tracker Trucks?
I got my first set of Trackers from Larry Balma and Dave Dominy in the mid '70s, and then went to work in the shop soon after that.

LMB: In the production shop?
Yes, I was grinding trucks, doing assembly and the dreaded delivery. I remember Lance Smith was so happy I started doing the delivery. He said, "I'm done, I'm burnt, get me outta here."

LS: What was it like when you got your first precision bearings? Which were the first urethane wheels you rode?
My first urethane wheels were the small Road Riders, then the OJs came out and Road Riders were done, because the big Road Riders were too tall and too tippy for the banks and pools. The OJs were a little smaller, and they had the rounded edge with the bevel on the backside. They were coping-friendly and made out of good urethane. I rode some Tunnel Rocks. They were insanely fast, but they got flat spots easily. Then the big boom came with the Kryptonics.

LS: So, did you go from the Fultrack to the Midtrack? Yeah.

LS: How did the Midtracks feel?
The Haftracks were a little narrow, so I went to the wider wheels, to make them wider. But, the wider wheels had too much drag, and didn't have the same response. Then I went to Midtracks, so I could cut down the width of the wheels, and there was just enough truck in between the wheels to fit the coping really well and held you in. You'd come up and grind, and your bottom wheel would

hook you in. The Fultracks came about with pool riding, because the boards went from 7 ½" and 8" wide to 10" and 11" wide, so that's why everybody went to the Fultracks. But, the hang up with them was you had too much space in between your wheels, and you'd hit your kingpin. That's why Tracker made Copers and Lappers.

LS: Did you get a chance to use the Lapper or the Coper?
I didn't like them. I remember burning out a set of Copers to the axles in a weekend.

LMB: The Rockit Man was gnarly! So, which was your favorite terrain?
My all-time favorite was the Escondido reservoir, and the El Cajon skatepark. It had some awesome snake runs and bowls with smooth, rounded tops that you could do no-hand power slides across the lip. Backyard pools were always exciting, because you never knew what you would get. Some were like riding big waves at Mavericks. Spring Valley had one of the best skatepark pools, and Del Mar also had a great pool. It was a little rough, but it was all right. Long, concrete halfpipes like Anaheim. When the surf was flat, we'd just hit the streets, downhill with banked driveways. I also skated La Costa a lot, and messed around a little with freestyle. I liked the pools and banks best, though.

LMB: Why was Tracker so important in the history of skateboarding?
Prior to that, all we had was Chicago roller skates, and we ripped the old, crappy steel trucks off of those and converted them to our skateboards. Tracker was actually a truck that was made for skateboarding specifically and designed for the urethane wheels when they came out. Basically, Tracker Trucks revolutionized skateboarding at that point.

LMB: Do you have a favorite Tracker ad?
Yes, I do. At the Spring Valley pool, I did a big carve in the deep end, then came up, hit the little love seat and did a canyon jump across the open end of the shallow. My good photographer friend Bruce Cooley shot the ad. That's my all-time favorite.

LMB: You were known as the Rockit Man. How did you get involved with Rockit?
When my brother and I were first skateboarding, before the pro thing, we shaped our own boards out of some marine plywood. Before the Rockit, boards were made out of oak hardwood. I destroyed two or three hardwood boards a day. And through the innovation of you guys at Tracker, that's when the first maple laminate boards came out. So, between my riding and input, and your guys' expertise at being able to research and build them, that's how the Rockit came about. It was kind of like a water ski laminate. I remember a guy down at the water ski shop….

LMB: Charlie Watson.
No, before that came Bob Sackit, then G&S got involved with it. Bob Sackit had a little ski shop and started building them down there. That's how all of that evolved.

LMB: So, you were the main R&D guy for Rockit. What were the first changes to

the boards in that first year there?
We had to determine which lengths were good for pools, and for freestyle. Some of the thinner laminates worked out better for shorter freestyle boards. I think we settled somewhere around 30" for a good pool board. The Rockit had many more laminates for more strength, which also gave it more flex and punch out of the bowls without breaking. We had a straight flat board, and then we had a board with a rocker like the old Zephyr.

LMB: Then we added the kicktail [which was originally developed by Larry Stevenson for Makaha in 1970].
The kicktail revolutionized skateboarding, like the double kicktail has since. When we first started out, we just had the flat boards and we shaped them like surfboards: swallow tails, pin tails, etc. We had no grip tape, so you had to monkey grip them with your feet to stay on. Then other brands started to put the wedge kicktails on the solid wood boards.

LMB: Part of the beauty of laminated boards was that you could build that kicktail right into the shape.
Yeah, you could heat press it right in, and it was a smooth transition, more of a hook to hold your foot.

LMB: Okay, we talked about the Rockit deck with a rocker, and then the hook tail, and then finally this Rockit deck with a molded kicktail.
The hook tail really worked good in the pools, because it would hold your foot in so you couldn't slide off. The only problem I had with that was when the hook wore down, it was

gone. But, since they went to the flat kicktail, it was a lot more friendly for freestyle and all-around cruising and riding. The rocker board worked good for giant slalom and downhill. It held you in really good.

LMB: The kicktail is what helped Alan Gelfand develop the Ollie.
Yes, it did. [Makaha, followed by] Rockit is where kicktails came from.

Read the full-length interview at trackertrucks.com

Above: **The Rockit Man, Russ Gosnell, gears up to shred the Tracker Ramp, circa 1977.** Photo: Lance Smith Opposite page: **Russ Gosnell stars in this special Tracker / Rockit Skateboards combo ad, December 1977.** Photos: Bruce Cooley

By Larry Balma + Lance Smith

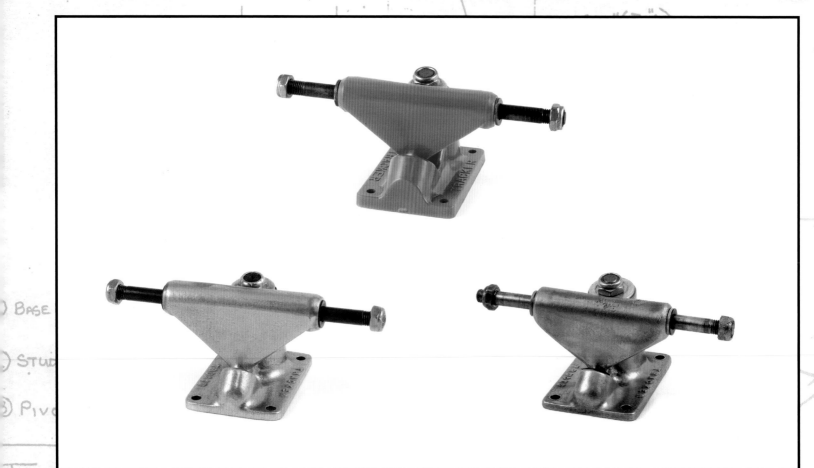

TRACKER DESIGNS LTD.

T-002 BASE HOUSE

MAY 1, 1975

L.M. BALMA

TRACKER
MIDTRACK
The Middle Way (1977)

Via a frontside air, Rodney Jesse lifts his wild hair above the chunky coping of the Kona Bowl in Escondido, California, circa 1977. Photo: Lance Smith
Opposite page, top: A Tracker Midtrack first production run truck, circa 1977.
Opposite page, bottom photo, clockwise from top left: An all-nylon Tracker Midtrack first production run truck, circa 1977. A Tracker Fultrack cut down into a Midtrack prototype with a floating axle, circa 1976. A Tracker Midtrack production truck with a second generation baseplate, circa 1977.

With a 3 3/8" (85 mm) hanger width, the next Tracker truck, which fell between the Haftrack and Fultrack, was aptly named the Midtrack. The Midtrack's axle height and roll center was likewise set between the Haftrack and the Fultrack geometry. Although we had actually prototyped the Midtrack along with the Haftrack, due to cash flow and marketing, we chose to launch one new truck at a time. Finally, we were beginning to think like businessmen! Bennett also came out with a wider truck, but they were still afraid to go as wide as the Tracker Fultrack. At 3" wide, the new Bennett Pro tried to compete with the Tracker Midtrack. Later, Bennett added axle extenders to reach the 3 3/8" width of the Midtrack. Trackers were already the most popular trucks; all we had to do was produce enough of them to meet demand! The Midtrack was the most popular Tracker in 1977 and into '78, when we began production on the Gnarly Tracker Midtrack, on which the 1/2" pivot added even more strength and confidence.

By 1978, wheels had become so wide that the Midtrack with wide wheels matched the current deck width of around 8". We knew that the decks would continue to grow wider, so we began work on a truck even wider than the Fultrack. If you look through skateboard magazines from the late '70s, you will find Tracker team riders on prototype trucks in various widths using long axles with spacers on Haftrack, Midtrack and Fultrack hangers. As boards quickly grew wider, the Fultrack and then the Extrack took over.

In 1978, Tracker pattern maker Gary Dodds was experimenting with the Tracker Ultralite baseplate program, and since the Midtrack had the largest demand, he built an injection mold for the Midtrack hanger. Even though it had a Gnarly pivot, the early nylon hanger was not strong enough for vert. At the time, we only used it for slalom and later on some roller skates. In 1982, we ran an ad for the Ultralite Midtrack, when Per Welinder and Pierre Andre Senizergues were taking advantage of its light weight for all of the new flip tricks in freestyle. Not long after, Powell-Peralta's narrow 57mm roller skate wheels came into vogue in freestyle, which made the Tracker Fultrack the proper width for a freestyle board, thus the Ultralite Midtrack was short-lived in the marketplace. If you happen to have a set in your collection, consider yourself lucky, as they are quite rare! After Stacy Peralta's extremely successful documentary film *Dogtown and Z-Boys* hit screens in 2001, Hollywood decided to produce a dramatic version called *The Lords of Dogtown* in 2005. Skip Engblom, who was in charge of locating and replicating authentic skateboards and props for the movie, came down to Tracker and had us pull out old matchplates to produce Midtracks once again! In fact, thanks to Skip and the movie, we currently produce batches of Midtracks on a regular basis. —**LMB**

Top: **Mike Weed (RIP) performs a backside edger at Spring Valley skatepark in Spring Valley, California, circa 1977.** Photo: Unknown
Above: **Per Welinder curb grinds a set of Tracker Midtracks, circa 1981.** Photo: Unknown
Left: **The legendary inventor or the Outrageous Eight Wheeler, Lonnie Toft goes off the lip frontside in your face at Reseda Skatercross in Reseda, California, circa 1977.** Photo: Jim Goodrich

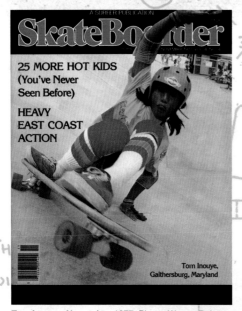

Tom Inouye, November 1977. Photo: Warren Bolster

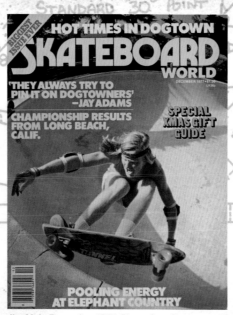

Jim Muir, December 1977. Photo: Stan Sharp

Brad Bowman, June 1978. Photo: Stan Sharp

This Arrow points the way to a gnarly frontside carve grind by Kent Senatore at Surf de Earth Skatepark in Vista, California, August 1978. Photo: James Cassimus

Jeff Tatum lifts a frontside aerial out of the Kona Bowl at Del Mar Skate Ranch in Del Mar, California, circa 1978. Photo: James Cassimus

Below **Chuck Edwall** built up this three-dimensional Tracker flying truck logo in order to accentuate his very first Tracker wing logo from 1975, which was two-dimensional. This 3-D view clearly shows that it is a wheel with speed lines flowing back. Chuck grabbed a Midtrack, stuck the wing logo on the axle and photographed it at an angle. It took many attempts by trial and error to build this logo the old fashioned way before the advent of desktop computers.

Bottom right: **A Tracker Midtrack sales flyer, circa 1977.**

TRACKER TRUCKS

MIDTRACK

The most recent truck from Tracker has already commanded a terrific response. To list the top name skaters that ride this truck would not only be lengthy, but would be a major effort to not omit anyone. The Midtrack combines best features of the original Fultrack and the Haftrack. At 3 3/8 inches between the wheels, the width, geometry and action of the Midtrack have proven it to be an outstanding all around truck. Of course, the Midtrack is made of the same A356 aluminum as the Fultrack and Haftrack, heated treated to T-6 castings and features heat treated chromemoly studs and axles.
The Tracker Midtrack, direct result of experienced skateboarders riding, testing and developing.

TRUCKS YOU CAN TRUST.

TRACKER TRUCKS P.O. BOX 398 CARDIFF-BY-THE-SEA, CA 92007

TRACKER TRUCKS

MAG MIDS
with **Copers** T.M.

If you haven't figured out why we make Midtrack Copers, you haven't met Steve Rocco yet. Tracker Trucks, P.O. Box 398, Cardiff-by-the-Sea, California 92007.

Dealers call (714) 481-9551.

Steve Rocco, May 1980.
98

Gregg Weaver, July 1977.

Russ Gosnell, August 1977.

Scott Williams, September 1977.

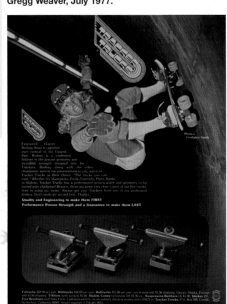

Rodney Jesse, April 1978.

Per Welinder, Primo Desiderio, October 1982.

Endless Sidewalk, June 1984.

The Genesis of Street Skating

In January 1980, *Skateboarder* magazine ran an article called "Curb Grinding and Other Joys," which was the first-ever coverage of a new phenomenon called street skating. Although skateboarding originally started in the streets in the early to mid 20th century, street skating as we know it today—skating on objects—first began around 1979. To claim that any one person invented street skating is preposterous. But, it is safe to say some early practitioners, among many, included Steve Caballero, Gavin O'Brien, Corey O'Brien, John Lucero, Neil Blender and Steve Rocco, the star of the Tracker "Mag Mids With Copers" ad from May 1980 (opposite page). Steve can be seen here pulling off a little handplant on a curb. It may look a little silly now, but, unless you were skating at the time, you have no idea how much of an influence this ad and the *Skateboarder* article were. Just

one example: they caused my friends and I to start shredding curbs immediately, doing 15 foot long boardslides on double-sided ones long before we saw anyone else do it. Not long after, Powell-Peralta released the Street Issue deck and Santa Cruz foisted the Jammer upon the public, followed by an increasing amount of street sticks from many brands. After its humble beginnings on curbs, street skating progressed through the mid '80s with wall rides, street plants and jump ramps. Finally, when Mark Gonzales employed Rodney Mullen's flatground Ollie to jump onto any and all objects, street skating finally matured, introducing the realms of handrails, stairs, gaps and ledges to skateboarders everywhere. The floodgates were opened and pandemonium ensued, fueled by the unlimited imagination and bravado of four-wheeled urban terrorists.—**GSD**

Alva sez: Trackers Blaze Anywhere!

TRACKER TRUCKS

PERFORMANCE PROVEN CHOICE of CHAMPIONS!
Fultracks $22.00 per pair, Midtracks $22.00 per pair, Haftracks $21.00 per pair, T-Shirts (with pocket) $5.50, Slalom Cones (min. 10) $1.00 ea., Suspension Rubbers (4) $1.00, Sticker 25¢. Free Brochure and Order Form. Out of State add $1.50 shipping; Hawaii, Alaska and Foreign add $3.50 shipping. California residents add 6%. Send Cashier's Check or Money Order ONLY to: Tracker Trucks, P.O. Box 398, Cardiff-by-the-Sea, California 92007.

Tony Alva, June 1978. Photo: Wynn Miller
100

Born in 1957, Tony Alva started skateboarding and surfing in the mid '60s. During the sport's second explosion in the following decade, this raging Z-Boy and Dogtown legend thrived in the eye of the hurricane. Brandishing a 1977 World Champion title and a *Skateboarder* magazine poll win, Tony's rep soared into the stratosphere as he went on to found Alva Skates, the first eponymous skateboard brand owned by a skateboarder. With photographer Raul Vega and designer Eric Monson, Alva Skates pioneered the first conceptual artistic advertisements in skateboarding history. As if all of that weren't enough, Tony also piloted the first ever frontside air on vertical above pool coping when no one even knew if it was possible, garnering him instant legend status in the process. A skate rat until the day he dies, Alva has never stopped shredding in the decades since. Read on for a little peek into the life and times of a true skateboarding icon.—GSD

Tony Alva
INTERVIEW

GSD: How did your pro skateboarding career get started?
When I graduated from high school in 1975, I wanted to be a professional surfer so bad. I just wanted to live on the North Shore of Oahu in the winter. I remember living in a station wagon, in tents, sleeping on people's floors and just whatever I could do to get by. We were barely scraping by, living on rice and whatever fruit we could pick off of the trees and fish from the locals. I can remember if you were lucky enough to have a decent skateboard, that was a real treat. It's kind of a trip to look back on those days. I went through a lot of boards and wheels. I might not have had a good place to live or had a lot of healthy food to eat, but I always had a nice skateboard. If you had a nice set of Trackers back then, dude, those trucks would last for five or six boards.

GSD: Was that before you were making money from skateboarding?
Definitely. I hadn't even had a picture in *Skateboarder* magazine until I went skating one day at Wallos. I was there with the surf photographer Steve Wilkings. I got a double page spread and it said, "The electric Tony Alva." That was the picture that put me over the top. That was the first big one that just said, "Check out this guy, the way he looks, his style and approach to what he is doing. This is the guy!" A two-page spread was huge when you were a kid. HUGE. I wasn't really aware of it, because I was living that lifestyle I just described in Hawaii. After that, people were knocking on my door. It was like that was it, it was on. That's when I got the hook-up with Torger Johnson and Bruce Logan, and started training a lot for competition through the Logan Earth Ski team. That's when I started to really progress and get really good, which is what it took to be a professional skateboarder. That Logan team is what formed my future. As soon as I won the big contest at Carlsbad, that was when the money guys came. "We'll pay you to do this, this and this."

LMB: How did you join the Z-Boys?
Well, I always wanted to be on the Zephyr surf team, because they were the coolest surf team in town—especially on the South side, because they were the only guys who could surf POP pier. It was the team to be on. I wanted to be on the surf team so bad, but I wasn't good enough at that point. So, I back-doored it by being a good skateboarder. They decided to start a junior division of the surf team that ended up being the Z-Boys skate team. Kent Sherwood, who was Jay Adams' stepfather, and Jay, Jeff Ho, Skip Engblom and all of the boys, put our heads together and said, "Why don't we make an extruded fiberglass version of the Makaha board?" It was a banana board with a full rocker, double kick, and a baseplate riser beam. Later, I formed a partnership with Pete Zender, who was making the best laminated skateboards at the time. We had a garage and we had $25,000 to play with. We also got a loan, so we had $25,000 on top of our first $25,000 and we started Alva skateboards. So, I went from the station wagon and barely being able to afford a pair of shoes to the ditch photo to all of a sudden—boom!—I was a rock star, with the ladies, the limo, the drugs.

LMB: Were you credited with the first frontside air?
I was credited because I was documented doing it first. I think there were a few other guys doing it at the same time, but it wasn't documented. I was probably the first guy to land it who had it documented. I was fortunate to have Craig Stecyk and Glen Friedman around and then eventually Warren Bolster, the editor of *Skateboarder*, too. We had some super 8 footage of me doing it on film, so that's how I ended up getting credit for it over Kevin Reed or George Orton. There were a few other guys doing airs at the same time, but I'm not sure if they actually landed them. I know they were blasting out and going for it. I know for a fact that when I landed it at the Dog Bowl and skated away, most of the guys who witnessed it—whether they were friends of mine or not—their jaws hit the ground. They were baffled, and said, "I can't believe you just did that!"

GSD: Did it come about from an accident?
Yes. I was trying to hit the lip super hard, and I actually grabbed the board while I hit the lip and it bounced me out. So I started grabbing around my knee similar to the way I surf. I like the tuck knee style. Michael Peterson and the old Australian surfers influenced me a lot on that. I also found out that the farther up the rail I grabbed, it seemed to naturally pop out, like the Tracker ad I did with the Darth Vader sticker on the board at Gonzo's pool. That was a couple of years later when I could actually go straight up, pop out, 180 it and come back in. When I first started doing airs in the Dog Bowl, I was just carving, there was no 180 going on. It was just an air carve. And that was a bigger pool, too. It was wider, a little bit higher and had a smoother transition, which gave you more room to move. Gonzo's was pretty tight with a very quick transition and quicker vert, so I needed to develop a different technique.

GSD: Wasn't the Dog Bowl at a mansion?
Yeah, this kid named Dino lived there. He had a terminal illness. We used to bring him bags of weed, and he'd sit in his wheelchair smoking joints and watch us skate. He had a little girlfriend who was his "nurse." She would roll him joints. Dino was not a surfer or skate-

boarder at all, he was just a kid we met who was from an oppulent family. His parents were very well educated and they had this huge mansion with an empty pool. Somehow, we found out that it was cool to skate there and he gave us permission. We became friends with him, but not just to skate the pool. He was a real friend of ours. When he did die, it was pretty emotional. We all felt there was a piece of us missing. He really got a lot of enjoyment having skateboarders around, and there were a lot of dogs. It got called the Dog Bowl because there was always a pack of dogs there that would circle the bowl. A lot of times when people took pictures, they would stick their faces right in the lens.

We ended up being called the Dogtown boys because of the affiliation with that rich neighborhood. Santa Monica was not a big place, and there were lots of invisible lines in town where you went from million dollar houses to studio apartments to a ghetto just like that. There was a mixture of ethnicities. It wasn't just all white people like on the North side. The Zephyr shop and skate team was so multi-ethnic because it was from the other side of the tracks. Those guys were not from the North side. I was the only kid from the North side, but I wasn't from a wealthy family. My dad thought he could keep me out of the riff-raff side of town, so we moved to the North side, which put us just a block outside of the zone. He thought that I would go to the better schools, be around white kids and not get into all kinds of trouble. But, come on, I was a latch key kid and my dad was working third shift for Hughes Aircraft most the time. I ran amuck and did pretty much whatever I wanted. My dad knew that I was aspiring to be a professional surfer or skateboarder. He looked at me and said straight to my face, "There's no future in skateboarding." I was like, "Wow." So, I spent the whole time from the age of 17 until my dad passed away in 2011 trying to prove him wrong.

The thing for me was being an entrepreneur at 19 years old. Stacy Peralta and I were the first pros to brand our names onto skateboards; that whole thing didn't come out of spite. That came out of our creative energy and our ambition. My ambition at such a young age was very aggressive to the point of crossing that line into greed. I wanted it all. I wanted the whole cake, and I didn't want to share it with anybody else, including Stacy. It's kind of a trip to look back on it now and see the way the skateboard industry has changed and see that there's a slice for everybody. Your slice might not be as big as everybody else's or as big as it used to be, but it doesn't really matter at this point, especially to see how big skateboarding is internationally. Everybody's got their little slice and I'm happy with the slice I have now. I like to look back on those days and learn from all of that, "Gimme, gimme!" I'm much happier now than I was back then. When you're 19 years old, you think you can do it all yourself, and boy do you learn the hard way, man, because there's a lot of mistakes you make along the way. It's like being in a band: you can't play all of the instruments yourself. You've got to have a good drummer, a good guitar player, and I'm the bass player. A lot of guys who live really ambitious, greedy lifestyles don't realize it leads to a spiritual malady. I don't want to get stuck in that.

Read the full-length interview at trackertrucks.com

By Larry Balma + GSD

Top and bottom: **A comparison between Tracker and Lotus trucks. Lotus were one of many indentical knock-offs of Trackers.**
Right: **Unwanted: Imitation Trackers flyer, and a Lotus ad, both circa 1978.**

UNWANTED
Imitation Trackers

It's true. Due to the popularity and widespread demand for Tracker Trucks, some less-than-ethical manufacturers are producing IMITATION Tracker Trucks. A number of these IMITATIONS may even have our name on the base plate. Here at Tracker, we are worried that you will be fooled. We do not want you to buy these PHONY trucks expecting our strength and quality—only to discover that you are not riding Tracker Trucks and are not covered by the Tracker guarantee.

There have been COUNTERFEITERS for a long time, and it has become necessary to learn the distinguishing factors between the real and the copy. Think of how carefully you would inspect a hundred dollar bill, or a diamond if it came from a questionable source. That is what we are asking you to do when you buy new Tracker Trucks: INSPECT CLOSELY. Of course, you should always look for a reputable authorized Tracker Trucks dealer and keep relying on established distributors.

nylon insert lock nuts on stud and axle

black axle with dimple in one end

thin black bearing seat washer

durable pivot bushing

black stud with dimple in end

"Tracker Trucks" written on top of base plate

good symmetry

quality finish

high gloss

GUARANTEED MADE IN U.S.A. printed on bottom of base plate (sometimes appears in a box)

all Tracker Trucks come with grey Space Pads (9/16" for Fultrack and Midtrack; 5/16" for Haltrack)

AUTHORIZED

TIRED OF WAITING?

LOTUS FAST-TRACK
5¾" AXLE

CALL—LOTUS—WE DELIVER

LOTUS DELIVERS—Lotus Wide Track and Lotus Fast Track Trucks.
LOTUS DELIVERS—A sand cast, heat treated, 356 aluminum alloy truck with a hardened axle.
LOTUS DELIVERS—A heavy duty design with full 9/16" red action rubbers.
LOTUS DELIVERS—A truck you count on, fully guaranteed against breakage.

LOTUS WIDE-TRACK
6⅝" AXLE

For O.E.M. Distributor, and Dealer pricing call:
LOTUS International, Inc.
1122 N. Gilbert Ave
Anaheim, CA 92801
(714) 635-2733 (213) 897-9951

Pigg Products
15976 South Anaheim Blvd.
Anaheim, CA 92805
(714) 761-3477

Skateboard Specialties
15029 Leffingwell Road
Whittier, CA 90604
213/941-4658

Bike-A-Lot
227 Laurel Street
East Northport, NY 11731
516/757-3265

Tract Continental Skateboards
7900 W. Nise Ave.
Baltimore, MD 21222
(301) 285-5688

Lotus of California
2168 W. Broadway
Anaheim, CA 92805
714/776-7463

black axle with dimpl

thin black beari

GUA
on
ap

MADE IN USA

in end

written

ase plate

good symmetry

quality finishing

high gloss polish

102 all Tracker Trucks come with grey Space Pads 9/16" for Fultrack and Midtrack; 5/16" for Haltrack)

TRACKER TRUCKS

AUTHORIZED DEALER

COUNTERFEIT TRACKERS
Unwanted Imitations (1977)

In 1976 and 1977, the demand for Tracker Trucks was so great that we could not produce enough to satisfy it. Although we had ramped up production, we still needed more. Increasing production was not as easy as you might think. An order for parts had to be placed at least three months before we received them. We had to be careful how many parts we ordered, because we had to have the money to pay for them when they arrived. Business is always a gamble. The steel that we used for our axles had to be ordered from the steel mill six months in advance. One time, a railroad bridge collapsed in Ohio with a load of our axle material on the train car, so we were out of luck. In response, we worked on securing two suppliers for every truck part we needed to protect our parts flow. By 1978, we were successfully producing 40,000 trucks per month and could meet the demand.

Prior to 1978, there were unscrupulous entrepreneurs who actually built counterfeit Tracker Trucks. They would cast their counterfeit parts directly off of our castings. There is a known amount of shrinkage in the aluminum alloy, and the counterfeit parts measured exactly that amount smaller than a real Tracker. An actual counterfeit truck would display the Tracker name on the base. An exact truck copy had no name or some other name. Either way, Tracker had a design patent that covered everything. Of course, just like printing counterfeit $100 bills, counterfeiting a product is an illegal act. The difference is that we had to do our own policing, thus we chased down companies from Orange County, California all the way to Rockaway Beach, New York, and even across the pond in Great Britain.

We hired private detectives to chase down leads until we found the source. Tracker lawyer Steve Angus and salesman Keith Hagen even went to New York and Maryland to dig through dumpsters in alleys. Looking back on it now, they could have been shot in the process! Every time we found the source, the business folded and opened the next day under a new name, so no one was ever prosecuted. It was like a game of whack-a-mole. In England, however, the patent and trademark division chased the culprits and shut them down, arresting the perps and seizing all of the counterfeit trucks and shipping them to us to melt down. Brits protect patent holders and get the job done. All hail the Queen!

Some other companies copied Trackers, but instead of using our name, they simply put on their own and sold them at a discount. Although most of the copy trucks were made of inferior metals, some were built pretty well because they just copied our design. We spent a lot of time and money chasing down the counterfeiters, only to learn that our cash would have been much better spent increasing our own production more quickly. We figured it just wasn't worth our time and money to fight these guys in court anymore. —**LMB**

It's simple.
From the very beginning,
the development of skateboarding has depended on the creative energy of some very real people. TRACKER has always supported the pursuit of better products, and we devote the majority of our creative time to designing and building gear that further advances the sport itself. I have the highest respect for others who have contributed their ideas and skills to the advancement of skateboarding. I feel a great deal of satisfaction working with these people . . . the skaters, photographers, writers, designers and manufacturers who have a real love for skating. Even when directly competing, it seems the desire to further the sport draws many of us together. A look at the roster of the ISA will attest to this.

Many people have contributed (and continue to contribute) their energy, creativity and skill in the development of TRACKER TRUCKS. Three years ago, my partners and I carefully designed the TRACKER FULTRACK with performance, strength and beauty as our foremost considerations. More recently, we brought you the HAFTRACK and MIDTRACK models, incorporating the same principles and distinctive shape with their own respective geometries. The shape of TRACKER TRUCKS was our solution concerning beauty, and that shape functioned to set them apart from other trucks. When somebody else copies the shape of a TRACKER TRUCK with the hopes of capitalizing on our efforts, they are taking that which I believe is rightfully ours . . . the shape we created to identify the products of our own efforts. After all, it's just as easy to make skateboard trucks that don't look like TRACKERS.

At TRACKER, we take pride in seeing the TRACKER name on all our products, letting you know that what you're buying is a thing you can trust from a company with integrity. I assure you that TRACKER will continue to stand behind our products, taking the time to make each truck in our own shop, inspecting it, and knowing we've used the best designs and materials available. We ask you, in turn, to help us promote our sport and to discourage imitation. Even if your supplier happens to be sold out of TRACKER TRUCKS, don't settle for less. Insist upon original TRACKER TRUCKS and make your stand by not accepting look-alike substitutes. Let's all take positive steps toward keeping the spirit of skateboarding alive.

Thanks

Dave Dominy

For fast facts, write in Reader Service Card No. 76

Dave Dominy, January 1978.

103

Dependent on
TRACKER

ing forever." We respectfully disagree. Anyone who is familiar with skateboard history knows the truth: Tracker invented the game that all other skateboard trucks play in. And from now on until the end of time, all skateboard trucks will be dependent on Tracker's innovations for their own success.—**GSD + DH + LMB**

Here they are. Take a good look at the Three Musketeers of Independent, the most iconic team riders that brand ever had: Rick Blackhart, Steve Olson and Steve Alba. Hell, back in 1978, by giving Independent's founders advice on how a skateboard truck should work, Blackhart and Olson practically designed their first truck for them. But, where were Blackhart, Olson and Alba in the years before that? On Trackers, of course—you know, the original skateboard truck. The one that started it all. Simply put, Tracker innovated the features that all other skateboard trucks, including Independent, copied—including the A356 aluminum casting, fixed kingpin, triangle truss, four-hole mounting pattern, Gnarly pivot, chrome moly axle, etc. All Independent did was slap the Chicago / Bennett geometry on top of Tracker's innovations. Then they coined a brilliant name, drew up a strong, iconic logo based on the iron cross and carefully crafted a hardcore image—a winning combination that resulted in strong brand loyalty and sales, which set the stage for an intense rivalry between Independent and Tracker (and Nor Cal and So Cal) that would rage on through the '80s. Just like the Sperm Whale vs. the Giant Squid or Tyrannosaurus vs. Triceratops, the intensity of it could get pretty heated at times. We never heard of it coming to blows, but a lot of teasing, ridicule and vibes were hurled back and forth regularly.

For example, at one point, Tracker printed up a sticker that consisted of the international "no" symbol containing the words "Trackers Only" and a clear background that fit perfectly over an Independent sticker. Then Independent published an ad featuring a drawing in which one of their founders, Fausto Vitello, ran over one of Tracker's founders, Larry Balma, with a Mack truck. That was so brutal! And so it went back and forth. The funniest part was that most people didn't know that Larry and Fausto were actually good friends.

Another common barb hurled by Independent riders is that "Trackers don't turn," which is flat out not true. We've always effortlessly turned our Trackers all over the place. They *really* turn and remain stable, while Independents flop side to side like a nervous, jittery speed freak on caffeine. In fact, the turning angle between the two trucks is the same. Lastly, in the book *Built to Grind*, which is one of the best skateboard books of all time, by the way, the authors claimed that Independent was "the truck that changed skateboard-

Dear Dave Dominy,

Thanks allot for the stuff you sent me. I appreciate it. Could you please send me a shirt and more stickers. Oh don't worry about me riding TRACKERS, cause there the only trucks that work at Upland. I'll be riding at the contest for sure!!!! Got to go. See you at the 'Upland Contest. Me and Dunlop will blow your mind.

Steve Alba

3/30/78

TRACKERS ONLY

Top: **A letter from Steve Alba to Dave Dominy, dated March 30, 1978.**
Above: **Steve Alba frontside grinds Spring Valley Skatepark in San Diego, California, circa 1977.** Photo: Jim Goodrich
Opposite page, top: **Steve Olson preferred Trackers in 1977.** Photo: Glenn Miyoda.
Opposite page, bottom: **With his feet a-flappin', Rick Blackhart wows a demo crowd with some precarious frontside edgework, circa 1977.** Photo: James Cassimus

"I am proud to have been a Tracker rider. —Rick Blackhart

NEW GNARLY TRACKERS

Tracker Strong
Tracker Smooth
Tracker Dependable
Tracker Beautiful

• New Gnarly Extrack
Full 5" Span Wheel to Wheel!

• Gnarly Fultrack

• Gnarly Midtrack

• Gnarly Haftrack

Gnarly Trackers are also available, cast from Super Light Magnesium!
Tracker Trucks, the trucks you can trust since 1975!

New Inner suspension grommets Now 3 hardnesses to choose from, firm is made of urethane!

New strengthened base plate and new gnarly pivot with 2 pivot bushing compounds to choose from!

New guarantee/maintenance card and space pad come attached to truck with new tap pin.

New cupped retainer cap and conical outer suspension grommet, urethane in all the new gnarlys!
New lighter and stronger axle housings in all the gnarly Trackers!

Tracker has been working on these new trucks for 3 years, testing and preparing them to be the finest, smoothest and strongest Trackers possible. Each truck is built with fully inspected, hand-crafted castings, hardened to T-6 specs. Our axles and studs are manufactured with the finest chrome moly, spring steel. The threads are rolled, not cut, producing stronger more dependable threads. We use only nylon insert aircraft lock nuts and our unbreakable space pad is included with each truck.

The new gnarly Trackers, the pros have NO choice!
Send 50¢ for a Sticker, Brochure and Order Form to:
Tracker Trucks, P.O. Box 398,   Dealers call
Cardiff-by-the-Sea, California 92007.   714-481-9551

New Gnarly Trackers, February 1979.

All of the first trucks made by Tracker had a small pivot pin that measured just under 3/8" diameter. The pivot was the only part of the truck that had increased only slightly in size from the roller skate trucks that preceded Tracker. If you fell off your board going downhill, it could shoot out from under your feet with tremendous speed. If the board impacted the curb at speed and hit on only one of the wheels, sometimes enough force and shock load could cause the small pivot pin to snap or maybe crack. If a hole was struck severely while riding and the pivot already had a crack, it could fail. Since all of the other trucks at the time were prone to breakage, this was not a huge problem. Even so, as we always strived to improve our products, we could not sit still for this. We immediately made a batch of prototype trucks with a huge pivot pin that was 1/2" diameter and gave them to our team guys at the Signal Hill downhill race in 1976. Everyone said they looked Gnarly, so we had our name. As the Rhino team was launching airs out of the bowls at Carlsbad skatepark and landing up on the deck with tremendous force, they were the next guinea pig to get the Gnarly Trackers.

In 1975, Tracker had debuted the winged truss on the face of the hanger that gave them a unique look that was unlike any other skateboard truck. This truss added superior strength to the hanger, which was necessary

GNARLY
TRACKERS
Here's the Beef! (1978)

Right: **The Rhino Team were early test riders for the Tracker Gnarly prototype trucks, circa 1976.** Photo: Warren Bolster

Below, clockwise from top left: **Gnarly Tracker Haftrack and Midtrack production trucks, circa 1978. Gnarly Tracker Fultrack prototype truck, circa 1976 (note shallower pivot boss). Gnarly Tracker Fultrack production truck, circa 1978. The Gnarly Tracker Extrack is shown on page 112.**

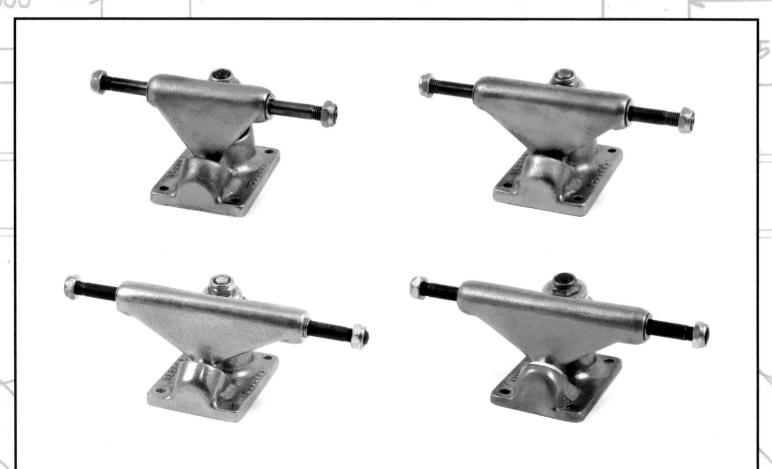

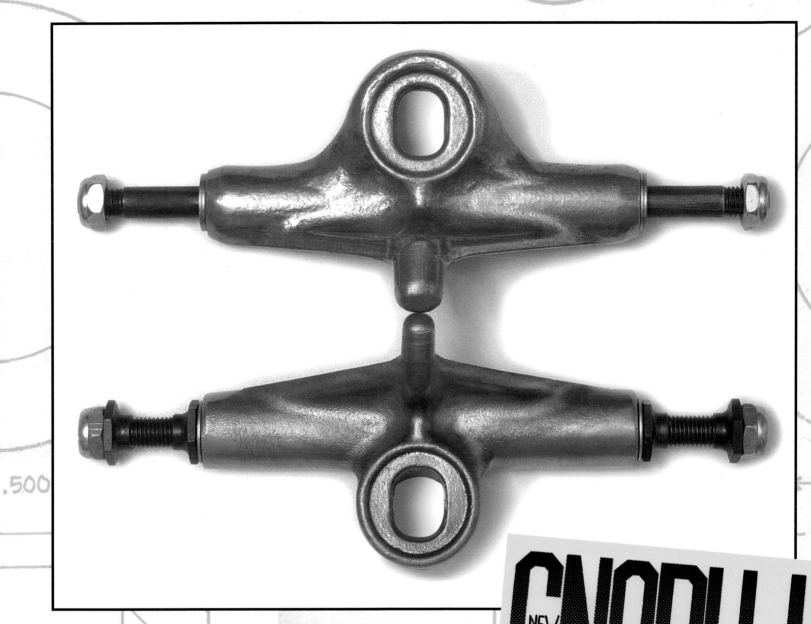

Above: **A comparison displaying the dramatic difference between a Gnarly Tracker Fultrack prototype hanger from 1976 and a Fultrack first production run hanger from 1975. Notice the cushion ring wings and beefed-up pivot added to the Gnarly hanger, as well as the pivot boss and bushing on the Gnarly baseplate.**
Right: **A Gnarly Tracker sales flyer, circa 1978.**
Opposite page, bottom: **Three Gnarly Tracker t-shirts, circa late 1970s-early '80s. The Banco typeface used in the Get the Picture? ad and the white and yellow t-shirts was adopted by *Thrasher* a couple of years later for their cover logo. Coincidence? The world may never know.**

Bert Lamar, Gregg Ayres, August 1979.

to support the width of the axle. However, the rear of the first production Tracker Fultrack truck had a cushion support ring with no truss. If you rode your trucks extremely tight like a downhiller, there was a chance that this ring could crack. On the Gnarly Tracker axle hangers, we added a truss in the form of beefy wings to the rear cushion ring and a conical outer cushion to eliminate squished cushions. Over the next year, we refined the aesthetics of our Gnarly Tracker prototype trucks by lengthening the pivot boss on the baseplate and adding clearance around the cushion ring. All the while, our hardest skating team riders fed us input. We finally launched the production Gnarly Trackers to the skateboard world in early 1978. The design of Tracker Trucks was now fully realized, and every model to follow was built with the Gnarly innovations. To recap, up to this point, Tracker invented the performance wide skateboard truck with a fixed kingpin, four-hole mounting pattern, triangle face, cushion ring wings, conical outer cushion, and Gnarly pivot. Although these features may sound trivial to the layman, they're really not, for the Gnarly Trackers went on to profoundly influence all skateboard trucks that followed.—**LMB + GSD**

109

WHAT'S IN A NAME?
Gunnair, JT Air, Tracker Air

The Gunnair

"I watched Jay Adams do his little backside airs at the Fruit Bowl around 1976, which influenced me to try them. Since my legs were a little long, my board would sort of tweak out from under me every time I grabbed the outside rail with my front hand. So, I reached in between my legs and grabbed the inner rail with my back hand, and the next thing you know, I was upside down and getting flight. I was doing it at the Valley Center Pool, at Kona, and I really worked on it a lot in the Spring Valley Pool. I did it in the Spring Valley contest, then did a frontside air right after it. Nobody had really done consecutive wall-to-wall airs yet—everyone would carve and set up for an air.

"In mid 1978, James Cassimus took a photo of the Gunnair at Vista Skatepark. It ran in the Focus section of the August 1978 issue of *Skateboarder*. I was already going several feet out of the top of the pool. Then UFO ran the 'UFO Flips Out' ad, and there I was, holding the inside of the board. Two years later, the trick was renamed the Indy air. I didn't understand it. I've had an interesting relationship through the Internet with Duane Peters. I've never spoken to him once, but I've followed everything he's said about me. Someone posted a video where he just ranted on me big-time, but it got pulled.

I didn't understand why he would do that. Surfers know their history so well, if something is out of line, somebody speaks up. But, in skateboarding, there's no accountability. They're called credit thieves.

"I first saw photos of the Indy air in *Action Now*, *Thrasher* and *Trans World Skateboarding*. I went to talk to *TransWorld*'s editor, Kevin Kinnear, and Grant Brittain was working there, too. I showed them all of my photos, and said, 'This trick has been done before. It's not called the Indy air. I invented it on Tracker Trucks, and it's called the Gunnair.' I was basically told, 'Too late, it's already in the magazine. It's not your trick anymore.' Still, to this day, if I run into Grant Brittian, he says if it wasn't for Duane Peters, that trick would never have been popular. They pretty much just ignored me."—**Gunnar Haugo**

The JT Air

The JT Air, which was later called the backside Ollie, was invented in San Diego, California in 1977 by Jeff Tatum, without any knowledge of Alan Gelfand's frontside Ollie that was invented in Hollywood, Florida around the same time.

"The JT air is a variation of a backside kickturn. Backside kickturn went over the light. Backside kickturn went to the tile. Backside kickturn went to the coping. Backside kickturn went to one wheeler. Backside kickturn went to edger. Backside edgers went to blow-outs and you made 'em, and everyone said, 'Whoa, dude! You got a little air!' I was around 20 or 21, and I would have dreams of doing a kickturn in the air, and one day, it came true. A lot of people—especially younger kids—associate the backside and frontside Ollie as one trick. But, as you know, that's not true at all. They're two completely different tricks. A frontside Ollie is a lot easier, for one thing. It's easier to stay on your board. Backside, it takes some real finesse and jibing with centrifugal force just to make it work. It's weird you brought up the whole thing about invention in general: Does any one person ever invent anything? The telephone, sex, punk rock—it's the same with skate tricks. I don't know if anyone ever totally invents anything in this world. It always happens in three places at the same time and somehow comes together."—**Jeff Tatum**, as told to Jeff Grosso in an episode of *Grosso's Love Letters to Skateboarding*, courtesy of Vans.

The Tracker Air

Info on the Tracker air is elusive. It was originally invented by a deaf skater named Chris Weddle. Most people called it the mute air in tribute to him. Some folks down in San Diego dubbed the trick the Tracker air, possibly as an answer to the Indy air, but the name never stuck. Sorry, Charlie. Better luck next time.—**GSD**

Above: **Gunnar Haugo hangs on to a Gunnair at Surf de Earth Skatepark in Vista, California, circa 1978.** Photo: James Cassimus

Left: **Jeff Tatum pops a JT Air at Surf de Earth, circa 1979.** Photo: Lance Smith

Opposite page: **Bobby Reeves descends a Tracker air over a typical vert ramp of the early '80s.** Photo: Grant Brittain

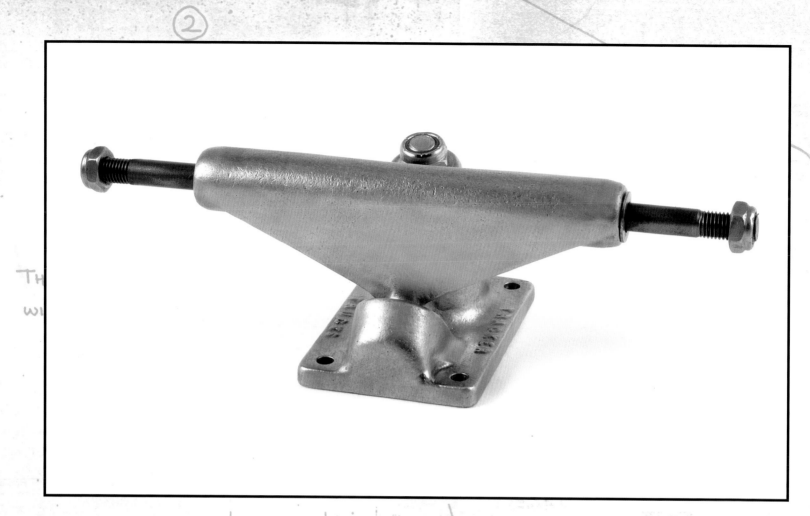

TRACKER DESIGNS LTD.

T-002 BASE HANGER

TRACKER EXTRACK
A Little Extra Width (1978)

Employing his new Tracker Extrack landing gear, Bert Lamar flies out of the pool at Oasis in San Diego, California, summer 1979. Note the spacers on his rear truck to research and develop axle width for the upcoming Tracker Sixtrack.
Photo: Jim Goodrich
Opposite page, top to bottom: **Tracker Extrack production truck and prototype,** both circa 1978.

In 1975, when we launched our 4 1/4" wide Tracker Fultrack truck, we rocked the skateboard world. The width was so shocking to most skaters at the time, we had to spend the next year designing and building tooling for a narrower truck, the Haftrack, which would be accepted by the masses. In the interim, we had to move our production facilities from our garage to an industrial setting to fill the growing demand. From the day our first Fultrack shipped, we were also working on more prototype trucks, using different geometries and axle widths. Led by Tracker co-founder Dave Dominy and team manager Lance Smith, the most prominent team riders tried all of these truck variations on every type of terrain. Tommy Ryan, Chris Strople, Tom "Wally" Inouye, Russ Gosnell and several others could often be seen in the pages of skateboarding magazines with weird-looking Trackers of various widths. These riders provided us with constant feedback. Luckily, our testing was ahead of deck size evolution, which was growing wider rapidly. By 1977, all of our prototype truck designs were established; our chore was to build new tooling to be able to drop them into our already established manufacturing production machine.

By late 1978, deck widths had increased to over 9", which inspired Tracker to introduce the Extrack to the market. Measuring in at a full 5" (127 mm) wide, the Extrack was designed for skateparks and pools. After prototyping the Extrack using extenders on the Haftrack, Midtrack and Fultrack models, we ultimately chose the same geometry and roll center as the Midtrack, which tucked away the kingpin nut to keep it from scraping against the coping. Debuting with the Gnarly Tracker line in 1978, the Extrack was our first truck that was never made with a small pivot. By the time the '80s rolled around, the Sixtrack took over as the de facto Tracker for ultra wide decks and vert riding, while the Extrack became the truck of choice for street skaters. This whole situation was highly ironic, as the Extrack was originally intended to be a vert truck. The Extrack also worked perfectly on mini-model decks designed for kids. One memorable Tracker ad from 1985 featured a prototype of GSD's original Tracker signature skateboard, which was the first pro model street deck, with a pair of Extracks that he had ground all the way through the hangers and halfway through the axles— and they still held up! This was a testament to the superior strength of Trackers. Thanks to street skating and mini-models, sales of Extracks held steady throughout the '80s. In fact, we continue to produce them today, so you can still live the dream.—**LMB**

Tom Inouye lays out a vert Bert in the pool at Boulder Skatepark in Boulder, Colorado, circa 1979. Photo: James Cassimus

Opposite page, top: **Shreddi Repas performs an early stand-up grind at Skatercross in Reseda, California, circa 1979.** Photo: Lance Smith

Opposite page, bottom left: **Kelly Lynn pilots a frontside air at Sensation Basin in Gainesville, Florida, summer 1979.** Photo: Glen Friedman

Opposite page, bottom right: **Lonnie Hiramoto lifts a fine frontal out of the keyhole at Marina Skatepark in Marina del Rey, California, May 1979.** Photo: Craig Fineman

114

Mike McGill, July 1980.

Extracks Best, August 1983.

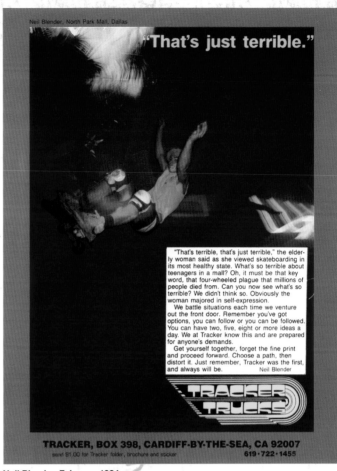

Neil Blender, North Park Mall, Dallas

"That's just terrible."

"That's terrible, that's just terrible," the elderly woman said as she viewed skateboarding in its most healthy state. What's so terrible about teenagers in a mall? Oh, it must be that key word, that four-wheeled plague that millions of people died from. Can you now see what's so terrible? We didn't think so. Obviously the woman majored in self-expression.

We battle situations each time we venture out the front door. Remember you've got options, you can follow or you can be followed. You can have two, five, eight or more ideas a day. We at Tracker know this and are prepared for anyone's demands.

Get yourself together, forget the fine print and proceed forward. Choose a path, then distort it. Just remember, Tracker was the first, and always will be.   Neil Blender

TRACKER TRUCKS

TRACKER, BOX 398, CARDIFF-BY-THE-SEA, CA 92007
send $1.00 for Tracker folder, brochure and sticker   619·722·1455

Neil Blender, February 1984.

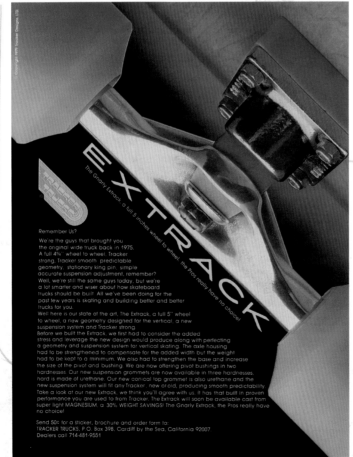

EXTRACK
The Gnarly Extrack, a full 5 inches wheel to wheel, the Pros really have no choice!

Remember Us?

We're the guys that brought you the original wide truck back in 1975. A full 4¼" wheel to wheel. Tracker strong, Tracker smooth, predictable geometry, stationary king pin, simple accurate suspension adjustment, remember?

Well, we're still the same guys today, but we're a lot smarter and wiser about how skateboard trucks should be built. All we've been doing for the past few years is skating and building better and better trucks for you.

Well here is our state of the art, The Extrack, a full 5" wheel to wheel, a new geometry designed for the vertical, a new suspension system and Tracker strong.

Before we built the Extrack, we first had to consider the added stress and leverage the new design would produce along with perfecting a geometry and suspension system for vertical skating. The axle housing had to be strengthened to compensate for the added width but the weight had to be kept to a minimum. We also had to strengthen the base and increase the size of the pivot and bushing. We are now offering pivot bushings in two hardnesses. Our new suspension grommets are now available in three hardnesses, hard is made of urethane. Our new conical top grommet is also urethane and the new suspension system will fit any Tracker, new or old, producing smooth predictability. Take a look at our new Extrack, we think you'll agree with us. It has that built in proven performance you are used to from Tracker. The Extrack will soon be available cast from super light MAGNESIUM, a 30% WEIGHT SAVINGS! The Gnarly Extrack, the Pros really have no choice!

Send 50¢ for a sticker, brochure and order form to:
TRACKER TRUCKS, P.O. Box 398, Cardiff by the Sea, California 92007.
Dealers call 714-481-9551

Tracker Extrack, March 1979.

Box 398   Cardiff, CA 92007   (619) 722-1455

Send Dollar

RECENTLY, SOME UNKNOWN PERSON PAID TRACKER THE ULTIMATE COMPLIMENT. THEY STOLE ANOTHER ONE OF G.S.D.'S PERSONAL SKATEBOARDS.   TRACKER TRUCKS: THEY'RE GUARANTEED FOR A REASON.

GSD, June 1985.

117

In the late 1970s, Sierra Madre, California native Chris Strople was one of the top pro vert skateboarders in the world. The inventor of the alley-oop and rock 'n' roll boardslide, he was also a faithful Tracker test rider who could often be seen piloting prototype trucks in many a magazine shot. A skateboarder for life, Chris still embarks on road trips to this day, hitting up skateparks near and far.—GSD

LMB: When did you start skating?
I started in 1966, when I was six, on a neighbor's Hobie Vita Pakt board with clay wheels. I skated hills and bombed his steep driveway. The first time I skated a pool was with my brothers at an abandoned motel across from the Santa Anita racetrack. It was a huge 12-foot deep keyhole. I skated barefoot, so we called it the blood bowl due to all of the wipe-outs. The first time I carved over the light, which was nine feet high, I was a vert skater from then on. I competed in downhill and slalom. I still have my trophies. Wally Inouye lived in Montebello. That's when he skated for Sims. He gave me my first set of Haftracks. Wally is one of the most tried and true Tracker guys through the last 40 years.
LMB: When did you first come down to the San Diego area?
Wally brought me down here in 1976, when I met Lance Smith and Gunnar Haugo at the Kona Bowl. Through Wally, I also met Rodney Jesse, Murray Estes and Sonny Miller, and we all skated the spots down here. I was skating for Sims at the time, but I broke every board he gave me. So, Curtis Hesselgrave introduced me to Billy Caster, who was very anal about quality—his craftsmanship was incredible. Soon after I got on Caster, I moved into a house in Cardiff with Curtis, Waldo Autry and Brad Strandland. I was the kid in the bunch. After the Cardiff house, I lived in Tom Stewart's garage, then in the San Elijo campgrounds for a while.
LMB: I was looking at a bunch of photos of you in skateboard magazines of the '70s. You were riding prototype Trackers with hanger extensions when we were going through the stages of widening our trucks.
The reason for the extensions was because each Tracker truck had a different pivot angle. In order to get a feel for which turning radius we wanted in the truck, we would slap some eight-inch axles on a Haftrack with

extensions to see how they worked. I actually rode them in a contest at Winchester. I took a bunch of axles up there and we had some other ones set off to the side, so in case I bent them, I could change them out really quickly in between runs. The lightness of them with the magnesium baseplates was also unique. Plastic baseplates didn't work too well. Bennett figured out that, but he kept on making plastic baseplates anyway. I think the first major product liability suits in skateboarding were against Ron Bennett for his plastic baseplates.
LMB: At the 1978 *Skateboarder* magazine awards, they called Mr. Bennett up, gave him a trophy, and the base of it fell off onto the floor. Everyone burst out laughing, because they were very familiar with the infamous broken Bennett baseplates.
There were very few truck companies back then. Tracker was it before Indy was even around.
LS: Bennett might have beaten us by a month or so.
Yeah, but Bennett never progressed. Tracker just took over. Bennetts didn't work too well in bowls. Tracker was always good to me and helped pay my rent so I could surf and skate all the time.
LMB: Why was Tracker so important in the history of skateboarding?
Tracker was the first real truck that was made for bowl riding and downhill. Bennetts weren't as well-made to take the abuse that skating had evolved to dish out. Tracker was the first to make a truck with abuse in mind. All of the others progressed from Chicago to Oak Street to ACS to Bennett. But, with that plastic baseplate, Bennett just couldn't take the abuse. Tracker was very important for forging a whole product line with modern materials. Tracker was definitely part of the whole history of skateboarding, and progressed it with the trucks. Independent should have given you guys some credit. Thanks for having faith in me to be a good skater for you guys.
LMB: Did you invent tricks on Trackers?
The alley-oop and rock 'n' roll boardslide were definitely invented on Trackers. Most of the tricks that I did later on were forged, for lack of a better term, on Tracker Trucks. Due to their durability, there wasn't a better truck at the time. Plus, the guys building them were great, too. They were actually skaters, and it made a big difference. As we knew back in those days, a lot of guys who got into the skateboard business didn't understand skating, so it was quite a pleasure to work with people at Tracker to help on the research and development, and make them better. You guys were always open to listen, which made it a lot better. All of the other truck brands didn't listen to the skaters about what was right and wrong, and how they could make their trucks better.
LMB: You rode all of the Tracker prototypes, then you came back and told us about which geometry worked better at which width.
What turned better and what worked on the street would not necessarily work in a bowl.

Around that time, Del Mar was built, and San Diego had a lot of great places to go skate, to test out the trucks in different mediums. You could go ride downhill on them, race some slalom, go to a skatepark, do some freestyle. Tracker had a truck for each kind of skating, but no one else did at the time. It was "one truck fits all."
LS: Did you skate Mt. Baldy much?
Yes, but not the widow maker, which is a huge run-off channel in case the dam overflows. You can't even walk to the top of it. You have to go up the side because it's so steep. Guys always wanted to bomb it. I saw somebody try it and get helicoptered out of there. I remember there was no graffiti the first time I went to the Mt. Baldy pipeline in 1975, and there was no tar on the bottom. I also remember seeing the Upland Pipeline skatepark—especially the 15 bowl—chalked out in the dirt. I couldn't fathom it. Then when they dug the hole for the 15 footer, we realized nothing had ever been dug that deep at a skatepark before. I wondered, "Are we going to be able to get to the top of that thing?" Then there was the Vertibowl at Paramount, which had eight feet of vert. It was fun to draw lines around skateparks back then.
LMB: Back then, there were no videos, so guys didn't know how to do tricks until they saw it in real life.
Yeah, which reminds me of something really sad. Wally had a huge collection of super 8 movies of skating, but, for some reason, someone took them. Wally had incredible footage of the pipes in Arizona, the Fruit Bowl and other epic spots, but we can't find them. And they're getting to the age that if they're not stored right, they'll be gone. We used to film ourselves in super 8 and go back and watch them to check our style like people do with iPhones today. I feel sorry for the current generation. The top guys don't get as much out of it as they should. Skateboarding should be in the Olympics. The X Games is ESPN's second-highest rated program besides football. That's their dirty little secret. What do you think people were watching in the Olympics: pixies doing triple axles, or snowboarders doing 20 footers out of the halfpipe?
LMB: Back in the '70s, you guys figured out how to fall, and Rector designed

By Larry Balma + Lance Smith

Chris Strople
INTERVIEW

safety gear based on that.
You're right. After I retired from skating around 1990, it took a good seven years to heal, if not longer. Eventually, the swellbows went down. I was wracked.
LS: You don't have permanent injuries?
I just had some surgery done on my foot. I tore up a ligament in my toe. I skate now, but I stay out of the air.

Read the full-length interview at trackertrucks.com

Above: **Chris Strople snaps a hot tail tap in Boulder, Colorado, circa 1979.** Photo: Unknown
Opposite page: **Chris pulls a frontside air in a Tracker Extrack ad, September 1979.**

The Cincinnati Kid, Garry Scott Davis (also known as GSD), moved from his native Buckeye State to California in 1982 to pursue his skateboarding dreams. The inventor of the Boneless One and the publisher of the first home-made skate zine, *Skate Fate*, GSD also boasted the first pro model street deck, which was issued by Tracker. During a stint toiling in the Tracker shop from 1983-'87, GSD was the Editor for *TransWorld Skateboarding*, and also the Art Director from 1988-'93. Since then, he's worked for companies like Sole Technology, played music in his bands Custom Floor and Carpet Floor, and enjoyed a lot of overseas travel.—LMB

When did you first start skateboarding?
The first time was around 1973-'74. Some kid in the neighborhood had the classic 2" x 4" with metal roller skate wheels nailed to it—you know, the full cliché—so I just rode that down a slight incline on the sidewalk one day. The weird thing is, I only rode it that one time. At the time, I really didn't think too much about it. How could I know then that skateboarding would become this all-consuming passion for my whole life? Three years later, during the big skateboarding boom of 1976, another friend got a little plastic Grentec skateboard for his birthday, and he brought it down to my house. The next day, I got one, and we were cruising down the sidewalk, doing 360s. Then I saw that movie *Freewheelin'* with Stacy Peralta—it was actually in the theater—and that got me way psyched on skating. The first issue of *Skateboarder* magazine I bought was the one with Tony Alva on the front doing a kickturn in the Soul Bowl. I got super stoked on Stacy Peralta's interview and CR Stecyk III's articles on Dogtown. That pretty much set the tone for the next several decades of my life.
In 1982, you came out to Del Mar just to watch the contest. How long did you stay out here?
Well, I moved to San Jose, because I was in touch with Steve Caballero, Gavin O'Brien, Cory O'Brien and Craig Ramsay through zines that we sent back and forth through the mail. I made *Skate Fate*, Caballero made *Skate Punk*, and the O'Briens made *Skate Scene*,

and we traded and wrote letters, so I was a pen pal with those guys. I moved out to San Jose in July 1982, just because there was a huge skate scene there. In August, I took the Greyhound down to San Diego to Del Mar for that Rusty Harris contest and I met Stacy Peralta, who was one of my skateboarding idols. It was amazing to meet him, and he introduced me to you, and got you to flow me a set of Extracks with red Copers. That's how our whole relationship started. At some point in early 1983, we started corresponding; you told me you were going to make a Tracker newsletter and that you wanted to use an editorial out of *Skate Fate*. Then, a couple of months later, the first issue of *TransWorld Skateboarding* showed up in the mail and I was blown away, because it was a magazine, and it had a color cover. *Thrasher* was all black and white then.
You wanted to come down to Oceanside to see about working at Tracker and *TransWorld*, so I sent you a bus ticket.
And I liked it, so I went back to San Jose, gathered all of my stuff, brought it down and started working for you.
Tell us about the infamous incident when you fell through the ceiling at Tracker.
That was in 1983-'84, when Bryan Ridgeway, Jinx and I had been sleeping on the floor at Tracker/*TransWorld*. You and Tracker Peggy Cozens would walk up the stairs every morning and see three bodies on the floor wrapped up in sleeping bags, and finally, after six months or a year, you got tired of it. You said, "Okay you guys have got to get out and rent a place." I only made minimum wage, which was $3.25 per hour then, so I couldn't afford to rent a room, buy food, bus fare and all of that stuff, so I had to keep staying there at Tracker. Sometimes, I would hide behind boxes and sleep upstairs until someone caught me. There was an upstairs bathroom with a ladder that went up to the roof; and in between the ceiling and the roof, there was a three-foot high crawl space up in the rafters. So, I climbed up the ladder, threw a piece of plywood onto the rafters and just started sleeping up there. I would shut the lid to the bathroom ceiling. One morning, as I was sleeping up there, I heard the plywood hatch open up, and Larry Balma's head appeared. The first words out of his mouth were, "You're busted, GSD." After that, I slept in the pools or Hi-Balls (enclosed trampolines) at Del Mar.
But, you must have rolled off of the plywood, because the ceiling got cracked and some dust fell down into the sink. That's when Peggy freaked out.
Then Craig Stecyk wrote in the Trash column in *Thrasher* that I had actually fallen through the ceiling and crashed down into the sink, which didn't really happen, of course. I just kept couch touring and sleeping at Del Mar. By 1986, I started living with Tod Swank for about a year, and then I bought a new Toyota truck and slept in the camper shell for a year. After that, I lived in houses.
Was *Skate Fate* really the first skate zine that got published and sent around?
Yeah, it was the first homemade one that was Xeroxed and published out of a skater's house. There had been a few before that made by skateparks and companies. But, *Skate Fate* was the first one I knew of that

was Xeroxed.
And it was the longest running zine. You did it continuously for how many years?
Well, I did it monthly for five years, and then it was annual for the second five years, because I got burned out at some point.
You designed Tracker ads on the back of every *Skate Fate* zine.
You know, what's funny about that is I never got a single one of those ads approved. I just did them. I was surprised you never got mad at that. I just winged them, and no one ever complained.
No, we enjoyed them all. So, you usually rode Extracks on street. Did you ever ride the other truck widths?
Well, when I started out in 1976, after I rode the Grentec, my first good board was a Logan Earth Ski Bruce Logan model with Bennett Hijackers and Sims Comps. The next year, my mom, dad and I drove out to So Cal on a summer vacation and I got them to take me to the Concrete Wave in Anaheim, and we also stopped by Kanoa Surf, where I bought a set of Haftracks and Sims Comp IIs. So, the first Trackers I ever rode were the Haftracks, and then at some point, I got Fultracks in the late '70s. Those first white Copers were really brittle. I remember smashing a layback grind into a bank to curb at the Doctor's Office and I just shattered that Coper into a million pieces. Later, you made them with a softer plastic. So, I rode Haftracks and Fultracks first before Extracks.
You could ride vert, but you concentrated on street.
Yeah, that's because in all of the swimming pools in the Midwest, the transition goes up and then levels out into a ledge that the vert wall sits on. The walls don't transition smoothly up to vert. I didn't have bowls or a vert ramp to skate, so I just concentrated more on street, banks and ditches.
Did you invent any tricks while you were riding on Tracker Trucks?
Yeah, in December 1979, I thought up the Boneless One. It was inspired by the backside footplant, which already existed. One time, my friends and I were sitting on the

Garry Davis
INTERVIEW

floor messing around with our skateboards, and I just thought, "What if you took off your front foot going frontside, like a front footed footplant?" But, I was thinking about it being done on vertical. We thought it would be impossible to get your front foot back on. Then we just forgot about it. A few months later, in March 1980, after the snow melted, some friends and I started doing it on a bank spot we used to ride called the Doctor's Office. It was super easy, especially on banks. It was actually way easier than doing a backside footplant, and you could boost way higher.

Read the full-length interview at trackertrucks.com

Above: **GSD cracks a tail slide onto a rock at the Shell Bowl in Oceanside, California, August 1984.** Photo: Neil Blender
Opposite page: **GSD pulls his trick, the Boneless One, at the Shell Bowl, early 1985.** Photo: Grant Brittain

Ray "Bones" Rodriguez pushes a smooth and stylish tail slide out over the coping at Marina skatepark in Marina del Rey, California, circa 1980. One of the most iconic skateboard decks of all time, Ray's first pro model was the first to feature skull graphics, which went on to be widely copied throughout the '80s and beyond. Photo: Jim Goodrich
Right: **Monty Nolder** busts a footplant on the lip of the halfpipe at Sensation Basin in Gainseville, Florida, circa 1979. Photo: Jim Goodrich

TRACKER MAGNESIUM
Gnarly Lightweights (1978)

After World War II ended in 1945, young hot rod enthusiasts returned home with knowledge of newly developed lightweight magnesium castings used in aircraft engines and wheels. Magnesium wheels were also cast for racecars, and, by the 1960s, cast aluminum wheels were built for street rods and muscle cars. These look-alike wheels were marketed as "mags," however, we all knew which ones were the real mags, and wished we could afford them. In 1978, Tracker partnered with racecar genius inventor Leonard Abbott, who built his own foundry to cast aluminum and magnesium parts for dragsters and race boats, to cast magnesium Trackers. With aerial maneuvers coming on strong in skateboarding, lightweight equipment was worth its weight in gold. (Aluminum alloy weighs 30% less than steel, and magnesium weighs 30% less than aluminum alloy!) Yes, Tracker magnesium trucks were very expensive because of the high cost of materials and the labor-intensive production process required, thus they were highly coveted. As soon as he began flowing out magnesium trucks, Tracker team manager Lance Smith suddenly became Mr. Popular, as many a team rider and other random skaters requested them. In fact, because of the mags' high value, Lance had to be really selective about who he gave them to, which forced him to keep them hidden under a blanket inside his car.

Because magnesium is highly corrosive when exposed to the elements, racecar parts made of magnesium were treated with an alodyne solution to prevent oxidation. Alodyne left an inconsistent, mottled, muddy yellow/green tint on our Tracker parts, so we had to find a different process to protect them. Harry Jackman Wheels was the first company to use an electrostatic powder coat on his aftermarket auto wheels and truck bumpers. Powder coating was the newest painting process available and worked perfectly to stop corrosion, thus all Tracker magnesium trucks were powder coated yellow by Jackman. No other truck brand painted trucks at the time, so the yellow Tracker magnesium trucks ridden by pros jumped off the pages of the skateboarding magazines just like they jumped off the store shelves.

Tracker magnesiums were produced in Haftrack, Midtrack, Fultrack, Extrack and Sixtrack widths for discerning skaters who could afford the price of admission. In fact, they were at least double the price of any other truck at the time. All Tracker magnesiums were built in

Below: **Ever since its debut in 1978, the Tracker Sixtrack magnesium was the most coveted truck by sponsored ams and pros. It was considered the cream of the crop of all Tracker trucks throughout the '80s up to today. With no full scale production since the late '80s, Tracker mags have gone on to become very expensive collector's items, with unridden pairs selling for hundreds of dollars each on eBay.**

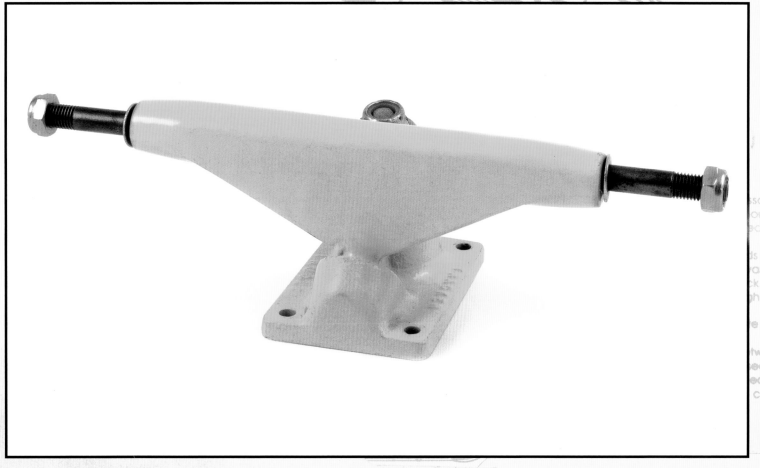

Alan Gelfand chucks a stylish frontside air out of Big O's capsule pool in Orange, California, May 1980. Photo: Ted Terrebonne
Opposite page, top: **Kent Senatore splays out a backside layback across the coping at Marina Skatepark in Marina del Rey, California.** Photo: James Cassimus
Opposite page, bottom left: **Brad Bowman flings a stylish early release frontside air out of Del Mar's keyhole in Del Mar, California, circa 1979.** Photo: Lance Smith
Opposite page, bottom right: **Mark Partain slaps a crail slide across the lip at McGill's Skatepark in Carlsbad, California, circa 1988. McGill's park was made of wooden ramps built over the old Carlsbad Skatepark, most of which was filled in with dirt. The only exception was this bowl that was, with the addition of vert walls, turned into a catfish pond.** Photo: Grant Brittain

MADE IN U.S.A.

Eat This!, August 1988.

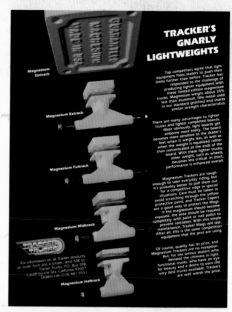

Tracker's Gnarly Lightweights, circa 1979.

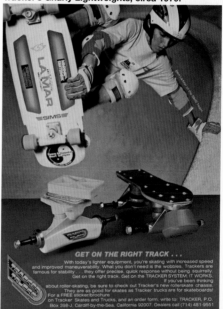

Bert Lamar, January 1980.

the Gnarly configuration; none were ever made with small pivots.

Tracker produced magnesium trucks for a full decade, from 1978 until 1987. Magnesium dust is highly explosive and could not be vacuumed into our conventional dust collection system. Thus, we had a separate grinding system for them. In the late '80s, Buddy Carr was the only grinder for the magnesium castings. While Buddy was on a trip home to Ohio, one of our aluminum truck grinders, Sigifredo, decided to try to grind the magnesium castings. He knew that they were ground on another system, but was unaware of the safety protocols, which included periodically cleaning up all of the highly flammable magnesium dust. Keep in mind when you watch huge fireworks shows on the fourth of July, the skyrockets with the bright white bursts and sparkles are made by exploding magnesium dust. Sigifredo did everything wrong and had magnesium dust piled all over himself. At break time, he lit up a cigarette, which instantly ignited the magnesium dust. Although we had a special extinguisher for magnesium fires, our shop foreman, who was standing nearby next to a tumble polisher hosing off some ground aluminum castings with water, glanced over, saw the fire engulfing Sigifredo, and instinctively turned the water hose directly at him. Magnesium burns at a temperature of 5610 degrees Fahrenheit. When the water hit the flames, it was instantly turned into steam, adding hydrogen and oxygen to the fire, which totally fried Sigifredo. Third degree burns melted away all of the skin from his arms and torso. After four months of skin grafts, the trooper finally returned to work. Tracker's insurance carrier forbid us to continue grinding magnesium from that day on. Despite the high risk, in recent years, I've been known to hand-grind new old stock Tracker magnesium trucks for collectors from time to time. —**LMB**

Neil Blender, circa 1980.

Doug Schneider, July 1979.

ALVA SKATES

714/957 0971

Tony Ava, circa 1980.

TRANSWORLD
SKATEBOARDING

FEB. '85 2.50
CDC 00586

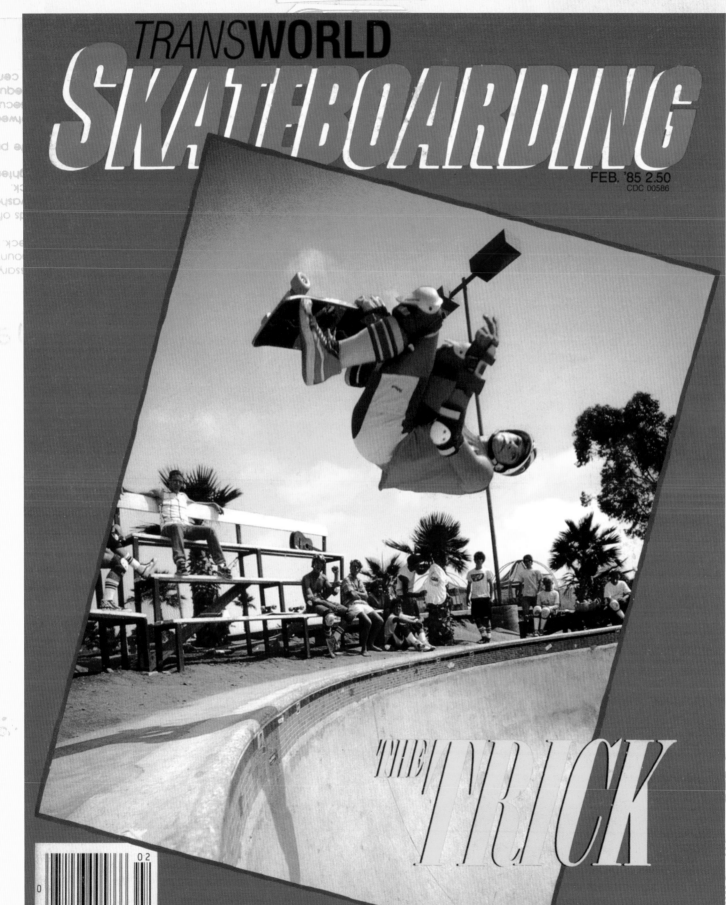

THE TRICK

In 1984, Mike McGill tore skateboarding a new keyhole when he unveiled the McTwist (540) to a stunned world, opening up vertical aerial maneuvers to multiple rotations for the first time. Born on September 2, 1964 in Brooklyn, New York, Mike moved to New Port Richey, Florida nine years later. Not long after, he started skateboarding, eventually getting sponsored by Powell-Peralta, for whom he co-starred in a series of groundbreaking videos like *Future Primitive* and *The Search For Animal Chin*. In the late '80s, Mike went on to open his own wooden ramp skatepark (built on top of the old Carlsbad skatepark), and McGill's Skate Shop, the latter of which is still open for business. Even though Mike's a dedicated family man, make no mistake about it, he still shreds as hard as ever to this day.—GSD

Mike McGill
INTERVIEW

When did you start skateboarding?
I think I was 9 ½. I borrowed a skateboard from this girl on the next block just about every day. It had steel wheels, but I still thought it was cool. My dad wouldn't buy me one, because he thought it was dangerous. I eventually showed him I could ride hers pretty good, so he bought me a board and a helmet.

Describe your first good skateboard.
It was a fiberglass deck with Trickeray wheels and BBs as ball bearings. I think I got it at Zayre's department store, which was kind of like Sears. I remember replacing the BBs with other BBs when they wore out.

When did you get your first Trackers?
During my first California trip with Alan Gelfand, Stacy Peralta told me to grab a Ray Bones board out of his garage at Venice Beach. It had Trackers on it, so my first set was hand-me-down ones, but they worked fine. I believe they were Extracks.

How did you get on the Tracker team?
Stacy told the people at Tracker about me and had them ship packages to me with notes on them from Chris Strople and Wally Inouye. That inspired me back in Florida.

Which Tracker models did you ride?
I started on Extracks, and then moved on to Sixtrack magnesiums and Aggro Quicktracks later on. I pretty much rode anything they ever made.

Tell us about your favorite Tracker ads.
I liked the ones back in the *Skateboarder* mag days like Tony Alva, Jay Adams and some of mine that showed skating, as well as some of the guys I skated with, like Alan Gelfand. I liked one that was taken at Big O, for sure. Back then, it was as big a deal to get an ad as it was to get a picture in the mag. There weren't as many companies, so if you were on a major one, it meant you were really respected. I liked some that were used inside product cards like Lappers and Copers, too. One was of myself doing a corner air at Upland. I was just as stoked on that as one in the magazine.

Did you invent any tricks on Trackers?
The McTwist and McEgg, primarily. I just like skating and adding my own style to tricks that already exist.

During your time on Trackers, what stood out about their performance?
They were very stable on vert. I knew I could depend on them no matter what I was trying. I never worried about anything breaking, and that's important when trying tricks higher and higher.

Tell us about some memorable times with the Tracker team.
In all honesty, I was going to ride for Indy after Cab did, but Tracker hired a guy named Bryan Ridgeway as their new team manager, and his dedication and support kept me on Tracker for nearly two decades, along with others who eventually worked for the company. There wouldn't have been many memorable times had they not got that guy as their team manager. It makes a huge difference when a company is supportive. Besides that, traveling the world, exploring new spots and meeting all of the people associated with that are the key memories. I'm still friends with people I met 30 years ago while traveling on those skate trips.

Tell us a couple of crazy stories from those trips.
When I was a teen, I was fortunate to have a radio station send me as an amateur to Venezuela to do a demo on the Pepsi ramp with Tony Alva, Tim Scroggs, Ellen Oneal, Alan Gelfand and Steve Rocco. What amateur got to do something like that in high school? All of the other contest and skate camp trips in Europe also stand out. But, for the most part, it was about skating as many hours as possible and having fun doing it. That natural high and stoke was more than enough!

Why was Tracker so important in the history of skateboarding?
Because they were innovators of products and were ahead of the curve, progressing to where skating would be headed. They made sure the riders had what they needed to keep progressing, too. The long list of great riders seemed to validate the legitimacy of Tracker products because the best were riding them. They supported events to keep the fire going in the industry, and even had the first full-time team trainer, Barry Zaritsky, who had a training house for rehabbing the riders. I know for sure he made it possible for me to participate in half of the contests I was planning on flying home from due to injury. I went from ready to disappoint all of my sponsors by not being able to compete, to placing in the top five by the end of it all. This happened time and time again, and I wasn't the only one he helped this way. He had us rehabbing correctly, had us eating right…the whole nine yards. Tracker was cool, because they let riders from other truck companies use the rehab facility and Barry. There's something to be said for that!

Which skaters inspired you the most?
I had photos on my wall in Florida of Stacy Peralta, Steve Olson, Tony Alva and Jay Adams. The most amazing thing to me back then was I would end up meeting all of them within two years after I got sponsored. As a little kid, I didn't think that would ever happen. They all had their own unique identities and styles, and I liked something different about each.

What have been the highlights of your time in skateboarding?
I was sponsored by some of the best in the business, traveled the world doing what I loved and was part of so many fresh things, like when the video age hit skateboarding, etc. I loved working on the Tracker video parts with Ridge and Keith Lenharr. Starting my shop back in 1988 was a dream I had for years and it still exists here in Encinitas, California today. I also owned and operated my skatepark in Carlsbad for years. I had several brands like Chapter 7 and Shaft that taught me plenty about the skateboard business inside out. I'm still skating today and having a blast when I do. I love seeing the other efforts being made to bring skateboarding to people around the world like those people of Skateistan. That's just all-around cool.

What are you up to today?
McGill's Skate Shop is where I spend my time. I also do demos for various charities, when possible. I still like those road trips, but I try to keep them within three to four hours away these days.

What do you enjoy doing besides skateboarding?
I'm a family man, so they are my priority. I like fishing and taking care of tropical fish, as well as hanging with the folks. Without their support over the years, I'm sure I would have never gotten this far in life with as much happiness as I've been afforded. They all know I need to get out and skate, though.

By Bryan Ridgeway

Opposite page: **Mike McGill, The Trick (McTwist), October 1985.** Photo: Grant Brittain
Below: **Mike McGill tosses up a Tracker air at his skatepark in Carlsbad, California, circa 1988.** Photo: Chip Morton

FOR A STICKER, BROCHURE AND ORDER FORM, SEND 50¢ TO TRACKER TRUCKS, P.O. BOX 398, CARDIFF-BY-THE-SEA, CALIFORNIA 92007.

POWELL AMATEUR STEVE CABALLERO

T R A C K E R

DEALERS CALL 714-481-9551

Steve Caballero, March 1980.
130

By Larry Balma + GSD

Shredding with Powell-Peralta for 35 years and counting, Steve Caballero easily lays claim to skateboarding's longest-running sponsorship. The inventor of such classic moves as the Caballaerial and the les twist, the Gentleman has also designed top-selling shoes like the Half Cab for his other longtime sponsor, Vans, and rocked out with his famous skate punk band, The Faction. It's safe to say Cab has skateboarding in his soul. Read on for the lowdown with a true legend of the magic rolling board.—GSD

Steve INTERVIEW
Caballero

LMB: When and how did you start skateboarding?

I first started out trying to be a BMX racer, but that didn't pan out, because I was so short for my age. I went to one race and I just figured out really quickly that those guys were two feet taller than me with longer legs. My friend had a skateboard and a ramp, so I tried it out and fell in love with it. Everyone around that time in the late '70s had the plastic skateboards. You know that famous red board with the steel wheels? I had one of those. I think the first wood board I ever had was a Free Former Ty Page. I would look through *Skateboarder* magazines and see all of these skateboard parks happening down in Southern California. I would try to emulate what they were doing by building ramps, but obviously my proportions weren't very good. The ramps I built had quick trannies, which made them super hard to skate. I ended up going to the Concrete Wave, across the street form Disneyland. After that, I was hooked.

LMB: How did you get your first Trackers?

I got my first set when I got sponsored by Tracker, which was through Mike McGill once I got on the Bones Brigade in 1979.

GSD: Do you still have one of your first pro model decks on Powell-Peralta with the propeller graphics?

I never kept an original one, but I do have the shirt that I wore in that ad.

GSD: They only made a few of those decks with the propeller, right?

I think they only made, like, six. I remember I had three of them. I gave one to my friend, and I remember seeing a picture of Tony Hawk riding one. I skated one, but never kept it. There's a guy in Australia who makes reproduction decks, and he made me a repro of it that looks dead on perfect. I want to get a pair of those Sixtrack magnesiums to put on that board with some Cubics and make a complete. Of course, I'll need the Copers and the Lapper, too.

LMB: Which Tracker ad was your favorite?

The most memorable Tracker ad that I had was a photo of me doing a backside air in the keyhole pool at Winchester. That was when Rectors first came out and I was wearing Rector elbow pads on my knees. If you look closely at the photo, my knees pads are really tiny, because I was wearing extra large elbow pads on my knees. I don't remember another Tracker ad. Was there a sequence?

GSD: You had a two-thirds page black and white ad of the Caballaerial in *Action Now*. When you invented the Caballaerial, was that inspired by someone you saw do a fakie 360?

The Caballaerial was inspired by a pro skateboarder from Nor Cal who rode for Tunnel named Robert Schlaefli, aka The Fly. One of the tricks that he used to like doing was an RB slide to fakie, then a fakie 360 kickturn. He would do it all the time in every run right above tile. I remember one time he did an RB slide to fakie, but had way too much speed. He pumped, went up and accidentally pulled a fakie 360 in the air as his board flailed away. At the time, I had already learned a new trick called the fakie Ollie, so I looked at what the Fly did on accident and wondered if you could actually pull it off—do a fakie Ollie and spin all the way around. So, I just got that idea in my head and became determined to do it. I just kept trying and trying it over and over again. At that point, I had learned a lot of the modern tricks, and I was looking around for new tricks to come up with.

This was in between the Big O and Marina del Rey contests of the Gold Cup. The Marina contest was going to be in the upper keyhole and sponsored by Powell-Peralta. I remember coming to that contest, and being very excited to introduce this new trick that Stacy just heard about from me on the phone. I guess he told Lance Mountain and Neil Blender, "Cab's got a new trick. No one has seen it and he's going to pull it out at this contest." So, I remember pulling up and Lance and Neil were just waiting there, saying, "We heard about this new trick. We want you to go up to the keyhole right now and show us." They basically put on my pads for me on the way up, because they were so excited to see it. I remember I bailed two or three before I actually landed one and they were just blown away. After that, they went back home to Whittier to try it, but they couldn't even come close. It was either Neil or Lance who said, "Maybe we can grab it." So, they ended up grabbing it, and because they had to grab to make the trick I had invented, they thought it was gay, so that's where the term gay twist came from.

LMB: Where did the name Caballaerial come from?

For the longest time, I just called it the fakie 360 Ollie, but it was Stacy Peralta who named it. We used to have this newsletter called the *Bones Brigade Intelligence Report*, and I remember Stacy had written, "Caballero wins Upland with the Caballaerial," so he called it that. I was so weirded out about having a trick named after me, for two or three years, I would just call it the fakie 360 Ollie.

GSD: Right when you started to learn the Caballaerial, how long did it take you to land one?

I don't really have a record of how long it actually took. I think I tried it for a month. I don't know if I tried it every single day, but I remember from the thought of it to actually landing it, I would get closer and closer each time until I turned around and just slid around and made it all the way. It probably took about a month to perfect it until I could actually show it. It's kind of hard to actually gauge how long it takes to learn a trick. There's a thought process that goes on before you even attempt tricks that you're not sure are even possible.

GSD: Well, the Boneless One didn't take that long. It was really easy. It only took one try (laughs). You were the first one to take it to vert, right?

Yeah, it was inspired by Garry Scott Davis, who at one point was living in San Jose for how many years?

GSD: I lived there for almost a year.

We were skating a lot of banks. Did we take you to Montague? Is that where you did the first one?

GSD: I invented it in Cincinnati, Ohio in 1979-'80. In San Jose, I first did it at the Sink or maybe the Bricks. Remember the Sink on my *Thrasher* cover?

I remember watching you do that trick and I was like, "That would be kind of a cool trick to take to vert." I went from learning it on a bank skating with you to taking it to my ramp, which was 12 feet wide and nine feet high. I tried it straight to coping on vert. I remember learning it, and then Palmdale was the next contest and I pulled out that trick to win the contest. That was 1983 and I was on Tracker.

GSD: Which was the first backyard contest, Joe's Ramp Jam?

No, the first backyard ramp contest was Palmdale; that's where the Boneless One came out on vert. The contest after that was Joe Lopes Ramp Jam, and that's where I pulled the Backside Boneless One.

GSD: Were you the first to do that?

Steve Caballero was the publisher of *Skate Punk* and *Speeed Zine*. These two issues are from June 1982 and 1984 respectively.

Steve Caballero, January 1981.

132

Yeah. I did the les twist at that contest, too. The les twist came from grabbing the opposite rail of a gay twist.

GSD: Tell us the story of how you left Tracker for Independent.

Around 1983-'84, I was getting a lot of attention from Fausto Vitello. He never asked me to be on the Independent team, he was just being very friendly and supportive and doing a lot with the industry itself with those backyard ramp contests. He was very involved and I was involved in the scene, as well. So, I got pretty close to Fausto. At the same time, I felt a little distant from you guys at Tracker only because I was up north. I was seven hours away from Tracker, so I never got to hang out down here. I was the only Tracker rider in Nor Cal, and believe me, I got a lot of crap for that. People would always tell me, "Dude, why are you on Tracker? You should be on Indy!" I was like, "Because they were the first truck company to give me a chance. I'm not going to leave them just to be on this cool company. I know I'm from Nor Cal, but I'm backing the company that backed me." For a long time, I took the hits from Nor Cal people. I didn't care what they thought; it was my life. But, from 1982 to '84, I didn't feel the love and support from Tracker, and I didn't think we [Larry Balma and I] were very close. The only person I was close to at Tracker was the team manager, Lance Smith [who left in 1982]. I don't know how much involvement you had with the team. My relationship with you was kind of like the one I had with George Powell. I didn't have a relationship with him, I had a relationship with Stacy.

LMB: In the '70s, Dave Dominy did the promotions and Lance was our team manager. Lance left in 1982 because we went through a real down time. At that point, I had bought out Dave and had to keep track of everything and make it all run, which was tough.

I guess when Lance left, I had no relationship and no communication with you guys. This was when Tony Magnusson and Tony Hawk were coming up, and I felt that you were putting a lot of energy into them. Because of the long distance relationship, they were closer, and I just felt left out. One time, Mofo said, "Dude, Fausto wants you to ride for Indy, and he's going to pay you!" I wasn't getting paid by Tracker, I was only getting free trucks. So, I said, "Get paid, too? That sounds like a good deal since I'm pro. So, yeah let's do this!" So, being from Nor Cal, getting paid plus the love and support I got from Fausto, it just seemed like the right transition for me. So, that's why I left.

GSD: How did you start up your zine, *Skate Punk*?

I went to Sweden one year with Mike McGill and there was a skater named Hans "Puttis" Jacobson who was making a skateboard zine called *Locals*.

GSD: Was it before *Skate Fate* came out in July 1981?

This was before that, because I had never seen *Skate Fate*. I saw *Skate Fate* when I started making *Skate Punk* and then we traded zines. My first issue of *Skate Punk* was in November 1981.

GSD: I remember I still lived in Cincinnati when I got an interview with you on a cassette tape from Craig Ramsay. He sent it through the mail for me to print in *Skate Fate*.

I didn't know about zines until Sweden, so I brought those back with me and showed Gavin and Corey. That's when we said we should make our own zine. Did Gavin and Corey even know you before that?

GSD: Yeah, we were pen pals because of the zines.

Okay, because Gavin and Corey were part of *Skate Punk*. We started *Skate Punk* and then after the second issue, we had some little rivalries. I was putting skimboarding, snowboarding and all of that stuff in there, kind of like *Action Now*. They were like, "No! Not having it!" So, they broke off and did their own zine called *Skate Scene*, and their subtitle was "No pedals, water or snow." So, I was kind of the *Action Now* of zines and they were the full hardcore *Thrasher*. Mine ended at issue number four. I took a break for a while, then we made *Speed Zine*.

GSD: Why did you change the name?

I don't know why. I think because I was not going to have punk rock in there anymore, and I wanted to start a whole brand new zine and make it just skateboarding.

GSD: How did your band The Faction get started?

I got into punk rock around 1980, before The Faction started. I wanted to get into playing music, so I started these little bands. I remember one of the first ones was called Xerox, which was based off of making my zine. Another one we had was called the Abandoned Children. The Faction started in 1982.

GSD: I used to see you play house parties all the time when I lived in San Jose.

Yeah, I drew that skeleton on the cover of our first cassette, or did you?

GSD: No, I drew the skeleton on the first Faction seven-inch cover.

Yeah, that's right. I remember we took photos at Adam's school, then we posed the photos in the cartoon that you drew for the cover. Those were good times, man. We toured the U.S. in 1984 and '85 with The Faction, which was pretty cool, because at the time, I had never toured even with Powell. We actually went on our own tour of the U.S. just in a small van with four guys before Powell even thought about doing tours. We made some 45s and a couple of albums. It was just that whole punk rock attitude, do-it-yourself attitude.

GSD: When did you get on Vans?

I got my first pair of Vans in 1979.

GSD: Did you get sponsored by Vans then or later?

Companies weren't into sponsoring then, they just flowed. So, even though I turned pro in 1980, I was just getting free shoes from them. Stacy would get shoes from Vans and he would give them to us. It wasn't like this direct relationship or involvement with the company. Around 1985-'86, Vans started really getting into BMX, breakdancing and all of that, so there wasn't much love. Stacy wasn't getting any more free shoes, so we just started searching out other shoe companies. We started wearing Converse. That's when Air Jordans came out, so I started wearing those. Tony Hawk and I even went out and bought pairs of Puma Prowlers at Big Five. I was wearing Pumas for a while. It was right around the time Airwalk started. I think Vans were losing market share of skateboarders and said, "We need to start getting back into this!" That's when Everett Rosecrans contacted me in 1988 and said, "Hey, we want you to ride for Vans and we want to pay you." I was like, "Sign me up! Getting free Vans and getting paid? Yes, that's a good deal for a professional skateboarder."

So, I signed up and about six months later, they approached me once again and said, "Hey we want you to have the very first signature skateboard shoe for Vans." I was like, "Cool! Let's do this!" Then I saw the contract, which said the more shoes I sold, the less royalties I got. I said, "That doesn't make any sense to me, because for the last eight years, I've been getting $1.00 per board from Powell, and the more boards that I sold, the more royalties I got. So, I'm not signing

this contract." Their whole thing to me was, "Oh, well. If the shoe sells, it's not because of your name, it's because we make a good shoe." I was like, "Okay, you can keep your contract." So, time went by and they kept bugging me, saying, "We need to make this Caballero shoe!" I responded, "Well, I'm not signing the contract." I remember I said to Lance Mountain, "These guys keep bugging me to make a shoe, but the contract sucks." Lance said, "Well, let's put it this way: What would you rather do, not get ripped off and make no money, or get ripped off and make a lot of money?" I was like, "All right, I'll sign." So, I signed the contract and—boom!—that's when the first Caballero high-top shoe came out in 1989.

GSD: That came out right after the etnies Natas, right?

I'm not sure when the time frame was, but when Natas got his shoe, etnies wasn't a U.S. company, they were in France, so his shoe only sold to Europe. So, I'm not sure which one came out first. They would have to go back and look at the actual dates, but they both came out in 1989.

GSD: How did the Vans Half Cab shoe come about?

Around 1992, vert started dying, and street skating started to become very popular. A lot of the street skaters who wore Vans were cutting off the Cab shoe half way. The trick the half Cab was invented by Kevin Staab and Tony Hawk. I didn't have anything to do with the name or the trick; they actually ended up calling it the Half Cab, because they were doing a fakie Ollie to 180, coming back fakie. I had already invented the Caballaerial, and in their minds, they were just doing half of a

Caballaerial, so they just called it a half Cab. So, that trick was already invented before the shoe was even thought of. In 1991, after I saw the trend of all these street skaters cutting down my shoe, I started cutting them down myself. They would put duct tape all around to hold in the foam; some used stickers and some even sewed it together. I was like, "Why don't we just make shoes like this?" I called up Vans up and said, "Hey, Steve, there's this new trend going on with my shoe. Everyone's cutting it down. Why don't we cut it down, put out new colors, and just call it the Half Cab, because it's half of the Caballero shoe." Vans went with it, and that's how the Half Cab shoe started. After time, we started developing new shoes, so the Half Cab went on the back burner. It was always in the line, but they didn't promote it that much. Close to 15 years ago, they started revamping it and doing collaborations, so it's kind of grown, and now it's the staple for skateboarding. It's still selling really well, and it's probably one of the most copied skate shoes on the market.

GSD: And you're still skating for Powell-Peralta?

I'm still riding for the Bones Brigade.

GSD: Do they still produce your deck models?

Stacy is back with George again, so Powell-Peralta are doing a lot of re-issues. Those are flying out the door like hotcakes. The collectors can't get enough of them. Every time we put out a new colorway, it's like, "I've got to get that colorway!" It's really cool to see what's happening at Powell, seeing them develop new colors and re-releasing those decks. It's not only stoking out the skaters who used to skate, but new collectors and even kids are getting psyched on those graphics that were so famous back in the '80s.

LMB: What were the highlights of your time in skateboarding?

One of the highlights of my skateboard career was being inducted into the Skateboarding Hall of Fame in 2010. That was a special night for me. All of my friends and family who I've met over the years of my career were all in one room. It was amazing growing up with these people for over 30 years, and still seeing them in the industry. People have come and people have gone, and to give a speech about my whole career in five minutes, there was a lot of emotion there. It was just an honor, because in my whole life, I never thought that I would make an impact, let alone be somebody in the sport. I just did it for fun, and for the love of it. I was very passionate about it, and I just wanted to do my best in every aspect of skateboarding. People recognized that, so I was very happy about it and very proud of all of the achievements and all of the blessings I've got from the industry.

Above: **Steve Caballero sails a lien air high above the coping blocks of the keyhole at Skate City in Whittier, California, circa 1980.** Photo: Glen E. Friedman

Tony Magnusson tweaks a sky high backside air over the Point X Mega Ramp near Temecula, California, circa 2005. Photo: Joe Hammeke

Born in Stockholm, Sweden, Tony Magnusson's love for the shred stick started during the big skateboarding craze of 1976. After re-locating to So Cal at the beginning of the '80s, Tony hooked up with Uncle Wiggley, turned pro and proceeded to fling himself far above the coping at every opportunity. In the late '80s, Tony realized skateboard companies should be run by skateboarders themselves, not suits, so he joined forces with his pal Mike Ternasky to form H-Street. The duo went on to pioneer the low-budget self-filmed skate video with *Shackle Me Not*, which had a profound influence on the next generation of street skaters. Today, Tony works as part owner of Osiris shoes, a relaunched H-Street, and still enters the occasional masters division in vert contests.—GSD

Tony Magnusson INTERVIEW

When did you get your first Trackers?
When I came to California, Variflex sponsored me, and the first thing I noticed was that it was really hard to make their trucks turn. It was frustrating. Dennis Martinez gave me my first free skateboard, and I ended up riding with Eddie Elguera, who I idolized in the magazines. So, it was really cool to be part of that team, because Variflex was the crew for a hot little minute there. It wasn't until skateboarding from the '70s kind of died in the early '80s that Variflex was all but gone. I probably got my first set of Trackers from Chris Strople and Wally Inouye, because they rode for Caster at the time, and they sponsored me for a little while. They said, "These are the trucks you need to ride." Everybody knew that the reverse kingpin Variflex trucks

just didn't turn. Then it was like, "Okay, this is how your skateboard is supposed to function in a pool!"

What about the performance of Trackers?
For me, it was more about having something that worked the way it was supposed to, and once it did, you didn't need to do a lot of thinking about it. My trucks worked, that's all I needed, so then it was all about skateboarding. That era of the early '80s was such an innovative time, thanks to the fact that

we skated with Tony Hawk—even though he was only 12. Before he was "Tony Hawk," he was amazingly innovative. There was so much development in tricks, lines and ways of riding that once your equipment worked, there wasn't a lot of thinking that needed to be done beyond that.

Did you invent any tricks on Trackers?
I think I was the first person to do a rocket air, but that's really Christian Hosoi's trick. He popularized it. The only trick that I really got credit for is a 360 Varial. Although it was probably done on Trackers, I don't have a trick named after me like the Hackett slash.

Why was Tracker so important in the history of skateboarding?
If you look at everything that happened in Sweden, it wasn't just that skateboarding came to Stockholm. We were also part of the first generation who broke away from the older generation in Sweden. A whole new music, punk rock, came to Sweden at the same time as skateboarding. There was a whole attitude of being able to express yourself in an individual way—not be part of a team, or follow rules or expectations that were set for you. You could go out and create your own future, and make your own life and art story, what you did was a piece of art, because you were the only one doing it that way. Skateboarding as a whole has embodied this individualism probably more so than any other sport, and it has more in common with musicians and artists who aspire to be unique. So, how does that tie into the equipment that you rode? Well, you had to have the equipment to make that happen. So, a few things happened that really created the whole foundation, and trucks was one of them. If you didn't have the trucks to make the board function, then it couldn't have worked. Obviously, the wheels on the board went through a lot of progress, too. Without the invention of urethane in the '70s, skateboarding wasn't going to happen. You would have never got the movement out of it with steel or clay wheels, as it was before—that's why skateboarding died in the '60s. So, urethane was important, and having trucks that could hold up to all of the moves that everybody was doing became the foundation.

Which Tracker ads were your favorites?
The one of Steve Steadham and I hanging out together in the t-shirt. That was pretty funny. I completely forgot about it until I saw it just now.

Do you still skate today?
I do. I've been fortunate to ride a skateboard my whole life, I live the American dream in California and I've been healthy enough to be able to ride a skateboard. As soon as I get out of here, I'm going to skate Bucky Lasek's. Look at how many skateparks there are now, and the terrain that's available to ride now. If you can ride a skateboard today, whether you're 15 or 50 like me, you're stoked.

You've made a living off of the skateboard industry, you've had several different board brands and you work on Osiris shoes. Is there anything you want to share about that?
Well, it was all out of necessity, because it was hard to get a job in 1982, and I didn't really speak English well. These dudes from

UCSD had a board brand called Uncle Wiggley, and they asked me, "Do you want to ride these really cool high-tech boards that we're building?" I said yes, and ended up working there and learning a bunch of stuff about how to build and sell skateboards. It went along well with my lifestyle. It's a little tough to have a nine-to-five job and try to be a pro skateboarder at the same time. Back in the early '80s, you couldn't make enough money from just riding a skateboard. So, I was in a really good position in the mid '80s when skateboarding really exploded. I had some ideas that a skateboard company should be run by skateboarders. When we started H-Street, we really had the opportunity to put that philosophy to the test: How would it work to run a less professional company? A couple of knuckleheads and some skateboarders running around with a VHS camera making videos. Will that work? Well, as it turned out, it worked pretty well. I've had a lot of people come up and compliment me and my buddy Mike Ternasky, saying, "Hey, we saw what you guys did, and it inspired me to start a company." It was a cool compli-

ment, but it was almost a backhanded one, like, "You guys were nobodies, so I figured I could do it if you could." It's been cool and humbling to know that a lot of people saw that as an inspiration. It wasn't exactly what we set out to do, but we were doing something that was authentically ours, and what we wanted to. It worked and it was an influence on how the skateboarding industry is run today. You want to have guys who ride to either own the company or be involved in some way. That's a good thing, and it puts a very unique mark on the skateboard industry. If I get part of the credit for making that happen, then I'm super stoked.

Read the full-length interview at trackertrucks.com

Above: **Tony Magnusson, Del Mar Skate Ranch, Del Mar, California, circa 1987.** Photo: Grant Brittain
Left: **Steve Steadham and Tony, August 1983.** Photo: Grant Brittain

By Larry Balma

Like a passenger train arriving full-speed at the station, Jim Gray extends his patented Gray slide across the capsule pool at the Big O in Orange, California, circa 1980.
Photos: Craig Fineman

By Larry Balma

A product of the late 1970s So Cal skatepark scene, Jim Gray proffered a clean cut image during punk rock's heyday in skateboarding in the '80s. Not only was Jim the originator of two tricks that bear his name—the Jim Jam and the Gray Slide—but he also skated pro for G&S then Blockhead, went on to found his own brand, Acme Skateboards, followed by a woodshop called ABC Board Supply. Today, Jim runs a sticker company called Inkgenda and still powers around the tranny like the tried and true barnstormer he is.—GSD

Jim Gray
INTERVIEW

When did you start skating?
When I was eight or nine, I got a little plastic Grentec board at the local drugstore. That was when I first rode a skateboard. I had a Black Knight before that, but it was just a skateboard to roll around on. I really started skateboarding somewhere between seventh and eighth grade. After I only skated for a few months, I got sponsored at Skatopia. That was the beginning of the skatepark era.

When did you get your first Trackers?
When I was riding Big O skatepark, Trackers were on some of the boards. I never bought a skateboard, other than the Grentec and Black Knight. I won a complete skateboard at a shop called Sunshine Skateboards in Fountain Valley. When I was done with that board, I took the trucks off of it. I don't remember what they were. I bought some wheels at the Vans store, and I made my own boards out of ash. Then we started making boards out of plywood and putting resin and sand on them for grip. After that, I got sponsored, so I never really went in and bought a pro skateboard deck anywhere. I made a bunch of them, but I never bought one.

One of my first sponsors was Pro-Am. They made a complete Tracker knock-off. Then I was riding for Powerflex when Lance Smith asked me to ride for Tracker. The ironic thing is Duane Peters asked me to ride for Indy at the same time, because we both rode Big O skatepark. I didn't give a shit about image or whatever anyone was saying, so I said, "Give me a set and I'll try them." I tried both trucks, and Trackers just worked better for me. My decision to ride for Tracker was based purely on riding them and liking them better than Indys, which were too squirrely for me. I didn't own a set of Trackers before I got sponsored by Tracker.

What's a Jim Jam? How and when did you invent it?
Some people call it a backslide sweeper, but I did the Jim Jam before the sweeper was even invented. So, a frontside sweeper is really a frontside Jim Jam. Duane Peters and I could argue about that one forever. During a sweeper, you set your tail down, but I never set my tail down in the Jim Jam, which is a continuously moving trick. You basically roll your wheels on the deck, pull on your nose and jump back on your board as you go in. Don't touch your tail on the deck or coping. That's the technical difference between a Jim Jam and a sweeper. I did it on accident

in the Big O clover bowl when I was probably 14, which was in 1977. I'd do tail taps and sometimes my back foot would slip off. I didn't want to jump off of my skateboard, so I tried to put my foot back on. But, it's easier to put your foot back on when you're going in than when it's on the coping. So, I'd stand there holding my board, then pivot and jump back on it. Somehow, after doing that a bunch of times, I got the confidence to just fling myself back on it. There are only a couple of young kids—Grayson Fletcher and Robby Ruso—who do it now. But, I'm stoked it's staying alive.

What's a Gray slide? How and when did you invent it?
Before the Gray slide, laybacks were done on the vertical wall, but I'd grab my nose as I grinded, put my back hand down, snap onto my tail and spread out like a layback on the coping—all continuously moving—then drop back in. So, it's really a high speed grind to layback on the coping. If you do it properly, your tail will slide for a block or two across the coping. You come in half sideways and straighten out on the way down the wall. I don't know when I invented it, maybe 1978-'79 at the Big O while I goofed off in the little bowls. It probably happened on accident—I have no idea how.

Any closing thoughts on Tracker?
My roots on Tracker were honorable. I tried Trackers and Indys and decided I liked Trackers better. I'm not one who caves in to peer pressure. Later, I started my own skateboard company and went completely against the grain, because I believed in something different. Some of our philosophies are the same. I'm not going to cower to friggin' piss ants who try to talk shit. To this day, I'll post a picture and some Indy guy will talk some shit. Dude, I will out fucking grind you and I will drill you into the hole if you fucking talk shit. If you can't ride your trucks better than me, then don't fucking talk about your trucks. I don't' care if you have an Indy tattoo on your balls. That doesn't make you cool. I know more kooks with Indy tattoos than I do with Tracker tattoos, so who's a bigger kook? The bottom line is they're just skateboard trucks. You make a choice. I think Trackers are well-built, and I don't like the way Indys turn. But, on the same point, Trackers turn differently. I know that, but they turn better for me. Trackers have a more proper steering, but they're slower. Indy's flop quicker, but flop constantly. When I made my Standard Trucks later in the '90s, they were kind of somewhere in between.

I remember Buddy Carr gave me a set of Tracker Darts after I had been riding Standard Trucks for years. The Darts were just sitting there in a box, and I needed to put together a new board, but I was hesitant, because I thought they were going to turn slow. I wasn't really aware of the changes that had been made to them. I remember putting them together, going out in the parking lot, and thinking, "Oh, fuck! These things fucking turn completely, with a quicker response than they had." So, I've been riding Trackers again. I was impressed the Track-

er Dart actually changed the game for me again. I don't know if I could ride the same original Sixtracks today for the way I skate now, because I do like my trucks looser. But, I like stability, I don't like squirrely. The Dart is stable.

The difference is the roll center, the Dart turns more, but the Indy flops.
The Indy flops, it always has. You can see the way the Indy pivot cushions wear side to side, because they drop left and drop right really quickly. But, I never liked the way they squirreled. I never had a squirrely feeling with Trackers. I know people buy Indys because lots of cool people ride them. Well, lots of cool people ride whatever other cool people get for free. Ride what fucking works, not what people get for free. Ride what someone would buy. What would you buy if you had to pay for it? That's probably the truest thing you could find out about a product: what would pro athletes buy if they had to put their own money on the table for it?

Everyone knows if you ride Indy, Thunder or Venture, you're going to get coverage in *Thrasher*. It was in some ways painful to know you weren't going to get coverage in *Thrasher* if you rode Tracker, and you probably weren't going to get coverage in *Trans World* either, because they so desperately didn't want to be like *Thrasher*. It was kind of a double-whammy. It was like, you get hit from Nor Cal and you get hit from So Cal. What the fuck? I would rather be part of something honorable than the fucking cow-

ards who did everything by shit talking and back stabbing people. I have honor, but I'm not as cool, so call me an honorable uncool guy, rather then a super cool shit talking back stabber.

Read the full-length interview at trackertrucks.com

Above: **"I'll huff and I'll puff and I'll blow your coping apart!" Jim Gray puts a pair of magnesium Tracker Sixtracks through the paces, circa 1988.** Photo: Grant Brittain

TRACKER
COPER
Coping With the Coping (1978)

In 1977, Tracker co-founders Dave Dominy and Gary Dodds developed the Tracker Coper. They did R&D using lengths of PVC plastic pipe machined to fit over the axle hanger and held on with stainless steel hose clamps. After extensive testing with team manager Lance Smith and the Tracker vert riders, Dave found that the only professional and cost-effective way to keep the pipe connected snugly to the hanger was to use stainless steel cupped washers at each end of the hanger. Gary designed the finished version of the Coper, which was initially made out of nylon 6, and the cupped washers that held the Coper securely as you tightened your axle nuts. In 1978, Tracker was the first company to bring Copers to the market. Designed to protect axle hangers from the heavy abuse of grinds on rough pool coping, the device also made longer 50-50 grinds possible while eliminating hang-ups and kingpin nut scraping. The Tracker Coper was molded in widths that fit

Steve Caballero flicks an Ollie out of the steep Kona bowl at Del Mar Skate Ranch in Del Mar, California, circa 1980. If you look closely, you'll notice the prototype Tracker Sixtrack Coper rings made out of PVC pipe. Apparently, the real plastic Coper rings hadn't made it into production yet. Photo: Grant Brittain
Right: **Allen Losi glides his Coper across a length of metal pipe, circa 1985. The proliferation of smooth metal and PVC coping in the mid to late '80s is one of the factors that made the Coper redundant and led to its demise.** Photo: Larry Balma

139

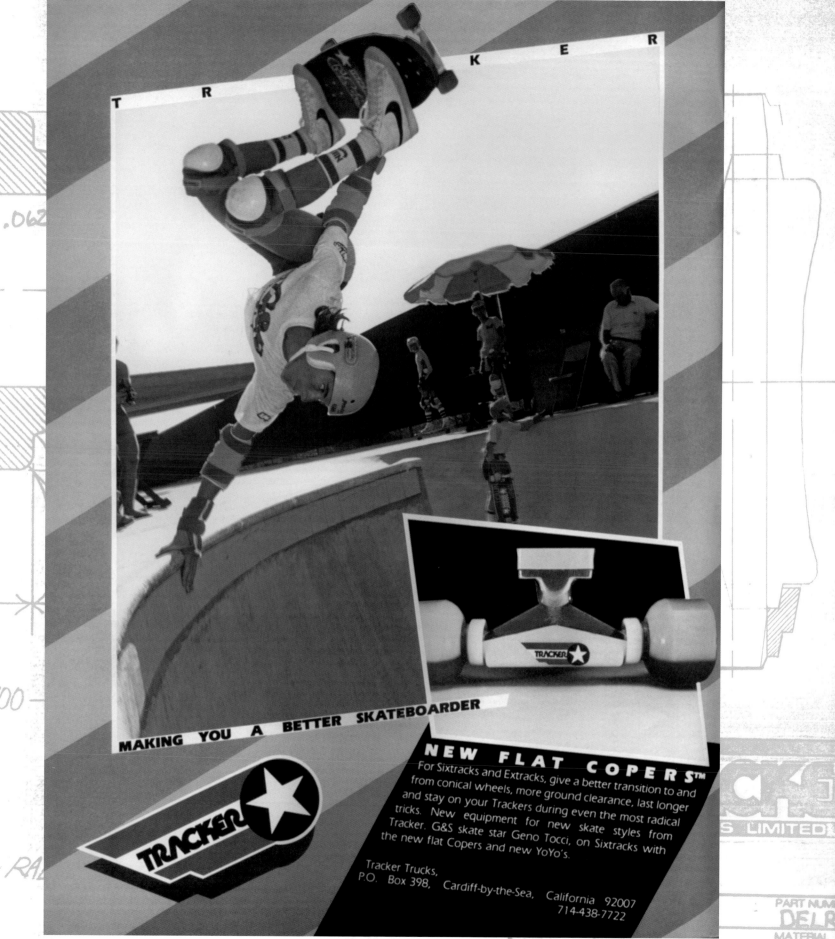

TRACKER

MAKING YOU A BETTER SKATEBOARDER

NEW FLAT COPERS™
For Sixtracks and Extracks, give a better transition to and from conical wheels, more ground clearance, last longer and stay on your Trackers during even the most radical tricks. New equipment for new skate styles from Tracker. G&S skate star Geno Tocci, on Sixtracks with the new flat Copers and new YoYo's.

Tracker Trucks,
P.O. Box 398, Cardiff-by-the-Sea, California 92007
714-438-7722

Geno Tocci, November 1980.

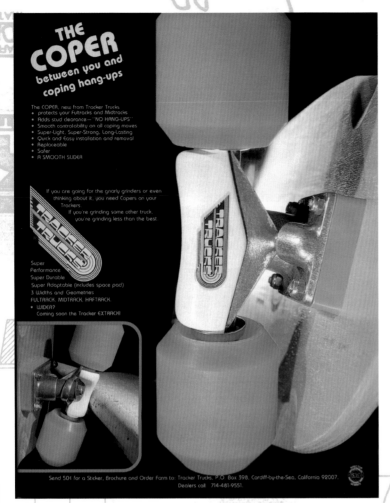

The COPER
between you and
coping hang-ups

The COPER, new from Tracker Trucks
• protects your Fultracks and Midtracks
• Adds stud clearance—"NO HANG-UPS"
• Smooth controllability on all coping moves
• Super-Light, Super-Strong, Long-Lasting
• Quick and Easy installation and removal
• Replaceable
• Safer
• A SMOOTH SLIDER

If you are going for the gnarly grinders or even
thinking about it, you need Copers on your
Trackers
   If you're grinding some other truck,
   you're grinding less than the best.

Super
Performance
Super Durable
Super Adaptable (includes space pad)
3 Widths and Geometries
FULTRACK, MIDTRACK, HAFTRACK.
• WIDER?
   Coming soon the Tracker EXTRACK!

Send 50¢ for a Sticker, Brochure and Order Form to: Tracker Trucks, P.O. Box 398, Cardiff-by-the-Sea, California 92007.
Dealers call 714-481-9551.

The Coper, January 1979.

Trucks you can Trust

Kyle Jensen, circa 1979.

the Midtrack, Fultrack and Extrack trucks. The following year, Gary designed a plastic ring that allowed the Extrack Coper to fit on the Sixtrack hanger—even when using wide, centered bearing wheels.

The first Tracker Coper to hit the market had a concave grinding surface that would tend to center the truck on the coping during a 50-50 grind. The Coper was also rounded from front to rear, and the underside was hollowed out for ease of molding and lighter weight. Some of these Copers shattered under heavy impact with curbs or pool coping because of the thin wall construction and brittle type of nylon we used. The second generation Tracker Coper Gary designed did away with the concave surface between the wheels and flattened the Coper front to rear, which added more grinding surface to allow skaters to grind anywhere between the wheels that suited their riding style. Gary also nixed the two hollow sections of the Coper on the back of the hanger to make the device fit more snugly. In addition, he found a new super lightweight Space Age nylon polymer with increased strength that also had excellent lubricating qualities and durability. Boasting so many design improvements, the "New Flat Copers," as they were marketed, were definitely new and improved.

Other truck companies produced cheap PVC water pipe-style Coper copies, but they would pop off while grinding, and the PVC was not as strong or as slick as our Space Age nylon. Tracker Copers were favored by vert skateboarders for the next decade. By 1988,

pros riding other brands of trucks that were not able to use Copers decided that Tracker pros using Copers were cheating! The long grinds that the Tracker Copers enabled were not as difficult as grinding the aluminum axle hangers on curbs and pool coping. Brandishing aluminum trucks worn down from countless grinds proved that you were a hardcore skater. At this time, halfpipe ramps, which were the dominant form of vert skating, were built using 2 1/2" diameter water pipe made of either steel or PVC plastic. Copers were simply too slick to grind on this already slippery coping. As the magazines and videos of the day portrayed the elite skaters riding without Copers, the use of them became uncool and, to some extent, unnecessary.

At that time, we were shipping 35,000 Copers per month. Manufacturing was booked three months out and we stocked four weeks inventory, as well. When Coper sales suddenly shut off like a light switch, we were stuck with 100,000 of them, many already packaged with the stainless steel cupped washers. Although we were able to recycle the unpackaged Copers, unfortunately, the washers and plastic bags had to be separated from the packaged ones before they could be sent to the recycler. We figured out that it was not worth the cost of labor to unpackage them all, so we ended up with a 20 foot long dumpster full of Copers that went to the landfill. It's too bad we didn't think to save a few thousand for collectors. The happy ending to the loss of Coper sales was that truck sales increased!—**LMB + GSD**

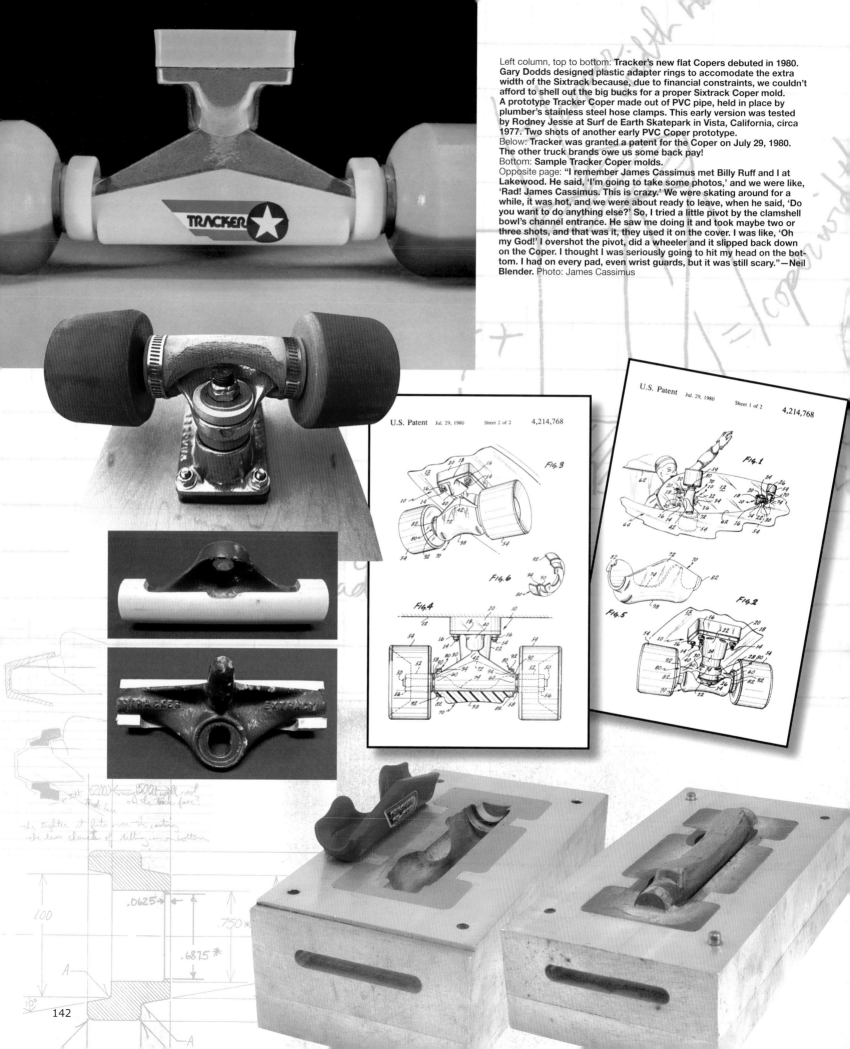

Left column, top to bottom: **Tracker's new flat Copers debuted in 1980.** Gary Dodds designed plastic adapter rings to accomodate the extra width of the Sixtrack because, due to financial constraints, we couldn't afford to shell out the big bucks for a proper Sixtrack Coper mold. A prototype Tracker Coper made out of PVC pipe, held in place by plumber's stainless steel hose clamps. This early version was tested by Rodney Jesse at Surf de Earth Skatepark in Vista, California, circa 1977. Two shots of another early PVC Coper prototype.
Below: **Tracker was granted a patent for the Coper on July 29, 1980.** The other truck brands owe us some back pay!
Bottom: **Sample Tracker Coper molds.**
Opposite page: **"I remember James Cassimus met Billy Ruff and I at Lakewood. He said, 'I'm going to take some photos,' and we were like, 'Rad! James Cassimus. This is crazy.' We were skating around for a while, it was hot, and we were about ready to leave, when he said, 'Do you want to do anything else?' So, I tried a little pivot by the clamshell bowl's channel entrance. He saw me doing it and took maybe two or three shots, and that was it, they used it on the cover. I was like, 'Oh my God!' I overshot the pivot, did a wheeler and it slipped back down on the Coper. I thought I was seriously going to hit my head on the bottom. I had on every pad, even wrist guards, but it was still scary."**—Neil **Blender.** Photo: James Cassimus

142

Progressive sports, people, music and way more!

ACTION NOW

$2.00

FEBRUARY 1982
VOL. 8, NO. 7

MODEL
NEL BLENDER

Poison or Antidote?
(Interview Inside)

The Great Ramp Hunt

Snowboarding: Have You Tried It Yet?

Lakewood's Last Stand

SnowWear For Winter

0 76956 14112   02

TRACKER RAMP
First Portable Halfpipe (1978)

In the mid 1970s, drainage ditches, irrigation reservoirs and full pipes were the main inspiration for the first generation of concrete skateparks that started opening across the United States. In 1977, inspired by the parks, Tom Stewart and Jon Landry built a couple of huge plywood quarterpipe ramps on each side of the street in front of his house in Encinitas, California. Then Tom got the bright idea to put them together and make a huge wooden U in his front yard. The result was the world's first halfpipe. Tom marketed a set of blueprints for his halfpipe under the name Rampage Ramps. As a result, backyard halfpipes caught on like wildfire, and started popping up from coast to coast.

Doug Firestone, of the Firestone Tire family, who owned a welding shop equipped with a steel bender, built some really cool quarterpipes for skateboarding consisting of a metal frame covered with a new Space Age clear plastic surface called Lexan polycarbonate. Always appreciating technological advancements, Tracker talked Doug into building the first portable halfpipe, the Tracker Ramp. Mounted on a trailer, it was affectionately called the Tracker Flytrap, because it folded up just like a Venus flytrap plant that captured its prey. The Tracker ramp measured 16 feet wide with no flat bottom. When it was folded up, it became a legal eight-foot wide trailer, which could be towed to a demo location and opened up, ready to skate in only five minutes.

After building the Tracker Ramp, Doug Firestone struck a deal with Pepsi to build huge halfpipes for their demo tours, as well as trailers to carry them on that were only eight feet wide. The slick surface, narrow eight-foot width and massive height of each Pepsi ramp was scary for the riders, but quite a spectacular sight for the crowd. Because ramp building was in its infancy, there was no flat bottom or rollout decks on the Tracker or Pepsi ramps yet. Despite that, we used the Tracker Ramp for a full two years to do demos, and even drove it down the Coast Highway in Encinitas in a parade while skaters shredded away. We ultimately sold the Tracker Ramp to the Vans skateboard team in the early '80s, who added folding rollout decks. Everett Rosecrans towed it on demo tours to Vans stores all over the country. To recap, 1978 was an unbelievably productive year for Tracker, as we brought to market the Gnarly Trackers, Magnesium Trackers, Extrack, Copers and the Tracker Ramp—an explosion of of innovation unrivaled in the history of skateboarding.—**LMB**

Left: **Back in the days before halfpipe ramps had flat bottom or rollout decks, Chris Strople precariously dangles a rock 'n' roll over the edge of the Tracker ramp at the glider port in La Jolla, California, circa 1979.** Photo: Lance Smith

Tony Alva taps heat on the Tracker ramp in Sorrento Valley, San Diego, California, circa 1977.
Opposite page, top to bottom: Russ Gosnell flies across the Tracker ramp, circa 1977. Backyard halfpipes like the Rampage "were death traps. They were only eight feet wide with rough transitions, too much vertical, and usually made out of old, splintery plywood. But, that's all we had until things like the Tracker ramp came along. It was cool. It was 16 feet wide, eight feet high, and the wheels gripped really good on the Lexan surface. We made the coping out of an oak banister. Stacy Peralta and I used to travel for a bank doing promotions and skateboard exhibitions on it. It was mounted on a trailer, and the two sides folded up and together. It looked like some sort of airplane wing. As we drove down the road, people had no idea what it was. That was the funnest ramp I ever rode. It was probably one of the first ramps to be user-friendly. It really worked. There were a lot of terrible ones out there for years. I rode some of the Pepsi ramps, but at eight feet wide and 20 feet tall, they were death traps, too."—Russ Gosnell
Stacy Peralta lays back on the Tracker ramp at the glider port in La Jolla, California, circa 1979. All photos this spread: Lance Smith

147

TRACKER HAFPIPE

This was prepared so that you will better understand what it means when Dave Dominy says you can borrow the Tracker Hafpipe.

Tracker will deliver and return the trailer. All costs will be billed to you. This will include a driver and helper at $50.00 per day. This will include a driver and helper at $25.00 per day and $.20 per mile. You will also be responsible for overnight expenses in case of wind or unforeseeable circumstances that hold up the driver.

We will set the trailer up where you wish, if it is possible. A large flat area is necessary. When the Hafpipe is folded out, it is 16' X 16'. We suggest you keep your audience well away, at least 10' to 30', to avoid flying skateboards. Even the best riders contribute to the problem. An area of 50' X 50' or a circle of 60' in diameter will be necessary.

DON'T LET YOUR SPECTATORS GET HIT!!!!

We must have a signed release of liability form in our file because once the ramp is open, it is to be your responsibility—according to our appropriately worded form. Have your attorney look at it if necessary. When the Hafpipe trailer is shut, it is our responsibility. When it is open, it is your responsibility.

We have professional riders available who are familiar with the Hafpipe and capable of putting on a good show. We will only recommend talented skaters with a mature attitude. If you should wish a recommendation from us, you should allow for this in your budget.

Thank you for your cooperation.

Dave Dominy

TRACKER DESIGNS LIMITED P.O. Box 217 Cardiff-By-The-Sea, California 92007 (714) 453-1834

Dave Dominy shreds the Tracker Ramp at the glider port in La Jolla, California, circa 1979. Photo: James Cassimus
Below: **Two views of the Tracker ramp, folded up for travel and open for skating, circa 1977.** Photos: Unknown
Opposite page, top row: **A concept drawing for a Tracker ramp brochure, which was realized with this photo of Bob Skoldberg, circa 1977.** Photo: Warren Bolster
A letter from Dave Dominy explaining how to use the Tracker ramp, along with a list of rules, circa 1977.
Opposite page, bottom: **Russ Gosnell gets stylish on a frontside off the lip on the Tracker ramp, circa 1976. Nice Jefferson Starship t-shirt.** Photo: Lance Smith

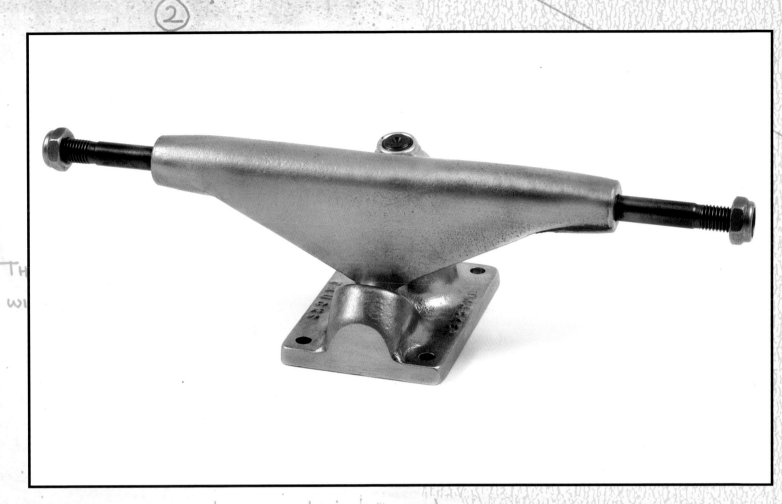

TRACKER
SIXTRACK
The Ultimate Tracker (1979)

Just like all previous Tracker models, the Sixtrack went through an extensive testing period before we put it into production. In fact, every Tracker product goes through a one to two-year prototype program in which many team riders give their feedback on all aspects of performance, feel and reliability before we begin production. For example, you can see photos in skateboarding magazines of the late 1970s of Tracker team pros riding Haftrack, Midtrack, Fultrack and Extrack axle hangers with different width extenders. Up until the Sixtrack, each new Tracker truck was about 3/4" wider than its predecessor. By 1979, based on ever-widening board and wheel widths, we added one full inch of width to the Extrack, the result being a new truck called the Sxtrack. Pronounced Sixtrack, we ultimately changed it to the correct spelling.

Debuting in 1979 with a 6" (152 mm) hanger width, the Sixtrack became the number one choice of pro vert skateboarders worldwide. With aerial maneuvers being blasted ever higher, the extra width of the Sixtrack combined with 10"-plus wide decks added landing stability. The Sixtrack employed the geometry and higher roll center of the Haftrack to keep the kingpin even further away from the coping. The Sixtrack became Track-er's all-time best selling truck model. By the late '80s we were shipping a staggering 50,000 Sixtracks each month—10,000 more than all of our other truck models combined. It was so popular, we even began offering up special colorways like Reggae, Tile Blue and Asphalt Black.

One time, Tracker's bank, which was located in Escondido, California, about 20 miles East of our factory in Oceanside, asked us to put some skateboards in a display window near their front door. We filled the window with an array of colorful skateboard decks, trucks, wheels and clothing; prominent in the display were our brand-new turquoise Sixtracks. The first night the display was up, someone smashed the window and stole all of our Tracker gear. The fact that someone was brazen enough to steal Trackers from a bank really spoke volumes about the high demand for our trucks! Well, breaking into a bank, even though it was only a display window, was a federal offense, which prompted the FBI to interview us. I told them that we had not yet shipped out any of the turquoise Sixtracks. So, the FBI cruised over to Escondido High School and busted the three guys who were riding on turquoise Sixtracks! I don't know what ever happened with those kids or our stuff, but I bet they learned a good lesson.

Jerry Valdez hangs a frontside air out of the keyhole at Marina Skatepark in Marina del Rey, California, circa 1979. Note the lack of plastic accessories on Jerry's skateboard (except for the Nose Bone), which was unusual for 1979. Photo: William Sharp
Opposite page, top: **A Tracker Sixtrack production truck, which weighs 400 grams.**
Opposite page, bottom photo, clockwise from top left: **A Tracker Fultrack extended into a Sixtrack prototype, circa 1976. A Tracker Haftrack extended into a Sixtrack prototype with a floating axle, circa 1978. A Tracker Sixtrack with axle extenders, circa 1985. A Tracker Sixtrack magnesium with a carbon graphite baseplate, which weighs only 290 grams, went into production in 1988.**

Ray "Bones" Rodriguez frontside grinds the clover bowl at Skate City in Whittier, California, early 1980. Photo: Unknown
Top: Tom Groholski and Dan Wilkes hoist twin eggplants in Vista, California, circa 1987. Photo: Chip Morton

BASE

STU

PIV

TRACKER DESIGNS LTD.

T-002 BASE HANGER

John "Tex" Gibson enters the descent stage of a classic invert at Oasis in San Diego, California, circa 1980.
Photo: Craig Fineman

Like all of the other Tracker hangers, the Sixtrack has evolved over the years. Since the axle was made a little bit longer to make mounting Copers easier, some of our team riders used extra washers to widen their Sixtracks. In response, we even offered cone-shaped aluminum axle extenders in 1989 that brought the truck's width out to 6 3/8" or 162 mm. That is just a millimeter wider than an Independent 169, whose numbers never do relate to actual millimeter measurements. Other minor refinements and functional improvements have been made to the Sixtrack over the years, but the original geometry has remained. You can still order the classic Sixtrack trucks from Tracker today.

Trackers in the Smithsonian

In 1987, Tracker Sixtracks were the first and only skateboard trucks to be put on display in the Smithsonian Institution. For 25 years, they've been featured in the History of American Sports Collection's "Material World" Exhibition in the National Museum of American History, Science, Technology and Culture. Two Powell-Peralta decks, each with Tracker Sixtracks, were donated by George Powell and I. Now, 25 years later, the Smithsonian has added an actual skateboard exhibit.—**LMB**

153

WALL

GRIGLEY

WIRES

ROOF

TRACKER
TRUCKS
™

SEND BUCK
TRACKER
BOX 398
CARDIFF, CA.
92007

John Grigley, October 1987.
154

Ray Underhill (RIP) smacks a knee-on high above the Vista ramp in Vista, California, circa 1988. Photo: Grant Brittain

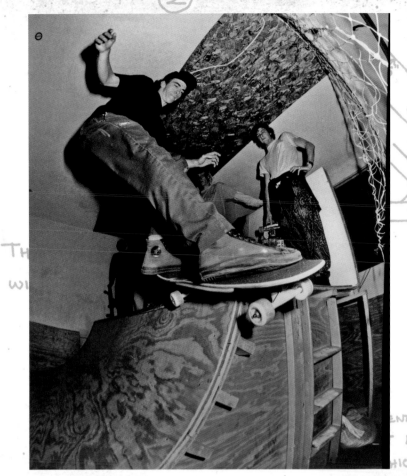

Steve Saiz tackles a fire hydrant, October 1989.
Photo: Steve Sherman
Opposite page, clockwise from top left: **Sam Cunning-ham hangs one over on a mini-ramp at Surf Ohio in Dayton, Ohio, circa 1988.** Photo: O
Rudy Johnson at play on a natural flat bar at School W in San Diego, California, circa early 1990s.
Photo: Steve Sherman
Mike Vallely goes to work on a streetstyle contest course, circa 1988. Photo: O
Guy Mariano enjoys visiting hours (front truck grind) at School W, circa early 1990s. Photo: Steve Sherman

ALAN GELFAND

POWELL/PERALTA Winner of SkateBoarder Magazine's "Most Spectacular New Maneuver" of 1978 for his "No Hands Ollie Aerial" Tracker congratulates Alan for his award and his choice of trucks.

TRACKER TRUCKS

For brochure, order form and a sticker, send 50¢ to: Tracker Trucks, P.O. Box 398, Cardiff-by-the-Sea, California 92007   Dealers call (714) 481-9551

PHOTO CASSIMUS

Haftracks (2⅝"), Gnarly Midtracks (3⅜"), Gnarly Fultracks (4¼"), Gnarly Extracks (5"), and Copers   Gnarly Magnesium Trackers, too

Alan Gelfand, June 1979.
158

Born in New York in 1963, Alan Gelfand is best known as the inventor of the most important trick in skateboard history, the Ollie. After moving to Hollywood, Florida in 1972, Alan debuted his innovative no-hands aerial a half decade later, just three years after he started skateboarding in 1974. Although it was conceived on vertical, the Ollie would go on to become the default launch pad most modern day street skating tricks blast off from. A card-carrying member of the original Bones Brigade, Alan's pro skateboarding career came to an untimely end in 1981 due to knee injuries. At that point, Alan transformed himself into a champion go-cart and racecar driver throughout the 1980s and '90s. After opening his Olliewood ramp in 2002, he's been enjoying time back on the shred stick. Read on for the full scoop.—GSD

Alan Gelfand
INTERVIEW

JG: When and how did you get your first set of Trackers?
Probably around 1976-'77. When Stacy Peralta came to Florida in 1977, I had already been skating on Trackers.

JG: How did you get on the Tracker team?
Stacy hooked me up; he had the connections for everything. I don't change much. I pretty much do the same thing all the time. Up until 2000, I didn't carve. I never carved in my life, because my trucks were so tight. I had an almost solid bushing on the bottom and a very small bushing on top, so I didn't turn. I always slid my front truck. It's kind of weird to see it in videos, but now they're so loose, it's ridiculous.

JG: Which Tracker ads were your faves?
The Ollie got voted Best Trick in *Skateboarder*, and I got a congratulations ad for that.

GSD: Do you remember which year?
A long time ago. Mike McGill has a memory for everything on Earth, but I have no memory. I've never done drugs in my life, but I have no recollection of anything I've ever done. I'd imagine that was in 1979.

JG: You and Mike McGill really caught everyone's attention sometime in 1978. Before that, we couldn't get *Skateboarder* to pay any attention to Florida.
That's because Stacy flew me out to California.

JG: Yeah, once you made it out to California, everyone paid attention to you. How did you invent the Ollie?
There was a skatepark in Hollywood, Florida called Skateboard USA with a snake run that was kinky and over vertical. I would do this trick called an Ollie pop where I'd pop off the over vert and land on top of the lip. Than I started doing Ollie airs. Also, I'd jump from the big bowl over this wall into the under bowl. It wasn't really an Ollie, but I could jump and the board would come up with my legs. A real Ollie is when you bring your knees up to your face. You've got to compress and the board has to come up to you.

JG: Well, that was your style. That's how you made it your own, and no one else could do it like you did.
For a while. Someplace in the world, some-one else probably did a no-handed aerial, but no one on Earth ever saw them do it. In the old days, if a new trick happened, we didn't see it on the East Coast until months later.

JG: Yeah, there was at least a three-month gap between the time I'd shoot a photo and when it would show up in the magazine. That kinked over-vert wall you were talking about, no one believed anyone could do much of anything you actually did on it.
That park was really big and rad for the day, but it was really over-vert and kinky. It reminds me of some of the crazy stuff they build nowadays.

GSD: Did Stacy tell you to learn the Ollie everywhere?
Stacy said, "When you learn how to do that trick all the time, give me a call. I'll fly you to California." At the end of the week, I called him and said, "I can do it every time." McGill and I went out there a few times and stayed at Stacy's house. He would drop us off at Marina in the morning and pick us up late at night.

GSD: When did you first do an Ollie on a vert ramp or pool with coping?
I don't know. I'm not sure which year we first built the Hollywood ramp. The Ollie took off there, for sure. Glen Friedman took a lot of photos there. But, that ramp was barely vert. It's harder to do an Ollie on a wall that's not true vertical than it is when it's vert. What's weird about when I did the Ollie back then was that my trucks were drilled far back, so I didn't have a long kicktail. My tail never hit. If it did, my board would have stuck straight out from the wall, because my tail was only three inches long. Some people think, "Oh, you hit the tail." No, it was just the weird way I launched. Look at the photos.

JG: That's what tripped out most people with your Ollies—they couldn't quite figure out what you were doing with your board. What stood out about Tracker Trucks' performance?
They didn't break. We had concrete parks that were tough on any equipment, and we skated so much for so long. Trackers were strong and light. I can't account for how much Trackers turned, because mine were so tight. Trackers just worked right. When the magnesiums came along, forget about it. One of the coolest days of my life when I was a little kid was when I went home from school and got this box from UPS with a case of magnesium Tracker Trucks. It must have been more than four sets.

JG: Which skateboarders inspired you the most?
The no-brainer was Stacy Peralta definitely inspired me back in the day and got us to be where we were—at an ability level and professional level. Mike McGill is also at the top of the list. We would push each other so much. McGill and I pretty much thrived off of each other. There were so many people who no one had ever heard of, too, like Jeff Deur and Kevin Peterson. This guy Jeff Deur was probably the best skateboarder who ever was, but no one ever saw him skate. He was doing five to six foot high backside airs when other people were doing one foot high airs. Steve Anderson was the funniest guy ever, and he was a great skater.

JG: Ed Wamble, George McLellen.
Yeah, all of those guys. I hate to mention one name, because there are so many others who were great. Steve Fisher was great.

GSD: Do you own a vert ramp?
In 2002, I built a ramp that was six inches higher than the Hollywood ramp. It was 10 feet tall with six inches of vert. Then a year later, it turned into a bowl that was 75 feet long and 45 feet wide. It's awesome. We over-built it, just like everything I've ever done. The thing has never had a kink or a loose screw to this day. Everybody says it's perfect. The Team Pain guys, who were friends of my wife, Sharon, built it on the side. One of the guys from Team Pain called it Olliewood, and we had a fake Olliewood logo like Hollywood. I relinquished care of that bowl two years ago, so now it's just private.

JG: What are you up to today?
After I got out of skateboarding in the early '80s, I got into go-cart racing, and I won the Grand National Championships in 1987. I also got into autocross car racing and endurance racing. I raced 12-hour and 24-hour races all the way up until 2002. When I got third place on the podium at Daytona, I quit.

JG: What made you quit? Did you just get burned out?
No, I met my wife and I wanted to grow up a little bit instead of just cruising. I made it to a place where I never thought I'd be able to get to: driving a Porsche at Daytona. I thought it was time to go on to the next step. All of my life, I've always strived and been obsessed. I thought, "After winning four 12-hour races and four 24-hour races in one lifetime, what else can I do?"

GSD: Where do you work today?
I have a shop called German Car Depot, where I've been selling and servicing Volkswagen and Audi cars for 25 years now.

GSD: What do you enjoy doing besides skateboarding?
Working. And when I'm not working, I like to work.

JG: You also have to support Sharon and the lifestyle she's accustomed to.
And a bunch of dogs, too, and their fancy lifestyle. I'm blessed to be able to look back at what I've done and the people who've helped me all along the way.

JG: Closing comments?
I never knew how much an 80-pound kid from Hollywood, Florida would affect so many people in a positive way. It's off the charts. I'm the world's most famous skateboarder who no one knows. That is the truth. Every single day of my life, I'm reminded of that when people say, "You're the guy who invented the Ollie?" On my ridiculous little web site called olliearmy.com, which is nothing but a one-page thing, 20 people per day sign up. They enter their name, address, phone number and say, "Please visit me," or whatever. In public, I try to shy away from stuff.

JG: Well, when you were inducted into the Skateboarding Hall of Fame in 2013, we had to drag you out from underneath the table to accept your award.
It was pretty funny. We were outside the hall, ready to go in, and I was thinking, "I don't want to be here around all of these people." So, I went off to the corner, and who did I see sitting next to me on the bench? Rodney Mullen (laughs). I wasn't trying to avoid the event. I appreciate it and I think it's really cool. I just don't like attention.

Read the full-length interview at trackertrucks.com

By Larry Balma + GSD

the mags came out right after. You can see photos of me on them in the brown bowls.

LMB: We made Extrack mags before Six-track mags, but it was close in that time.
Okay, it may have been the Extrack. I was too busy blasting airs to know which track it was. When I first went to Marina, I was riding Gullwing trucks with the two different axles on each side. Shogo Kubo was riding Gullwing Super Wides, so I got those after I had the Fultracks. I started riding wider decks, so I got those wide Gullwings. Then I saw Jay Adams with Trackers, so the Gullwings were gone. Gullwings couldn't turn. The only reason why I rode them was because Shogo did. It happened that fast. Within a few months from 1977 to '78, I switched from the Tracker Fultrack to Gullwings back to Trackers. That was pretty much it right then. I was a full-blown am all the way until I entered the pro ranks riding my Sims prototype model.

GSD: Favorite Tracker ads?
During that little period after I rode for Powell-Peralta then Dogtown, I rode the Tracker 777 board. I told Stacy I wanted to turn pro, but he said, "You can't turn pro for a couple of years." I replied, "A couple of years? No, I'm ready to take on those pros now." He said, "No, you're not ready." Then Dogtown asked me to ride for them. I was like, "If you give me a pro model, it's a done deal." My dad drew up my graphic, which we still have, then Dogtown went out of business. That's when I came to Tracker and said, "Let me ride that 777 for you guys." Then Tom Sims approached me, which was an amazing moment, because all of these stylish skaters like Brad Bowman and Doug de Montmorency rode for Sims. I was like, "If there's anybody I'd turn pro for, it's Tom." I went down to Santa Barbara and had a great meeting with him. Then he called me later and said, "I licensed Sims to Brad Dorfman." I was like, "Man, things are just not working out." It took a good year-and-a-half before I met with Brad in 1982, which is when he showed me the rising sun board and I was like, "Sweet!"

LMB: It became one of the largest selling skateboard decks in that era, too.
There have been some serious roller coaster rides in the industry. We went from seeing big time prize money to no prize money to $200 bucks for first place and we were skating our hearts out. We didn't care. We paid our way to get there and all the way home, and we were like, "Woo! That was the most amazing day in the world!" Who knew? We knew. Before that, the skateparks were closing down, but that just made skateboarding that much cooler. Skateboarding is aggressive; it's not your typical pansy sport in which you have to obey the rules. Our only rule was to break the rules. So, we went into the backyards to skate pools and build halfpipes. That's what really motivated us to keep going.

GSD: When you were riding Trackers, what stood out about the actual performance of the trucks?
I was blasting airs and jumping over huge channels and stuff like that, so I needed stability. I remember Pat Ngoho coming to the skatepark with a pair of Indys. He was like, "Dude, these trucks turn great." I got on them and couldn't even balance on those things, because they turned too quickly. They were super wide. I think they were 169s. I was like, "No, these Trackers are solid. They don't squirrel." Being 12-13 years old, I

Christian Hosoi INTERVIEW

Christian Hosoi floats a picture perfect Ollie out of Del Mar's keyhole in Del Mar, California, circa 1982. Photo: Grant Brittain

Who wore spandex, lace lingerie and danced on the coping? Not you. Who invented the body jar, Christ air and rocket air? Not you. Who started the weird-shaped board trend of the late '80s with the hammerhead? Not you. Who launched mega-high airs two decades before the Mega Ramp? Not you. Who is widely acknowledged as one of the greatest and most stylish skateboarders of all time? Christian Hosoi, that's who. So, sit back, relax and enjoy the nice, long chat we had with this man of many words about his colorful life and times.—GSD

LMB: When and where were you born?
I was born in Los Angeles, California on October 5, 1967.

LMB: When did you start skateboarding?
By the time I was six, we started building little quarter pipes in our backyards. We were trying to emulate what we saw in *Skateboarder* and *Skateboard World* magazines. When I was eight, I went to Skateboard World skatepark in Torrance for the first time. Marina del Rey opened in 1978. I went there two weeks before it opened and saw Tony Alva, Jay Adams and Billy Yeron just shredding the Dog Bowl. I snuck in there and I was

in heaven. It was euphoria for a little kid to sit there and watch the guys he saw in the magazines just recently live and in person. As a little kid, it was intimidating going into a major skatepark and trying to mesh in with the pros. It wasn't like I was a pansy, I was just intimidated because there was so much ripping going on. I'd watch the pros skate the Dog Bowl, and see local kids get localized. The pros would come in and say, "Get out of here. Beat it!" I was like, "Dang, this is insane. They're getting kicked out of the bowl. I'm not going over there. I can't even hit the coping in the deep end." So, I felt it out, saw the rust bowls and started skating them every day. I didn't even skate vert for the first few months. Then my dad talked to Dennis Ogden, the owner of Marina del Rey, and became the manager. That's when the floodgates of progression started for me. Marina became my backyard, but I could still only skate the little bowls. Then Jay Adams took me under his wing and put me on Z-Flex. Soon after that, Stacy Peralta asked me to ride for Powell-Peralta. By then, I was a little 12-year-old kid with long hair, who everybody thought was a girl, riding vert.

LMB: So, you started with the Tracker Fultrack trucks?
I think I had Sixtracks on the Z deck and then

needed the stability to pump and to get my strength going, because I was a small kid. I wasn't some big, tall guy full of muscles. For me to blast an air back then, it was all about finesse, timing and rhythm. Trackers turned smooth. I continued to ride them for a while, even when my friends were like, "These Indys are great for carve grinding." I'd respond, "Well, these Trackers are great for blasting big airs." I had to go with what I knew at that time. I skated for Tracker until 1982. Getting off of the team was tough, because it was prestigious and there was a loyalty involved.

It was an honor to ride for Tracker. It's funny how Tracker and Indy ran the industry. It was Indy = *Thrasher*, Tracker = *TransWorld*. Tracker was a natural progression for where I was at in my lifestyle then, and who I was hanging out with. At the time, there was this Nor Cal vs. So Cal rivalry going on. But, inside I knew that I was part of something special, and I was proud to be in Tracker ads. As the skateparks closed down, skateboarding crashed and transitioned into a new place, this dirty backyard culture. That's when I ended up meeting Fausto Vitello, Eric Swenson, Mofo, Kevin Thatcher and Craig Stecyk. That was my next thing to be a part of. There was no ill will involved.

GSD: How did you learn how to launch airs so high?
I remember David Andrecht doing that big method air at the Big O and seeing the photo of it in *Skateboarder* and just going, "Wow!" I was blasting some big airs. I was almost doing the highest airs in the world, and I was just 12 or 13. I felt like I was going higher. I would go out there every day and do a higher air. I was like, "When is it going to end? When am I going to stop going higher?" It really didn't stop. I kept going higher. That's when I knew I had figured out something about skateboarding, that I was going to propel it and be the one who goes the highest. So, when I saw David Andrecht, it inspired me. I thought, "Okay, you can go high." Then I went home to Marina to practice in the upper keyhole. When the lien air came out, that's when I could go higher. I was like—boom!— going straight up and straight down. It was like, "I'm not even trying."

In that new clam shell bowl at Colton, I was doing these big, fully tweaked tail method airs. That was the beginning of me really starting to figure out the landing. High airs are all in the landing. It has nothing to do with, "Okay, I'm going to go high on this wall." You have to land right. Even when we did the high air contests back in the day, it was in a regular halfpipe. We didn't have these huge, massive roll-ins. We didn't have the Mega Ramp, or jump 70-foot gaps to a 27-foot tall quarter pipe and do a 23-foot high air. We were on a 10-foot halfpipe, building up speed, pumping our lights out and just going 10 feet out on this literally 11-foot ramp. So, it's all about your landing. That's the focus. I figured it out, I breathed right, and I studied Bruce Lee's techniques, where he got his strength and power. My dad was a huge part of my training and thinking about how I could get the most energy when I was pumping. That's why I was able to take it and go to that next level of high airs. It took a lot of concentration and discipline to generate more energy.

That's also the influence that I used to create my persona and my character, be-

cause I didn't want to be a copier. I wanted to be authentic and original. I had to do things like wear spandex that separated me. At this one contest, I danced before I dropped in. I borrowed lace lingerie pants off of some girl and wore them in the Capitola Classic contest because I knew that no one had done it yet. That was my thing. I wanted to do things that no one had done. When I got those spandex pants, I was like, "No one is going to wear these," and sure enough, nobody has to this day. I haven't seen anybody wear spandex while skateboarding, especially in a contest. That's what's so special about skateboarding—you can be yourself.

GSD: Who designed the hammerhead?
That was me. I came up with the fish shape, too. I wanted a board that could do tail taps on PVC coping and not slip off. That was one of my favorite tricks, because Shogo Kubo did them amazingly. I included a flat nose because I did air tail taps and it was a good spot to put your hand. I cut out the sides just to make the board lighter and it looked sick. I was like, "Dude this thing looks sick." They said, "That thing looks freaky." When I started my own company, I said, "How can I change this shape? I need a handle for backside airs. How can I make a notch in the front for a backside air?" So, I cut out a little shape on a piece of foam paper with a flat nose with the hammerhead handles. I was like, "That doesn't look good at all." Then I looked at the swallow tail, and I looked at the nose, and thought, "Let's swallow the nose!" So, I cut out the nose, looked at it and was like, "Sick! That's a hammerhead!" It was like that—just that quick. It was all function and had nothing to do with, "I'm going to make a funny-looking board," or "I'm going to copy an animal."

GSD: Was it the first weird-shaped deck?
The only other shaped board was the Chris Strople winger. But the hammerhead was the first shaped deck in that time of skateboarding. I'm so stoked that I inspired the Tex Gibson, the John Lucero, the Rob Roskopp and all of those shapes that are so iconic today. I'm sure somebody would have done it, but I was glad that I was one of those who pioneered the shaped board.

GSD: What inspired you to do the Christ air and rocket air?
I was in a hotel room in Texas with Lance Mountain, John Lucero and Neil Blender, and we were all doing these crazy tricks on our beds like we always did. All of a sudden, I put two hands on the nose, two feet on the tail and said, "I'm going to be flying like this!" Somebody said, "Oh, yeah, that's like a rocket air!" I was like, "Let's try it tomorrow." I think Lance and I were the only ones who tried it. Boom! Lance went flying across the whole ramp, carving in the air while grabbing rocket, and I was like, "That was sick." That's when the Kahuna ramp was a massive behemoth with 10-foot trannies and two feet of vert, all metal and perfect. I just launched straight up and almost made the first one. Within three tries, I launched my first one head high, and landed it like it was nothing.

The Christ air came after I saw Monty Nolder and Tony Magnusson kick their feet

out on backside airs, but their feet were all whatever. I was like, "Dang! That's pretty sick. They're doing no-footed airs." But, I thought they were kind of ugly. I liked the way that Nolder did them. That dude skated strong. I was sitting there with Cab, coming up with all of these airs, when I thought, "Imagine doing a big old Christ air like this (arms and legs stretched out in the crucifix position). My name is Christian, my nickname was Christ, I wore a cross all the time, so I thought that would be pretty sick, and it just made sense, right? The Christ air. I went up—boom!— stuck out my arms—bam!—stuck my legs together straight down. I would do them as high as I could. After four or five tries, I made my first Christ air. That's the most profound and ironic trick to me, because it pertains to who I am today as a Christian and a man of faith. I'm a pastor, I believe in Jesus Christ, and then to think I invented the Christ air. And 25 years later, I'm into the knowledge of who Jesus Christ is. It blows my mind how things work out. I'm stoked beyond words to be the guy who invented the Christ air.

LMB: So, you're a pastor and skating for Vans. Tell us about your life today.
Today is great! I'm going to be 48 next year.

I've got four children, and I've got grandchildren. I'm a pastor at the Century Church right here in Costa Mesa. I've got multiple sponsors, and I run my own company called Hosoi Skateboards, which is something that I'm super passionate about. I get to create shapes, design graphics and stoke out kids when I give them boards or put them on the team. I'm building a team right now. I just want to be part of skateboarding. I just want to share the stories of skateboarding's past with people who are coming up after us so the stories won't become myths. That's why the Tracker book is so important, because future generations will be able to learn about skateboarding history—who was involved with it, and how it all happened. It will blow their minds. They will have a whole new appreciation for skateboarding and for those who made a sacrifice for it. Guys like us sweat, bleed and cry for our sport and our culture. Skateboarding is what we love, and projects like the Tracker book tell that story.

Read the full-length interview at trackertrucks.com

Above: **Christian Hosoi traverses the channel at Marina skatepark in Marina del Rey, California, late 1980.** Photo: James Cassimus

Back in April 1986, I designed a Tracker ad featuring Allen Losi barreling through one of his famously long stand-up grinds at Del Mar. The headline appropriately read, "Just One Page of Surl." The word surly, which means bad tempered and unfriendly, pretty much summed up Big Al's rocky relationship with the coping. Off board and face to face with humans, however, it was another story; he was always super friendly and mellow. Despite the notoriety of his burly grinds and lip slides, Allen's approach to skateboarding was not all brute force. As the inventor of the Ollie to fakie, fakie Ollie footplant, lien to tail and the luggage terminal (Elguerial to tail), he debuted some of the most progressive moves of the early '80s. To delve into more detail of his life and times, check out Grosso's *Love Letter* to Allen Losi on YouTube and read the following interview.—**GSD**

Allen Losi
INTERVIEW

LMB: Where and when were you born?
I was born in Sylmar, California in 1965.
LMB: When did you start skateboarding?
My neighbor across the street got a Black Knight with clay wheels and I fell in love with it that day. He got leukemia and died and his mom gave me his skateboard. My mom gave it back to her to remember her son by. I went to the store and bought my first skateboard and from then, on I've been skateboarding.
BR: Who came up with the Varibot name?
Duane Peters. It was funny; I liked it. My dad, Gil Losi, called the shots on us progressing,

and all of us obeyed. If we didn't, we would get pushed aside, so we became full-on Varibots. Instead of worrying about style, we just did tricks. Back then, people were really into hitting every wall of the pool. Your lines and how you looked doing them were just as important as what you did. But, by the time the Tony Hawk era and the NSA came around, that wasn't really a factor anymore, because we were going back and forth on vert ramps with flat walls, just doing maneuvers.
BR: Whenever we heard someone talking shit about Varibots, we were just like, "Well, that guy's doing rad stuff!"
It also became a media ploy that I enjoyed, to be honest with you. Duane would embrace us. He rode our wheels. It wasn't a negative "Let's fight each other!" thing. It was more publicity, so I rolled with it. Any publicity is good publicity.
LMB: How did Variflex get started?
A couple of years after I started skating, my uncle Ray, my dad, my brother and my cousin started Variflex. Ray just wanted to manufacture mass-market skateboards to make money, but my father Gil wanted to make good skateboards and travel around with the team. So, at some point, they had a disagreement, then my father left the Variflex program in 1982. After that, it was never doable. In my opinion, on the pro skating side, Variflex was all a farce. A while later, I was gong to leave Variflex to do Team Losi with Santa Cruz, but my family threatened to disown me, so I did Team Losi with the family. They hired some other guy to run it, so I don't even know where they got the boards made. They were the worst ones ever. I was arguing with my family about it when I broke my leg and they finally let me go. Then I started LSD, which stood for Losi Skate Designs. That was what I thought a skateboard company should be like, with a team that was cool to travel with.
LMB: When did you first ride Trackers?
1979 was probably the first time I rode a pair of Trackers. I rode everything: Lasers, Rebounds, Bennetts, ACS. I rode everything I could get my hands on to check them out.
LMB: So, when you stopped riding Variflex Connection trucks, that's when you joined Tracker?
We were at a contest at Kona and I wanted to skate, but I couldn't turn on those Connection trucks. Fausto Vitello gave me a set of Indys, and that's when I first got off of the Connections. Then when I talked to you (Larry), I got on Tracker. I never really rode for Indy. Fausto just gave me trucks. But, I was excited to be part of Tracker. Tracker was the best team and brand I ever rode for. My favorite part of that whole era was riding for Tracker, because it was comfortable, it was casual and it was good fun.
LMB: Were you riding Sixtracks?
Yeah. I remember you gave me a set of the magnesiums, then I went to the concourse in San Diego, where the police took my board and I never got another pair because the magnesium fire happened at your factory and it was over. Those

were the only magnesium trucks I ever had. They were cool and lightweight, and I liked them a lot. I wish I had more. I always groveled over that.
LMB: Favorite Tracker ads?
It was a Lester ad. Lester always had the best ads. To me, Lester *was* Tracker at that time. I hung out with Lester the most when I rode for Tracker.
LMB: During your time on Trackers, what stood out about their performance?
I came from riding Variflex Connection trucks, so I can ride anything that does or doesn't perform. I rode the worst-turning trucks ever made. And somehow I had to skate contests on them. By the time that happened, I could ride anything. My favorite Trackers were the magnesium ones. Man, those things were cool. They were a very good product. It was either Tracker or Indys—they were by far the top two products to ride. There was no other choice if you wanted to be on point. The reason I ended up leaving Tracker was because I thought if I got on Thunder, I would finally get photos in *Thrasher*, but Fausto never liked my family, so it didn't work. I just left a good company to be stuck someplace where I had nothing.
BR: Why is Tracker so important to the history of skateboarding?
Anyone who stood the test of time, stands out—especially Tracker, Indy, Santa Cruz and Powell-Peralta. The brands that hung in there are the ones that have my respect. Tracker was always an honest, straight shooter with people, whereas other people manipulated us and jumped on opportunities. Tracker was solid, legit, and always treated us well.
BR: How has skateboarding mentally trained the way you think?
Skating gives you self-confidence. Not only that, it opened my eyes to live my life instead of fussing about anybody else's. That's the best thing skating gave me. It gives you health, it gives you inner and physical strength, it gives you a peace of mind that nothing else fulfills. Music, snowboarding, I've tried everything I could, but nothing replaces skateboarding. Nothing. Only skaters who really feed on it know what it is. When you get older, it doesn't matter. You still feed on it. I love all of the old guy reunions. It's great to get together.
BR: What else do you want to talk about?
There is nothing better than the Tracker / Del Mar days. That was by far the best part of my life. I actually lived in the Del Mar pro shop. My bed was the slot car track. I woke up every morning and skated, then went to the beach. It was absolutely paradise.
LMB: Which years was that?
1984 to '86, right in that window. Man, it was good times. If the weather was good, I would sleep outside in the High-Balls (enclosed trampolines). But, I would usually sleep in the building. Then they took away the High-Balls, so I lost my bed.
LMB: Tell us that story about Jeff Tatum's backside Ollies.
I went to Del Mar for a contest. It was the first time I saw a backside Ollie. JT was charging up to the coping at Del Mar. He carried a lot of speed; it was crazy how much speed he generated preparing for this trick. All of a sudden, he would smack the tail and the board would fly through the air. Sometimes, it would not only flop off of his feet, but it would land on the wall, then he would

By Larry Balma + Bryan Ridgeway

land back on his board on the wall. It was wild. It was crazy! Every time he would throw up a backside Ollie, my heart went up into my throat. I just didn't know what was going to happen. I was afraid, but he would make them. As a spectator, though, it was incredibly scary. It was very frightening.

BR: You were good to see and hear skating at Del Mar. Those long-ass frontside grinds were a staple. I'd be walking down the sidewalk toward the keyhole and I could hear the clickity-clacking. Your grinds were well-known. I knew who was skating just from how long the grinding sound lasted. I could hear that fucking aluminum grind on the coping and knew it was Losi.

I like to hear that. That coping was chunky, too, man. There were some holes in that shit. I remember when they changed the coping, it was nice for about a week. Then it was clicky-clacky all over again. They didn't have the kind of coping they have today. It was a totally different world. Back then, if you saw someone with a skate shirt on, you probably knew them.

LMB: Closing comments?

I was embraced by Tracker. Everybody there treated me very well, better than anybody else I ever rode for. Even after my family treated you guys like shit, and my cousin manipulated you guys, as they did me, you guys didn't tie me into it. Where other companies in the industry blamed me for my family's activities, which I had no part of, you guys didn't even associate me with it, and that was great. Tracker products were great, and the people were great. In my opinion, Tracker was the cleanest, sharpest thing, and I was very grateful to be part of it.

Read the full-length interview at trackertrucks.com

Allen Losi blasts a sky-high judo air at Del Mar Skate Ranch in Del Mar, California, circa 1987.
Left: **Out take of a** *TransWorld Skateboarding* **Pro Spotlight portrait.**
Opposite page: **The layback air is an ugly trick. Allen Losi is well-known as the only person who ever made it look good. Del Mar, 1983.** All photos this spread: Grant Brittain

163

Neil Blender gets lippy at the Buena Vista pool near Santa
Cruz, California, circa 1984. Photo: Billy Ruff
Opposite page: Neil, looking uncertain about the lens and life in
general, circa 1980. Photo: Glen E. Friedman

AARDVARK RULES, FOR A DECEMBER DAY

Neil Blender is one of the most revered figures in skateboarding history. Channeling Pablo Picasso, Salvador Dali and Rod Serling, he's lived his whole life as a work of oddball art. In the early 1980s, when sharp, professional deck graphics ruled, Neil was the first to put a homespun, surreal twist on it, and he penned some hilariously bizarre yarns for his Aggro Zone column in *TransWorld Skateboarding* magazine. Likewise in *Skate Fate* zine, Neil's Mark

Neil Blender
INTERVIEW

Coonson comic strip foreshadowed exotic terrain and maneuvers like the ho-ho plant and skating handrails several years before it happened in real life. As if inventing tricks like the bean plant, no comply, jolly mamba, wooly mammoth and many more was not enough, Neil often blessed other people's moves with funny, perfect names like the luggage terminal (Elguerial to tail). He was also the first to do front truck grinds on coping back when it seemed impossible. Neil's sometimes erratic, always spontaneous behavior manifested itself in many ways: painting a cartoon face on a wall during a contest run, ripping tiny ramps inside a house, acting like a lizard on the flat bottom after a knee slide, pushing a silly rocket air over a little hump. Ultimately, Neil Blender's lasting legacy inspires all of us to be as creative as possible, and to not take ourselves, or life, too seriously. And that's what skateboarding needs now more than ever.—GSD

LMB: When did you get your first set of Trackers?
When I was really young, around 14, I had some Speed Springs, and then eventually Trackers just worked their way onto my board.
LMB: Was this before you got sponsored by G&S?
Oh yeah, I was just trying to get skateboarding working in my life, cutting out boards, no sponsors. Do you remember Brad Jackman? He got sponsored by Caster. He had a Tom Inouye board. He leaked it onto Skip Disney, who rode it for a year. The thing was battered. Then I got it, finally, and it was still rad, because it was a Fiberlam. It was so good! The Tom Inouye model is probably the raddest board even now—the shape, everything about it is good.
GSD: Was your first sponsor Powerflex?
No, my first sponsor was this dude who was trying to make a skateboard company called Dragon Skates. It was rad. He brought some boards down to the Big O, and he said, "Hey, man, I want you to try these boards I'm making." So, I rode the Dragon Skate for a while, and then never heard from that guy again. Woodflex came after that, and then Powerflex.
LMB: When did you get on G&S?

In the summer of '63 (laughs). No, I think it was around 1980 at a Big O contest. I had a friend named Dave Padorski who was on G&S. We'd always ride at the park together. The G&S team showed up, and Padorski was already sponsored. He said, "Hey, man, I can get you some Yo Yo wheels right now, if you want!" I was hyped. I skated in the unsponsored division, and I think I did good, because after the whole thing was over, Steve Cathey came up and asked, "Instead of just riding Yo Yos, do you want to be on G&S all the way?" I was like, "Yeah, man, let's do this." So, a box arrived a week later at the Big O with so much gear. Everything made by G&S was red and yellow. They still had that look going with the jerseys, but it was right at the cusp when they were getting rid of it, so all of this excess stuff was in their factory—all of those weird jerseys you'd see with the Christian fish logo. I didn't know about the whole religious thing with them.
GSD: How did Dick Tracy end up on your helmet?
I don't know. It was a little puffy guy that came out of a gumball machine that I stuck on my helmet. We were into putting weird things on our helmets. We'd cut out things that looked rad, like logos of food companies from the time that didn't even make sense. And then the Dick Tracy sticker looked pretty cool, so I just stuck him on there. I just kept him on and kept it going through different helmets.
GSD: So, you mostly rode Sixtracks?
Yeah, but when I first got ahold of Trackers, I had some Fultracks, but they were too wide for the board, and the wheels stuck out. So, I hack sawed the Fultracks on each side, hammered out the axle and shortened it, and it worked.
LMB: Well, you sort of made Midtracks out of them.
GSD: Did you like working for Tran-

BY GSD + Larry Balma

sWorld Skateboarding?
The Aggro Zone was fun. I liked being able to know there was going to be a rad photo to look at. That was the ultimate thing when I'd look through a magazine as a kid, like, "Oh, my God! That photo!"
GSD: Sometimes you wrote these strange stories like the Gerbil's Days.
That was just retardation, man. I look back like, "What was I trying to do?" It was a little weird when I start to look at it. I have to quit trying to do that.

GSD: Tell us about the lien air.
The lien air came about because John Lucero saw a picture in the magazine of this guy, Niko Weis, and it said, "wild Canadian air." [With his front hand, he was grabbing the lower rail behind his foot on a frontside air.] John said, "Hey, look at this." I said, "Yeah, it looks pretty lame." John said, "Try it grabbing in front of your foot and you'll be able to grab later, so it'll be easier." So, we started trying them, and Lucero was totally right. It was called the lien air because you have to lean in order to do them. Then [in an *Action Now* caption], D. David Morin spelled it like my name backward, so it seems like I got more credit on that one. What other moves are there? The gay twist was lame.

GSD: So, that one came about because you couldn't do a Caballaerial?
Yeah, it seemed retarded when we did it. It was just like taking Caballero's move and making it look really crummy. The way it felt, too, just struggling through the trick. We shouldn't have even tried it. Cab is too hot at those.

GSD: Did you ever end up making a Caballaerial?

No, it's really eating away at me now. I tried it for days, and then it was just too hard to figure out how to make the board stick to my feet. I tried them again maybe around seven years ago at Clairemont. I just tried to get into the position, and it's more understandable. I feel like maybe I could make one now, if I was lucky. It would take all day, though.

LMB: Did you ever land a ho-ho plant?
I never made one. There's no way. Ho-hos were too intense. Steve Schneer was an actual gymnast who was a skater. He was one of the first good guys I saw at Big O. Him and Duane Peters were the best dudes there.

LMB: You were so tall, which was a drawback to the ho-ho.
I don't know, it's the switching of the hands: starting out invert, then standing on both hands, then going in egg, right? That's how Schneer did it. He ended up walking around the deck on his hands. I think that's why people started hating him for a minute. They would get mad at him,

Neil Blender, August 1987.

Neil Blender, March 1983.

HA, HA. HA, HA!

SITCOM FRENZY

This mask doesn't scare me anymore.

Above right: **Sitcom Frenzy, circa 1995.**
Drawing: Neil Blender
Below: **Neil offers up a Gray slide at Sadlands in Anaheim, California, circa 1981.** Photo: Jim Goodrich
Opposite page, top: **Neil Blender hoists a stylish nose bone frontside air out of Skate City's keyhole in Whittier, California, circa 1982.** Photo: Brad Jackman
Opposite page, bottom: **Neil enjoys some quality time with his imaginary friends, circa 1984.**
Photo: Jim Goodrich

like, "The guy's just a freak, we don't care about him." Little did they know, he was seriously rad. He had a trick called the hospital, which was a 540 egg right along the tile—a tumbling egg. He never landed one, but he tried them so long ago.

GSD: Do you remember the luggage terminal?
Yes, Allen Losi's luggage terminal. It was an Elguerial [360 invert] to tail, right? Him and Eric Grisham were the only two guys I saw do fakie 360 taps clean, no wheel touching.

GSD: When you did the first front truck pivots at Del Mar in the mid '80s, I had never seen anyone do that before. Did you ever see anyone else do it?
I don't know, I don't think so. That came from when we were drawing cartoons. Visiting hours.

GSD: Visiting hours was a frontside front truck grind, invented by an alien called the Visitor.
Was it? That was the new deal. They turned it into that name, I guess. So, maybe that was the trick. I don't even know.

GSD: What is the jolly mamba? The frontside invert to something.
Yeah, frontside invert, and then you just turn it, so it feels more like you're coming in opposite foot invert. Even though you're going to fakie, you just try to make it turn into a regular invert.

GSD: And the woolly mammoth is?
Just fakie out to your nose, grabbing stale between your legs. Just speaking of rad moves in general, like Allen Losi's fakie Ollie footplant. That rates way up there, right?

GSD: So, what kind of art are you doing now? Painting, drawing, graphic stuff?
Yeah, just a little cartoonish, bigger outline painting style using brushes. I still draw with pens a lot. I usually do pen stuff for Vans. They use a lot of small line work and blow it up for t-shirt graphics. But, I do paint a lot, mostly with acrylics, just because it's easier to clean up, and it's pretty fine. I have to start making some boards and t-shirts. I did a run of t-shirts with the Heated Wheel logo, the trampoline guy. Did you ever see that one? He's doing a flip in a sleeping bag

on a trampoline. So, he's just all twisted up. There's no way he's going to land right. I'm going to re-issue that one. I think I made, like, 50 of them. I sold a bunch of stuff on eBay, but that was like two years ago.

GSD: How long did you keep riding Trackers after the '80s?
In the '90s, I moved to Ohio and I still rode Trackers when I was living there. I had some Aggros, and the hangers had more beef. Yeah, the Aggros were hot. I still have a bunch of those, but right now, I've got Indys on my super wide board—215s on the Olson—and then Ace trucks on another board. I don't even ride vert anymore. I just push around in the street on this little slalomy skateboard.

LS: Does it hurt too much to ride vertical?
In my mind, I can just launch right now, but I can't see as good, so my timing's off.

GSD: I saw you around 2005, and you had this funny little skateboard about 20 inches long and two or three inches thick with fenders and the baseplates were sunk into the deck. What was that all about?
Oh, my God! Peter Hewett did a frontside invert on that thing in the Claremont pool. The board is like 21 inches long, it's seriously tiny, and it's got small Indys and tiny wheels. It was a piece of 2" x 8". I routed it out to drop in the trucks so it would sit lower, so it's stable when you ride it. It's about the same height as a normal skateboard. I call it the Dictionary, because it looks like one of those red dictionaries you see around.

LS: So, what does Tracker really mean to you?
It represented people. All of the best dudes were riding them. Tracker was just so solid of a thing. It's like a Crescent wrench—something that's going to work. It's the rad tool.

Read the full-length interview at trackertrucks.com

MAKE A SHRINE FOR MY PADS

Jeff Phillips stalls an Andrecht, circa 1988. Photo: Chip Morton

Jeff Phillips, February 1987.

Jeff Phillips, June 1988.

Phillips, February 1986.

Jeff Phillips
TRIBUTE

Looking back on vert skateboarding in the 1980s, many people will agree that Tony Hawk did the most tricks, Chris Miller had the best style, and Jeff Phillips was the most powerful. Indeed, more beast than man, he relentlessly shook the ramp, pounded the coping and launched way above it with the utmost force and confidence. Even during high-pressure contests, "Philpod" would simply throw on a tie-dyed shirt topped with his famous self-painted skull and crossbones helmet, and unleash a startling display of spontaneous skateboarding genius, which often included his signature tricks, the straight leg frontside air and the Phillips 66, while high as a kite. Jeff even defeated the unbeatable Tony Hawk two or three times, which really wasn't all that important to him, as he just loved to skate whenever and wherever with whoever. Sadly, Jeff ended his own life on Christmas day in 1993. He is sorely missed by everyone who knew him. If Jeff Phillips were still alive today, he'd still be killing it on his skateboard. I just know it.—**GSD**

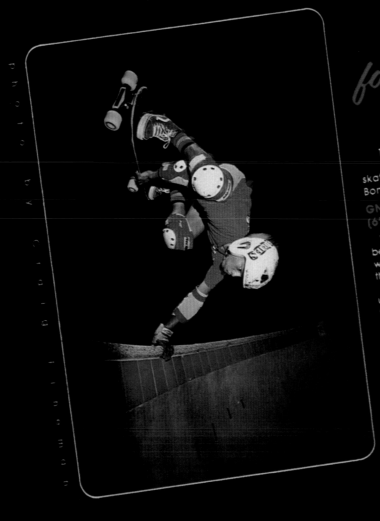

Landing Gear for the Bones Brigade

Top competitor in this year's Hester Series, RAY "BONES" RODRIGUEZ, skates on his own model board from Powell, with Bones wheels (of course), and Tracker's new

GNARLY SIXTRACKS—ST-1500
(6" between wheels)

When describing trucks, axle length alone can be misleading, so Tracker chose to measure the width of the axle casting itself, which is between the wheels.

If you're real observant, you'll notice that, unlike the other Tracker models, the triangular face of the SIXTRACK doesn't extend to the ends of the axle casting. You'll also notice that the ends of the axle casting are tapered. These subtle changes make it possible to use inset and center bearing wheels, as well as functioning beautifully with Copers.

The SIXTRACK's unique geometry offers the smooth and dependable Tracker feel, but we've made it quicker and even more responsive, with an increased turning ability.

Best of all, the SIXTRACK barely weighs more than the EXTRACK (Tracker's 5" model). We have carefully slimmed the castings down, watching to preserve the STRENGTH and DURABILITY inherent in the Tracker design.

All this works together to make the Tracker SIXTRACK the strong, light, high performance wide truck you've been waiting for.

The Sixtrack

TRACKER TRUCKS

Send 50¢ for a Sticker, Brochure and Order Form to: Tracker Trucks, P.O. Box 398, Cardiff-by-the-Sea, California 92007   Dealers call 714-481-9551.

Ray "Bones" Rodriguez, October 1979.
170

Tom Groholski, April 1987.

Mike McGill, January 1990.

TILE BLUE AVAILABLE NOW TRACKER DESIGNS LTD. P.O. BOX 217 CARDIFF, CALIFORNIA 92007

Tile Blue, September 1989.

Mark Partain, December 1988.

50/50, December 1989.

Chip Morton, Mark Hamilton, December 1988.

Shades of Performance, February 1985.

Mike McGill, December 1988.

Christian Hosoi, September 1982.

Tom Inouye, December 1979.

Marty Jimenez, June 1988.

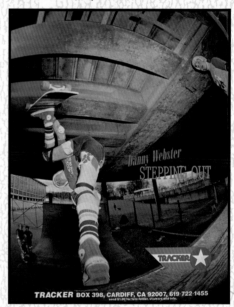

Danny Webster, October 1984.

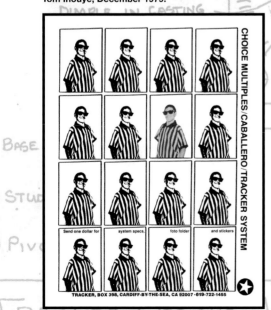

Steve Caballero, January 1983.

Rubber Stamp, August 1985.

Mike McGill, November 1983.

After growing up surfing and skateboarding in Orange County, California, Marty Jimenez, also known as Jinx, moved to the suburbs of Cincinnati, Ohio in the late 1970s. He sessioned Apple Skatepark until it closed, then Rob Roskopp's halfpipe, followed by the MESS Series. After moving back to So Cal in 1984, Jinx worked and / or skated pro for such brands as Tracker, Madrid and Vision. He even owned his own skateboard brand, Channel One, for a spell. Since the late '90s, Jinx has been doing art direction at Volcom and shredding the myriad public skateparks of Orange County.—GSD

Marty Jimenez
INTERVIEW

LMB: Where are you from?
I was born in Los Angeles, but I grew up in Orange County. In my last year of high school, I moved to Ohio. When I was living here in California, I was obviously into surfing and skateboarding and all of that fun stuff. When I moved to Ohio, I attempted to join the football team, but realized that was a bad move. So, I just got that much more into skating. This was during a low point in skateboarding when it tapered down in 1980-'81. It was a real bummer, because right before I moved to Ohio, I lived about a mile from the Big O. On the good side, when I look back, it actually worked out for the best, because if I would have stayed out here, there was a good chance I probably wouldn't have finished high school, because I was having too much fun. Living in Ohio opened doors for me to see the Midwest and the East Coast. I still had opportunities to visit California during spring break and holidays, when I was able to skate other parks, as well as the Big O. In the summer, I would stay as long as I could until it was time for me to go back to Ohio. It ended up being a good thing for me. I got exposed to Midwest skating and all of the friends that I still have to this day.

LMB: When did you first ride Trackers?
We started our own little skate series called MESS (Mid East Skateboard Series), which was a backyard halfpipe series. We might have had the first contest at Mike Hill's house. Rob Roskopp lived back there at the time. So, we connected these little backyard contests together, and after the third one, Bryan Ridgeway said, "Hey, I've got some Tracker magnesiums. Do you want to ride for Tracker?" I said, "I want to try em, for sure." So the day that I got on Tracker was the day the Ridge gave me those trucks. At the time, with the magnesium, Tracker seemed like they were on the forefront of technology and trying to push it, trying to do more than just settle for the status quo. Not to mention they already had an awesome team to look up to.

LMB: What year was that?
That was in 1983. Then we had the second year of the MESS, which changed because guys started moving out to California. I think GSD was the first to move out, then Bryan Ridgeway, and then Rob Roskopp. All of these guys who lived back in the Midwest started navigating their way out to California, like Joe Bowers, Chris Carter, Jeff Kendall and

eventually everybody. The whole crew ended up out here. I was supper stoked. I got hooked up with Tracker and not long after that, I ended up getting sponsored by Madrid. At the time, Madrid had a little cult following in the Midwest. They sponsored Bill Danforth, Rob Roskopp and myself. After that, it was Jeff Kendall. We had a little Madrid posse back then.

GSD: How did you get nicknamed Jinx?
Bob Pribble was actually the one who gave me my nickname, Jinx. Pribble was from Indiana, and I was from Cincinnati. We got to know each other through the MESS contests. We decided to take a road trip down to Tennessee to go see Ray Underhill and Britt Parrott. Pribble and Chip Jones came over to Cincinnati before we started the adventure, and we skated this ditch. It was super shitty and the bottom was wet, so Chip decided to try it anyways. He skated in, hit the flat bottom, which was slimy, and fell in the water. He instantly became Swamp Thing. On the trip, we all ended up getting nicknames, because goofy things like that happened. Although my last name, Jimenez, is really pronounced him-E-nezz, in the Midwest, its JIM-in-ezz. Somehow, Pribble got Jinx out of it, and then my nickname was Jinx from that point on. We had all kinds of funny names for Pribble, like Dribble.

LMB: What about the Cherry Lane Ramp?
The Cherry Lane Ramp was actually at Rob Roskopp's house. When I moved to Cincinnati, I was just trying to connect with skateboarders, which were a pretty rare commodity out there. I lived out in the boondocks, so I wasn't in Cincinnati proper. I went through the Yellow Pages and tried to find a skateboard shop. I finally got a hold of one called the Pachinko Factory, who told me about Rob. So, I called him, and he said he had a quarterpipe. He was just about to get out of skateboarding. But, we had something in common, and he did still love skateboarding.

Rob lived out on a big farm, and somehow, we talked each other into turning his quarterpipe into a halfpipe. We ended up having a couple of skateboard contests on it, including the MESS. When Rob moved to California, his ramp got taken down. That's also where I met GSD. He lived in Cincinnati and showed up one day and wanted to skate with us. We were like, "Oh, cool! Another guy. We've got a three-man session." From that point on, GSD came back and skated the ramp a couple of more times and turned us on to his zine, *Skate Fate*, which was awesome. That gave us the catalyst to communicate with other guys. We started networking with our own zines.

Eventually, I made my way back out to California thanks to you (Larry), GSD and Bryan Ridgeway, because we started the zine thing and everybody had moved to California. I was really struggling, thinking, "What am I going to do?" When I finished high school, I didn't have the balls to move out to California, so I ended up going to college. That's when I had an epiphany:

"As soon as I'm done with this, I'm moving back to California." I moved about a week after I graduated. You guys gave me the opportunity to work in the Tracker shop, and you had started *TransWorld Skateboarding* magazine, so there was some work we could do there. I packed all of my belongings plus Ridgeway's stuff in my tiny Renault Le Car, which was probably the smallest car ever made. Ridgeway and I drove down to Kona Skatepark in Jacksonville, Florida for a contest, then to Dallas, Texas to spend a couple of days with John Gibson and the crew there. That was super fun. We skated a bunch of stuff, and then drove cross-country to Oceanside. In the Tracker shop, we spent a better part of the day packing grommets, pounding axles in hangers and things like that. Later in the day, we'd work on the magazine then skate Del Mar every night.

LMB: Do you recall any memorable times with the Tracker team?
When my home base ended up being the Tracker factory. GSD, Ridgeway and I lived there for a while, even though we weren't supposed to. I was like, "Oh, my God! I'm working and living at this place that's literally three blocks from the beach!" So, I could surf again. I could also go skate Del Mar. It was Nirvana, and I was there with my buddies from the Midwest. Ridgeway ended up being the best man at my wedding, and he's still one of my best friends to this day. GSD is from Cincinnati, did the same thing, and made it in skateboarding. It's pretty mind-blowing that we actually lived our dream. When you're in it, you don't realize until you get a little older, when you reflect back and think, "Wow, we really did what we wanted to do."

LMB: Any closing comments?
I just hope the Tracker legacy lives on. It's

rad you're doing this book, because there's so much history attached to the brand. Skateboarding history is good for everybody, whether you're a kid just now getting involved, or for us older guys to refresh our memories on the good old days. It's a great idea and long overdue.

Read the full-length interview at trackertrucks.com

Above: **Marty Jimenez slaps a red curb with a backside bert, circa 1987**. Photo: Unknown

By Larry Balma

Randy Stahlecker blazes on Tracker Tracks with Midtracks at Del Mar Skate Ranch in Del Mar, California, circa 1979. Photo: Lance Smith
Bottom left: **Peggy Cozens and Larry Balma sell Trekkers at a roller skate trade show, circa 1979.** Photo: Unknown
Bottom right: **A Trekkers size chart, circa 1979.**
Opposite page: **A Trekkers product shot and ad, October 1979.**

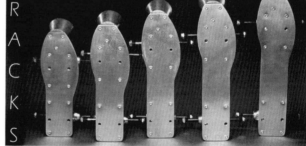

High performance rollerskate chassis by Tracker Designs, Limited

Tracker Tracks are very strong and very light skate chassis. We think they're the most durable skates ever made. They are strong enough to withstand prolonged outdoor skating, and intense skateboard park riding. The stresses that shatter other plates and trucks and bend other axles don't even phase Tracks. This inherent strength is due to meticulous engineering and manufacturing. The plate itself is a space-age maple/aluminum sandwich that is strong, light, and able to absorb shock while retaining its rigidity. The trucks are highest quality in every detail ... right down to the aircraft nylon insert locknuts. These trucks have wheel clearance and axles sized for the new generation rollerskate and skateboard wheels. After all, the new technology doesn't benefit you if you have outdated plates that don't fit. Tracker Trucks are so stable you can ride them tight or loose without wobbling, even during tricks. In total, Tracks provide a ride so smooth and maneuverable, they meet the performance demands of indoor skating. There's never been a skate like this before.

Tracks are available in five sizes ranging from Women's 2½ to Men's 13. They can be mounted on any well-chosen boot or shoe. They come complete with toestops. Many fine tuning accessory items and replacement parts are available from Tracker and wherever Tracks are sold.

| | Approximate Shoe Sizes | | Overall | |
	Women's	Men's	Length of Plate	Wheel Base
Track 302		10-1/2 to 13	11-7/8 in.	8 in.
Track 282	9-1/2 to 11	8-1/2 to 10	11-1/8 in.	7-1/4 in.
Track 262	7-1/2 to 9	6-1/2 to 8	10-5/16 in.	6-7/16 in.
Track 242	5-1/2 to 7	4-1/2 to 6	9-1/2 in.	5-5/8 in.
Track 222	2-1/2 to 5	1-1/2 to 4	8-3/4 in.	4-7/8 in.

GENERAL RULE: The optimum TRACK model for your boot or shoe will be the longest one possible; the plate should be equal to, or slightly shorter than the sole of the boot or shoe. Always mount the TRACK plate flush at the heel.

In the mid 1970s, Tracker co-founder Dave Dominy was inspired to roller skate in bowls after he watched Kenny Means do it employing a side-stance style. Kenny rode Snyder skate plates, which were the top-of-the-line roller skates of the day, precision designed and machined and constructed using grade 8 hardware, much like our Tracker Trucks. Dave quickly learned how to skate side stance, so we built some prototype Tracker roller skate boot plates that could accommodate our wider hangers, which ultimately helped push the limits of vertical roller-skating. Working with Taylor Dykema, we developed an extremely light and strong plate utilizing technology pioneered by Tom Sims and George Powell for slalom skateboards: Two plies of maple topped with a 7075 aluminum alloy. Tracker produced five sizes of roller skate boot plates with Tracker baseplates riveted in place. When Tracker pattern maker Gary Dodds built a mold for the toe stop base, we had a finished new product that we marketed as Tracker Tracks.

In 1979, at the same time skateboard sales were giving way to the new sport of BMX, an outdoor recreational roller-skating boom was occurring. The problem for recreational roller skaters was that they had to put on boots, which was a laborious process. We were already familiar with the old clamp-on roller skates that were tightened onto street shoes. When you were done skating in them, you'd simply un-clamp the skate plates and walk off. When we were kids, we had used the cheap steel wheel clamp-on skates to build our first skateboards. The clamp-on skates worked reasonably well with hard sole shoes, but by 1979, hard sole shoes were not the norm. Everyone used canvas rubber sole shoes for active sportswear. Needless to say, clamp-on skates could not be tightened to hold onto a soft rubber shoe sole. Eager to sell to the roller skate market, many skateboard manufacturers bolted canvas shoes to roller skate plates, which were more comfortable and less expensive than boot skates, but they did not solve the problem of having to carry around a pair of shoes to wear after you removed your skates. So, Tracker set out to design a modern clamp-on style of roller skates. The result was called Trekkers.

We utilized our lightweight boot plate and made it wider in order to

TRACKER TREKKERS
Roller Skates (1979)

make a solid platform without the shoe being bolted in place. Dave Dominy experimented with all variations of straps to hold the shoes securely in place. There were many strap configurations that would work; however finding a combination that was adjustable and simple was not so easy. We settled on a strap system that worked quite well, as any type of shoe could be attached to our Trekker skates. I even skated our Trekkers barefoot for a Channel 8 news release! Our first strap system was not foolproof. The rear strap was not intuitive, which made it difficult for many people to correctly re-attach if it came completely undone, as few of them kept the instruction card. The final version of the strap was fixed to the rear of the skate with a Velcro patch for easy adjustment.

By 1980, Tracker Tracks skate plates and Tracker Trekkers were experiencing robust sales with vertical roller-skating promoters like Duke Rennie and Fred Blood, and recreational skaters from Venice Beach to New York. We advertised Trekkers in trade magazines and roller skate magazines around the globe. Tracker took the next step in marketing to the roller skate industry by attending a trade show in Hawaii to market to roller rinks. Roller rinks carried rental boot skates for their patrons who did not own their own skates. They had to stock 13 men's sizes and 10 women's sizes with multiple pairs of skates in each size to maximize the amount of skaters on the floor. Imagine pulling on a pair of sweaty boots that the last skater had just heated up after an hours-long session.

Trekkers solved the problem of the roller rinks' rental stock. Four Trekker sizes covered all of the rental needs and worked for both men and women, and each skater could wear his own shoes! The rink owners were ecstatic. They lined up to make orders with our sales manager, Keith Hagen. We returned from the show and placed parts orders to build Trekkers! We even purchased automatic rivet machines and tooled up to meet the demand. But, as it turned out, unbeknownst to us, Tracker had upset the apple cart of the roller skate industry power players, whose history went back 100 years. Chicago, Sure Grip and other industry big boys got together with their insurance company that insured all of the roller rinks. Using the liability card, they invented a reason to cancel the insurance of any rink that used Trekker skates for rentals. All of our rink orders were cancelled, which threw Tracker into a major downsizing move to focus on survival within the dramatically shrinking skateboard industry.—**LMB**

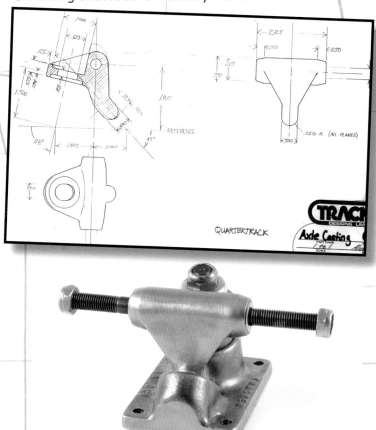

Tracker Quartertrack Prototype (1980)

In 1980, Dave Dominy made a hanger drawing and Gary Dodds built a master pattern for a narrow roller skate truck called the Tracker Quartertrack. Measuring in at a tiny 2 1/8", the Quartertrack axle hanger was as narrow as we could go with our original Tracker baseplate with the built-in bottom cushion boss, as anything narrower would allow the wheels to rub against it. The Quartertrack was developed for Tracker's roller skate program but was never put into production. Although we did cast maybe a dozen sample Quartertracks, we never gave them to anyone outside of the Tracker staff or built any production tooling, so you'll likely never see one!—**LMB**

Above: **A Tracker Quartertrack truck for use on Trekkers roller skates, circa 1980. This is one of only two in existence.**

176

TRACKER SYSTEM
Pegboard Delights (1979)

In 1979, we created the Tracker System, which was marketed to skateboard shops as a point-of-purchase display containing a complete collection of trucks, replacement truck parts and packaged accessories mounted on Masonite pegboards. Up to this time, even the smartest shops carried only cushions or kingpins. The nylon insert aircraft locknuts that we used on our axles weren't even available at hardware stores. The Tracker System offered all of the nuts, washers, cushions and bushings—most of which fit any truck—and even our baseplates and hangers. By offering a packaged deal for parts plus a display, we opened up a whole new point of sale for stores. In addition, skateboarders with quivers were able to swap hangers from deck to deck without having to buy full set-ups. Also used as an ad slogan on and off over the decades, the Tracker System still exists today.—**LMB**

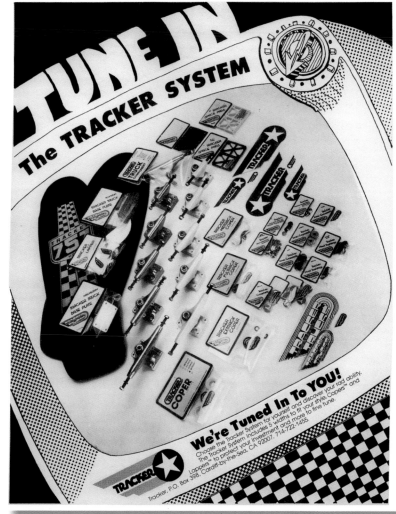

Tune in to the Tracker System, April 1982.

NOT JUST A TRUCK COMPANY,

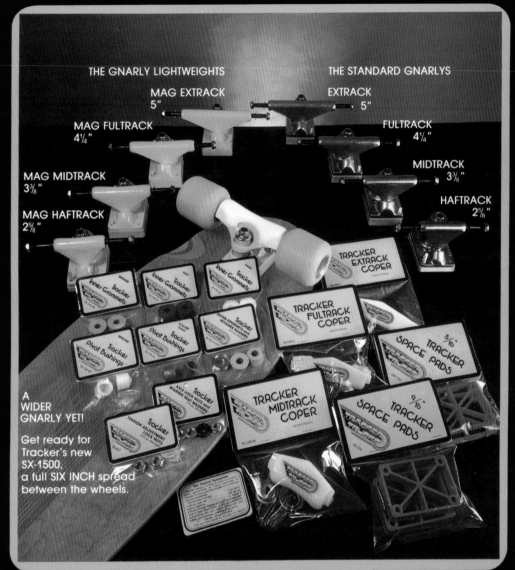

THE GNARLY LIGHTWEIGHTS

MAG EXTRACK
5"

MAG FULTRACK
4¼"

MAG MIDTRACK
3⅜"

MAG HAFTRACK
2⅝"

THE STANDARD GNARLYS

EXTRACK
5"

FULTRACK
4¼"

MIDTRACK
3⅜"

HAFTRACK
2⅝"

A
WIDER
GNARLY YET!

Get ready for
Tracker's new
SX-1500,
a full SIX INCH spread
between the wheels.

BUT SKATEBOARDERS WHO HAVE DEVELOPED
THE TRACKER SYSTEM

for skateboarding. We're talking about a performance proven group of components designed by some of the best skaters around. The Tracker system isn't for everyone It's designed for the skateboarder who takes his sport seriously

Once you've dialed into the Tracker system you have dialed into optimum performance tuning to your personal style That's adaptability Tracker wants you to be able to make your trucks do what YOU want them to, because you're going to be riding them. We've got our own Trackers tuned the way we like them

Control is what our sport is all about and Tracker wants you to have all the control you want and need. Dial into the Tracker system, if you haven't already and dial into confidence. Confidence is what makes our sport so much fun

For a sticker, brochure and order form, send fifty cents to: Tracker Trucks, P.O Box 398, Cardiff-by-the Sea, California 92007 Dealers call 714-481-9551

1980s
Skateboarding Timeline

1980 · As skateparks close down left and right, the popularity of skateboarding continues to wane. A few dedicated hardcore enthusiasts skate streets and build their own backyard wooden halfpipes, which keeps skateboarding going at a grassroots level. The large skateboard brands suffer huge losses, forcing many to go out of business while others manufacture other random items in addition to skateboards to stay afloat.

· Vision signs a licensing agreement with Tom Sims to market Sims skateboards.

· Tracker debuts the Lapper, the first truck form-fitting plastic anti-hang-up device, which spawns many imitators.

· Gullwing makes a comeback as one of the top three truck brands through heavy marketing, truck design improvements, and rebuilding their team with top riders like Chris Miller, Jeff Phillips, Mark "Gator" Rogowski and Billy Ruff.

· In July, *Skateboarder* changes its name to *Skateboarder's Action Now*, and eventually to just *Action Now*, and begins to focus on a variety of action sports like BMX, motocross, surfing, etc. in order to widen the magazine's appeal outside the dying skateboard market.

· DEVO films a video for their song "Freedom of Choice" featuring David Andrecht, Eddie Elguera and other top pros ripping Marina Skatepark.

· The Gold Cup Series takes over where the Hester Series left off, holding super-intense contests at skateparks all over Southern California, including Oasis, The Big O, Colton, Marina and Upland. Eddie Elguera wins the pro overall while Billy Ruff sweeps am.

· Steve Caballero blows minds with the Caballaerial (fakie 360 Ollie) on vertical.

· Upcoming talent includes Carabeth Burnside, Steve Caballero, Scott Foss, John Gibson, Jami Godfrey, Jim Gray, Roger Hickey, Duane Peters, Steve Rocco, Jay Smith and Mike Smith.

1981 · Skateboarding enters the middle of a deep underground phase. After the demise of *Skateboarder*, skaters everywhere heap hate and ridicule upon its successor, *Action Now*. Even a TV show called *AN on TV* doesn't help. In response, Independent's Fausto Vitello and NHS's Rich Novak launch *Thrasher* to address the lack of a dedicated skateboard magazine in the marketplace. Due to the sport's economic downturn, *Thrasher* starts off as a black and white newsprint rag, a step down in quality that *Skateboarder* is unwilling to take.

· *Thrasher* inspires skateboarders to create their own homemade photocopied skate zines, which explode in popularity over the next few years. Some prominent titles include *Bend*, *Karmaboarder*, *Powerhouse*, *Skate Fate*, *Skate Punk*, *Skate Scene*, *Swank* and many more.

· A $49.95 complete skateboard called the Jammer keeps NHS (Santa Cruz) and Independent going through the downturn, while Tracker manufactures mechanical beds on the side to stay afloat.

· A form of punk rock for skateboarders, skate rock begins to appear, pioneered by bands like The Big Boys, JFA and the Faction.

· Upcoming talent includes Neil Blender, Tony Hawk, Christian Hosoi, Allen Losi, Tony Magnusson, Lance Mountain, Billy Ruff, Bob Serafin and Kevin Staab.

1982 · After their February 1982 issue, *Action Now* magazine ceases publication.

· *Thrasher* publishes their infamous "Skate and Destroy" article by CR Stecyk III and an Independent ad featuring a naked girl with Indy stickers on her nipples. After *Thrasher* refuses to run a counterpoint article called "Skate and Create" written by Tracker co-founder Larry Balma's sidekick, Tracker Peggy Cozens, the latter launch *TransWorld Skateboarding* bi-monthly the following May to portray a more positive side of skateboarding. Starting with its first issue, *TWS* sports glossy paper and a full color cover, and promotes skateboarding from around the world.

Allen Losi powers through one of his burly stand-up grinds during a huge contest at Del Mar Skate Ranch in Del Mar, California, May 1986. Photo: Tod Swank

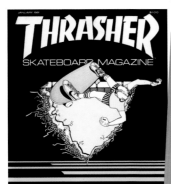

• Titus Dittman launches *Monster* skateboard magazine in Germany. Later, his Munster Monster Mastership becomes Europe's largest skateboard contest.
• A tribute to a photographer who passed away, the Rusty Harris Series includes vert contests at Upland, Whittier and Del Mar.
• On the cover of *Thrasher*, Rodney Mullen debuts the flatground Ollie, which will go on to have a profound impact on street skating a few years later.
• Upcoming talent includes Lester Kasai, Keith Meek, Chris Miller, Rodney Mullen, Jeff Phillips and Mark Rogowski.

1983 • By now, almost all of the 1970s skateparks are closed and 'dozed except for Del Mar and Upland in California and Kona in Florida.
• The first backyard ramp contest, The Great Desert Ramp Battle, goes down in Palmdale, California. Steve Caballero takes the first place trophy.
• Small versions of vertical halfpipes called mini-ramps begin to appear. Typically, they feature eight-foot transitions cut off at six feet with metal pipe coping and ample flat bottom.
• Powell-Peralta releases Bones Swiss bearings, which have been the gold standard ever since.
• Stacy Peralta produces an unreleased short film called *Skateboarding in the '80s*, a precursor to the first official Powell-Peralta video, *The Bones Brigade Video Show*.
• *Thrasher* debuts the first street skating contest at Golden Gate Park in San Francisco. Tommy Guerrero claims the top spot.
• The ASPO Series goes belly up.
• The MESS Series debuts in the Midwest as the first backyard ramp series.
• Channel handplants become popular on vert ramps.
• Upcoming talent includes Jeff Grosso, Tommy Guerrero, Craig Johnson, Eric Nash, Monty Nolder, Rob Roskopp and Steve Steadham.

1984 • Airwalk debuts and becomes one of the biggest selling skateboard shoe brands of the decade.
• *TransWorld Skateboarding* hires David Carson as art director to give the mag a much-needed facelift. In the '90s, Carson goes on to be a world famous graphic designer for *Ray Gun* magazine, Nike, Pepsi, Armani, etc.
• In June, *Thrasher* prints its first four-color cover.
• Stacy Peralta and CR Stecyk III pioneer the first skateboard video, Powell-Peralta's *The Bones Bri-*

gade Video Show, which helps to promote the sport to a whole new generation of kids.
• Frank Hawk launches the National Skateboard Association and the California Amateur Skateboard League, which will go on to organize many a contest series across the United States for years to come.
• Dozens of new manufacturers spring up in the industry. Mark Gonzales, Natas Kaupas and Tommy Guerrero take street skating to new heights, while Rodney Mullen dominates freestyle.
• Mike McGill sends shock waves through the skateboarding world when he unveils the McTwist (540) on vertical, which opens up aerials to multiple rotations for the first time.
• Upcoming talent includes Adrian Demain, Mark Gonzales, Claus Grabke, Tom Groholski, Natas Kaupas, Ken Park, Owen Nieder, Danny Webster and Dan Wilkes.

1985 • Skateboard shoes from Airwalk, Vans and Vision become hugely popular.
• Tracker debuts the first pro model street deck, the GSD.
• Blockhead markets a street deck with a four-inch nose, hinting at the popsicle sticks to come in the '90s.
• Skate Rags is launched by Mike McGill, Rex King, Peggy Cozens and Larry Balma. First offering padded skate shorts, the brand expands into casual skate clothing.
• Chris Miller suffers one of the gnarliest slams ever after he locks up on a backside air into the corner at Upland's Combi Pool.
• Lance Mountain sets the tail of his skateboard on fire and wins the Terror at Tahoe backyard ramp contest.
• Mark Gonzales blows minds by using Rodney Mullen's flatground Ollie to jump up onto benches and over sidewalk gaps.
• Tony Hawk one-ups Mike McGill's McTwist (540) with the McHawk (720), which inspires an arcade video game of the same name, 720, in 1986.
• Upcoming talent includes Steve Claar, Bill Danforth, Steve Douglas, Nicky Guerrero, Jason Jessee, Jeff Kendall, Jesse Martinez, Allen Midgett and Buck Smith.

1986 • Known as the Big Five, Powell-Peralta, Vision/Sims, Santa Cruz, Tracker and Independent grow to be the biggest brands in the industry. Board royalties and contest winnings escalate, netting some pros as much as $10,000 per month.
• Christian Hosoi designs a new hammerhead-shaped skateboard, which inspires a plethora of crazy deck shapes throughout the late '80s, culminating in the Mark Lake Nightmare and the Schmitt Stix Saw Blade.
• etnies Footwear is launched by French footwear company Rautereau Apple. Converse, which had been a popular skateboard shoe in the 1960s, sponsors Christian Hosoi and Rodney Mullen.
• Vision launches its own apparel line called Vision Street Wear, which becomes popular worldwide.
• Chip Morton launches a line of super baggy drawstring pants called Limpies, which starts a worldwide fad.
• Held at the Expo 86 World's Fair in Vancouver, Canada, the TransWorld Skateboard Championships are the first truly international skateboarding contest, bringing together pro and amateur skaters from 16 countries to compete in various events.
• While Christian Hosoi surprises the skateboarding world with his Christ and rocket airs, a myriad of lip

tricks enjoy a resurgence on vert.
• Street skating progresses with street plants, wall rides, launch ramps and fun boxes.
• Upcoming talent includes Mike Crescini, Ken Fillion, Reese Simpson and Mike Vallely.

1987 • After losing its insurance, Del Mar Skate Ranch gets bulldozed, ending a nine-year run.
• Mike McGill opens a skatepark consisting of wooden ramps built on top of the original Carlsbad skatepark, which was buried.
• Wooden bowls and ramps with round corners become popular, as do fish-shaped decks.
• A number of top skateboarders and former pros leave their sponsors to start their own skateboard companies. One example is Steve Rocco, who leaves Vision / Sims to launch the Rocco division of Skip Engblom's Santa Monica Airlines, which later turns into World Industries.
• etnies debuts the first pro model skateboard shoe, the Natas by Natas Kaupas. The Vans Steve Caballero model follows soon.
• In their December issue, *TransWorld Skateboarding* publishes "From Hands That Bite," the first survey of fine art (as opposed to comic strips) produced by skate-

boarders. In the '90s, numerous art galleries and magazines follow suit, mounting shows by Ed Templeton, Chris Johanson and many others.
• Powell-Peralta's *The Search for Animal Chin* video introduces the first combo / spine vert ramp. Spines go on to become a very popular feature on mini-ramps; the video, featuring a cheesy plot and acting, becomes a cult classic.
• Mark Gonzales stuns the skateboarding world with an Ollie boardslide down a handrail, the first handrail move that singlehandedly creates the future course of street skating for decades to come.
• Indy nose-picks and various other front truck tricks

Above: *Thrasher*, **January 1981.** Drawing: Kevin Thatcher
TransWorld Skateboarding, **May-June 1983.** Photo: Frank Hawk. **The first Powell-Peralta video.**
Jimi Scott and Steve Saiz enjoy a little launch ramp madness, circa 1987. Photo: Jim Goodrich
Left: **A G&S Neil Blender Coffee Break deck, circa 1986.**

on mini-ramps and vert become popular.
• Upcoming talent includes Bod Boyle, Randy Colvin, Jeff Hartsel, Jeff Hedges, Andy Howell, Scott Oster, Bryan Pennington, Steve Saiz, Ben Schroeder, Julian Stranger and Sergie Ventura.

1988 • Island Water Sports opens the United States' first skateboard camp in St. Louis, Missouri.
• Larry Balma and George Powell donate two Powell-Peralta skateboards with Tracker Trucks and Bones wheels to a permanent exhibit at the Smithsonian's National Museum of American History. These are the first skateboards in the Smithsonian.
• After existing for years as homemade toys, fingerboards are marketed by various skateboard brands, predating Tech Deck by a decade.
• The inventor of Makaha skateboards and the kicktail—both in the 1960s—Larry Stevenson launches *Poweredge* magazine as an alternative to *Thrasher* and *TransWorld Skateboarding*.
• H-Street premieres *Shackle Me Not*, which influences many other start-ups to produce their own hand-held low-fi skateboard videos.
• The first mini-ramp contest goes down at Richmond Skate Ranch in Vancouver, Canada.
• Street skating becomes more technical with kickflip variations like Jason Lee's 360 flip.
• Upcoming talent includes Ron Allen, Ray Barbee, Blaze Blouin, Matt Hensley, Frankie Hill, Tom Knox, Bucky Lasek, Jason Lee, Danny Sar-

gent, Chet Thomas and Danny Way.

1989 • After 12 years of service, Upland Pipeline skatepark gets bulldozed, ending a long list of '70s skateparks to fall under the blade.
• In business since 1970, the Woodward gymnastics camp in Pennsylvania opens a skateboard camp.
• Mini-ramps with spines pop up everywhere.
• World Industries debuts the Mike Vallely barnyard skateboard, the first double kick deck since a few tiny ones in the mid '70s, which paves the way for the popsicle stick era of street skating. Mark Gonzales launches Blind skateboards, backed by World.
• Tod Swank starts Foundation Super Co. and later Tum Yeto.
• After six years of bi-monthly publication, *TransWorld Skateboarding* goes monthly with its August issue and launches *TransWorld Skateboarding Business*, an industry-only newspaper
• Santa Cruz releases their *Streets on Fire* video, featuring Natas Kaupas' legendary Ollie to fire hyrdrant spin.
• A Hollywood-backed movie centered around skateboarding called *Gleaming the Cube* is released, starring Christian Slater and featuring the shred sled skills of Tony Hawk, Mike McGill, Rodney Mullen and Mark Rogowski. Stacy Peralta is the second-unit director.
• Upcoming talent includes Sal Barbier, Ron Chatman, Buster Halterman, Omar Hassan, Jeremy Klein, Alphonzo Rawls and Ed Templeton.

John Gibson presides over one of an endless stream of huge vert ramp contests that went down in backyards and homegrown wooden skateparks throughout the 1980s. Shut Up and Skate, Houston, Texas, 1986. Photo: Grant Brittain
Inset: When he Ollied onto a handrail for the first time in 1987, Mark Gonzales broke through a barrier that opened the floodgates to modern street skating. Photo: O

One of the founders of the street plant craze of the mid 1980s, Mike Vallely stands one tall out in front of the United States Capital, Washington DC, 1988.
Photo: O

181

TRACKER
LAPPER
The Lap of Luxury (1980)

In 1980, Tracker unleashed a new product called the Lapper, a plastic anti-hang-up device that facilitated many curb hop, fakie rock, lip slide and other re-entry maneuvers. The Lapper was originally inspired by a simple, crude metal bar skateboarders bolted onto the bottom of their decks that ran up at a 45-degree angle and fastened under the truck's kingpin nut. This type of device was marketed under the name Lip Slider. An-

Tracker, and marched him straight over to the Lapper station—right after an all-night red eye—for the first of many an eight-hour shift. "I felt like I was in purgatory. I didn't understand what I was being punished for," claims GSD. Two years later, Buddy Carr learned the process from Pierre André Senizergues on his first day on the job, and Bryan Ridgeway put in some hard time on the Lapper press, too.

The Tracker Coper could only be used on Tracker Trucks, but the Lapper would fit on any brand of skateboard truck, thus Lapper sales soared throughout the first half of the '80s. Many imitators appeared, including a direct knock-off called The Bird. By 1988, we finally built an injection mold that produced a beautiful Lapper without all of the tedious labor. Then, as the use of Copers became uncool and looked down upon as cheating, the Lapper followed suit. Longer noses on skateboards facilitated re-entry over the coping during lip tricks, and Ollies up curbs became commonplace, rendering the

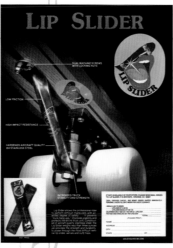

other version called the Clyde Slide, named after Florida skater Clyde Rogers, was fashioned out of a huge piece of PVC pipe. Both of these unwieldy designs appeared around 1977, along with many others. Tracker co-founder Dave Dominy and I knew we could come up with something simpler, lighter and more functional. Although some of the Tracker Lapper prototypes were pretty clunky, Dave and the team put them to the test, and the shape and design evolved and improved during this process. The final design of the Tracker Lapper was held in place by two of the rear truck mounting bolts; there was no need to bolt it into the bottom of the deck. The Lapper extended up snugly over the rear of the truck, and perfectly covered the kingpin stud and nut.

Each Lapper was die-cut from a high-density polyethylene sheet, warmed in a small toaster oven (!) until it was soft, then clamped into a custom press. We formed the curves into 12 Lappers at a time, and, as each one cooled, we dropped it into a barrel of cold water to hold its shape. (Since Tracker was in a huge amount of debt during Lapper development, we simply didn't have the money to pay for expensive injection molds.) The Lapper press and packaging station was the entry-level job at Tracker. When GSD moved from San Jose, California down to Oceanside to work at Tracker in May 1983, the shop foreman picked him up from the Greyhound bus station at 7:00 a.m., drove him to

Lapper obsolete overnight. In fact, the first sample run of injection-molded Lappers came out right when Lapper sales died off, so none were ever shipped. Unfortunately, we had to scrap the expensive molds, and throw thousands of pre-existing packaged Lappers and Copers into a huge dumpster bound for the landfill. No more lap of luxury!—**GSD + LMB**

Ray Underhill puzzles all onlookers with an obscure move called the ice plant to fakie during a contest at Del Mar Skate Ranch in Del Mar, California, circa 1985. Photo: Grant Britain

Opposite page, center, left to right: **Stacy Peralta enthusiastically shows off his homemade lip slide helper, circa 1977.** Photo: Jim Goodrich. The Lip Slider, July 1978.

Mike McGill brandishes a Clyde Slide at Clearwater Skatepark in Clearwater, Florida, circa 1979. Photo: Jim Goodrich

Boasting another variation on the lip slide device, Christian Hosoi blasts an Ollie out of the Brown Bowls at Marina Skatepark in Marina del Rey, California, June 1980.
Photo: Ted Terrebonne

Opposite page, bottom: **An original clamp from the Tracker Lapper press of the 1980s. Unfortunately, the jig that held the Lappers in place got dismantled and tossed during one of Tracker's moves.**

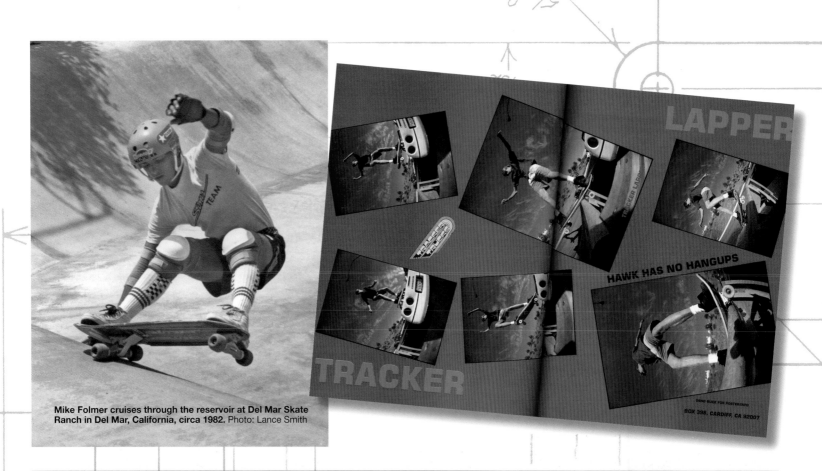

Mike Folmer cruises through the reservoir at Del Mar Skate Ranch in Del Mar, California, circa 1982. Photo: Lance Smith

LAPPER

HAWK HAS NO HANGUPS

TRACKER

BOX 398, CARDIFF, CA 92007

Above right and below: **Tony Hawk stars in a two-page spread ad for the Tracker Lapper, plus an out take, December 1987.** "One of my funniest Tracker memories was when Larry Balma drove over to my house, because he thought Lapper sales were slacking and said, 'We've got to do an ad with a Lapper.' He had this state-of-the-art Corvette, and he asked, 'How about if you do a street plant on my Corvette, then hang up on it?' As a skater, I knew that just wouldn't work at all. But, I thought it was a hilarious idea. 'First of all, I'm going to trash your car. Secondly, you can't really make that.' I didn't know how that would highlight the Lapper anyway. So, Larry brought his car to my house, and I figured I could Ollie off the trunk of the car into my jump ramp, hang up on the jump ramp, and come in with a Lapper. That actually worked pretty well, as cheesy as it seems now."—Tony Hawk Photos: Miki Vuckovich

CORVETTE

Top left: **An elusive injection-molded Tracker Lapper, circa 1988. Only a few samples were ever produced.** Above: **A youthful Tony Hawk winds his way around the keyhole at Del Mar Skate Ranch in Del Mar, California, circa 1981, as a Tracker 777 complete looms above.** Photos: Unknown

185

TRACKER DECKS

777, 757, 707 (1980s)

After the Rockit Skateboards debacle back in 1976 (see page 86), we decided by 1980 that enough years had passed, so it was high time for us to make skateboard decks again, this time directly under the Tracker brand. Dubbed the 777 and 757, our first two Tracker decks' names were borrowed from Boeing aircraft of the same designations. 777 and 757 also happened to be the deck length in millimeters. The Tracker 777 and 757 debuted during a low point in the economy and near the bottom of the second commercial downturn of skateboarding. Measuring in at 30 5/8" long and 10 1/2" wide, the Tracker 777 was made of a seven-ply hard rock maple laminate dyed one color. We kept the price point as low as possible by avoiding pro endorsements, and by decorating the deck with a simple, one-color silk-screened graphic designed by Tracker artist Chuck Edwall. Although the first version of the 777 was flat, the second run featured a new concave in the front half. The concave added strength to the deck and offered more wheel clearance, so wheel wells were only necessary on the rear truck. But, we added front wheel wells later anyway, just for shits and giggles. At 18 degrees, the kicktail on the 777 was steeper than most decks of the day.

In January 1980, *Skateboarder* magazine ran an article called "Curb Grinding and Other Joys," which offered up the first-ever coverage of a new phenomenon called street skating. Although skateboarding originally started in the streets in the early to mid 20th century, street skating as we know it today—skating on objects—first began around 1979. Launched together in 1980 with the Tracker 777, the 757 was our first street deck. This versatile shred sled was a more traditional skate-anywhere design, but not really a vert board by 1980 standards. Measuring in at 757 mm, 29 3/4" long and 9" wide with a 15 degree kicktail, the 757 boasted a flat deck and wheel wells front and rear. Later versions sported concave and grew to 9 1/2" wide.

The 757 graphics featured a vanishing checkerboard supporting a Tracker 757 road sign. In 1983, we dropped the checkerboard pattern and left the road sign, which was augmented with some colorful paint splatters. After work, I would lay out a bunch of 757 decks on the floor of the Tracker factory,

Above left: **A beauty shot of the Tracker 777 and 757 decks, circa 1980.**
Left: **A rare photo of Dave Dominy, Larry Balma and Chuck Edwall silk-screening Chuck's graphics onto a bunch of Tracker 777 decks, circa 1980.** Photo: Unknown

Tony Magnusson pilots a Tracker 777 prototype deck high above the coping of the keyhole at Del Mar Skate Ranch in Del Mar, California, circa 1982. Photo: Grant Brittain
Below right: The two Tracker 777 decks with graphics designed by Chuck Edwall, circa 1980-'81.
Opposite page, left to right, top to bottom: Two different Tracker 757 deck graphics, circa early 1980s.
Neil Blender shows off some one-off hand-drawn Tracker 757 graphics, circa 1984. Photo: Grant Brittain
A chrome ball incident involving the Tracker 757—a board graphics concept drawn by Neil Blender that was never used, circa 1983.
In the early '80s, Neil Blender's main street deck was the Tracker 757. Here he throws out an Ollie on one at Sadlands in Anaheim, California, circa 1983. Photo: Jim Goodrich

WISE UP!
Choose the Tracker System for yourself

TRACKER ★

THE TRACKER SYSTEM
includes 5 widths to fit your style, Copers™ and Lappers™ to protect your investment and more to fine tune. Tracker, P.O. Box 398, Cardiff-by-the-Sea, CA 92007, 714-438-7722.

THE TRACKER DECKS
STREET WISE 757
POOL WISE 777 concave

Ray "Bones" Rodriguez, October 1981.

crank up some Led Zeppelin and splatter a wide variety of paint colors on them Jackson Pollack style! No two 757 decks ever looked exactly the same. My dad, Maurice, Tracker Peggy and GSD were also known to splatter a few from time to time! An ardent fan of the 757, Neil Blender could often be seen riding this deck on the street. He even hand-drew some 757 graphics on one of his personal decks.

The shortest deck in the series, the Tracker 707 was just 27 3/4" long and 8" wide with a 15 degree kicktail and wheel wells front and rear. Tested by a few Tracker team riders circa 1983, the 707 was never released for sale to the public, as it was simply considered too small. It's a shame, too, because mini-versions of pro model decks for little kids became all the rage just a few years later. During development of the 707, Neil Blender doodled a couple of graphic concepts for the deck, which GSD kept for safekeeping in his collection for three decades. That blew away all of us. Today, Neil makes a living off of his art, and since we had a few boxes of new old stock 707 decks from 1983 collecting dust in the warehouse, we decided to team up with him to produce a very limited-edition run available through Kickstarter. Unfortunately, only a few very lucky collectors got their grubby hands on one!—**LMB**

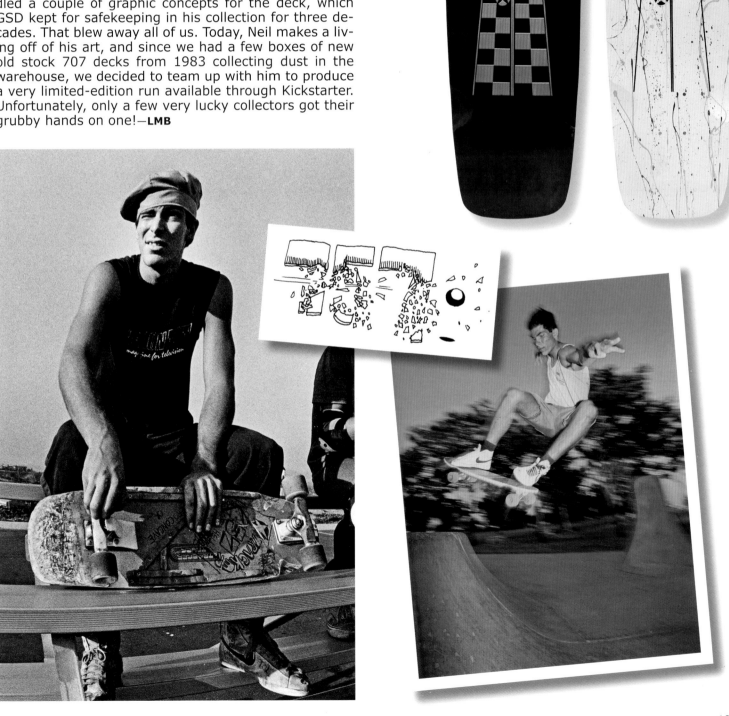

Mike McGill, December 1981.

Mike Folmer, January 1982.

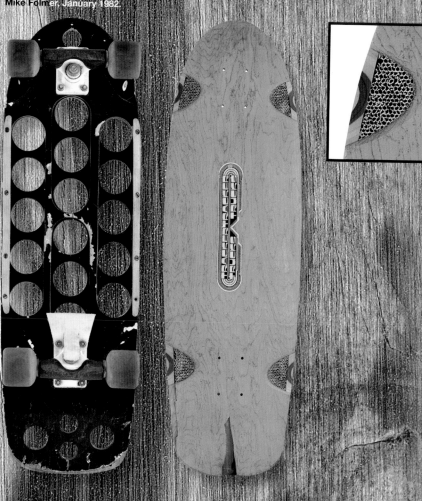

NEIL BLENDER-^{TEAM}G&S AND TRACKER

SEND FOR A BROCHURE, 2 FREE FULL COLOR GLOSSY PICTURES AND 2 FREE STICKERS.
PLEASE ENCLOSE 75¢ POSTAGE & HANDLING.
TRACKER TRUCKS P.O. BOX 398, CARDIFF-BY-THE-SEA, CA 92007 714-438-7722.

Neil Blender, May 1982.

Right: The ultra rare Tracker 707 deck that never went into full production. Only one short run of 48 of these 707 decks was manufactured back in 1983, only to have someone decide the deck was too small. The graphic idea submitted by Neil Blender (above) was never silk-screened onto them, and the project was literally shelved. In 2014, Neil re-worked the graphics (right), which were promptly screened onto the original 48 decks and offered to rabid collectors.

Bottom row across whole spread, left to right: One of three aluminum decks designed and made by Rohr, an aerospace company, circa early 1980s. Machined out of solid 1/2" aluminum alloy, each of these decks weighed only two pounds! (A seven-ply maple deck of the same size weighed three pounds.) NASA actually sent one of these aluminum decks on a Space Shuttle mission, for which it was outfitted with Tracker Sixtrack mags and skinny wheels so the astronauts could belly board back and forth on a track through the cramped and cluttered cargo bay.

Two experimental seven-ply maple decks with multiple large drilled holes for weight reduction.

Another seven-ply maple deck with a layer of aluminum honeycomb added for weight reduction.

The Tracker Alarm Clock, Screaming Flower and Street Specimen were cruiser boards shaped by Peter Kiss, circa 1989-'90. Artwork on the former was drawn by Dean Kegler, the latter two by Rick Froberg, who did graphic design work for Tracker and *TransWorld Skateboarding* back in the early '90s. Rick is best known for his guitar and vocal work in the bands Pitchfork, Drive Like Jehu, Hot Snakes and Obitz.

Below: Rick Froberg cruises on a longboard behind the offices of *TransWorld Skateboarding* in Oceanside, California, circa early 1990s. Photo: Unknown

What Do these three skaters have in common?

Answer: **TRACKER TRUCKS**

Box 398, Cardiff-by-the-Sea, Ca 92007

Good Grief, circa 1983, Auckland, New Zealand.

CHECK 'EM OUT!

Skate Attack, issue 9, December 1983, Cincinnati, Ohio.

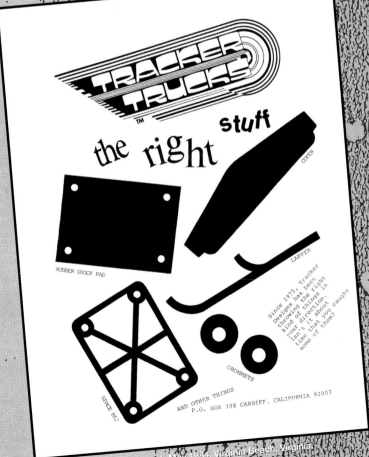

TRACKER TRUCKS ™

the right **stuff**

COPER

RUBBER SHOCK PAD

LAPPER

Since 1975, Tracker Designs has been throwing the right kind of things in your direction. Isn't it about time that you caught some of them?

GROMMETS

SPACE PAD

AND OTHER THINGS
P.O. BOX 398 CARDIFF, CALIFORNIA 92007

Kamikaze, Volume 1 Number 1, May, 1984, Virginia Beach, Virginia.

Air, issue 2, circa 1984, Solana Beach, California.

TRACKER
ZINE ADS
Advertising Alternatives (1980s)

The word zine is short for magazine. A zine is a small, humble, homemade publication usually printed on a photocopy machine. At the beginning of the 1980s, during skateboarding's second depression, the full-color *Skateboarder* magazine died off, soon to be replaced by a black and white newsprint called *Thrasher*. In their June 1981 issue, *Thrasher* ran an editorial that encouraged skateboarders to document their own scenes via the "do it yourself" approach. Soon, Xerox machines were humming from coast to coast, resulting in an explosion of homemade photocopied skate zines. Tracker ads frequently appeared in these publications, and although most of them were unofficial and unapproved, we really liked the homegrown feel, which served as a nice contrast to our professionally designed ads. By the mid '80s—fueled by the backyard ramp revolution and the maturation of street skating with the Ollie—skateboarding lifted off into its hugest phase of popularity thus far. *TransWorld Skateboarding*, which launched in 1983 as a full-color glossy, inspired *Thrasher* and later *Poweredge* to step up their games. Despite this general commercial upsurge, the homemade skate zine scene continued to expand exponentially with dozens of titles. There was a base underbelly of skateboarding that needed exposure, and homemade zines filled in this gap nicely with no nods at all to advertisers, parents or authority. As the '80s wound down, skate zines appeared less frequently until, by 1990, the scene became but a small murmur of its former glorious self. The time had come for the old vert and street pros of the '80s to step aside for a new breed of young street technicians. As the world of flip tricks, handrails and gaps inspired little in the way of homegrown photocopied napkins, the focus turned to high-quality magazines full of sharp sequences and, especially, videos to document the ever-increasing complexity of modern street skating. By the mid-1990s, a vast majority of the nutty zines of the previous decade had all but disappeared.—**GSD**

Death Zone, circa 1985, Gutersloh, West Germany.

Bail, issue 1, circa 1984, San Jose, California.

TRACKER

WHITE

BLACK

SEND DOLLAR

BOX 398   CARDIFF, CA. 92007   (619) 722-1455

Tracker Man, December 1985.
194

TRACKER **MAN**
Offspring of a Genie (1985)

Ah, the mid 20th century: advertising's goofy age, a time when enormous, campy character statues were deployed in front of businesses to attract customers driving by. As new homes popped up all over the Los Angeles basin to house the largest influx of residents ever to hit California, this burgeoning population, dubbed the baby boomers, needed carpet for their new homes. Serving their needs was a familiar sight all over the southland: a chain store called Carpeteria that opened in 1960. Towering 25 feet tall, their mascot, the Carpeteria Genie, hoisted the store's name high aloft on upstretched arms, beckoning potential customers to enter its shaggy lair. Fast-forward 40 years. By the time the 2000s rolled around, the company had filed for bankruptcy, and most of the Genies had all but disappeared, taking off on a magic carpet ride somewhere.

Inspired by the Carpeteria Genie, the Tracker Man logo was conceived and designed in 1985 by artist CR Stecyk III, who was best known for his corrosive articles and photos in *Skateboarder* magazine in the '70s, and his ad and graphic work for Powell-Peralta in the '80s. Craig's vision was to create a pre-Columbian-style man holding up the Tracker logo similar to the Genie. His finished design for the Tracker Man logo portrayed a symbol of strength with historical roots, which was a powerful metaphor for Tracker. Craig is a master at invoking meaning using symbols without a need for words.

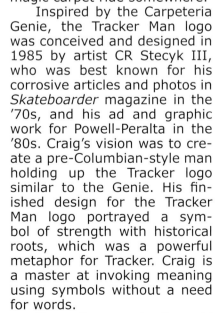

One afternoon in the mid '80s, I was riding the Amtrak train between Oceanside and Los Angeles when I happened to pass by the sign company that built the Carpeteria Genies! There they were, standing tall against a building next to some railroad tracks somewhere in Santa Ana. I picked out landmarks so that I would be able to drive back at a later date to track down the exact location so I could buy one of the Genies. It took me a whole day to weave my way around Santa Ana until I finally found the sign company. I gave them my sales pitch, and after several letters and phone calls, I signed a release to purchase one. In subsequent years, the Genie appeared in several Tracker and Invisible ads and videos, and on Fuel TV. I still have it today, partially dismantled out in my avocado grove in East Oceanside.—**LMB + GSD**

Above: **CR Stecyk III rolls on through skateboarding's first Dark Ages, 1967.**
Below: **Stecyk portrait, 2014.**
Opposite page: **Stecyk with surfboard, circa 1970s.** All photos courtesy of the CR Stecyk III archives.

By Larry Balma + GSD

it into the Skateboarding Hall of Fame, which was an honor, and in my speech I figured I had to tell the truth about how I started skating. So, I apologized to my cousin for stealing her skates back in the day and playing it off like I didn't. She did eventually get to be Miss Texas, so her luck turned out good.

As our addiction grew, we scoured roller rink trash cans looking for broken shoe skates. Alleys provided fence planks and old drawer fronts to harvest for decks. The cobbled together boards were then ridden and traded. Mark Richards was the first guy I ever saw who assembled and sold skateboards in a retail environment. He started Val Surf, the first multi-brand off the beach surf shop. Around the same time, Larry Stevenson launched Makaha, Vita Pakt did Hobie Super Surfer while surf shops like Greg Noll, Gordon and Smith, Jack's, Gordie and Dewey Weber were also doing it.

The first commercial skateboard I ever possessed came from Stevenson. He was a lifeguard who founded Makaha and *Surf Guide* magazine and promoted the Surf Fair. Larry later also patented the kicktail. I benefited in that I was granted a local boy's de facto sponsorship by him. Of course, I in turn would give boards to my friends. I had a lot of Malibu cartel surf associates, and would pass boards along to individuals like Jamie Budge, Denny "River Rat" Waller and Miki Dora. Larry would occasionally observe, "Where are all of your skateboards going?" and I'd offer up some inane excuse, but Stevenson was a savvy fellow and he knew what

CR Stecyk III is skateboarding's Wizard of Oz, a mysterious puppet master behind the curtain, pulling the strings, guiding skateboarding in myriad ways over the decades. Stecyk is a walking encyclopedia of the "sport," and throughout the 1970s, '80s and beyond, his hidden influence was, and is, far-reaching. A surfer, skateboarder and artist since the late '50s, Stecyk co-founded Zephyr surfboards and skateboards with Jeff Ho and Skip Engblom in 1968. He got his start in publishing in 1975, penning a series of highly influential articles in *Skateboarder* magazine about the Dogtown scene, in which he sprinkled bits of arcane knowledge into his intellectual, stream-of-consciousness rants. After *Skateboarder* died in 1980, Stecyk wrote for *Thrasher* at the same time he designed ads for Tracker Trucks, two very different outfits run by rivals. Few others ever pulled off anything like that. Stecyk's raw "Skate and Destroy" article in *Thrasher* caused Tracker to launch a whole new magazine called *TransWorld Skateboarding* just so they could publish a clean cut rebuttal called "Skate and Create." Employing his eccentric conceptual art background, Stecyk also played a major role in the creative direction of Powell-Peralta, one of the most important brands of the '80s. He named their team the Bones Brigade, and produced the first skateboard video, *The Bones Brigade Video Show*, with Stacy Peralta. They followed that up in 2001 with the documentary *Dogtown and Z-*

Boys. As if all of that were not enough, Stecyk is also co-founder of *Juxtapoz* art magazine, and one of his hand-painted surfboards is in the permanent collection of the Smithsonian. As of 2014, you can find CR Stecyk III doing graphic art work for Hurley, where he sat down with us surrounded by his psychedelic hand-printed posters to record the epic interview that follows.—GSD

LMB: Where are you from?
Ocean Park, California, which is a district located between Santa Monica and Venice.
LMB: Did you surf before you skated?
I grew up in a surfing community. The first people I knew who skated were surfers, so it was always intertwined for me. I had a scooter before I had a skateboard, but I didn't really know what to do with it until I surfed proficiently. When I started in 1958, they still called it "sidewalk surfing."
LMB: What was your first good skateboard?
(Laughs) Are there bad skateboards? Well, you're supposed to say the project with your dad where you make the fruit crate scooter with steel skates nailed onto a wooden 2" x 4". In the beginning, I'd go up on the hill, ride down, try to turn, and one day the box came off. It's been downhill ever since. After that auspicious beginning, my Machiavellian chicanery led to me stealing roller skates from girls, prying off the truck assemblies and putting them on my boards. Those transgressions put me in this tortured afterlife. My version of Hades is the Devil interviewing me about skateboarding. I made

was up. The Hilton Brothers were located just up the beach and they were the nucleus of the Hobie team. Baby Dave Rochlen did time as the Makaha and Hobie team manager, and he later scored me a 500 mm Takumar telephoto lens in Japan that I still use. The world champion, Danny Bearer, was in my kindergarten class. Squeak Blank was on my Little League team. I ran with Steve Hilton all through high school, and still see him. I knew Torger Johnson, the Saenz Brothers, Johnny Freis, Jimmy Fitzpatrick, Ray Flores,

CR Stecyk III
INTERVIEW

Cris Dawson, Coleen Huff, Jimmy Ganzer and Woody Woodward. What of the industry that evolved? The Logans were stalwarts on the Makaha team. Skipper Boy Engblom used to brand the Makaha Phil Edwards models in the factory. Jeff Ho worked for Roberts in Playa del Rey and Weber. The Hurley brothers laid up skateboards for Wayne Brown. Ned "Bones" Evans rode eight-wheeled Dewey Webers. Herbie Fletcher carved concrete for Jack Haley. It just goes on and on. Its origins date back to the 1930s, when ancestral types like Indian Jack Quigg rode cut-down doors with roller skate wheels on them down the Santa Monica hills. La Jolla had a booming sidewalk surfing scene in the '40s. Ask around, there were a lot of surfers who seriously skated. Carl Ekstrom, John Van Hammersveld, George Downing, Mike Doyle, Phil Edwards, Butch Van Artsdalen, Joey Cabell, John Severson, Skip Frye, Miki Dora and David Nuuhiwa are all people I encountered around skateboarding in those dark ages.

In the '70s, there was Roller Sports back in Florida, and we'd seen their urethane wheels at rinks. Cris Dawson was riding precision bearing Roller Sports on the street. Your buddy Frank Nasworthy started putting the Cadillac imprint on urethane rink wheels and marketing them for skateboarding, which was a brilliant call. We were all using old Chicago or Sure Grip trucks. There was a good eight-year period after skateboarding went out of fashion in the late '60s. That was the most fun period for me, because there were thousands of skateboards to be had for free. You didn't have to do anything, just pick 'em up and ride. Once the urethane and the Bahne extruded fiberglass boards hit, things blew up. Jeff Ho, Kent Sherwood, Jay Adams and myself laid out the contours for the Zephyr flexible fiberglass board on the curb on Main Street in Ocean Park. The team were the neighborhood kids. It was like that everywhere with people spontaneously trying to innovate.

GSD: Who was the first person you heard of skate a pool?
I know about 300 people who claim they were the first person to skate a pool. And they're probably all telling the truth, as they see it.

GSD: So, everyone has a different story.
Yeah, Herbie Fletcher skated in the Airport pool. He'll show you a photo of it. Gary Swanson skated his dad's pool in Bel Air and hosted sessions. Jimmy O'Mahoney lipped the Olympic Pool in Exposition Park. Danny Bearer rode the Bird Bath. All of the guys I

mentioned previously skated pools before anyone else they knew of had done it. The last person who ever skates a pool is the guy you want to find.

LMB: Why was Tracker so important in the history of skateboarding?
It's hard to realize there was a period when there were no products engineered specifically for skateboarding. For many, Tracker was the first successful truck designed by skaters for skateboarding. Tracker survived. There may have been some other people who thought they had designed a viable truck, but their products didn't hang around long enough to impact. Many early skateboard trucks were thinly disguised Chicago or Sure Grip trucks. Most of those guys went out of business. Tracker was one of the first companies to come out that was run by skaters, and they also stayed in the business and contributed to how the activity developed. Mr. Bennett had a truck.

LMB: Did he ever skate?
I don't think Ron Bennett skated, but he was constantly proclaiming his own genius. Rich Novak and Doug Haut certainly surfed and skated. You've got to give NHS and those guys credit as they have had great success, but truck-wise they came in as a manufacturer a little later. Tracker trucks looked like Tracker trucks from the beginning, and you could use them to do a lot of things. The first Independent was an amazing spring suspension truck, and they later they evolved them from slalom into the vert and street market. Original Independent trucks with the springs are hard to find. Slalom guys still love those trucks. A vastly avant-garde suspension truck was the ultra rare Stroker. Salamini designed it, and Fausto Vitello and Eric Swenson engineered and brought it to market. They were so adept, that they subsequently became involved with several other truck brands like Independent, Venture, and Thunder.

LMB: What do you remember from your time around Tracker?
The most storied Trackers were the magnesium ones. There was a voodoo atelier aspect to their creation. They were outside of the box and technically adroit, right up to that decisive explosive moment.

LMB: I've been known to grind a few to this day.
A magnesium fire is the worst industrial disaster to deal with. Balma, you used to warn me about magnesium fires, then one day, I had one of my own. Total engulfment happened in seconds, it was beyond belief how hot that thing burned. Taking a fire extinguisher or spraying water on it only increased the flames. Magnesium fires are pretty radical.

LMB: Magnesium is the bright white stuff that explodes out of fireworks.
I worked another major magnesium fire down by the 5 freeway that burned for a couple of days. Intensely bright white flames went up for at least a hundred feet and super-heated mag hot rod wheels shot up into the air like rockets. Any fireman will tell you

a magnesium fire is one of the worst kinds to fight in terms of it being ultra hot, plus the constant threat of explosion. It's the real deal. So, it's little wonder that the Tracker mags are so highly sought after by collectors.

LMB: You designed Tracker ads for 10 years. Do you have any favorites?
I can't remember anything prior to last Sunday, so I'd have to see them. Tracker was an interesting group to work for, because they were open ended. There wasn't any censorship to speak of, other than the great Tracker Peggy, who monitored everything. Luckily, she didn't have anything to do with what I worked on.

LMB: She didn't censor the Crutch Sweeper ad. She performed in it.
Yeah, she was the old lady in the Crutch Sweeper ad, which was interesting, because she was viewed as the moral barometer for modern skateboarding, going back to her legendary "BE GOOD, BE GOOD" campaign in the inaugural issue of *TransWorld Skateboarding*. That admonition was influenced by an Independent ad featuring a naked girl with Indy stickers covering her nipples. There

was a rumor that I knew that girl, but how could I tell? She was wearing sunglasses.

GSD: Which Powell-Peralta ads that you worked on stand out as favorites?
(Laughs) Any one that George Powell participated in would be my favorite. You should go talk to George. He's in the middle of writing an 800-page book. We once burned a Cadillac in his mother's front yard in Bel Air. That was good fun. We drove the car up and torched it. Ray Bones, Stacy, Cris Dawson and I all knew what was going on, but I don't know if George ever told his mom we were going to burn it in her chic front yard. It was a case of spontaneous combustion. To his credit, George went over and calmed the hysteria. Being the quarterback at Hollywood High School in his youth, he was a leader of men.

GSD: Did you ever get arrested by the skating policeman?
(Laughs) I know several of them. I am acquainted with several LAPD officers right now who skate. I don't know if they would say on the record that we're friends. But, we get along pretty well.

LMB: So, your dad supplied vehicles to custom car builder George Barris. Was

your dad an artist? Where did your creative genes come from?

Yeah, my dad worked at the Ford motor company and was in business with George Barris. My mother was an artist. She had a ceramic studio in back of the house and we lived in an artistic community. I think that was part of it. My father was a photographer and he was big on modified cars. Our house had clay tools, kilns, spray guns, welding equipment and sanders—everything you needed to make cars, skateboards, surfboards or artwork. In our neighborhood, a lot of guys fixed up cars. I grew up in the middle of all of that.

LMB: When did you first meet Ed Roth?

Ed Roth knew my father, so I was around Big Daddy from when I was young. He was always a venerated figure. Pops had a business with George Barris who had a shop called Kustom City in Lynwood, where Von Dutch was employed at various times. Roth had his shop over in Maywood. Gene Winfield, Ed Iskenderian, Dean Moon, Jocko Johnson, Dean Jeffries, Gil Ayala, Vic Edelbrock…that was the scene my pater inhabited. Robert Williams and his wife Suzanne also worked for Ed Roth and were integral people on *Choppers* magazine. They're very good friends of mine to this day. I did projects with Ed later on. I was lucky to be around all of those guys. Years later, I curated museum shows which had Roth, Barris, Von Dutch and the Williams twins in them.

LMB: You were pretty out there with your art and stories. When did that begin? In high school?

My uncle ran a bar. In the European tradition, wine was served with meals. Socialization and oratory were part of everyday life. There were a lot of parties filled with interesting people, so that's probably where the stories came from.

GSD: When did you first start having art shows in galleries?

In 1966, at Immaculate Heart College, if you're talking about a piece of something called art with your name on it being presented. I'm confused about what art is. I don't even know what I like.

GSD: For your art piece Road Rash, you skinned a dead animal, bronzed its innards, stuck the pelt back on and glued it to a roadway like some kind of macabre speed bump. Who or what inspired those kinds of site-specific art works?

You get to do whatever you want to do in this life. Everyone is doing what they want to, whether they admit it or not. I was raised around tools, we didn't have much money and I wasn't very motivated in terms of getting a job, because I thought it would take me off the beach. The ocean was interesting to me, so I got a job as a rental raft wrangler for Ely's Beach Rental at Santa Monica Pier, which meant I got to keep my surfboard there for free. So, I didn't have to carry my board around and was well situated to hustle tips from the tourists. The gig was that I would go pick up the mats after hours from the people who rented them. And the other gentleman in the enterprise down at the Ocean Park Pier to the south was Jay Adams' stepfather, Kent Sherwood. I knew Kent from when we both worked at Dave Sweet Surfboards. So, I would go down there and wrangle the rafts, and that's how it worked. Art is just another aspect of human enterprise. You look for the lost floating raft on the ocean's surface while the sun sinks on the horizon. And when you find it, you epoxy it to the surface of a freeway on ramp.

LMB: Did Sherwood design aircraft?

Later in his career, Kent was recognized by the United States government for his unique ability to precision form foam structures. Kent's done well and holds a number of patents. He designed the wings of the Pegasus missile. It traveled six times the speed of sound and they described it as essentially being built with surfboard technology. So, Kent and I worked for Dave Sweet, who was the first guy to make foam surfboards in a modern manner, meaning polyurethane foam surfboards shaped to order. He sold them when the other people in the industry were still using balsa wood. I grew up around Kent, and was involved with Jay Adams since he was three. I knew Jay for over 50 years.

LMB: Describe Jay as a skater.

(Laughs) Jay never changed as a skater. He was always completely extemporaneous, interactively changing up stuff. Adams would never do the same thing twice. That was the beautiful thing about Jay, he lived life to the fullest because he had to do it that way. He didn't have a choice. Even when he screwed up, there was an honest beauty to it. He was magnificently remarkable. Jay never whined or never complained.

LMB: It seemed like he always pushed as hard as he could push, no matter what.

Kent Sherwood grew up in Waikiki and raised Jay like he was a Hawaiian kid. Adams was absolutely immersed into water sports from the time of his birth.

LMB: What about Dogtown? Do you have anything to say about the Zephyr days?

Ah, the Zephyr days. Every town's got its wit and wisdom, its glory and gore. Ocean Park, Santa Monica and Venice were no different. We just reflected it as it happened around us.

Bryan Ridgeway: Back to your artwork, what influenced it? What triggered you to have such a great understanding of your surroundings?

That's a well-thought out question. I grew up at the end of Route 66, which was a famous road that started in Chicago, went across America and ended up at Santa Monica beach. I watched people come down that road and run down to the ocean. Some of them couldn't swim very good, if at all. Bad outcomes awaited the unprepared. The first time you help pull a dead body out of the ocean, it changes you. So, you learn to watch your surroundings, because it makes sense. At Santa Monica pier, there was a hill we skated down, and if you didn't turn at the bottom, you'd hit the railing and go in the ocean. Learning where the suicide cracks were in an old wooden pier was an essential survival skill. If you got off your line while skateboarding down a hill on clay wheels, you'd dag into those pier pits on the side. So, you had to pay attention, that's all.

LMB: What was that story about you and a bomb?

That was a sculpture that looked like a Soviet bomb, which they discovered at Santa

Monica beach. Fortunately, I was able to defuse it and get it out of there before it hurt anybody. If you can't risk a bomb for the rest of humanity, what kind of artist are you? Or if you have a really bad aesthetic idea, why not go dump it in the ocean and say it's art?

LMB: How old were you when you pulled that stunt?
Seventeen. There was a hotel magnate who had a large mansion on Sorrento Beach who believed that a Russian torpedo-like weapon had showed up submerged in his swimming pool, but we were unable to verify that.

LMB: You and Stacy were an amazing marketing duo. Do you still do research at Disneyland?
I still have a pass to Disneyland. There was a two-year time period when I ran my entire life from a bench there on Main Street. I'd show up every day, pay my way in, and go sit on the bench, take my pathetic phone calls and draw on napkins. Being at the Magic Kingdom every day, it seemed like I was eventually gonna learn something. My belief was that I was just this anonymous guy in the Magic Kingdom. But, I guess the park employees noticed me. One day, I was there during a severe downpour. It was a magnificently dreary and depressing day. So, I decided I'd go into the Snow White ride, which was a little kid ride that I'd never been on. There was absolutely nobody there. So, I'd ride around, get off and go back to the beginning of the empty line area and get on it again. I was the only guy riding it. I repeated this cycle about 10 times. Finally, the woman who was operating the ride said, "You know, you can stay in your seat and not move." So, I sat there and rode the Snow White ride and tried to discover what I could learn from it. It was a dark ride, so there's not much in there. Hours later, they stopped the ride and I thought, "The park must be closing." But all of the kids who ran the ride brought out a little cupcake with a plastic Snow White statue and a burning candle on it, and said, "You have ridden this ride more than anyone in the history of the park, and we want to thank you." Since they were so kind, I stayed on the ride until the park closed, because I realized they thought I was a special person. It would hurt their feelings if they discovered I was just a cynical guy trying to stay out of the rain.

LMB: So, back to you and Stacy. In 1984, you guys rented a video camera, made the first skateboard video, _The Bones Brigade Video Show_, and helped relaunch skateboarding. Do you still film?
Yeah, I film all the time just for myself. If my movies show in a cultural institution, people say I'm an art guy. But, if I film while I'm riding the Snow White ride, they'll say I'm intellectually lacking.

GSD: Have you ever launched a magazine?
Having not learned from the _Swindle_, _Thrasher_, _TWS_ or the _Surfer's Journal_ and _Rodder's Journal_ crews, all of whom had launched magazines, I did foolishly participate in launching _Juxtapoz_, an art magazine.

GSD: Why was it foolish?
It's far more fun to read magazines than to make 'em.

GSD: Was it fun to read _Breakout_?
Wow, _Breakout_ magazine! Kevin Kinnear.

LMB: When _Breakout_ went out of business, a plumbing company took over their office and lined the front window with porcelain toilets.

I would have liked to have seen that.

GSD: You said _Breakout_ was the most boring magazine of all time.
It's telling that I once said _Breakout_ was the most boring magazine of all time, then later did not even remember that I ever said it (everyone laughs). The hubris of youth. It could have been my mentor, the great thespian John Barleycorn, who inspired me to say these outlandish things. Fortunately, the meds they have me on now make me placid.

GSD: Do you still write the Trash column in _Thrasher_?
No, I stopped writing that years ago and have no idea what goes on there. I've contributed to different magazines over the years with no malicious intent or reasonable thought. It would be inaccurate to say I've ever written anything, because I was not paying attention the entire time I was doing it, so it couldn't be called writing in the traditional sense. I don't participate in the running of any magazine or determine editorial content.

GSD: Do you still have your collection of _Skateboarder_ and _Thrasher_ magazines and hand-painted surfboards, skateboards, and other stuff you worked on

over the decades?
No, those were parting gifts to girls who appeared on the old _Stecyk Variety Show_. I don't save a lot of stuff. Here's a funny story: All of the women in my life at one point decided I needed to clean up the piles of old skateboards I owned. I argued, "These things are going to be valuable someday." Mom said, "Nope, son. Get that shit out of here." So, I filled five 50-gallon oil drums with skateboards—pretty much all of them were excellent examples. I put them out in front of the house with the trash truck coming down the street. A minute later, I was driving down Ocean Park Boulevard and saw Jay Adams. He said, "I'm going to start collecting skateboards. Do you have any old ones?" I told him that he was in luck and that they were out in front of my mother's house. So, he ran up there, but the garbage men had already passed by and the drums were all empty.

LMB: That tells me you didn't learn anything from the Dave Sweet factory experience.
When Dave Sweet decided he was going out of business, he had hundreds of new and

used surfboards. Dave was uber-focused on his new radio-controlled glider wing business. They call those long mission tactical drones now. Sweet's business outlook changed overnight and he instructed me to dispose of all of the shop surfboards. So, suddenly, I had 500 of them. All I could think of to do with them was take a sledgehammer and break off the fins so we could fit more of them in the back of the trash truck to take to the dump.

Jim Gray: You didn't realize your retirement fund was right in front of you.
Instead, I chose to break pine fin Phils and red fin Hynsons into small, useless bits. It was a savage frenzy, and I loved every moment of it. We laughed at Dave's obsession for those gliders, but if you look at what the world is doing now, he was pretty far ahead of the game.

LMB: What have been the highlights of your time in skateboarding?
Anything that is driven by gravity is a good thing to do. Skateboarding is an accessible sport, as you can do it pretty much anywhere. So, I was never bored skateboarding. Skateboarders are successful on the planet because they're the kind of people who make their own entertainment. You can go anywhere in the world and skate. That's the reason skateboarding doesn't go away, and the reason people keep doing it.

LMB: So, tell us about your spot here.
We're in an anonymous room at Hurley in Costa Mesa, California, making prints. This is the Printing Press, which is an open atelier program that allows the public to print using letterpress, serigraph, thermal printing and hand technology. They also have similar programs here for audio production, video production and surfboard shaping.

GSD: Do you sell these prints?
Nothing here is for sale. I just make prints and put 'em up on telephone polls. I've printed thousands of 'em. I don't know if that has made the world better or worse.

JG: More interesting.
Well, it gets you through the day.

BR: In _Butch Cassidy and the Sundance Kid_, Paul Newman said, "I have vision, while the rest of the world is wearing bifocals." What did he mean by that?
Paul Newman started a food company and gives back all of the profits to charity every year, which was a pretty good vision. _Butch_ is a Hollywood film, and you can't believe anything you see in the movies. I think people are all the same. Some are more interesting than others, and some approach things differently than others. Ed Roth, who was a significant cultural exponent, and built a lot of cars and also changed media in many different ways, claimed that the only people who advance things are the one-percenters. He said the one-percenters are the people who get it, and 99 percent of the people don't get it. Roth believed that there are some high-performing people in the upper five percent, but the one-percenters are the ones who change everything. Ed claimed you don't have a choice. You do what you do, and if you're a one-percenter*, it'll be the right thing.

Opposite page, top to bottom: **Stecyk straddles a hog, circa 1970s, and poses with his hand-printed posters at Hurley, 2014.** Photo: Grant Brittain
Above: **Stecyk installs one of his Road Rash speed bumps, circa 1980s.** Photos courtesy of the CR Stecyk III archives, except as noted.
*Not to be confused with Wall Street one-percenters!

Tony Hawk, August 1986.

Sick of Heavy Trucks? May 1983.

John Gibson, October 1986.
200

Duralite Baseplate, February 1990.

Tony Hawk, October 1986.

ULTRA LIGHT

BOX 398, CARDIFF, CA 92007, 619 · 722 · 1455
Send $1.00 for system specs, stickers and foto folder.

Ultralight, September 1983.

TRACKER
BASEPLATES
Let's Touch Base (1977-2007)

By the time we marketed our line of Gnarly Tracker Trucks in 1978, our aluminum baseplate had gone through five evolutions. The first baseplates had a kingpin hole drilled all the way through, in which we screwed a grade 8 kingpin using Loctite to keep it in place. We soon changed it by drilling a blind hole that our custom formed grade 8 kingpin would die into using the Loctite once again. Even though our kingpins were stronger than the grade 5 kingpins that most skateboard trucks used, ours could still snap under extreme loads. The hanger of the first generation Gnarlys had a narrow kingpin slot that could bind on the kingpin with enough leverage to cause it to snap at the baseplate. Skateboarders snapping kingpins on other trucks were used to pounding them out and pushing in a new kingpin bolt from the underside of the base, so by 1983, we modified our baseplates to accept grade 8 kingpin bolts. Our counterbored hole allowed the kingpin to be pressed into the aluminum without the need for Loctite. The bolts, which were actually cheaper than our earlier custom kingpins, were stronger because there were no threads where the bolt emerged from the cushion boss. The bonus to our skaters was that they knew if they ever did experience a kingpin failure, they would be able to replace it themselves. Today, Tracker aluminum baseplates always come with removable kingpins. Newer design evolutions have produced even stronger and lighter aluminum baseplates.

In 1977, Tracker began design and development using polymers as a substitute for the base metals used in truck manufacture. Gary Dodds purchased an injection-molding sample machine to add to our prototype shop in Sorrento Valley. Other companies had used plastics because of their ease of manufacturability and lower cost, which resulted in parts that were much weaker and cheaper than aluminum trucks. Tracker, on the other hand, was more interested in developing a baseplate that would be much lighter and stronger than aluminum or magnesium. Through years of testing, we found out that there was no commercially available plastic that could meet these requirements. The material had to be tough enough to withstand the punishment of curb grinds, ditch transitions, six-foot high aerials and harsh landings. After four years of testing, finally some mad chemist locked away in an underground laboratory somewhere worked with ultra-light, high-impact

Baseplate Evolution

1975 - small pivot top

1975 - small pivot bottom

1978 - Gnarly top

1978 - Gnarly bottom

1978 - magnesium bottom

1979 - magnesium bottom

1982 - Vydynyte top

1982 - Vydynyte bottom

1983 - pressed kingpin

1983 - mag pressed kingpin

1986 - Vydynyte top

1986 - Vydynyte bottom

1988 - carbon graphite top

1988 - carbon graphite bottom

1990 - Aggro Quicktrack top

1990 - Aggro Quicktrack bottom

1991 - Aggro Street Track top

1991 - Aggro Street Track bot

1992 - B-52 top

1992 - B-52 bottom

1995 - B2 top

1995 - B2 bottom

1996 - Hawk top

1996 - Hawk bottom

1999 - Dart top

1999 - Dart bottom

1999 - Axis top

1999 - Axis bottom

2002 - Racetrack X top

2002 - Racetrack S top

plastics for use in the aerospace industry, only to invent a new super polyamide compound called Vydynyte. A select group of Tracker pro riders thrashed this new compound for a year and a half before it passed the test for quality, durability and performance. In 1982, Tracker released the first generation of the Tracker Ultralite baseplate, which was 52% lighter than magnesium and 65% lighter than aluminum.

The design of the first Ultralite baseplate copied the shape of our aluminum casting. Since riders who rode their trucks extremely tight noticed some flex in the base and the kingpin, I got out the clay and began to design ribs to strengthen it. Gary Dodds offered his engineering expertise as he went to work on a new mold that added more structural ribs and strengthened the entire base—especially the cushion boss. The result was a completely new Ultralite base that performed extremely well, although it still flexed a bit. Later, in a third evolution, we added even more ribs. Our production of Ultralite trucks grew from 2,000 per month in 1982 to over 40,000 per month in 1988. Our total production of Trackers, including the all-aluminum trucks, was over 60,000 trucks per month. Every month, we sampled new materials and, by 1988, we had perfected an elastomeric compound containing carbon graphite fiber that was bulletproof and did not flex at all. This new carbon graphite base, called the Duralite, could not be molded in the wide variety of colors we were used to, thus it was offered only in satin black. Since our competitors pushed aluminum baseplates so hard in their ads, and we couldn't convince consumers that the Duralite baseplate didn't flex, we were forced to stop the production of it in 1991 and go all aluminum with our new trucks, the Tracker Aggro Quicktrack and Aggro Street Track.—**LMB**

Above: **Omar Hassan guides a 5-0 to the promised land, circa 1991.** Photo: Unknown
Below left: **Kyle Jensen gives the keyhole's coping a workout at Del Mar Skate Ranch in Del Mar, California, circa 1979.** Photo: Lance Smith
Below right: **From 2007, the Tracker Fastrack baseplate is longer than all other Tracker baseplates.**
Opposite page: **Notes on Tracker Trucks Baseplate Evolution.** From 1978 on, all baseplates were built for Gnarly pivots, including post-1989 ones, even though they weren't advertised as Gnarly. Due to occasional breakage, a bar was added to the magnesium baseplate in 1979 for strength. Magnesium is lighter than aluminum but is also more brittle. We made kingpins replaceable in all metal baseplates from 1983 on. The 1988 carbon graphite baseplate was marketed as the Duralite. Although we designed a few prototype baseplates that never went into production that we couldn't fit here, you can see one for the Tracker B52 E-Clip Floater on page 262. You may wonder why we didn't show the bottom of the Racetrack baseplates. Well, the bottom of the Racetrack X baseplate is the same as the Axis, but with six holes; and the bottom of the Racetrack S baseplate is the same as the Hawk, but with six holes.

2007 - Fastrack

PATTERN
RECOGNITION
Larry Balma Gets Schooled in the Fine Art of Pattern Making (1980s-1990s)

Over the years, we at Tracker have always made improvements, both big and small, to our truck designs based on input from our team riders. For example, when we made them wider, we designed stronger wings on the cushion ring. Changes like these required alterations to the master patterns. By 1985, Tracker co-founder and pattern maker Gary Dodds was too busy with his new company, Tri-Industries, molding all of our composite parts, as well as parts for other industries, to build our master patterns. So, I began working with a retired pattern maker in Valley Center, California until he passed on. Pattern makers are few and far between, as California is not friendly to the foundry trade because of the toxic emissions created by smelting metals and pouring it into molds. In the early '90s, I met a pattern maker in Los Angeles named Jerome Selseth, and we immediately forged a friendship. (Ha-ha! Get it? Forged!) Over the next several years, Jerome mentored me on a weekly basis until I became a pattern maker myself! Although I was already a journeyman machinist, building master patterns and molds was quite challenging, as it requires knowledge of draft angles, cope and drag, metal flow characteristics and shrinkage. It's all very complex, and you always have to think in three dimensions in both negative and positive, so there's always some trial and error. But, I love a challenge, and love working with my hands and machines, so I consider it very rewarding to be able to create a product from inception to production. Throughout the '90s and '00s, I was able to design many new Tracker Trucks from start to finish, even some that we never produced, while also designing trucks for for brands like Orion, Ruckus, Mercury, Torch and others.—**LMB**

Left: **Craftsman and master pattern maker Jerome Selseth kept the evolution of Tracker Trucks rolling along efficiently for 25 years while he taught me his trade.** Spread: **Here we have 40 years' worth of Tracker master patterns and molds displayed on my 4500-pound granite surface plate. Granite is the most stable material on earth. It does not stretch or warp, and the surface is ground flat to within 1/10,000 of an inch from one corner to the other. Every master pattern begins life on a surface plate. The 1971 Lamborghini Muira S in the background sits in my workshop as a design inspiration.**

PLAY IT!

Lou's Records in Encinitas carries all the latest sounds. Ask for the FLIP SIDE at your record store or most any quality skateboard shop. Freestyle to music just for fun.
PER HOLKNEKT has exquisite taste in his ladies, his music, his cars, and of course his skate equipment.

That's why Per rides Tracker products.

Quality & Performance = FUN!

Send $1.50 for Tracker folder, sticker, brochure and Flipside sticker

619·722·1455

TRACKER, BOX 398, CARDIFF-BY-THE-SEA, CA 92007

TRACKER FLIPSIDE
Freestyle Deck (1982)

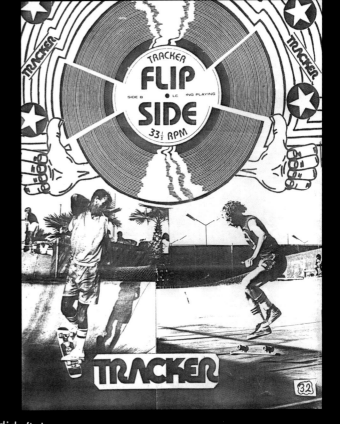

Measuring 26 1/8" long and 7" wide with a 4 7/8" flat nose and a 5 1/8" slight kicktail, the Flipside was Tracker's first freestyle deck. Although it was 666 mm long, we just couldn't bring ourselves to call it the 666. Tony Magnusson and Per Holknekt rode the prototypes and skateboarder / artist Pete Finlan came up with the original graphics, which featured a vinyl LP record that he airbrushed by hand onto every deck. After a short while, custom airbrushing every deck became too costly, so Tracker graphic artist Jamie Briggs drew up a line art version of Finlan's design that we could easily silk-screen. At some point, we gave pro freestyler Per Holknekt his very own colorway of the Flipside featuring his signature on a red or black deck with a gold record.

"Flipside" was a term that radio station DJs used to identify the song on the back side of a 45 rpm hit single record, which had just one song on each side. Popular from the 1950s through the '70s, the single, which measured 7", was slightly larger than a CD or DVD, which didn't become popular until the '80s and '90s respectively. Perfect for DJs and jukeboxes, singles were also inexpensive, which contributed to their popularity. We actually used a 12" LP record size for our Flipside graphics, since singles were on the decline. Still to this day, some discerning music aficionados prefer the warm sound of analog vinyl records to the digital sound of our modern age. The name Flipside was also a double entendre, as flip tricks had become popular with freestylers who were thinking up new moves all the time. Tony Hawk was the first to take flip tricks to vert, and a bit later, street skaters applied them to obstacles. Throughout the '80s, Tracker was one of only a few companies that cared about freestyle skating. We even gave a pro model deck to French freestyler Jean Marc Vaissette, who went on to form V7 Distribution with his father. —**LMB**

Top right: **A Tracker Flipside ad in *Go For It* zine starring Shane Rouse and Per Holknekt, circa 1983. Bottom row, left to right: A rare Tracker Flipside deck airbrushed by Pete Finlan, a silk-screened Flipside production deck and a Per Holknekt pro version, all circa early 1980s. A Tracker Jean Marc Vaissette pro model, circa 1986.**

The first time I ever rode a skateboard was around 1973 in Cincinnati, Ohio, where I grew up. I was 10 years old. I stood on a friend's 2" x 4" with metal roller skate wheels nailed on and awkwardly wobbled down the sidewalk on a little hill in front of his house. I only skated that one day and never set foot on a skateboard—or even thought of one again—until a few years later. I started skateboarding for real in May 1976, when my friend Ray Coombs got a plastic Grentec board for his birthday and brought it down to my house. The first deck I ever built myself consisted of a sheet of masonite pegboard glued to a slab of scrap wood, which I named the Hot Dog Shark. After painting the Hot Dog Shark logo on the bottom and mounting the trucks and wheels, I stood on it and, not surprisingly, the middle of the deck sagged to the ground. I'm sure it shattered not long after. The Hot Dog Shark was the best thing ever. After that, I went through a long line of decks. Although a couple of them were name brands like a Bruce Logan model by Logan Earth Ski in late 1976 and a Steve Caballero model by Powell-Peralta in 1981, most of the decks I thrashed were home made.

The first, called Sun Skates, were Sims Taperkick-inspired decks made by my friend Dave Gibson. Unlike

TRACKER
GSD DECK
First Pro Street Model (1985)

the Sims Taperkick, however, Sun Skates did not have a ply of maple running through the center to keep the horizontally laminated hardwood strips from separating under the stresses of skating. By 1978, laminated seven-ply maple decks became popular and took over skateboarding. So, Dave and I started making Sun Skates out of that. After he moved to California, I continued making Sun Skates for the next couple of years.

Around 1981, I started drawing new, non-Sun Skates graphics on my decks. I remember painting this one bright yellow with a big, red Tyrannosaurus on the bottom. That was the first-ever dinosaur graphic I drew, which is surprising, since I loved dinosaurs since third grade. After moving to San Jose, California in summer 1982, I relocated to the North San Diego County area in May 1983 and began working at Tracker and *TransWorld Skateboarding* magazine. In 1984, after cutting out a slew of non-descript handmade shapes, I made a fictitious pro model deck for a cartoon character of mine named Kent Watson. This deck measured 9 3/8" x 30" and gradually curved inward on the sides going

Opposite page: **The Crutch Sweeper ad was another one of CR Stecyk III's brilliant ideas. He talked Tracker Peggy Cozens into dressing up like a little old lady and instructed GSD to knock her over with a well-placed Bert. There's nothing like a little slapstick comedy to brighten your day! June 1983.**
Bottom row, left to right: GSD's homemade Kent Watson deck, circa 1984, plus a complete collection of Tracker GSD decks including the Eyeball from 1985, Pterodactyl from 1987, Airplane Safety from 1988 and Fish from 1989.

GSD, July 1985.

back toward the tail, abruptly curving out just before the rise of the kick—giving the overall shape the vague appearance of a bomb. I spray painted the deck yellow, then stenciled and magic markered on a simple eyeball graphic with cartoony lettering in white and blue—all topped off with Kent's signature at the bottom. I made the Kent Watson deck mainly because I thought it would be pretty fun and funny to skate around on a pro model for a pro that didn't even exist. I ended up riding it for quite a few months.

The following year, Tracker, who I had been sponsored by since 1982, asked me if I wanted a pro model. Who would say no to such an offer? I quickly shrunk down the Kent Watson shape a bit to 9" x 29 1/2" and refined the eyeball graphic, replacing Kent Watson's name with my initials, GSD, in the same cartoony lettering, all supported by a Tracker logo that I designed exclusively for this deck, plus the words "Banks / Curbs" and my signature. As it turned out, the GSD became the first-ever signature model street deck.

In 1986, I changed my graphics with an enlarged, close-up photo of part of my face covered with drawings of pterodactyls flying around, which was inspired by my lifelong love of prehistoric life. Since fish shapes were becoming all the rage, I completely re-designed the GSD model into more of a fish shape in 1987 with a really pointy nose and pointy tail corners. Back in the '80s, it was really important for each pro model shape to be quite different from the others. My 1987 graphics were inspired by the drawings inside an airplane safety pamphlet, which I saw quite often, as I flew to a lot of contests in those years.

1988 brought one more graphic change on the fish-shaped GSD deck: a rough line drawing of, appropriately, a fish spanning the entire bottom of the board. My pro model fizzled away sometime the following year without much fanfare. Throughout the '90s to the present day, I've always ridden whatever decks I could get for free. As for the future, I've been thinking about making some unusual-shaped decks with hand-painted graphics for cruising around on, but I don't know if I'll ever make the time to do it. Maybe someday my life will come full circle and I'll once again find myself putting the finishing touches on another Hot Dog Shark. Hopefully, the new one won't sag all the way to the ground.—GSD

Top left: **GSD boosts his trick, the hazard, out of the reservoir at Del Mar Skate Ranch in Del Mar, California, circa 1983. The hazard, which was a handplant / footplant combo, was one of several tricks that led up to the street plant craze of the mid '80s.** Photo: Grant Brittain
Left: **A GSD guest artist deck from Krooked, circa 2008, and two GSD tribute decks from Scum, circa 2011, and Pete's Pigs, circa 2013.**
Opposite page, bottom left: **GSD frontisde grinds the Fallbrook Ramp in Fallbrook, California on a prototype of his fish-shaped deck, circa 1987.** Photo: Grant Brittain
Opposite page, bottom right: **Russ Pope designed the shape and graphics on this GSD tribute deck for Transportation Unit, 2015.**

Under You, Near You, Around You, December 1986.

GSD, October 1988.

Maurice Balma, June 1989.

By Larry Balma

Born and raised in the Lone Star State, Dan Wilkes is known as one of the burly Texans, a group of hard-skating friends that includes such skateboarding legends as Jeff Phillips (RIP), John Gibson and Craig Johnson. Like GSD, Dan is a lifelong fan of dinosaurs, which inspired the two of them to festoon his two pro planks on Tracker with prehistoric life. Although the hearse that Dan drove back in the '80s may be history, his aspirin-damaged psychedelic zine, *THC*, lives on, as does his penchant for shredding apart any skatepark that gets in his way.—GSD

When, where and how did you start skateboarding?
I started skateboarding when I was about 10 years old. My next-door neighbor, Leo Mesack, who was retired (he was in his 70s), was an amazing woodworker. He built my first skateboard with a metal wheeled roller-skate that he cut in half and attached to the end of an apple crate. We put lime green shag carpet on it for traction. This all happened in Dallas, Texas.

When did you get your first Trackers?
My first set of Trackers, which were Fultracks, came from the Skateboard Shop at Valley View Mall in maybe 1976-'77. They were sold to me by Al Coker, who is still my friend to this day.

Who gave them to you?
My grandfather bought them for me. My whole family was very supportive of my skateboarding obsession.

Which Tracker Truck model did you ride most of the time?
Probably Sixtracks or Aggros, which I still ride!

During your time on Trackers, what stood out about their performance?
People always talked about quick turning (squirrelly), but I wanted smooth, solid, even turning. That is what has always stood out to me.

Why was Tracker so important in the history of skateboarding?
Tracker laid the groundwork everyone followed. Their designs still hold up today—that is what makes history.

Which Tracker riders influenced you? Who were the guys you looked up to?
Chris Strople, Tom Inouye and Stacy Peralta always influenced me with their flowing surf style, which was important to a landlocked Texan. (I live 300 miles away from the Gulf of Mexico!) I like Tony Alva now, but I didn't like him at all during his peak. The guys I look up to the most are my friends, the guys who push me to do something better, the guys I grew up skating with.

Did you invent any tricks on Trackers?
Ask Neil Blender where the ho-ho came from.

Tell us about some memorable times you had with the Tracker team.
The East Coast demo tours! Travelling from one mom and pop skate shop to another and just getting to skate with local kids was what I enjoyed the most. There is something about places that have harsh weather half the year that makes you appreciate skating

Above: **Dan Wilkes on the cover of** *Skateboard Plus* zine, February 1985.
Below left: : **A Tracker Dan Wilkes ad colored by Dan himself for his zine,** *THC*, circa mid 1980s.
Below: **A collection of Tracker Dan Wilkes decks** spanning from 1986-'88, plus a tribute from Cockfight, circa 2011.
Opposite page: **Dan Wilkes offers up a Tracker (mute) plant, circa 1987.** Photo: O

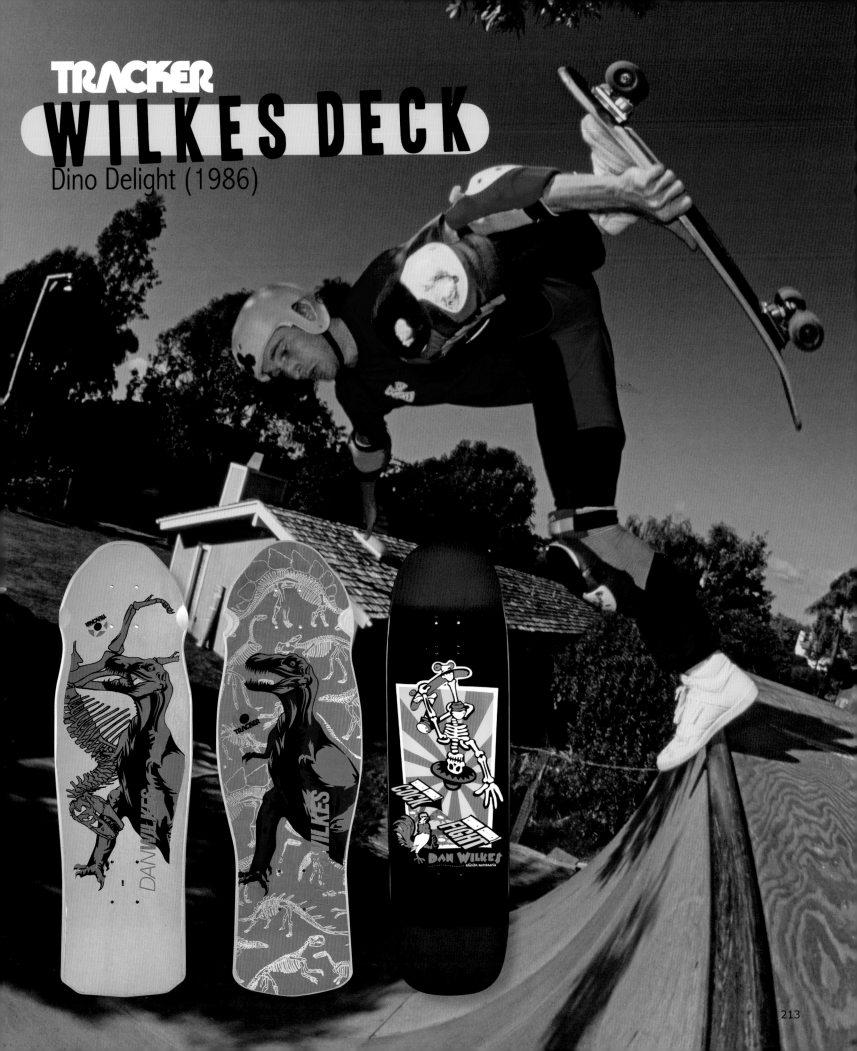

TRACKER
WILKES DECK
Dino Delight (1986)

more. I also remember skating with GSD in Dayton, Ohio on some Sadlands-type structures with snow on the ground.

Which Tracker ads were your favorites?
Non-skating: Jeff Phillips with the ski mask and Uzi. Skating: Me doing a mute footplant (who knew?) in the August 1988 *Thrasher*.

There was a Tracker ad featuring you dressed up in a caveman outfit, battling a dinosaur. Where was that shot?
The ad was shot at Dinosaur Valley State Park in Glen Rose, Texas. I still go there two or three times a year with my kids. It is an incredible place to bike, hike, and camp. The T-Rex holding my board in the ad came from the 1964 New York World's Fair before it was moved to Glen Rose. There's also a Bronto-saurus there. I have always been fascinated by dinosaurs and the Flintstones, and it just

seemed like a likely place for an ad, but I think Bryan Ridgeway might have pushed me into it.

How did you decide to have Tracker produce your deck model?
I actually started riding for Tracker thanks to Don Singer of Donel skateboard distributors and Stuart Singer's father. I worked at the Skateboard Shop where I got my first Trackers, then at Donel. I did well in local contest series and started travelling more with Jeff Newton of Zorlac. Newton was my first sponsor and everything else took off from there.

Did you request dinosaurs as your Tracker deck graphics, or did GSD foist them upon you?
Yes, Dinosaurs were always in the back of my mind. I even had a 777 deck with

a T-Rex on it. When I saw what GSD drew, I knew that was it. The original was slightly different, and I seem to remember a dino-saur doing a sweeper also. Garry's artwork has always amazed me.

Tell us about the Cadillac hearse.
Just like skateboarding, I have always had a passion for old cars, motorcycles, and scooters, mostly from a mechanical point of view. The hearse was a 1961 Miller-Meteor with a Cadillac 390 (first year). It was fun to travel around in and could carry about nine people, as the rollers in back for the coffins flipped over and turned into seating, but the gas mileage was a killer.

Back in the '80s, you made a zine called

Dan Wilkes, February 1988.

Dan Wilkes, February 1988.

Dan Wilkes, February 1988.

Dan Wilkes, December 1989.

Dan Wilkes, August 1988.

Dan Wilkes, June 1986.

THC. What inspired it? Is it true that you would intentionally not give a copy of every issue to any one person so no one would have a complete collection?

THC is still an ongoing experiment. It's not the THC (tetrahydrocannabinol) you think. It's just three letters with a different title each time: #1 *THC*, #2 *The Hallucination Continues*, #3 *The Hell Chronicle*, #4 *Texans Hate California*, #5 *Through Hypnotic Control*, #6 *Truly Harsh Contortions*, #7 *To Hallucinate Correctly*, #8 *Testing Heavy Currents*, #9 *Terribly Hideous Creatures*, #10 *The Helpful Computer*, # 11 *Typical Hypocritical Conclusion*, #12 *Time Has Come*, #13 unnamed as of yet. I gave copies (I made only 13 of each issue) to different people who knew others with a different issue. So, if you happen to have an issue, you do know someone else, besides me, with a different issue. You also know people with the same issue

who know people with different issues. *THC* was a subliminal social media experiment before its time.

Do you still skate today?
Yes, but not as much as I would like to, though. I still skate Texas, with its new resurgence of skateparks. I'll skate where ever I am and with whomever will put up with an old man snaking them!

Do you have any closing comments?
I am very lucky to have been part of Tracker's history, and I thoroughly enjoyed the time that I had with everyone at Tracker. It's like being part of an extended family.

Opposite page, clockwise from top left: **Dan Wilkes and his hearse, circa 1987.** Photo: Grant Brittain
Original line art for Dan Wilkes' first pro model deck on Tracker, and a t-shirt graphic, both drawn by GSD, circa 1986-'87.
Dan, channel eggplant, April 1986. Photo: Grant Brittain

FAVORITE DISH:
CHIPS-N-GUAC

MEAT TEAM MEMBER
BUDDY CARR
KEEPS 'EM BURNIN'

WHEELS XENO

CHOICE THANES

SEND A BUCK FOR A BUCKS WORTH OF MUCK TO: A-1 MEATS BOX 1262 OCEANSIDE, CA 92054

Back in 1973, the loose ball bearing cone nut set up used on skateboard wheels was cheap, but very difficult to install and adjust properly. The bearings were slow and dust would stick to the oiled bearing balls, causing them to wear down until they spit out as you were skating, which would seize up the wheel and make you slam. Sometimes, when your board started to slow down or vibrate at speed, you could look down and actually see the tiny ball bearings fly out. If you reacted quickly enough, you could run it out, as long as you weren't going faster than 15 mph. The precision bearing, pre-lubricated with dust seals installed, was another very important evolution to advance the sport of skateboarding. When Tracker co-founder Dave Dominy and I began our skateboard project in 1973, we set out to make precision bearing urethane wheels and new wider trucks. Dave coined the name Saturn Wheels for them. At the time, I had no experience working with plastics, and as it turned out, we had our hands full just building up the company to produce Tracker Trucks. So, we were forced to put the precision bearing wheel project on the back burner for a while. From 1974 to 1976, I was machining Stoker urethane wheels on a lathe to fit center set R8 sealed precision bearings for our slalom and downhill racers. The R8 bearings measured 1 1/8" or 28.575 mm on the outside diameter and 1/2" or 12.7 mm inside, and 8 mm wide. The 1/2" inside required me to machine a custom bearing sleeve / spacer that would fit over a 5/16" axle. Dave was working with Henry Laruccia of IDI-Power Paw wheels to develop our Tracker wheels. Henry made 4" diameter downhill wheels for Signal Hill that utilized our R8 bearings and spacers.

One day in 1976, Rich Novak and Jay Shuirman from NHS (Novak, Haut and Shuirman, a big distributor for Tracker Trucks) made a trip down to the Tracker factory in Sorrento Valley, San Diego, California and saw the Stoker precision bearing wheels that I was machining, along with some prototypes from IDI. At the same time, Rich and Jay had been secretly working on a precision bearing wheel with Creative Urethane, which they were just about ready to launch. Called the Road Rider, their wheel boasted a much smaller bearing called the 608, which had an almost 7/8" or 22 mm outside diameter and 5/16" or 8 mm inside, with a 7 mm width. Available in quantity, this bearing was very inexpensive, and contained a large enough inside diameter to slide over the axle without any special spacer. A much better solution for the everyday skateboarder, the 608 bearing is still in use today.

Rich and Jay freaked out that we

Stoker wheel

R8 bearing

608 bearing

TRACKER
WHEELS
Adventures in Urethane (1986)

were working on a precision bearing wheel. They convinced us, and rightly so, that it would screw up the market if there was more than one bearing size. They encouraged us to stick to building trucks and that NHS would make the wheels. They immediately released the OJ wheel, for which Tracker was the master distributor. Tracker advertised and shipped OJs by the truckload

for about six months until NHS started selling OJs directly to shops and successfully cut us out of the wheel business. Fast forward to 1986, when I partnered with Tracker pro skater Jim Gray to create a company called Brainstorm Designs. Jim's first project was to set up a wheel program for Tracker. Speed roller skater Tom Peterson left his position at Kryptonics wheels in Boulder, Colorado and moved to Huntington Beach, California to establish a new wheel company called Hyper Wheels. The first 'thanes we designed were called Tracker Ollie Wheels; we also launched Tracker Lester Marbles at the same time. Our initial order with Hyper was for 60,000 Ollies and 20,000 Marbles. We sold out of all of them in three weeks and had to reorder! By comparison, in 2014, a big first order of a new wheel may be 4,000 pieces.

By 1988, the Tracker brand had become so hot, we could sell anything with our name on it. The problem was to attract a team for the wheels. If a skater wasn't a Tracker truck rider, he probably wouldn't want to ride Tracker wheels. Marc Hostetter, who became the Tracker wheel program's product director, and Beau Brown re-

LESTER

MARBLES

61mm x 42mm

92A, 95A, 97A

6mm RADIUS

EDGES

CENTER SET

REVERSIBLE

Lester Kasai, August 1989.

Matt Hensley, September 1989.

Chuck Dinkins, October 1989.

Baird Bergenthal, Sal Barbier, January 1990.

Marc Hostetter, April 1989.

Baird Bergenthal, Tuan Nguyen, August 1989.

Making Wheels Important, January 1993.

ally whipped it into shape. We packaged Tracker Ollie wheels with our Ready-to-Shred-Kits, which contained trucks, wheels, bearings, space pads, a wrench and mounting hardware. After a while, we came up with Tracker Sex Wheels and eventually dropped the Tracker name off of the wheels entirely. At that point, we launched A1 Meats as our new wheel brand. That's when our wheel sales really blew up. At the dawn of the '90s, Marc Hostetter worked closely with our wheel team, many of whom were street skaters. He scored the hottest name of the day, Matt Hensley, to ride for A1 Meats, which put the brand over the top. In fact, in its prime, A1 Meats had over 100 team riders, including other legends like Kris Markovich, Sal Barbier, Mike Carrol, Kien Liu and Jason Dill. The most popular wheel that really grew A1 Meats was the King 55 mm, featuring graphics by Wrench Pilot artist Andy Jenkins. Around this time, our wheels became so sought after that one day Steve Rocco called Marc Hostetter to inquire about having us make World Industries wheels.

Since the Ollie maneuver had become the starting point of almost every street trick, and a low center of gravity made it easier to pop an Ollie and perform flip tricks, Marc started designing smaller and smaller wheels like the Nut Huggers, some of which were as tiny as 45 mm and even 38 mm! It wasn't long before the whole skateboard industry followed the trend. I met with Stacy Peralta and CR Stecyk III to discuss a problem with the tiny wheels: The small diameter worked well on a smooth, flat surface, but would not roll over a rough surface like asphalt with cracks. Street skaters would often skate a smooth spot, then pick up their boards and walk a block or two to the next smooth spot. As it turned out, the tiny wheels were killing the essence of street skating. By 1994, we agreed to increase diameters into the 50 to 60 mm range and promote the bigger wheels with our team riders and advertisements, which was definitely a healthy move for the future of skateboarding. Due to cash flow problems, we had to put our wheel program on hiatus a few times in the mid to late '90s so we could fund the deck brands Invisible, Neighborhood and Sixteen. However, since the early '00s, Tracker branded wheels have been back in the mix.—**LMB**

Above: **The Tracker Ready-to-Shred Kit was marketed mostly to sporting goods stores that didn't carry any components, circa 1989.**
Below: **Various large size Tracker and A1 Meats wheels, circa 1989-'90.**
Right: **Various small size A1 Meats wheels, circa early '90s.**

Adrian Demain vaults a lien air high over Lester Kasai at the Fallbrook Ramp in Fallbrook, California, circa 1988. Photo: Grant Brittain

MATT GOLDSBY
Mini-Ramp Ace
Vertical Speedster
McGill Skatepark Local
Day Dreamer

ADRIAN DEMAIN
Street Ripper
Mini-Ramp Rager
Vertical Flare Boy
Very Courteous

RICHARD SALAZAR
Pool Slasher
Sad Land Local
Stylish as heck
Likes the girl across
the street from
Lester's house.

WHEELS
LESTER "MARBLES"–97A
95A
92A

STUFF
T-SHIRTS
STICKERS

**HOUSE LINE
DECKS**
KASAI-FULL SIZE - 31½ x 10½
MINI - 29½ x 9½
DEMAIN-FULL SIZE - 31 x 10½
MINI - 29½ x 9¼
H.O.K. STREET - 31⅝ x 10

LESTER KASAI
Leader of the House
All Around Shredder
Arm Wrestler
Pool Shark
Hates Ironing

JON JON BRYAN
AM
1st House Member
Bionic Airs
Mexican Food Addict
Nickname "Rocky"

KEVIN CHAN
Vancouver Canada
Artist
Street Urchin
Silent One
(Not Pictured)

send buck/get stuff
HOUSE OF KASAI
BOX 398, CARDIFF, CA 92007

Matt Goldsby, Adrian Demain, Lester Kasai, Ricard Salazar, Jon Jon Bryan, March 1990.

HOUSE OF
K A S A I
The House Lester Built (1986)

Lester's new sponsor?"

A bit later, Joe Johnson and Powell-Peralta skaters Tony Hawk and Adrian Demain started talking with Lester; seems they were getting the itch to start their own companies. Although the team manager of Powell-Peralta, Stacy Peralta, was not into it as he didn't want to lose Tony or Adrian, I saw it as the next evolution. After all, back in the late '70s, Stacy himself had also made the move from pro skater to company owner. I didn't sugar coat the discussion with these guys about how difficult it was to run a business. Overwhelmed by the prospect of too many responsibilities, Tony ultimately decided to stay with Powell to concentrate on being the best pro skater he could.

After talking to his parents and grandparents, who passed on the stories of their Samurai family heritage, Lester chose the oak leaf for his first Tracker graphic. The oak leaf is the Kasai family's coat of arms and signifies strength and wisdom. The graphic also featured an ankh, which symbolizes peace and love, and Japanese characters that spelled out "happy ever after," which is how Mr. Kasai lives his life. Lester's board went into production soon after and sales went through the roof. We then decided to build a team for Lester called the House of Kasai, which we launched with House guest Adrian Demain's model. Again, we enjoyed immediate success. Soon after, we released Tracker Lester Marbles wheels, which worked well on vert and sold as good as the decks! The House of Kasai was definitely one of the high points of the Tracker legacy.—**LMB**

In 1985, Tracker rider Lester Kasai came down to the factory one day, bummed out at his deck sponsor. So, I grabbed an unscreened Tracker 777 deck, spray-painted Lester in bright letters on it, set it up, gave it to Lester and sent him down to the Del Mar Skate Ranch to practice for an upcoming contest. After wheeling and dealing with Lester and making a phone call to our deck manufacturer to determine if they could handle the heavy workload, we decided to market a Lester Kasai vert model. Our first ad featured Lester blasting a huge air with a drawing of chopsticks holding a question mark, which implied the question, "Who is

By Larry Balma

Another product of the So Cal skatepark boom of the late '70s, Lester Kasai went on to become one of the top vert skaters of the '80s. With an aptitude for amplitude, Lester could always be counted on to blast sky-high airs above the pools and vert ramps of America, weather permitting. After putting in a stint riding for brands like Sims, Lester joined forces with Tracker in 1986 to form the House of Kasai, a very successful endeavor that flourished until vert skating got buried by handrail kids in the early '90s. Never one to throw in the towel, Lester continues to slay the latest skatepark pools on a reissue of his classic first Tracker deck.—GSD

Lester Kasai
INTERVIEW

Where did you grow up? When did you get your first set of Trackers?
I grew up in Anaheim, California. I actually bought some of my own Tracker Fultracks when I started skating in 1977. So, I rode Tracker Trucks as an amateur. I tried some of the other trucks, and then you guys hooked me up, probably during the ASPO contest series in 1979-'80. The big thing for me back then was those events. That's where it all began. And I stayed loyal to Tracker all of that time because I loved the trucks.

Why was Tracker so important to the history of skateboarding?
As a young teen learning about skateboarding, I looked at all of the magazines we had back then, and I remember the Tracker ads, and the guys who were on the team. Back then, one of my favorite teams that I would watch and read about in the magazines was the Bones Brigade, with their bright florescent boards, Cubic wheels and Tracker magnesium trucks. For me, it was kind of magical the way Tracker advertised all of their hardware. It was just so cool. The Copers, Lappers and the whole thing were like a system. It was the Tracker System, and they were all packaged so beautifully, the way everything went together. I was like a little kid in the candy store.

Did you save any boards?
I pretty much kept all of my stuff. I threw away some stuff, but I have all kinds of *Skat'n News* newspapers from the ASPO contests, and I look through those. I have all of my old magazines. My prized possession is my Neil Blender coffee break fiberglass bottom deck. I have all of my Tracker boards and everything. It's all wrapped up, and I'm going to keep them forever, I guess.

Let's talk more in-depth about your skateboards. You were skating for Sims.
Tom Sims called me up at my home. I don't know how he got my number. I was an amateur, and he asked if I wanted to skate for him. I was so stoked to be part of the Sims team, with the Sims jerseys, the urethane gloves, skating with Brad Bowman and all of those guys. I got to go to the Sims factory in Santa Barbara. It was amazing. Then Sims got licensed out to Brad Dorfman and Vision. So, yeah, I was part of Sims. It was a good time; it was fun, and pretty successful.

Then it was time for me to leave. I was really tight with you and Tracker, and I remember we did that ad with my board with the question mark on it. Once again, that was your idea [Larry]. You had such great ideas. That was the beginning. I was a free agent at that time, and I remember people like Santa Cruz, Tony Alva and Christian Hosoi were calling me up—you know, all of these other companies who wanted to work with me. But, I had such faith and loyalty to Tracker, and we came up with that whole concept—you and your ideas—and we went with it. That was a great time, a very successful time for both of us, and it was a lot of fun.

Do you remember the first prototype Tracker Lester deck? We had a Del Mar contest coming up, and you didn't want to ride your old board, so we just sprayed-painted that one. Regardless of what you were doing brand-wise, that was the board you rode in the contest.
Yeah, and we also did one with the question mark ad. You and I were still stewing on what we were going to do. Basically, back then you were my support system, and I think we figured it out.

We had a lot of fun when you got together with Adrian Demain.
Yep, we wanted to keep things very fun and fresh, so Adrian climbed onboard, and I think we created something very special. I still hear from a lot of people to this day, I'll meet them in some other country, and they'll say, "I was a member of the House of Kasai. It was so cool, we got these newsletters and stickers." Once again, it was another one of your ideas, and it worked really well.

Do you remember around 1987-'88 when Tony Hawk talked with you and Adrian? He wanted to start a new company backed by Tracker. But, when we were all hyped up to do it, you told me how much work it was to manage a company, and you really just wanted to skate.
That was another reason why I could go skate: you and everybody else from Tracker supported me and focused on the business stuff, so it worked out good. I was still a young kid, too, and I had all of these people pulling at me, and I didn't know who to trust. All I wanted to do was skate. You took care of me, and I appreciate that to this day.

Yeah, we had a run there. We made a lot of skateboards, and we did the Marbles wheels.
Those were cool. I remember working with Jim Gray on those. Actually, some guy told me he still has a set of Marbles, loves them, and actually skates them. So, I still hear people saying they have Marbles or the Lester boards. It's pretty cool to know it's been this long and people still have a set rolling around somewhere.

Tell us about Frankie goes to fakie.
That's one of the tricks that I came up with and named. It was a cross bone air to fakie. That's all it was (laughs). Back then, we just came up with all of these tricks and tried to get people to like them. And no matter what the trick was, we always tried to name it something interesting, or name it after some kind of trend that was going on then. So,

Frankie goes to fakie was a take-off on that band called Frankie Goes to Hollywood.

What is the Bennihana?
I'm not sure what year that was, maybe 1983-'84? That was a fakie Ollie tail grab taking off your back foot. It actually won the Dale Smith award at a Del Mar contest. I think nobody made up any new tricks at that contest, so he gave it to me. That was obviously named after Bennihana, the restaurant that Tony Hawk and I would always go to. We loved it so much. Again, we were just having fun with tricks, having fun with names. That's what it was like back then. The Bennihana actually became a very popular trick with street skaters.

What's your secret to launching bio airs?
Growing up watching skaters like David Andrecht, who was one of my favorites. He was one of the guys who started breaking the barrier of going high. I remember watching and thinking, "Wow, that's just so amazing. I can't believe how high he's going!" It looked so fun. I just wanted to do airs. I wanted to go as high as I could possibly go, because it was so exhilarating. So, I always tried to go as high as I could, and tried to build some momentum wherever I could. I prefer doing airs more than a lot of other tricks.

We ran that one ad in which you went so high you flew off the page.
That was actually super cool. I still have that at home. You put part of it in the front of the magazine and the other part in the back. So, when you got to the back, you'd be like, "Oh, okay." That was super clever. You had a lot of little clever ideas like that.

Do you recall any other memorable times with Tracker?
What I really remember was having such care and support from Tracker, from Peggy and

Ridge. I was a young kid growing up in this industry, this environment of skateboarding, and these people took care of me like family. They taught me, they supported me—that's what I remember. All of that care and love, that's what I remember the most—going to a contest and just having that. That's the fondest memory I have of Tracker.

Read the full-length interview at trackertrucks.com

Above: **Grant Brittain, Lester Kasai and Pierre Andre Senizergues on tour in Japan, circa 1988.** Photo: Linda Prettyman. Opposite page: **Lester Kasai hucks an Ollie out of Del Mar's halfpipe in Del Mar, California, circa 1984.** Photo: Grant Brittain

Above: **It's goof off time with the Tracker team: Mike McGill, Marty Jimenez, Tony Hawk, Kevin Staab, Adrian Demain, Jim Gray and Lester Kasai.** Photo: Unknown
Above right: **Lester Kasai and Adrian Demain double their fun, circa 1988.** Photo: Chip Morton.
Decks across whole spread, left to right, top to bottom: **Lester Kasai Designs, 1984. Lester Kasai contest deck spray-painted by Larry Balma, 1985. Tracker Lester Kasai prototype, 1986. Tracker Lester Kasai first production deck, 1986. Tracker Lester Kasai Dragons 1, 1988. House of Kasai Street Cleaner, 1989. House of Kasai Street Model, 1989. Lester Kasai Dragon 2, 1989. Lester Kasai Fireball, 1989. Adrian Demain 1, 1988. Adrian Demain 2, 1989. Adrian Demain 3, 1989.**

Mike McGill's
Skate Shop
ENCINITAS.CA. (619) 943-7738

226

First sponsored by Uncle Wiggley back in 1983, Del Mar local Adrian Demain was one of very few six-ply plank riders to ever leave the Bones Brigade for a greener lawn. Come 1987, the invitation from his pal Lester to be the first guest in the House of Kasai proved to be too good an opportunity to pass up. Bringer of the judo / anti-judo and big hair under the helmet, Adrian is also an accomplished guitarist who has jammed with the likes of Lee Rocker, Billy Watson, Thee Corsairs, the Forbidden Pigs and the Cheap Leis.—GSD

Adrian Demain
INTERVIEW

LMB: When did you start skateboarding?
I really started skateboarding right at the end of 1978.

LMB: When did you get your first set of Trackers Trucks?
My first set of Trackers was with my first Powell-Peralta Steve Caballero board. That was probably around 1982. They were Tracker Sixtracks. I had to have Sixtracks with the Copers to go with my orange Caballero board. At that time, everybody who I was influenced by rode Trackers, which led me to want to ride only Trackers. Nowadays, kids look at Copers and ask, "What is that? Look at all of that stuff on there." But I thought Copers were so futuristic. It was way more of a system, it was high tech, and the best skaters used the Tracker System. I wanted to ride that.

My first board sponsor was Uncle Wiggley, which I referred to as UWS, because I was afraid to call Uncle Wiggley my sponsor. I didn't want to ride for Uncle Wiggley, I wanted to ride for Powell-Peralta. So, I was already riding Trackers and Bryan Ridgeway approached me and said, "Do you want to ride for Tracker?" Of course, I replied yes, and told him I wanted Sixtrack mags. He said, "We don't have those, but we have Extrack mags." I just wanted magnesium trucks, so I rode Extrack mags in 1983-'84. At the time in 1983, they had already started phasing out the mags. They were too expensive to make, there wasn't really a demand for them and things were changing. They came back later.

LMB: Ultimately, you ended up skating for Powell-Peralta.
Yeah, thanks to Mr. Tony Hawk, I got on Powell, which, as you can imagine, was a dream come true—to be on the team with Caballero, Hawk, Mike McGill and Lance Mountain. I tell this story a lot, because I'm really proud of it. There was a contest at Del Mar and everybody always stayed at Tony's house. They just put everybody up, because the Hawks were so great. So, we were all sitting at the house watching TV, and Tony got up and left the room. Rodney Mullen was over in the corner with his ear on the phone for about a half hour. Eventually, he put down the phone very quietly, stood up, walked over to me and said, "You're going to get on Powell." Then he walked out of the room. Sure enough, when I got home, there was a message at the house. My mom said, "Stacy Peralta called." I was freaking out: "Stacy Peralta? Do you

know who that is?" So, I got to ride for Powell-Peralta.

GSD: Was there ever talk that you'd get a model on Powell?
There was, but unfortunately, that was right at the time when everything was kind of blowing up, and suddenly, the Powell-Peralta team was really huge. Then things began to change, especially when the videos started coming out. Tommy Guerrero got really popular, and they were kind of like, "Oh, we have to follow this lead." They sort of tried to mold me in that direction, but they knew they had to go with what was brewing. Even then in 1986-'87, the team was up to 30 riders. So, you know the difference from 1984 to '86, when there would be 15 people to 30 people to 60 people to who knows how many people were on the team. So, my model just kind of fell through the cracks, but I have experimental shapes at my house.

GSD: So, you moved over to the House of Kasai in 1987?
AD: Yeah, I guess it was at the beginning of 1988. I think I was on the Powell team through '87, and then shortly thereafter, I started talking to Lester Kasai about riding for the House of Kasai. That started off as sort of an off-handed comment, because we were both talking about how the industry was changing. I talked about how I felt I was getting lost in the shuffle and I just jokingly said, "I should just ride for you," and he was like, "Would you ride for me?" I said, "Yeah." That was how we came up with that "house guest" line in my first ad, because we were joking that I could be the house guest in the House of Kasai. Lester and I skated together for so many years before, and we hung out a lot, so it seemed like a natural progression.

GSD: Of your House of Kasai pro model boards here, which one came first?
This one was the first. It's pretty much just like the Captain Harlock comic book I bought when I was in Japan. Unfortunately, I don't remember who did the graphics on this one. In fact, I don't remember who did the first couple, but that's what this one was based on. It's anime, but it didn't really have that sort of title at the time, because it was just Japanese animation. Captain Harlock was a space ranger or something like that. I really don't know why I was drawn to him. I think it started out that I just liked the style of the Japanese animation. And then there was this [pointing to the pyramid]. I still have a letter someone wrote to me about the pyramid with the sevens, saying that I was a money worshipper. Of course, I had no idea that was associated with the Illuminati. I just thought it was cool, and it was my ode to Steve Vai, who I was a huge fan of back then.

For my second graphic, I just wanted it a little cleaner looking. I came back from Japan with this vampire video, which I still know nothing about, which inspired part of the artwork. I just liked the way the vine looked. I think Rick Farr did this one, or at least this part of it. I can't remember if it was him or Ron Lemon. Then somebody put

a cat and bird in there. It was an inside joke. It was basically the same graphic except with my signature. Truth be told, I practiced that signature a lot until it came out how I wanted it. Rick Farr definitely did my final graphic. This one was my favorite. I told him just to run with it. I said we should keep the guy in there, but we weren't married to the image. I didn't feel the need to keep it as a series. He came up with this, and I really loved what he did with it.

GSD: Rick did the lettering?
Yeah, he did it completely from scratch. I didn't give him any guidelines whatsoever, except that we should keep the guy, the Illuminati and the money, of course. That's what it was all about—that I was going to make so much money off of all of those people. I really liked the way it came out. Thankfully, I don't have my last graphic.

GSD: There were four?
There were four, and I did the artwork for the last one unintentionally, because Ridge said, "We need to make your name bigger, because we need to see it on the shelf." So, I drew this horrendous big sort of Superman-shaped thing with my name huge. Maybe it was a joke to myself. The guy from my other graphics was really small in the middle, crouched down but still holding the pyramid—hoping for the money, I guess. So, yeah, he was tucked away in the corner, my name was really huge, and I said, "Here, how about this? Maybe you can make something with that." Then I got the first production board and it was pretty much exactly as I had drawn it. I said, "Oh! You were supposed to make it better. The lettering is all unbalanced." I didn't know about that sort of stuff. I know they made at least three, because I rode one and Lester actually rode one for a while, because he liked my shape better than his. Plus, one of his friends up in Orange County who rode

for the House had one, so there are three.

GSD: Can you remember some of your favorite Tracker ads?
I only remember my least favorite ad: the street airwalk off of a sidewalk bump. They used the wrong photo. My board was only about an inch off the ground.

Read the full-length interview at trackertrucks.com

Above: **Lester Kasai and Adrian Demain enjoy some fakie fun at Sadlands in Anaheim, California, circa 1988.** Photo: O. Opposite page: **Adrian flings a table top Gunnair at Mike McGill's skatepark in Carlsbad, California, circa 1989.** Photo: Unknown

By Larry Balma + GSD

Adrian Demain, December 1989.

House of Kasai, circa 1989.

Lester Kasai, June 1987.

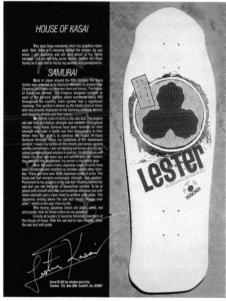

House of Kasai, October 1986.

Lester Kasai, circa 2009.

Lester Kasai, October 1985.

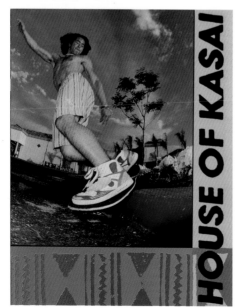

Lester Kasai, September 1989.

Lester Kasai, December 1987.

Adrian Demain, May 1990.

Adrian Demain, April 1990.

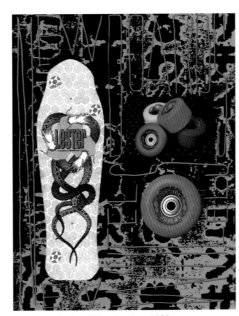

New Boards New Wheels, circa 1988.

Lester Kasai, February 1986.

Lester Kasai, June 1988.

Lester Kasai, December 1986. Lester blasted so high, we had to run the top of the photo on another page.

Lester Kasai, October 1983.

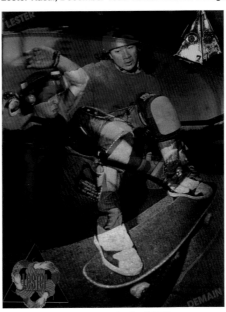

Lester Kasai, Adrian Demain, April 1989.

Lester Kasai, Adrian Demain, August 1988.

229

BOBBY REEVES

GSD + The Ridge, November 1982.

The proven leader
Coast to coast
Planet to planet

Send 1.00 for foto folder, stickers and system specs to:
TRACKER, P.O. BOX 398, CARDIFF-BY-THE-SEA, CA 92007 · 714-722-1455

TRUCKS YOU CAN TRUST
TRACKER
SINCE 1975

Bobby Reeves, September 1989.

Send 1.00 for foto folder, stickers and system specs to:
CARDIFF-BY-THE-SEA, CA 92007 · 714-722-1455

Team Building With
THE RIDGE

In the late 1970s, most skateboarders outside of California had no way to see how the pros actually pulled off tricks. There were no skate videos, and very few, if any, movies that made it out to our neck of the woods. Of course, there was no YouTube or even a web then either. All we saw were still photographs. Just like every kid from coast to coast who skated, I studied every photo in *Skateboarder* magazine intensely. With the long Huntington, West Virginia winters in full effect, I had plenty of time to try to figure out how the latest skateboard tricks were done based on the physical positions the pros were photographed in. Sequences were not shot of every trick, so sheer imagination played a pretty big role. I studied the transitions they were skating as well as the equipment they were using, and noticed that every skater I really admired rode Trackers, even though I respected skaters who rode other brands. Stacy Peralta, Tony Alva and Jay Adams were the most notable of the first wave, and the photos of them were always cool to see.

In the front end of the '80s, I visited the Midwest's premier pay-to-skate facility, Apple Skatepark in Columbus, Ohio, as often as our little squad's parents could make the two-hour drive. Occasionally, I ran into Bobby Reeves from Florida and Jami Godfrey from Cherry Hill skatepark in New Jersey at Apple, both of whom rode for Powell-Peralta and Tracker—teams I really admired. Other young Powell / Tracker upstarts like Ray "Bones" Rodriguez, Alan Gelfand and Steve Caballero were busting out onto the scene in California, as well. As far as truck brands went, Tracker had built a rep for sponsoring tons of the best riders. They had a tight group of guys, and a diverse ethnic group, as well. That fact, along with serious product development, was what attracted so many skaters to Tracker. I knew that a good skater could ride any brand, but it seemed like if you rode Trackers, you had an edge, because Tracker was well-known as the leader of skateboard truck innovation.

I remember when I used to mail a buck to Tracker for some stickers, they would include a personal note of encouragement with the goods. Over time, those notes would become one of my only connections to skaters outside of my hometown, where most had curtailed their skating activities for the lure of getting some tail. Eventually, Tracker put me on their truck flow team and sent me the latest products before they were even out on the market. That was an insane feeling. In November 1982,

Ridge, Steve Rocco and Jinx peruse the pages of *Thrasher*, circa 1984. Photo: Grant Brittain

I even appeared in a full-page Tracker ad in *Thrasher* with another Midwesterner, GSD, which let people know that there were Tracker skaters in the heart of the country. Believe it or not, it was a big deal to represent Ohio and West Virginia in a Tracker ad, especially back then!

This all shaped who I would become when Tracker hired me and moved me to Oceanside, California in late 1983. It was never my dream or aspiration to become a team manager, but I naturally gravitated toward those responsibilities, because I knew how it had impacted me as a skater living in the hills of West Virginia. There I was, working at Tracker performing a variety of tasks for the team, and the brand. I quickly discovered that Tracker team skaters had been treated the same way for years. That personal touch is something that stuck with me. When you included a personal note of encouragement in their box of flow product, it offered support and the feeling that you were actually helping the skater progress. In my opinion, skaters from different pockets around the country deserved as much attention as California riders. In fact, I wrote a feature article in *TransWorld Skateboarding* called "East Meets West" to that effect. After that article, and the subsequent exposure of so many of those skaters, it was good for all truck brands to know there were great skaters outside of California.

And I knew precisely which ones I wanted on Tracker, starting with Ray Underhill over in Tennessee, Allen Midgett and Henry Gutierrez in Virginia Beach, Marty Jimenez in Ohio, Keith Lenharr up in Pennsylvania and John Grigley down in Florida. Ray Underhill was important for more than just his skating. When he got on two of the best teams of the time, Powell-Peralta and Tracker, he proved again that great skaters existed in the Midwest, which was a breakthrough. Rob Roskopp from Ohio was right there, too, with Madrid and Independent until Santa Cruz got a hold of him! The bottom line was, it showed everyone in the world that skaters could come out of the Midwest and be respected. Being on Tracker was part of that respect. When it became valid to get sponsored in new pockets outside of California, people around the world knew they could get recognized, too.

Through my connections in our national network of skate zines, I had a pulse on which skaters and areas were advancing, so when I arrived at Tracker, I already had an idea on how to recruit, develop and support skaters. I studied how great teams had been built in the past in skateboarding, as well as other sports; for example, the way Lakers general manager Jerry West constructed his winning teams. I also spoke with Stacy Peralta about how the Zephyr and G&S teams had been run, as well as his strategy in building the Bones Brigade. Pros like Mike McGill, Tony Hawk, Tim Scroggs and Rodney Mullen and ams like Ray Underhill, Bucky Lasek, Chris O.P. Moore, and Donny Griffin, in addition to the names mentioned in paragraph two, were all among those who were on both teams. After Tracker co-founder Dave Dominy and team manager Lance Smith laid the groundwork in the '70s, I wanted to build on Tracker's elite team image. This was measured in terms of skating ability, style, competitive desire and determination, innovative instincts and, most importantly, personality. It was pursuit of this perfect mix that led me to develop the intangibles of projecting how far a skater might advance over time while they were with Tracker. I was also into having a diverse group from all areas around the globe.

I worked on how to maintain consistency whenever skaters joined the team, switched to other teams or transitioned out of their prime. I also developed different levels of support for our riders. There were different levels for pros, different levels for sponsored ams, and perks for team flow riders who I helped develop with their other sponsors. My overall goal was to maintain the ability to acquire top pros and ams and be able to project talent ahead two to three years once I saw them skate. John Gibson and Jeff Phillips, both of Texas, came on board, which was important to lock in the next generation of Texas riders like Bryan Pennington and David Nielsen. This same process went down for the rest of the United States and Canada and eventually all around the world as skateboarding became more international. One thing that attracted riders to Tracker was the image of who was on the team, and who had been. Even if, from their perspective, some riders said they weren't the right fit for Tracker, they still said they were honored to have been considered, and those who felt it was the right fit were downright stoked.

Chris Carter pecks a frontside grind in the L Bowl at Apple Skatepark in Columbus, Ohio, circa 1980. Photo: Mark Underwood

As for upcoming talent in general, I wanted anyone who already rode for Tracker to root for the team to score the next great rider, i.e. there is no I in team. I wanted their experience with Tracker to be so great that they wanted Tracker to always have a legacy of great skateboarders and skateboarding. The key was to show appreciation for those who may have put a guy on the team who would replace them someday. The deal was to enjoy the experience while you were on Tracker and not worry about when you retired. You were always part of something great as long as you looked at it as some of the best times in your life. There was a natural evolution and cycle to team riders coming and going, and I couldn't have ever been so successful at recruiting if I didn't have the help of those who were thinking of the future for Tracker.

Although vert dominated skateboarding throughout most of the '80s, by the middle of the decade, street skating and contests had taken root. As some of the vert skaters crossed over into street, early street skaters like GSD were joined by Mike Vallely and the Gonz, who changed the whole game forever when he first jumped up onto handrails. Freestylers like Rodney Mul-

len pushed the limits, too, rounding out the rock solid Tracker team. In the '90s entirely new breeds entered the fold, like Willy Santos, Rob Dyrdek, Lance Conklin, Mike Dahre, Bucky Lasek, Duane Pitre, Sal Barbier Armando Barajas, Julio de la Cruz, Shorty Gonzalez, Laban Pheidias, Ron Chatman, Jeremy Klein, Dan Rogers and many others. I worked with Stacy Peralta quite a bit as he gathered intel from a network of skate shops worldwide. One in particular kept him abreast of an evolving group of skaters who Stacy eventually sponsored: Paulo Diaz, Guy Mariano and Gabriel Rodriguez. Stacy would steer some riders my way and some to other truck brands he thought would benefit the rider with various support. Jim Fitzpatrick was also a great asset over at Powell; we worked well together coordinating their Bones Brigade touring events while actively scouting for Tracker prospects even when Powell's team was booked up. It was a resource that we could only have had if we shared a great relationship and a passion for skateboarding. That's how Bucky Lasek was found.

In the late '80s and on into the '90s, Tracker still had a great reputation for taking care of team riders. Most deck brands wanted some of their guys on Tracker because we provided a level of support that even some of them didn't. At Tracker, we had great relationships with team managers of most of those brands. I went to every event to watch riders sponsored by them, always looking out for new Tracker team members. Whether Tracker or the deck sponsor discovered an upcoming young skater, we would work together to see if our teams were a good fit for the rider. Although it was the skater who had the talent, it was all of the sponsors who joined forces to give the rider a support group so he could take his skating further. We worked closely with the deck sponsors, showcasing their riders in our ads and videos and, of course, we got the same treatment from them. We always had more Tracker riders than we had ad pages, so, luckily, when we began making those raw Tracker videos in the late '80s, we were allowed to highlight all riders, not just the elite ones who would make it into our ads, thus our videos were very helpful with rider retention.

By 1987, Tracker was rolling well enough that we could hire an assistant team manager, Chris Carter, from West Virginia. He knew what was up, so he and I both collectively made key team and marketing decisions during those years. It was like having two team managers! In 1989, we pulled a highly respected skater out of Pennsylvania, Keith Lenharr, who had high credibility in the Northeast. Keith was so respected that once people found out he was working at Tracker, the sponsor me tapes increased tenfold. We picked up more guys in New Jersey, Pennsylvania, Virginia Beach, Maryland, Georgia, North Carolina and Florida—Fred Gall, Fred Reeves, Derek Krasauskas and Phil Rouchard being some prime examples. Keith was instrumental in us getting some key regional guys who would in turn help us with future generations of skaters. By having team managers who were living it and skating every day, Tracker had credibility world-wide. In the late '90s, Julio de la Cruz stepped in from South Central Los Angeles to help with Tracker's street team. He was instrumental in hooking up Jesus Fernandez, Quim Cardona, Daniel Lebron, Fabian Alomar, Lee Smith, Alfonso Fernandez, Jason Barr, Joey Suriel and the list goes on. After some team riders left Tracker, we maintained relationships with them, and since they knew how well we supported our team program, they always sent riders to be looked out for by Tracker. This meant pro or am skaters who were in positions within the industry after their skate careers were over. It also meant ex-employees like Chris Carter once he started Alien Workshop in 1990.

With 40 years of Tracker history to reflect back on, it's safe to say that the brand was affiliated with a high percentage of the best skateboarders who ever stepped on a deck. It was a pleasure having so much fun with all of them, as well as making it through some tough spots in life together. Tracker allowed us to help skateboarders in many more ways than merely shipping out a box full of trucks, t-shirts and stickers. We all went through life together; we were the skateboarding brotherhood. There are other truck brands with great riders, but from the '70s through the '90s, there is no question Tracker lead the way on every level, as well as pushing other brands to do their best!

To all who have slammed and gotten right back on board, to all who have gained something from building yourselves up from the inside out, to all who share in the joy of seeing new generations tap into what you've already laid down, to all who have supported advancing the cause of skateboarding and what it brings, to all of the brands that have come, contributed, gone, or are still with us today, to all of the skaters who have come before us but are no longer with us, I salute you all! Just as we ourselves are ever-evolving, so is skateboarding. It's the ulti-mate ride!—**Bryan Ridgeway**

Keith Lenharr fries up some tasty hot eggs on a gnarly backyard ramp, circa 1987. Photo: Pensinger

233

1990s
Skateboarding Timeline

1990 · Almost all skateparks of this period consist of wooden vert ramps, mini-ramps and launch ramps.

· Burnside in Portland, Oregon emerges as the first huge concrete skatepark built illegally guerilla-style under a bridge.

· Former G&S and Tracker employees Mike Hill and Chris Carter launch Alien Workshop out of Dayton, Ohio as an oddly creative alternative to California skateboard brands. Featuring artwork by Hill and Neil Blender, the Workshop grows into one of the most respected brands / teams of the '90s. John Lucero starts up Black Label.

· A few people quietly begin building collections of mint, unridden skateboard decks from previous decades, most of which can be acquired for really low prices this early in the game.

· Created and produced by original Z-Boy Nathan Pratt and directed by Stacy Peralta, a skateboard variety show called *SK8 TV* launches on Nickelodeon featuring interviews at the Pink Motel pool.

· Roger Hickey makes the *Guinness Book of World Records* for downhill speed runs: 75.3 mph on a luge and 55.4 mph stand-up.

· Danny Way almost lands a 900, but no cigar.

· Upcoming talent includes Paulo Diaz, Rob Dyrdek, Mike Frazier, Rudy Johnson, Neal Hendrix, Ocean Howell, Kien Lieu, Colin McKay, Duane Pitre, Jordan Richter, Wade Speyer and Remy Stratton.

1991 · The skateboard industry largely abandons vert to concentrate on street, which is much more accessible to kids everywhere.

· The city of Palo Alto, California builds one of the first free public concrete skateparks in the United States. Fortunately, this concept will expand to other cities and states through the rest of the decade and completely explode in the 2000s.

· Mark "Gator" Rogowski turns himself in for the murder of Jessica Bergston.

· Blind and Plan B launch to become two of the premiere street skating teams of the '90s. Simple shoes debut and channel their inner hippie.

· Steve Rocco's World Industries pushes the limits of good taste with deck graphics displaying full frontal nudity, crack pipes, racism and Satanic imagery, ushering in the era of small brands that surpass the sales of '80s giants like Powell-Peralta, Santa Cruz and Vision. Stacy Peralta and many of his team riders leave Powell-Peralta.

· Santa Cruz launches their Everslick line of plastic bottom decks, killing slider rails overnight. Within months, the whole skateboard industry follows suit.

· Skateboards slowly morph from wide vert decks into narrower street decks.

· Blind releases *Video Days*, one of the most beloved videos in skateboard history. Beautifully melding old school style with cutting edge street skating, Mark Gonzales' part is often cited as an all-time favorite. *Video Days* also helps launch Jason Lee's acting career.

· Alien Workshop premieres *Memory Screen*, which puts them on the map and introduces artsy found footage to skateboard videos.

· *TransWorld Skateboarding*'s Master of Gravity vert ramp debuts at the ASR trade show, bringing skateboarding to the show floor for the first time.

· Upcoming talent includes Salman Agah, Ray Barbee, Sal Barbier, Josh Beagle, Tim Brauch, John Cardiel, Ron Chatman, Peter Hewitt, Frankie Hill, Frank Hirata, Rick Howard, Jeremy Kline, Eric Koston, Jason Lee, Guy Mariano, Kris Markovich, Brian Patch, Laban Pheidias, Dan Rogers, Willy Santos and Chris Senn.

1992 · A hideous facet of this period of skateboarding history manifests itself in the form of tiny

Tony Hawk fires up a Gunnair at a Vans Triple Crown contest, 1995. Photo: Unknown
Below, left to right: **Around 1992-'94, small wheels and big clothes ruled skateboarding. The first issue of** *Big Brother***, circa 1992.** Photo: Spike Jonze
An early World Industries logo.

wheels, huge baggy clothes (Blind, Fuct, New Deal and Plan B are the main apparel offenders), focusing decks, pressure flips, etc.

· Just as curbs enjoy a resurgence, street skaters start launching themselves en masse off gaps of the roof, stair and parking lot variety. Kris Markovich becomes known for riding extra long rails.

· Skateboard deck evolution finally settles into the standard popsicle stick shape, while noses grow like Pinocchio's until they're longer than tails.

· New skateboard brands include Birdhouse, Blue, Channel 1, Chapter 7, Consolidated, The Firm, Milk and TV.

· Venture pioneers low trucks for street skating, featuring a new shorter hole pattern with the bolts moved back from the nose and tail.

· Vans releases the Half-Cab, one of the most popular skateboard shoes of all time.

· Freestyler Pierre André Senizergues strikes a licensing deal with etnies' French founder, Rautureau Apple, to begin designing etnies in the U.S. He calls the brand etnies USA, then etnies America.

· As the economy enters a recession, big skateboard brands shrink to make room for small ones, and magazines' page counts dwindle. Despite the adversity, *Slap* launch-

es as a newsprint zine, only to grow into an actual magazine later. Ditto *Big Brother*, founded by Steve Rocco, which goes on to publish scads of controversial content like how to kill yourself or make a fake ID card, upskirt shots, etc. in addition to skateboarding. A decade after the demise of *Action Now*, TransWorld Publications launches *Warp* magazine (the first issue was called *Blast!*) to cover a similar array of action sports and music with the subtitle, "the Surf, Skate, Snow Experience."

· Jason Lee, Guy Mariano and Spike Jones star in Sonic Youth's "100%" music video.

· Dan Field organizes *Degenerates*, the first gallery art show to feature the artwork of skateboarders, in-

cluding GSD, Mark Gonzales, Andy Jenkins, Lance Mountain, Tod Swank and others. Aaron Rose's Alleged Gallery opens in New York City and goes on to host the art of many prominent skateboarders.

· Upcoming talent includes Jason Adams, Matt Beach, Ronnie Creager, Jason Dill, Mike Frazier, Neal Hendrix, Geoff Rowley and Jeremy Wray. Simon Woodstock emerges as skateboarding's official class clown.

1993 · Popular proving grounds of street skating include the EMB plaza and Carlsbad gap in California, and LOVE Park in Philadelphia, Pennsylvania.

· Some new brands making headway include Evol, Flip, Girl, Invisible, Maple and Toy Machine. Droors and Fuct bring the apparel.

· Sector 9 and Gravity launch, both offering longboard cruisers, which had been ignored by manu-

TIM VON WERNE

Tim von Werne, December 1995.

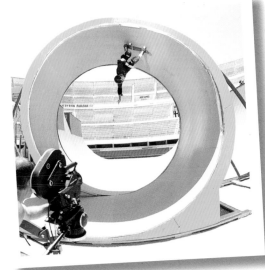

Tony Hawk, 1999. Photo: Atiba Jefferson

facturers since the mid '70s.

• Skateboarding's dirty little secret: planks of the cruiser, longboard and downhill variety quietly—and hugely—outsell street decks for years to come.

• Tracker markets the B52 Floater and B52 E-Clip Floater, the first floating axle truck and first e-clips to replace axle locknuts.

• Skateboard wheels start to grow bigger again, as low-top skate shoes sweep through the industry.

• To capture increasingly technical street tricks, magazines begin to run video grab sequences. Noticing the absurdity of printing video on paper, New Deal's Steve Douglas launches *411VM* as skateboarding's first video magazine, publishing copies of each issue on actual VHS tapes. *411* fills in the gaps between brand videos, and helps many kids learn tricks easier than print mags, which really raises the level of street skating in years to come.

• Switch stance begins to infiltrate street skating, just as its young practitioners develop an openly hostile attitude toward anything that involves old school, downhill, tranny or vert. In response, *Juice* magazine launches with the motto "Pools, Pipes and Punk Rock."

• Upcoming talent includes Steve Berra, Mike Carroll, Mike Crum, Jerry Fowler, Rune Glifberg, Rudy Johnson, Heath Kirchart, Steve Olson, Chris Pastras, Tom Penny, Duane Pitre, John Reeves and Jamie Thomas.

1994 • Similar to the guerilla-built Burnside skatepark in Portland, Oregon, locals start work on FDR in Philadelphia, Pennsylvania after the heat comes down on LOVE Park.

• Jeremy Klein debuts Hook-Ups, a deck, shoe and apparel brand widely known for its Japanese animation-style female characters and monsters. Girl spins off a subsidiary called Chocolate.

• Rob Dyrdek introduces Orion trucks with Kareem

Sector 9 longboard, Sixteen popsicle stick.

Campbell, Eric Koston, Kris Markovich, Tom Penny and others.

• Damon Way and Ken Block start DC Shoes, which grows into one of the biggest footwear brands in skateboarding. etnies unveils one of the most beloved skateboard shoes of all time, the Sal 23. Other new shoe brands include Duffs, and Globe in Australia.

• Kevin Lyman debuts the first annual Warped Tour, a huge traveling show featuring bands and skateboarding.

• *TransWorld* launches Board AID, the first board sports charity event, featuring pro vert skateboarding and snowboarding, plus a full-on rock concert, all in a carnival-like atmosphere on the snow. Board AID donates over $696,000 for AIDS education and awareness and goes global in 1997.

• After a decade, the organizer of many a skateboard contest series, the NSA, calls it quits, to be replaced by World Cup Skateboarding, formed by Don and Danielle Bostick, who continue to run a true world championship series all over the world.

• Tampa Am debuts and goes on to be the premier amateur skateboard contest.

• The Alleged gallery in New York City presents Ed Templeton's first art show.

• Upcoming talent includes Donny Barley, Chad Fernandez, Marc Johnson, Josh Kalis, Paul Sharpe and Clyde Singleton.

1995 • The El Toro handrail wars are in full swing with soldiers deploying increasingly technical tricks down its huge spine.

• Public skateparks start to become more common.

• Online auction web site eBay launches, which causes the price of vintage skateboards to soar in subsequent years.

• Tum Yeto becomes the first major skateboard company to launch a web site. Owner Tod Swank follows it up with skateboard.com, encouraging the whole skateboard industry to embrace the burgeoning World Wide Web.

• Popsicle stick street decks bottom out at around 7.25" wide as slick bottoms disappear.

• Pierre André Senizergues launches éS Footwear for the technical street skating market, while Tim Gavin and 118 Boardshop debut DVS. Puma gets in on the skate shoe game, as well.

• The maker of etnies, Rautureau Apple, is bought by a European shoe conglomerate, which is in turn acquired by an American company.

• Unknown Brazilian Bob Burnquist takes the vert event at Slam City Jam by storm, winning it with an astonishing display of switch stance skating.

• ESPN launches the Extreme Games sponsored by Nike, Taco Bell, AT&T and Mountain Dew. Chris Senn wins street, while Tony Hawk snags vert. Skateboarding says hello to huge corporate sponsors and influence.

• The Hard Rock Cafe and *TransWorld Skateboarding* produce the World Championships of Skateboarding. Tony Hawk takes the top prize. The contest later evolves into the Triple Crown of Skateboarding. Vans purchases the Triple Crown in 1998 and adds other board sports, making it one of the largest contest series.

• Jim Fitzpatrick establishes the International Association of Skateboard Companies (IASC) and is elected founding executive director. After two years of lobbying the California State Legislature with senate bills AB1296 and SB927, skateboarding is added to California's Hazardous

Recreational Activities List (HRA), providing liability exemption for California municipalities. The success in California becomes a model for the rest of the nation, which opens the floodgates for public skateparks across the USA.

• Produced by *TransWorld Skateboarding* in conjunction with the newly-formed IASC, the first Skateboard Industry Conference is held in Cabo San Lucas, Mexico.

• Upcoming talent includes Pat Duffy, Jason Ellis, Jim Greco, Marc Johnson, Chad Muska, Tom Penny, John Reeves and Andrew Reynolds.

1996 • Simon Woodstock skates in a suit made out of pennies for a Vans ad.

• Foundation builds the world's biggest skateboard, standing 30" tall x 48" wide x 142" long and weighing in at 450 lbs.

• Deck and wheel sizes begin to grow again into the 8" zone and 55 mm respectively.

• Dave Bergthold launches Sixteen, the first skateboard deck brand marketed exclusively to kids.

• Tracker debuts the Hawk Truk, the first pro model skateboard truck.

• Skateboard shoes become big business, with buttery two-page spread ads becoming common for new brands like Kastel and Osiris (formerly known

Ronnie Bertino, Orion Trucks, December 1995.

as Evol), as well as old pros like Vans and Airwalk. Rautureau Apple puts the etnies brand up for sale. Unsure of how his etnies America licensing agreement will be affected, Pierre launches Emerica, short for etnies America. A bit later, he buys the etnies brand name outright from Rautureau Apple then forms Sole Technology, an umbrella company for etnies, éS and Emerica.

• Toy Machine releases *Welcome to Hell*, which puts them on the map and, thanks to Jamie Thomas' part, moves handrail skating up another notch.

• ESPN changes the name of the Extreme Games to the X Games.

• Overzealous security guards and an aging street course cause pros to boycott the Munster contest in Germany.

send a buck for stickers and info p.o. box 398, cardiff, ca 92007

Ron Chatman, March 1994.

• Tom Penny front blunts a gnarly ledge on the infamous August cover of *TransWorld Skateboarding.* The only question is did he make it?
• Upcoming talent includes Brian Anderson, Jake Brown, Max Dufour, Erik Ellington, Bam Margera, Rick McCrank, Elissa Steamer and Lincoln Ueda.

1997 • After establishing himself as a legend, and at the height of his popularity, Tom Penny pulls a JD Salinger by disappearing into rural France for a couple of years.
• Osiris releases the D3, Dave Mayhew's pro model shoe, which goes on to become the best-selling skateboard shoe.
• Sole Technology launches Sheep shoes, aimed at the low price market. In sharp contrast to the overall serious tone in the skateboarding industry, Sheep portrays a more fun, playful image. The brand is shut down within a year. Axion shoes also debut.
• The publisher of *TransWorld Skateboarding*, TransWorld Media, is bought by Times Mirror. The original *TWS* staff remains in place.
• *Hustler* publisher Larry Flynt Publications buys *Big Brother* and, ironically, tones down the outrageous content to make it more acceptable for newsstands.
• Aaron Rose from Alleged art gallery publishes *Dysfunctional*, a groundbreaking book that takes a look back at skateboarding history through an artistic lens by showing deck graphics, stickers, zines and artwork in addition to action shots.

• The first All Girl Skate Jam goes down in Graffix warehouse in National City, California. Elissa Steamer wins street, while Cara-Beth Burnside grabs vert.
• Tony Hawk completes the first documented loop.
• Danny Way bomb drops from a helicopter into a vert ramp and blasts the highest air at 16.5 feet.
• Heath Kirchart kickflip backside lipslides a 10-stair handrail and lipslide shove-its a 13-stair.
• Jamie Thomas attempts the Leap of Faith (a giant stair gap) for a Zero ad, but gets broken off.
• Upcoming talent includes Ali Boulala, Jason Dill, Cairo Foster, Pierre Luc Gagnon, Kerry Getz and Darren Navarette.

1998 • Skateboard shops begin to sell a crap ton of blank decks, inspiring Powell to release mostly blank mini-logo pro decks to combat the problem.
• Evol and Plan B skateboards go under.
• Chris Miller launches Adio shoes with Steve Berra, Tony Hawk, Jamie Thomas and Jeremy Wray on the team.
• Sluggo completes the first back flip on vert.
• Upcoming talent includes Alex Corporan, Sam Hitz, Daxter Lussier, Kenny Reed, Bastien Salabanzi, Ed Selego and Daniel Shimizu.

1999 • Upland's combi pool is recreated (with more tranny and less vert) at a Vans skatepark inside The Block, a mall in Orange, California.

• The Skatelab skatepark and skateboard museum opens in Simi Valley, California.
• One of the most legendary street spots of all time, the EMB plaza in San Francisco, California, gets demolished.
• The high demands of landing tricks down huge stairs and gaps inspires skateboard shoe designers to employ technical elements of running shoes and cross trainers like puffy tongues, air bags, etc.
• Chad Muska leaves éS Footwear to launch C1RCA. His pro model debuts as one of the fastest-selling skateboard shoes ever. Mike Carroll and Rick Howard introduce Lakai footwear.
• Michael Brooke publishes *Concrete Wave*, a book on skateboarding history.
• Birdhouse destroys a van and themselves filming their most famous video, *The End*.
• Mark Gonzales dons a strange all-white outfit to do a demo in the Munchengaldbach modern art museum in Germany, creating the first—and probably last—example of skateboarding as performance art.
• At the X Games, Tony Hawk lands the first 900, launching himself and skateboarding in general into the mainstream. Activision debuts *Tony Hawk's Pro Skater* video game.
• Heath Kirchart lipslides the massive El Toro rail.
• Upcoming talent includes Mark Appleyard, Diego Bucchieri, Danny Garcia, Jerry Hsu, Arto Saari, Kristian Svitak and Stevie Williams.

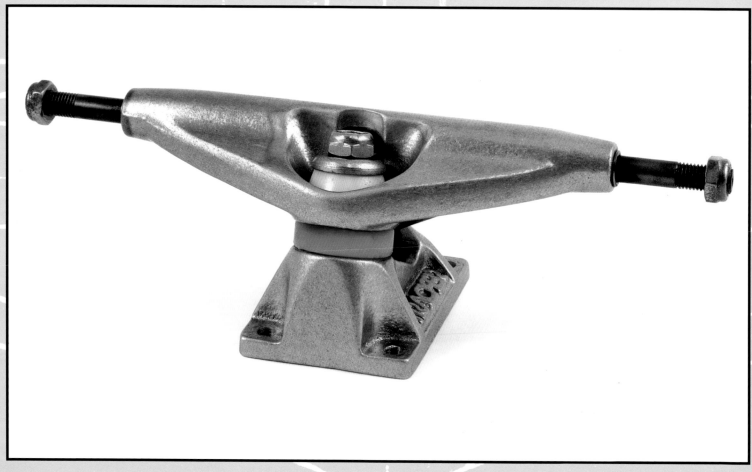

TRACKER AGGRO
QUICKTRACK
a Completely New Truck (1990)

As the best-selling truck of all time, Tracker was still perched on top of the skateboard world in 1990. Producing 60,000 trucks per month, we were so successful we decided to launch a completely new model called the Tracker Quicktrack. Our sales staff always wanted a new product to push, so we gave it to them! The look of the Quicktrack hanger was dramatically different from all previous Trackers. In order for the Quicktrack to be really strong and light, we added huge trusses around the cushion ring so we could hollow out the whole underside of the hanger. At 6 3/8" (161 mm) wide, the Quicktrack was slightly wider than the original Sixtrack, and the same width as our latest Sixtrack with the conical spacers. The new sand cast baseplate that came with the Quicktrack was named Aggro, which was designed with ribs on the top and also hollowed out on the underside to be strong and light. The Aggro baseplate featured an increased steering angle of five degrees, which made it turn quicker than classic Trackers. All of our original Gnarly truck hangers would also fit on the new Aggro baseplate, which resulted in a slightly quicker turning response than the original baseplates offered. During research and development, the Tracker team tested the Quicktrack for a whole year and really liked the prototypes. Then we got our marketing in place, our foundry orders in stock and began production.

Heat-Treating Disaster
1991: The Year Tracker Broke

The heat-treating facility that had worked on Tracker Trucks for years decided to put our new Quicktrack axles on the graveyard shift. The only problem with that was the guys in charge of the night crew were on drugs. Along with a lot of aircraft parts, they failed to heat-treat our axles over a 30-day period, sending them out with false certifications.

Throughout Tracker's history, we always required a heat-treating certification on our axles. Unfortunately, by the time we released the Quicktrack in 1990, we became overly confident in our vendor, and failed to pull sample axles to perform a Rockwell hardness test ourselves. By the time we found out that there was a problem, we had built and shipped out 30,000 Quicktracks all over the world. The non-heat treated axles bent, which caused the hollowed out aluminum hangers to crack. We tried to have our distributors and dealers return the trucks to us for replacement. We tried to explain what happened at the heat-treating facility. We even added a visual design change to the cast-

Top left: **Paulo Diaz vaults over a plastic trash can at School W in San Diego, California, circa 1990.**
Photo: Steve Sherman.
Above right: **Top views of Tracker Aggro Quicktrack hangers before and after the addition of axle rings.**
Left: **Tony Hawk brandishes a set of Tracker Aggro Quicktracks on the cover of** Thrasher, **January 1991.**
Photo: Scott Starr. Opposite page, top and bottom: **Tracker Aggro Quicktrack front and back views.**

239

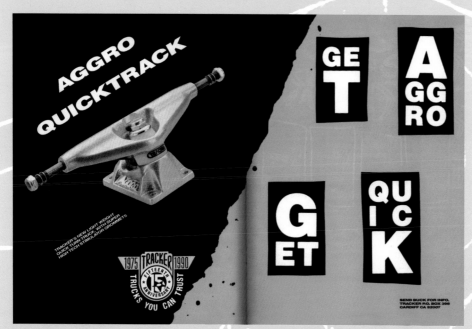

Tracker Aggro Quicktrack, June 1990.

Bucky Lasek, Kyle Anderson, March 1991.

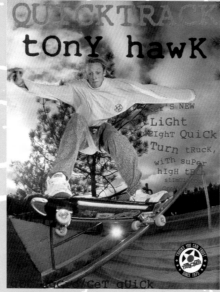

Tony Hawk, June 1990.

Omar Hassan, Tony Alva, June 1991.

240

Tracker Eurotrak Tour madness, circa 1990.

ing that also strengthened the hanger. Of course, the real problem was the first axles that were not heat-treated, which caused people to call our new truck the Quick Crack. Right when our customers' confidence dropped, Independent's sales climbed, which made it the best-selling truck for the first time in history.

The heat-treating company night shift also failed to heat-treat aircraft and aerospace parts. Again, these were sent out with bogus certifications. The Federal Aviation Administration seized the heat-treating company and closed it down. By the time we found out what happened, we had no recourse. That was a lesson we learned the hard way. Ever since, all Tracker parts are sample checked for quality control no matter how busy we are, even though we receive certifications from the supplier! Because of our problem with the sand cast Quicktracks with the non-heat-treated axles, we decided to change the casting process, the look of the hanger, and the truck name itself. I had already been working on some new hard steel permanent molds to cast the Aggro baseplate and Quicktrack hanger, a process that took over nine months. As it turned out, it was an extremely eventful year as we put our marketing team in gear to launch a new Tracker Truck.—LMB

The Tracker Eurotrak Tour Fiasco

In 1990, Lester Kasai, Adrian Demain and I went on a Tracker tour through 12 or 13 countries in Europe. We had guys like Matt Goldsby and Omar Hassan from other teams like Blockhead with us. We took 12 big boxes of t-shirts everywhere we went, gradually depleting them. We had to carry all of those, plus our luggage, on the train through Spain, France, Italy, Switzerland, etc. We didn't get rid of all of the t-shirts until we got to Norway at the end of the trip. What a hassle it was to take all of this stuff with us, blocking exits of the train so people couldn't get off. We couldn't even fit into a seat on the train, because we had too much shit. Nobody could go to the bathroom in our car, because we had boxes stacked up and were sleeping on them!

When we arrived in Barcelona, after a 10-hour overnight train ride, we got off and unloaded all of the boxes, because we were going to do some sightseeing all day. Omar Hassan, who was just 15 years old, had a lot of pent-up energy, so he did a little boardslide on a nearby bench. Then a cop came up and yelled, "What are you doing? You broke that bench!" Even though it was made out of cast iron, it was already tilted and warped. Then the cop said, "You have to pay $3,000 for that!" We were like, "What?" We only had eight hours in town, and they took Omar to the train station jail. Francisco Bergo from Sessions tried to bail him out. We were stuck there for eight hours, when Omar finally got out 10 minutes before we had to catch the next train out of town. Needless to say, we didn't get to do any sightseeing or go to the demo.—**Bryan Ridgeway**

The Tracker team hams it up in Larry Balma's Corvette during a photo shoot for the 1990 Tracker catalog. Photos: Miki Vuckovich

Emerging on the So Cal skateboarding scene in the late 1980s, Omar Hassan was one of the few young upstarts who kept tranny skating alive during the "all handrails all the time" era of the '90s. Always standing his lip tricks tall on the coping and blasting bodacious aerial maneuvers far above, it's obvious Omar learned his lessons from the Jeff Phillips school of power skating. Read on to hear about how Tracker impacted this all terrain ripper's formative years.—GSD

When did you get your first set of Trackers? Who gave them to you?
I got my first Trackers from Jim Gray. I was probably around 12 or so, and I started skating all of the local ramps in the neighborhood. I was probably around 13 when I really got on the team, then I rode Trackers through the late '80s and early '90s. Once I turned pro, Tracker had actually purchased Blockhead skateboards, which at the time was one of the most cutting-edge new deck brands that had more artistic graphics and progressive riders. So, Tracker and Blockhead were always a huge part of my life that made me who I am today.

What was it like skating for Tracker back in the late '80s and '90s?
Tracker had a lot to do with my upbringing. It was weird how skateboarding was back then in the '80s, because there weren't a lot of clothing brands, and shoe brands weren't as involved as they are now. Back then, hard goods really drove skateboarding. So, if you rode for Tracker, Indy or Gullwing, they were one of your main sponsors. You wore their shirt and stickers. No one had rights like the

clothing brands do nowadays, where you have to wear their stuff. There weren't so many sponsors out there, just decks, trucks and wheels. Maybe the clothing and shoes were trickled in there a little bit, but decks and trucks were the main thing. The West Coast, and where I lived in the Orange Country area, was really driven by Tracker, especially when I was growing up. Tony Hawk on Tracker represented the elite from San Diego, and Christian Hosoi on Indy repped Los Angeles, so you had the Hawk vs. Hosoi / Tracker vs. Indy thing.

One thing I do remember about that whole rivalry is that I got the cover of Thrasher when I was riding Trackers. I'll never forget, it was a huge deal at the time, because Thrasher had a stronghold on Indy. I got to know Fausto Vitello and the guys who ran Thrasher through all of those Back to the City contests that they put on. Back then, contests were thrown by skateboarding-affiliated companies. You didn't have all of these energy drink brands and other corporate sponsors like today. It was a tight-knit group of people. If you had a contest in San Francisco, Thrasher and those guys ran it. Since Blockhead was out of Sacramento, I spent a lot of time there and in the San Francisco area, so I felt like I broke the mold a little bit on the Tracker vs. Indy thing, because I had friendships with those guys. It got to the point where the rivalry was, "Either you're cool or you're not," so when I got the cover of Thrasher with Trackers on my board, that was a big way for me to be accepted. The point was it doesn't really matter what you ride or who you back, it's all still a huge part of the love of skateboarding. Even before that, it got to the point where everyone was strong-arming each other so hard with the truck thing. I never played into it, so I got really lucky to get a Thrasher cover, because there was a lot of politics involved. That was super cool, and I'll never forget how stoked everyone was.

Do you recall any memorable times with the Tracker team?
I learned a lot from what Tracker did for me, with Bryan Ridgeway especially. Ridge and Jim Gray really molded me into realizing how to turn skateboarding into a career. When I got on Tracker, they sent Lester Kasai, Adrian Demain, Matt Goldsby and I on a seven-country European tour. Ridge had to go to my school and talk to my principal to get the homework I needed to be gone for a month. Back then, doing something like that was not the norm. At the time, you were kind of an outcast even if you were a skateboarder. It wasn't a very mainstream thing to do; it was more of a tight-knit group of people doing something different. It wasn't so networked out to where everyone knew what skateboarding was. There were so many memorable times for me, but that European tour was incredible. It opened up my eyes to see what skateboarding was about, especially in foreign countries. We did so many demos and met so many people; it's

hard to express how much Tracker, being the elite truck brand, meant to skateboarding.

Once I really got into skating and understood it, riding for Tracker was one of the raddest things, because they actually did stuff for me that other truck brands didn't do for their riders, like sending them on seven-country tours to Europe for a month. Tracker was an elite brand to ride for, especially at that time, because they did have a roster of skateboarders who backed up the truck and the brand. Once you got the okay to actually be on Tracker, you were in an elite class of skateboarders. It was really an honor to ride for Tracker back then. I had a group of friends who wore Indy pride and a group of friends who wore Tracker pride. At the time, that drove skateboarding even more than the boards. There wasn't a huge rivalry with boards, because there were enough board brands to appeal to everybody. But, when you have two major truck brands, and both have a roster of the most elite skaters, then it forms this rivalry that was cool to be a part of. You have to be from that generation to understand how intense the whole Tracker vs. Indy thing was.

It was interesting that, as time went on, the whole truck thing in general faded away, because it got so saturated just like boards did. There were so many brands; everyone started making their own trucks, and the Tracker vs. Indy rivalry fizzled out a little bit. Today, trucks don't have that big of an influence on skateboarding. That was a special time. Skateboarding was so new, there wasn't much competition, so Tracker really had a corner on that market, especially having Tony Hawk. I mean, you can name a million guys like Jeff Phillips, Mark Gonzales, Rudy Johnson and Guy Mariano; the roster of people who came out of that camp was pretty awesome. To be a part of that history was super-humbling.

Which tricks did you invent on Trackers?
I came up at the tail end of the early '90s, when most of the tricks were already invented. Everyone already had the trick names out there, so everything else just became variations of tricks. There's not one I'm going to throw out there and have someone else say they might have done it first.

You're more of a stylist, like Christian, compared to Tony, who was more trick-oriented.
One thing about Tony Hawk and his influence: you asked me about inventing tricks. Well, Tony invented half of the tricks I do.

Tracker was a perfect match for me, because we had Lester Kasai, who, in my mind, was the closest we had to Christian Hosoi. Tracker had all of their ducks in a row with every type of skater on their team, and I was lucky to be a part of that.

Read the full-length interview at trackertrucks.com

Above: **Omar Hassan shows off a set of Tracker Quicktracks on the cover of Thrasher, December 1990.**
Photo: Scott Starr

By Larry Balma

Omar Hassan flicks a huge Ollie off of a curb cut, circa early 1990s. Photo: O

It was back in the late 1980s when Sal Barbier crawled up out of the swamps of Louisiana to start his skateboarding career on rickety backyard vert ramps. After moving to So Cal in 1990, Sal went on to find fame and fortune as one of the most prominent street skaters of the 20th century's final decade, when he designed the most beautiful skateboard shoe of all time, the Sal 23, for etnies. Brandishing a riding style smoother than butter and always looking sharp, Sal Barbier is a true style icon both on and off the skateboard.—GSD

Sal Barbier
INTERVIEW

Where did you grow up?
Baton Rouge, Louisiana.

When and how did you start skating?
I was hanging out with friends in the ninth grade who introduced me to skateboarding. I was getting into BMX freestyle and my mom decided to ground me from my bike for having bad grades, but she didn't say anything about the skateboard.

Describe your first good set-up.
My friend Kevin Falk found and sold me a Variflex Arrow deck with Tracker Trucks and Kryptonics wheels in 1985. I started on vert. I could do inverts, sadplants, backside Boneless Ones, little Ollies, frontside airs and lipslides. I was riding a Zorlac board. This was during that era when I was watching *The Bones Brigade Video Show* and I was trying to learn a lot of stuff they did in it. For that era, I was okay on ramps. I had one friend

who was really good on vert and I skated with him all the time. We built our own half-pipe right from the *Thrasher* ramp plans. It was only up for a week when the kid's dad had to tear it down for insurance reasons. After that, most of the guys quit skating. I probably did it by myself for two-and-a-half or three years. There was nothing, no ramps or anything. I had a small quarterpipe in front of my house and the closest mini-ramp was an hour away.

Which Tracker model did you mostly ride?
The Sixtrack without the removable kingpin.

Which Tracker riders influenced you?
I'm from the south, so Bryan Pennington influenced me the most to ride them. I looked up to him. I would travel to Houston, pad up and try to skate the ramps. He was the best guy I had seen in person, and he was more impressive than what I had seen on video tapes. If you saw him back then, you'd know exactly what I'm talking about. At the Shut Up and Skate contests, he would kill it. He and Jeff Phillips were my favorites and still are today.

Before you moved to California, were you busting handrails in Louisiana?
Yeah, I was never impressed by anything in the magazines or videos until I saw that H-Street *Shackle Me Not* video. When you live in a place like Louisiana and you don't have anyone to skate with, you watch videos all the time. It's just kind of weird when you're watching them and you don't see any new tricks in there that you can't really do. So, I got into handrails pretty early. I tried it right after I saw that Steve Saiz photo, which was the first photo I saw of someone sliding down a rail. I tried it on this two-stair rail and it was so short that when you got on, you'd just be right off. I was out of town when I did it. I told this one kid that I had done it and he didn't believe me. When I got back to town, he had picked out this seven-stair rail with a gnarly kink at the end, and it was pretty high, too. That was probably the first real one I did. It was pretty gnarly. I broke my rib on it, so I got back up and I did it again. Every day, I'd go back there just to do it so I wouldn't be scared of it.

When and how did you turn pro?
In 1990, I snuck out to California. I told my mom I was going to visit a friend in California, but there was no friend. I met a young man named Mike Ternasky, filmed a part for an H-Street video, and was given a signature model soon after.

Did you invent any tricks on Trackers?
Yes, kickflip boardslides.

Why was Tracker so important in the history of skateboarding?
Almost everyone rode them at one point, like Mark Gonzales, Tony Hawk, Jeff Phillips and Bryan Pennington, just to name a few. Of course, there were more from different eras.

Do you have any other comments about Tracker?
Can someone please explain how to

install those Copers? I've been trying to figure out that one for years.

Back in the mid 1990s, you designed the Sal 23 for etnies, which turned out to be one of the best-loved skate shoes of all time. Tell us about that.
I worked on the design of the whole shoe: the sole, the logo, everything. The reason I usually designed shoes was because I would find things wrong with other ones, and I wanted to make 'em the way I thought they should be made. I was a pretty stylish guy, and I liked everything I was wearing except my shoes, so I would just need to correct them. It would drive me crazy. I'd think, "If this was that way, and if that was in this color." I would cut up other shoes, draw on shoes and make markings of where I wanted panels to

be. I also wanted a rubber piece on the side so it wouldn't tear apart, because by the time most skate shoes break in, you have to get a new pair because they're all ripped-up. Then I went in and worked with the guys at etnies. After the shoe finally came out, it seemed like everyone had a pair at some point, which was cool. A couple of years later, when the Sal 23 wasn't out anymore, a lot of people would ask me if they knew where they could find a pair or if etnies was going to make 'em again. It was kind of cool to really work hard on something and have people understand it and appreciate it for what it was, rather than just putting my name on it and trying to get some money. It wasn't about that.

Who all was riding the Sal 23 when it came out?
Mike Carroll and a lot of my friends were wearing it back then, so I think almost everyone had 'em. It was cool to open up the magazine and see a lot of people riding the Sal 23. Maybe some wore it because they respected my name or they liked the way it skated or the way it was designed.

Who are your current sponsors?
I ride for Skateboard Veteran and Independent trucks.

Which are your favorite skate spots?
'80s era vert ramps. Do you know where I can find one?

What have been the highlights of your time in skateboarding?
Meeting people—everyone from musicians to distributors, shop owners, kids, women, and skaters from earlier generations who were hanging on my wall.

What do you enjoy doing besides skateboarding?
I study music, guitar and piano. I also like to surf.

Above: **The etnies Sal 23 shoe designed by Sal Barbier.**
Left: **Sal Barbier, circa 1990.** Photo: Miki Vuckovich

SAL BARBIER

AGGRO
AGGRO
AGGRO

GETTING AGGRO GOT THE QUICK

1975 TRACKER 1990
FIFTEENTH
15
ANNIVERSARY
TRUCKS YOU CAN TRUST

Sal Barbier, August 1990.

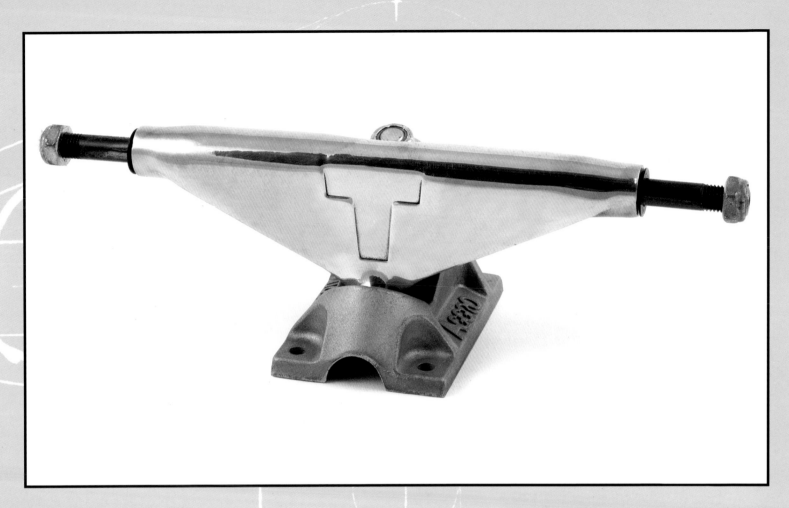

TRACKER AGGRO
STREET TRACK
Strong as Hell! (1991)

Launched in 1991, the Tracker Aggro Street Track was a lighter, stronger and more refined version of the Quicktrack, as well as boasting the first Tracker hanger with a cast-in axle. Although the truck was made out of the same A356 aluminum heat treated to T6 hardness, the parts were cast in a state-of-the-art hard steel permanent mold, as opposed to all of our earlier trucks, which were cast from sand molds that were

broken open during the process and had to be re-made after each pour. With an increased turning angle of five-degrees, the Street Track featured the same geometry as the Quicktrack. The incredible strength of the Street Track inspired the advertising tag line, "Strong as Hell!" In fact, the truck was so durable, Tracker's *The Brotherhood* video featured a clip of me pounding it repeatedly with a sledgehammer, only to find it in perfect condition afterward.

Measuring 6 3/8" wide (161 mm), the Street Track was primarily a vert truck that could also be ridden on the street before street boards evolved into enlarged freestyle decks that were affectionately called popsicle sticks. Of course, all of Tracker's original Gnarly hangers would also fit on the new Aggro baseplate, which resulted in a slightly quicker turning response. When we launched the Aggro Street Track, we were building about 40,000 of them per month. This slowed to less than 15,000 per month after some financial trouble we experienced during the economic downturn. As time went on, we produced and sold fewer and fewer Street Tracks as we brought out new truck models geared to the rapidly evolving street skating scene. —**LMB**

Above: **An original Tracker Aggro Street Track logo overlay.**
Left: **See Mr. Pallet standing tall. Watch Jeremy Klein make him fall with a well-placed Ollie to tail slide, circa 1992.** Photo: Dave Swift
Opposite page, top and bottom: **Tracker Street Track front and back views.**

John Pryor, September 1991.

New Street Track, September 1991.

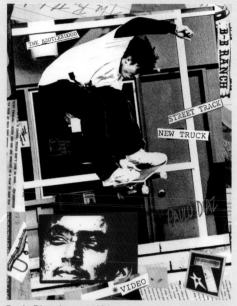

Paulo Diaz, August 1991.

Armando Barajas, 1992. Photo: Steve Sherman

Gonz, Chatman, Klein, October 1991.

Omar Hassan, February 1992.

Armando Barajas, July 1991.

Larry Balma, November 1991.

Tony Hawk, December 1991.

248

Rob Dyrdek, January 1992.

Mark Gonzales cavorts within the hamster wheel of infinity, circa 1992. Photo: CR Stecyk III

Mark Gonzales, November 1991.

A Missed Opportunity

Around 1991, we had the greatest street skater of all time, Mark Gonzales, riding Tracker Aggro Street Tracks. Around that time, Mark met with Tracker team manager Bryan Ridgeway and presented his idea to design a street truck. I sat down with Bryan and the Gonz for lunch and they both gave me their sales pitch. Gonz made some sketches of his truck idea on a napkin and, as soon as I looked at it, I could tell that he didn't understand how truck geometry worked, or how moving around the axle would affect turning. Gonz was so excited about his sketch that he didn't listen to my input. All I could see was how much effort it would take for me to build up prototypes and proceed through months of testing—like I had already done many times over the years—just to bring Gonz up to speed on truck design.

I looked at Gonz's drawing and said, "This truck won't turn." I thought about how Tracker's main competitor over the last 15 years, Independent, always said, "Trackers don't turn." Now Gonz unwittingly wanted us to build a truck that *really* didn't turn. He just wanted it to be low. I spent the time to build a prototype of his design, but he said it sucked and suggested we try something else. But, I just couldn't go on as I was still struggling to stay afloat after some financial difficulties the year before. Since my time every day had to be spent

thinking about dollars coming in, planning for the future was a luxury. Plus, I figured if there was going to be a pro model truck in this world, shouldn't it be for Tony Hawk?

In hindsight, I should have made a truck that was low like Mark Gonzales wanted with limited turning and named it the Tracker Gonz model. I'm sure he would have ridden and accepted a truck I built that would work, maybe with only a few aesthetic changes, so he could feel a sense of ownership. As it was, I was too stressed with another looming financial disaster to be able to focus clearly. As it turned out, Gonz talked to Fausto Vitello of Independent and, although Fausto would not give him a pro model truck either, Fausto and his partner Eric Swenson did design the Venture truck, which was also low with minimal turning. Unfortunately, Gonz became a Venture skater and I learned yet another hard lesson in business.—**LMB**

Ridge's View

The Gonz was excited to talk about a designing a truck with the owner of a legendary company like Tracker. Although he had a crude design, and a point about function and why it was necessary for the next generation of street skaters, he was intimidated going in. With those variables on the table, I thought Larry could use his wealth of knowledge and experience to break down the pros and cons after gathering more and more info from the Gonz. Instead, he wasn't aware of how sensitive the Gonz was, and how easily the Gonz could be put off by someone, yet again, talking to him like he was, in the Gonz's mind, an uneducated kid who knew nothing about anything. Whenever you design anything, there are three things to consider: what's necessary, what's available, and what's possible. It's about closing the gap on all three in order to morph it into the next viable solution. I knew this then, but couldn't communicate it before the Gonz felt slighted. Coming from Larry, the truck design jargon was all too technical. It wasn't Larry's fault, he just didn't know how to talk to the Gonz.

Larry was correct about Tony Hawk, but didn't realize the full potential of having the greatest street skater. Vert was fading and, yes, Hawk "deserved" it. But, in the 1990s, it was about selling to street skaters in a huge way, and the Gonz had the greatest influence at the time. Larry was into big name popularity, while I was into leaders of disciplines and their perspective popularity. Also, I'm not sure Larry even wanted to do another truck. He was so slammed by being the owner of TransWorld, Skate Rags, Street Rags, Limpies and Mammoth mountain bikes, that the amount of focus needed for Tracker was overwhelming. Larry ran out of steam and he was still reeling from a financial mess. Larry really liked the Gonz and what he represented, but I think the fire to stay at the forefront of truck brands had diminished a bit due to Larry's other responsibilities and stress. Like they always say, hindsight is 20/20. Everyone learned from that one! Miscommunication is a bitch, and sometimes you only have one chance to get it right. At least now we know we were right to push for the Gonz truck. Look at all of the pro truck models out today. Tracker was still first with the Hawk truck, though.—**Bryan Ridgeway**

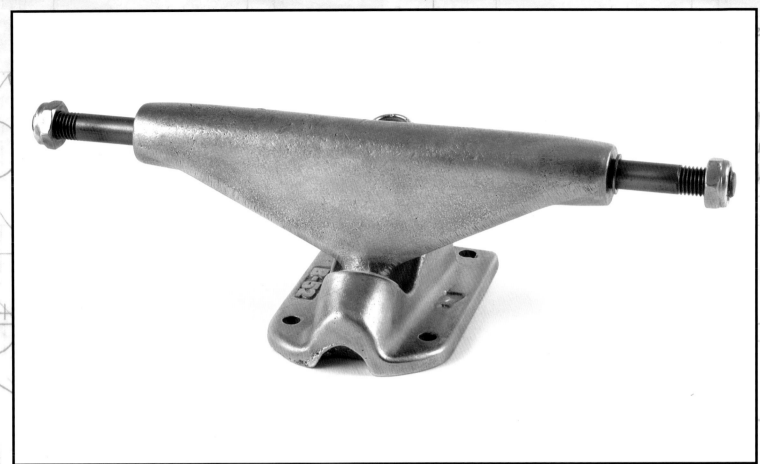

TRACKER

JOHN REEVES

B52 FIXED
AXLE TRUCKS
129 139 149

Send $1.00 for catalog
and sticker fix
P.O. Box 398 Cardiff, CA 92007

John Reeves, December 1993.

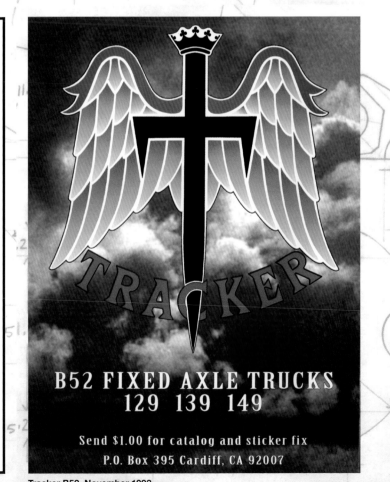

B52 FIXED AXLE TRUCKS
129 139 149

Send $1.00 for catalog and sticker fix
P.O. Box 395 Cardiff, CA 92007

Tracker B52, November 1993.

252

TRACKER B52
Down Low in the Street (1992)

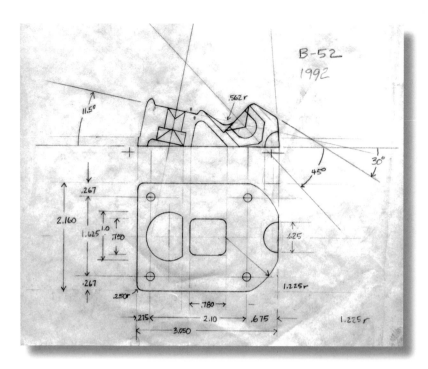

Although vertical ramps dominated skateboarding throughout the 1980s, by the early '90s, after a brief lull in the sport, street skating had begun to fuel the beginning of the third growth cycle. The basic trick that initiated every move in street skating was the Ollie. The tiny diameter wheels that were becoming all the rage made it easier to Ollie, and, likewise, new popular trucks for street skating were being designed with a low center of gravity and roll center and a slow turning angle; the key word being low.

Debuting in 1992, the Tracker B52 employed the original geometry of the classic Gnarly Tracker base, but lowered it 1/4". We also shortened the kingpin 1/4" along with the outer cushion, which allowed more kingpin clearance while using the lower Extrack hanger geometry. The outer cushion was even harder than the inner cushion and the truck was ridden tight. This made for an ultra-low roll center truck that worked, but only because the wheels had become so small and cushions so hard that they increased the board's flip potential without any wheel bite. The B52 was also the first Tracker baseplate to change to the shortened four-hole mounting pattern that was sweeping through skateboarding like wildfire. When street skaters did blunt, tail and nose slides on curbs and ledges, the mounting hardware got

all ground up and came loose. Thus, we shortened the hole spacing from 2.5" to 2.1," which moved the front mounting bolts out of the way. We also rounded off the front of the baseplate for less drag. Although the hardware was no longer a problem, the rounded front of the B52 baseplate made it more difficult to lock into blunt slides, so we changed it back to square again on our next truck, the Tracker B2.

The Tracker B52 name was borrowed from the Boeing B-52 Stratofortress long-range bomber first flown in 1952 and still in use today by the US Air Force. With the B52, we labeled axle hanger widths in millimeter sizes for the first time: 129 mm, 139 mm, and 149 mm. All of these sizes were based on the Tracker Extrack geometry. In fact, the B52 with the Extrack geometry hanger was the lowest Tracker ever produced. All of the B52 truck versions came in what we called a raw finish. Since we did not polish the base and hanger, the result was a smooth but dull aluminum finish, just as it came out of the tumbler machine. This saved us money, which allowed us to offer the trucks at a reasonable price. Remember, we were still struggling to get out of the hole after experiencing some financial problems during the economic downturn, and all of our manufacturing costs had risen. With our low level of sales, profit margins were almost non-existent and, much to Tracker team manager Bryan Ridgeway's dismay, our promotional budget was shot. Despite the bleak outlook, the time would soon come for Tracker to rise once again!—**LMB**

Below: **Tracker B52** baseplates master molds.
Opposite page, top: **Tracker B52.**

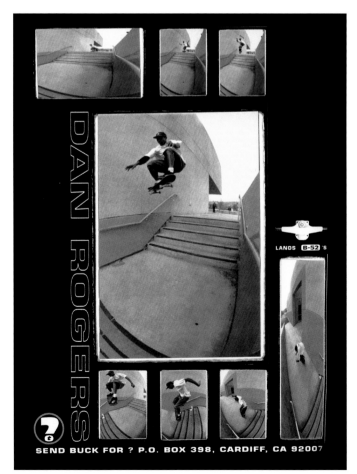

Dan Rogers, August 1993.

253

Back in the 1990s, Ron Chatman, Jeremy Klein and Dan Rogers were the triad of Tracker. As some of the top street skaters of that decade, they acted as a hub for the brand that attracted established legends like Mark Gonzales as well as major upstarts like Guy Mariano, Rudy Johnson, Andrew Reynolds and Jim Greco for a short time. (Essentially, when the latter five left Tracker, they went on to help make other trucks like Independent, Thunder and Venture more popular.) Born in East Los Angeles, California in 1971, Ron Chatman grew up in Long Beach, riding for brands like World Industries, Milk, ATM Click and 60/40. Also starting out on World Industries, Jeremy Klein, who was born in Torrance, California in 1971, went on to skate for Birdhouse. He eventually formed his own deck and shoe brand called Hook-Ups, which he still runs today. Beginning life as a military brat in Bethesda, Maryland in 1970, Dan Rogers ended up in So Cal by way of Iowa, eventually landing on Invisible. When we approached Ron, Jeremy and Dan about doing their interviews for the Tracker book, they came up with the bright idea to do it all together while revisiting and skating one of their old stomping grounds in Huntington Beach. Still in contact after all these years, they invited Bryan Ridgeway, longtime friend and Tracker team manager, to join in.—GSD

MD: When did you start skating?
RC: I started in 1978. I got a membership to Lakewood Skatepark in '79.
JK: I saw the *Bones Brigade Video Show* when I was in seventh grade and haven't stopped since I saw it.

JEREMY KLEIN

SEND BUCK FOR STICKERS AND INFO
P.O. BOX 198 CARDIFF, CA. 92007

254

DR: A kid named Rich Chleebek, who's dead now from a car crash, moved to my town. Everyone in Iowa dies from drunk driving car crashes for some reason. I was a sophomore in high school and had two Powell-Peralta boards, a General Issue and a Ripper. The first thing I did on a skateboard was ride off of five stairs, grabbing the nose and rail. Retarded kids today would say I grabbed Indy.
MD: Describe your first good set-up.
RC: An Alva deck with Tracker Trucks and Kryptonics wheels.
JK: A yellow Mark Gonzales with Gullwing trucks and black Rat Bones.
DR: A Rob Roskopp III with Gullwing trucks and red Powell-Peralta 3 wheels (worst wheels ever) from a shop called Kar City Big Wheels. The guy who owned Kar City was named Don. He spoke with an awesome speech impediment and would go down into the basement of his shop all the time with kids in the store. Why did he do that? With hindsight, probably to sip whiskey. The first time I went into Brooklyn Projects and met Dom, he had an old PK Ripper on the wall with a Kar City sticker on it. I was like, "No way, it couldn't be! Dom's from Brooklyn." When I asked about it, Dom said, "Yeah, this cool old guy in Iowa used to send me stickers and help me out with the race stuff. He basically sponsored me." When I told him my connection, we both tripped out.
MD: How did you all first get involved with the Tracker family?
RC: For me, it had a lot to do with Bryan Ridgeway. As a kid, I would always see Ridge at the events with all of the Tracker guys and I thought that was cool, just that whole friendship vibe. There were always two team managers at every event, Todd Hastings from Powell-Peralta and Ridgeway. In the end, Jeremy Klein pulled me in, but Bryan was a huge factor.
DR: I think I got on very similarly, through Ridge and Jeremy. Ridge took me up to Los Angeles to skate with Mark Gonzales, Ron and Jeremy, and a few other guys. At the end of the day, Ridge put it out there, "Why don't you just skate for Tracker?" I actually rode for Indy at the time and I was one of the only San Diego skaters to be featured in *Thrasher* regularly. As a kid, I really didn't think much of it. I thought, "Everybody gets in *Thrasher*." But, the reality was that wasn't the case. So, basically, when I quit Indy, *Thrasher* blacklisted me. I know they were pissed. I'm not sure if it was a personal thing, but the vibe with them definitely changed.
RC: But you got the cover of *TransWorld* right after in 1991!
MD: Do you remember the trick?
DR: Yes, it was a boardslide on a curved rail in Oceanside, California. I remember Grant Britain called me and said he had a flat bar to shoot a photo on. Then we showed up and it was this 10 or 11-stair curved rail. I was a little intimidated by it, but as usual, Grant convinced me that the shot would be good, so we went for it. I guess it paid off with the cover.
MD: Some kids cut the knobs off

that recently and are skating it again!
DR: It's pretty crazy to think that those kids skating it today were not even born when we shot that pic.
MD: What about you, Jeremy? How did you end up riding for Tracker?
JK: In all honesty, I was riding for Thunder and I wanted to get paid. Thunder didn't want to pay me, so I think I called Ridge and told him Ron Chatman and myself wanted to ride for Tracker and we wanted to get paid.

Ron Chatman
Jeremy Klein
Dan Rogers
INTERVIEW

I'm pretty sure that's where Mark Gonzales came into the mix, as well.
MD: Can any of you elaborate on what happened with Mark Gonzales and Tracker? It seems like there was a missed opportunity in there somewhere.
DR: The missed opportunity would have been the signature truck. Mark drew a truck for Ridge on a napkin. At the time, no one had signature trucks, so for Tracker to come out with two signature trucks, one for Tony Hawk and the other for Mark Gonzales, seems like a no-brainer today. But, back then there was nothing like that, so it probably seemed like a big risk, because people were not even really getting paid by their truck sponsors. If it would've happened, Tracker would've set the bar for all other truck brands.
BR: I gave the design and logo to Larry Balma and he did work on it, but it just wouldn't work on a functional level. But, I know he did start the process. Eventually, the design was shut down and Mark parted ways with the company.
RC: I personally still don't understand that whole thing. I think Tracker blew it 100%. Think about it: you make kung foo suits and Bruce Lee comes to you with a design. What do you do? You make golf clubs and Tiger Woods comes to you with a club design. What do you do? To me, that whole thing was gnarly. I honestly felt bad about bringing my buddy Gonz into the equation.
MD: Did you invent a trick on Trackers?
DR: "Invented a trick" is a stretch, but I was doing frontside 180s to switch crooked grinds really early. I thought I may have made them up, then I went to San Francisco and saw Henry Sanchez doing them at the EMB curb / sculpture thing with metal coping on it. He was the only other person I saw do them at the time.
MD: Which Tracker truck models did you guys skate?
RC: I used to like to skate the magnesiums, because I would always see them in the magazines when I was a kid. I liked to skate those on vert. On street, I rode whatever they gave me, but I do remember riding the B52 first, then the B2.
JK: I think I was basically a guinea pig. Most trucks are the same to me.
BR: Whenever there was new stuff com-

ing out, I would give it to Jeremy to test out, so he tried out pretty much everything. Guinea pig fits.

JK: I remember one time I wanted a longer Extrack hanger, because I was skating a 9.5" board, so Larry rigged one up with a longer axle and extra spacers. They looked ridiculous, but they worked. I was stoked on that. But, I remember riding the B2 truck a lot, and I guess from what you told me, I also rode the Tony Hawk signature truck. I have such a bad memory.

DR: I also rode the B52, B2 and the Hawk Trucks. If I remember correctly, they were pretty similar. But, I do want to bring up what I think was the most ridiculous thing, truck wise, for a bunch of engineers and guys who fix things to do, which was making trucks that were broken. "Instead of stopping your axles from slipping, we're going to make it so they slip all the time and rattle like a fucking freight train." Not to mention they would fall out and you would die! What was the other thing they made with the little clip and little slit at the end of your axle? You would barely touch your axle on something and those things would pop off with force. They were horrible, at best. How about going 100 mph and the stupid fucking e-clip falls off in between tricks, which makes your wheel fall off mid-nose blunt slide, and leads to your leading shoulder being driven into the ground with catastrophic force.

MD: Tell us about some memories that come to mind when you think back on your time with Tracker.

JK: We used to make a lot of videos for the new product that was coming out. Obviously not full production movies, but I remember those being fun times. Just getting picked up by Ridge, cruising around to spots and skating with no pressure, and possibly hit a Fuddruckers afterward.

RC: The actual skating and hanging with Ridge, Jeremy, Dan and the rest of the crew was fun, because come on, who doesn't like skating with your friends?

DR: For some reason, it seems like we were always skating at South Bay schools, but being from San Diego, I actually thought we were in Los Angeles. That's where all of Jeremy's banks were that he skated. Some were good, some were so bad you couldn't even ride up them, but he could somehow rip them all!

MD: Favorite Tracker ad?

RC: It was a kickflip tailslide at Gardena, and it was all because of this guy, Dan Rogers. You had more of a jock mentality and at the time I had started piling out a little, drinking and partying more than I should have, and you would always call me out, telling me I was blowing it. So, that was the motivation behind getting that particular trick, to show you that the party guy could still throw down. In fact, I actually called out the trick before shooting it and you called bullshit on me, remember?

DR: Yes, I actually do remember that.

JK: Was I there?

DR: Yep, he did it so fucking good. It was a frontside flip, not backside. So gnarly!

RC: Yes, frontside. I was so stoked skating with these guys. It was so fun, but they still pushed you! Dan got me so mad, I was like, "I can do this easy." That was seriously one of the sickest things I've done, and it was a video grab, so that was also the beginning of that era.

DR: My first Tracker ad was with Dave Swift. It was a backside 5-0 facing the camera with the Horsemen Forever logo on the wall.

[At this point in the interview, without any questions being asked, Ron Chatman proceeded to talk about the problems he had riding for Tracker.]

RC: It was simple: we weren't able to be paid money that we were promised.

DR: You and Jeremy were getting paid, and you wanted to get more, because you had been getting paid the same for two years.

JK: We wanted a raise?

DR: We just wanted a raise! It seemed fair at the time, because we had been on Tracker for a long time.

RC: We were doing our jobs skating and there were a lot of things happening in the company to show that the money was there. You're saying you can't pay us but you have the money to start up new projects like Neighborhood, etc. You can piss down my back and tell me it's raining but I can tell the difference. I was the one out of us three who was overly adamant about trying to get us the big pay. I got on Ridge's back to the point where I developed animosity toward him, because I felt like he wasn't gunning for us the way he should have, or at least what I expected. So, out of the three of us, I was the most bitter and angry.

DR: I think you have to understand that Ron was a little older than Jeremy and I. He was

looking at skateboarding as a career and felt like he was being exploited as a professional. Meanwhile, Jeremy and I were like, "What's exploited?" We just wanted to skate and have fun. We weren't looking at it from the same angle as Ron. So, basically, we had this meeting with Ridge. When did you meet Larry?

BR: At the Del Mar Rusty Harris Series contest in 1982.

DR: Okay, so Ridge hooked up with Larry in 1982 and had already seen skating rise and fall twice. Then there we were and Ron was speaking for all of us, because we all felt that way. Ron said, "Hey, we should be getting more money." We all agreed, but we didn't really understand how to make it happen. So, he talked to Ridge, who said, "Sorry, baby, it ain't gonna happen." So, Ron was like, "Fuck that! We want to meet with Larry." So, there we were—Ron, Jeremy, Ridge and myself—upstairs in some office at Tracker headquar-

Dan Rogers nose slides the hump of the Camel Bridge somewhere in San Diego, California, circa 1992. Photo: Grant Brittain

ters. Poor Larry had no idea about the intelligence he was about to deal with. He thought he was gonna deal with kids who were just gonna be like, "Whatever you say, you're a big business man. You have to know what's right. You're not taking advantage of us at all." It was obviously a different outcome.

JK: What exactly happened? I don't actually remember. Did we get paid or did we quit?

RC: I don't remember either.

DR: At the time, Jeremy was getting $150.00 per month and Ron was getting $150.00 as well. I wasn't getting anything, maybe $50.00 per month.

JK: No, Ridge actually got me a lot of money to start off with.

DR: Really? So, you were getting $500.00 or something like that?

JK: Yeah, it was something like that. [It was actually $300.00.] It was a decent amount of money to where I was pretty stoked.

Ron Chatman guides a frontside 180 Ollie to switch 5-0 in Long Beach, California, circa 1992. Photo: Dave Swift

DR: So, anyway, Jeremy was getting paid, Chatman wasn't getting paid enough, and I wasn't getting anything. So, we went into this meeting, and for whatever reason, Larry was all, "Well, you know guys, times are tough," and Ron just stopped him in his tracks by saying, "How can you say times are tough? You're starting up this company, you're starting up that company!" It was like a record had screeched to a stop! The ultimate confrontation: old man verses young lion. So, Ron threw out, "What, you want me to be happy? You're feeding me scraps," like, "Aaaaah, don't fro me offa da plantation, massa Larry!" That is a verbatim quote directed toward Larry, who probably had not been expecting to get hit with the race card. Long story short, we all got a raise that day. Thanks to Ridge for doing what he did and to Ron for taking charge.

BR: Well, you deserved it.

JK: I can't believe that race came into this. That's crazy. I understand not having money to run a company. Running a company costs tons of money. I'm giving him the benefit of the doubt. He might have been starting those companies…

RC: So, now you're going to back peddle and defend him?

JK: No, I'm just telling you back then I didn't own a company, so I didn't know how difficult it was to make money.

RC: I never owned a company, but my dad ran motels, so I knew how business worked. Even to this day, that was bullshit. I'm not a genius, but I was raised with a lot of common sense.

JK: Well, I've owned a skateboard company for more than 20 years, so I've seen how the money is, and there isn't much.

RC: Well, that's just business, period. That's all I'm getting at. Business, skateboarding or not, if you have a hotdog business…

DR: You're being negative, Ron.

MD: What are your thoughts on the Tracker book being released?

RC: I think it's rad. I think its good, because skateboarding is growing so big, and there are already so many kids who don't know the past. The roots are important, so any way you look at it, it's good for the family of skateboarding as a whole.

JK: Can we get a copy when it's done?

MD: Yes, of course. We will get you each a few copies.

JK: Well, I only want one. But, if it's good, I'll take a couple!

MD: Which skateboarders inspired you?

RC: Everyone from the '70s and '80s, mainly Bobby Valdez, Steve Olson and Tony Alva, because I was young and they looked rad. All early street pros.

JK: Mark Gonzales and Tony Hawk. To me, they are the best—rad trick selection and creativity.

DR: When I was a kid? Christian Hosoi, of course, Mark Gonzales, Natas Kaupas, Jason Jesse, Matt Hensley.

MD: What have been the highlights of your time in skateboarding?

RC: Skating itself is a highlight.

JK: Going on tours across America and destroying stuff.

DR: I took every opportunity I had to avoid joining the real world and lived every moment like it was the last. I was always the last to go to sleep and the first to wake up.

MD: What are you up to today?

RC: I still skate, raise my kids and pay bills.

JK: I've been doing my own company, Hook-Ups, for the past 20 years.

DR: After skateboarding, I wore a suit and tie for too long and, luckily, finally had the opportunity to work in skateboarding at a brand I truly love, Emerica. I've been around the brand for so long by default, so to actually be able to have some impact was really fun and frustrating, but amazing overall. Currently, I am the Global Sales Director at Asphalt Yacht Club. It's definitely a challenge running around preaching the gospel of skateboarding, meanwhile making the brand succeed in big box stores. We are the United Colors of Benetton for skateboarding. It's never been done, so we'll see if I can help pull off the impossible.

MD: What do you enjoy doing besides skateboarding?

RC: I enjoy reading, drawing, watching movies and listening to music.

JK: Video games, junk food and dogs.

DR: Outside of skateboarding, I have a wonderful family, first and foremost. I know the whole kid thing is boring, but I have two—a son and a daughter—and they rule. Their lives are magical and hopefully one day they will think I'm cool. I mean, how many kids do you know who have uncle Lance art painted in their rooms? The thing I'd really like to put out there for those who don't know anything about me is that I love skateboarding to a fault. I never cared in the past—I just lived to shred—and didn't care about the industry one bit. When I had my son and he started rolling with me, I realized that skateboarding might be one of the only things I'd ever fight for. It has given me my whole life, everything I have. It all comes from the greatest thing ever invented.

a kickflip by Dan Rogers

257

Dan Rogers, September 1995.

Armando Barajas, November 1992.

Billy Valdes, December 1992.

TRACKER B52 FLOATER

No More Axle Jams (1993)

By 1993, skateboard wheels had become so tiny and narrow that the axle nut stuck out past the edge of the wheel. As a street skater tried to master all of the new flip tricks, the skateboard would often land on its edge and impact the protruding axle nuts with such force that the wheel bearings would jam and become unable to roll. The skater would then pound the opposite side of the axle on the ground or any nearby object to loosen the bearing jam. Tracker's solution was the B52 Floater, in which we reamed out the hanger so the axle could slip freely from side to side and the wheels would never jam. What a great solution! One drawback to our innovative floating axle was that skaters needed to have two 1/2" wrenches to properly adjust their wheels. But, what a small price it was to pay for trucks that would never jam. Another drawback for some skaters was that the floating axle made more noise while skating, which attracted unwanted attention during stealthy nocturnal filming missions. The Tracker B52 Floater came in 129 mm, 139 mm and 149 mm widths, set on the B52's ultra-low roll center baseplate.—**LMB**

Paulo Diaz, January 1993.

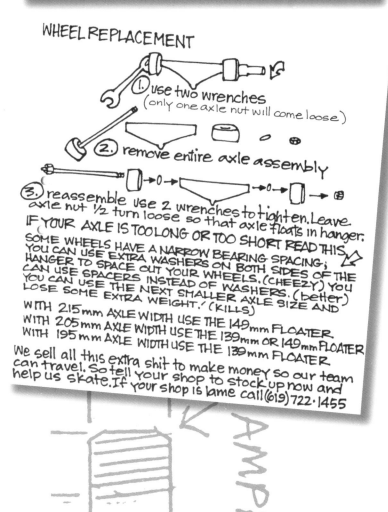

Above: **Tracker B52 Floater instructions.**
Opposite page, top: **Tracker B52 Floater.**

Jeremy Klein, Ron Chatman, October 1992.

FLOATER 139 AND 149

EXTRA KINGPIN CLEARANCE

INVERTED CUP WASHER AND SHORT CONICAL FOR INSTANT SNAPBACK RESPONSE

EXTRA MEAT FOR NOSE SLIDES

CUSHIONS - ULTRA REBOUND URETHANE

HOLLOWED OUT ALUMINUM BASE PLATE = LIGHTER WEIGHT

HOLLOWED OUT GRAPHITE BASE PLATE = LIGHTEST WEIGHT

BUSHING EJECTOR POINT

FREE SPINNING FREE FLOATING QUICK TURNING

HOLLOWED OUT AXLE CAVITY = LIGHTER WEIGHT

PRIME AIRCRAFT GRADE ALUMINUM (NO TIN CANS)

PIVOT - STRONG AS HELL

FREE FLOATING AXLE
AXLE WIDTHS = 215mm, 205mm AND 195mm

WHEEL REPLACEMENT

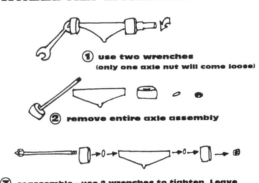

① use two wrenches (only one axle nut will come loose)

② remove entire axle assembly

③ reassemble - use 2 wrenches to tighten. Leave axle nut 1/2 turn loose so that axle floats in hanger.

USERS AND ABUSERS:

HAWK	BERRA	DACLIN
BUCKY	GALL	KEKICH
LABAN	PRYOR	PLASS
CHATMAN	KLEIN	WAAGE
DUFF	SANTOS	EVANS
ARMANDO	VALDES	PALACIOUS
	PAULO	

STRONG AS HELL TRACKER

tracker p.o. box 398 cardiff ca 92007   ph. 619-722-1455

Tracker Floater 139 and 149, circa 1992.

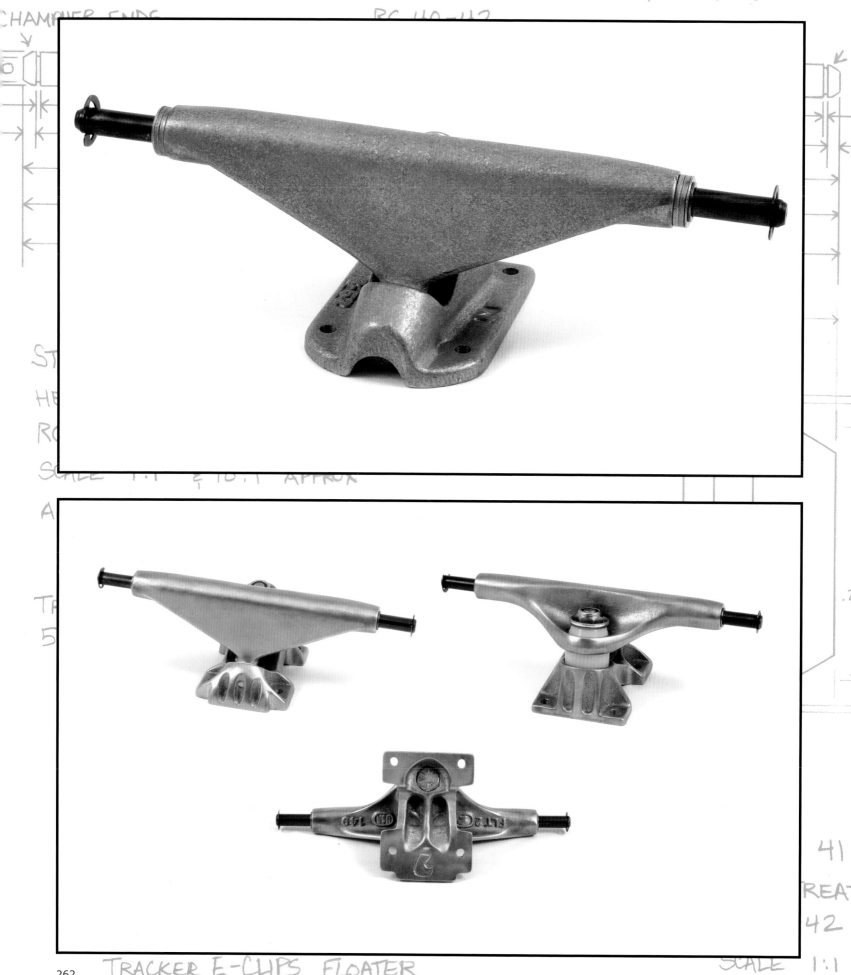

TRACKER E-CLIPS FLOATER

5-10-93

TRACKER B52 E-CLIP
FLOATER
What, Are You Nuts? (1993)

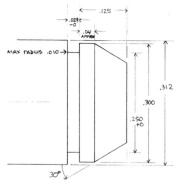

TO INSTALL **E-CLIPS**
Use screwdriver, key, nail, etc. Use the proper amount of washers to space wheels to the end of axle. Pop E-Clip into the groove. Hold opposite end of axle with finger and turn E-Clip in groove to <u>be sure E-Clip is snapped fully into place</u>.

TO REMOVE **E-CLIPS**
Use screwdriver, key, nail, etc. (Take care not to damage your bearing seal.) <u>Cover E-Clip with fingers</u> – (E-Clips are spring steel and can spring away.)

(Pro Tip—Carry extra clips in your wallet in case you screw up & lose one.)

The Tracker B52 E-Clip Floater was a brilliant evolution of the floating axle concept (see the previous chapter). An e-clip is a standard industrial bearing restraint that can be installed using only a screwdriver. The extremely narrow e-clips we used virtually eliminated axle nuts, thus the axle would seldom be able to contact the ground because it barely protruded past the edge of the bearings housed within the tiny, narrow skateboard wheels of that time. We had a groove machined in near each end of the axle to hold the e-clips in place. The original e-clips that we used were black and really thin. Since the shock loads from landing on them was too great, sometimes they would pop off. Soon after, we switched to heavy-duty gold e-clips that were thicker and stronger. We also added a slightly longer chamfered axle end, which solved the problem of e-clips popping off. However, most skaters who ever had one of the black e-clips pop off refused to try the new,

stronger gold ones. The e-clip turned out to be too foreign a concept for skateboarders, thus Tracker's aircraft nylon insert locknut, which it debuted in 1975, went on to remain the most popular choice for skateboard truck axles to this day. In all three iterations, the Tracker B52 sold fairly well, but ultimately, the truck's unusual innovations confused the market. This forced us to slowly phase it out in favor of a new, more normal truck.—**LMB**

Opposite page, top: **Tracker B52 E-Clip Floater with a fixed axle.**
Opposite page, bottom: **Tracker B52 E-Clip Floater with rare protoype ribbed baseplates that never went into production because everyone who saw them said they looked too different and high-tech.**

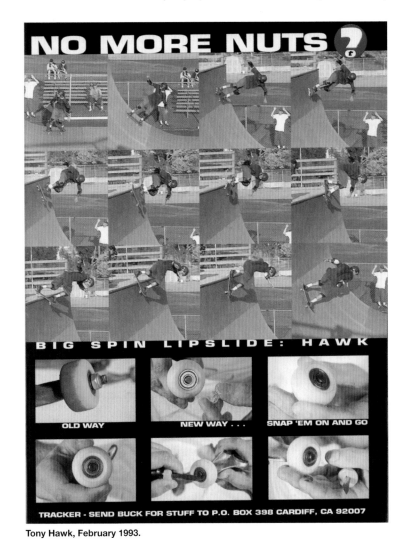

Tony Hawk, February 1993.

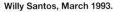

Willy Santos, March 1993.

Jeremy Klein, Bucky Lasek, Laban Pheidias, The Ridge, Armando Barajas, Tony Hawk, Dan Rogers, Ron Chatman, October 1993.

264

At the dawn of the 1990s, when street began to eclipse vert in popularity, a young whipper snapper by the name of Willy Santos was climbing up through the pro ranks, doing his part to help usher in a new age of skateboarding. Born in Subic Bay, Olongopo City, Philippines, Willy grew up in San Diego, California, where he started skating in the mid '80s. Not long after, he joined the Tracker team, for whom he still skates to this day.—GSD

How did you start skateboarding?
I started when I moved from the Philippines to San Diego, around 1985. I got into skating from watching someone do a boardslide on a double-sided curb. I thought it was the coolest thing ever. I instantly wanted to learn how to ride.

Describe your first good set-up.
It was a white and pink Skull Skates Christian Hosoi hammerhead with clear grip tape, black Gullwing Super Pro III trucks and Bones III wheels. I forget what color they were, but I do remember being so happy that I had to sleep with my board.

When did you get your first Trackers?
My first set of Trackers was actually a hand-me-down from a friend. I was always attracted to the trucks—keep in mind this was the mid '80s—and Copers were all the rage. There was just something about the Tracker Ultralites with Copers on there. As lame as people think using Copers is today, I get it—they just looked really cool to me. I think I remember Tony Hawk taking off the Coper and leaving the washers from it on. That was a cool sight, too! Another thing about the Ultralite that was appealing was the light weight, which allowed me to get that extra pop I wanted!

So, you were actually skating on Track-ers before you were sponsored?
Yes, definitely. I think at one point, I was riding a Tracker truck and a Thunder at the same time. I don't come from a rich family, so I would work with what I could get! When I did get hooked up with Tracker, it was definitely an honor. Tony Hawk, Jeremy Klein and I think Mark Gonzales rode for them at the time, so it was a no-brainer to ride 'em.

Who introduced you to the idea of riding for the Tracker team?
I think it may have been Bryan Ridgeway. I was skating with Rob Dyrdek a lot and filming the Birdhouse *Feasters* video with Jeremy and Tony, so it was a combination of things, just a natural progression.

When and how did you turn pro?
I turned pro for Gordon & Smith (G&S) in 1991. I was placing really well in the am circuit and getting loads of coverage in the mags.

Tell us a couple of crazy stories from road trips.
Some of the most memorable were on the early Birdhouse and Hook-Ups tours. Imagine skating and touring with Tony Hawk, Jeremy Klein, Steve Berra, Ocean Howell, Andrew Reynolds, Matt Beach, Jim Greco, Dan Rogers, Mark Gonzales, Paul Zitzer, Bucky Lasek, etc.

Why is Tracker so important in the history of skateboarding?
Well, number one, there's the history. It's set in stone, and you can't take that away!

Did you invent any tricks on Trackers? I was riding Trackers when I did what I think was the first frontside 360 heelflip over a hip. It was documented in the first issue of *Big Brother* magazine, as well as in *Feasters*.

Which are your favorite Tracker ads?
One advertisement that really stands out to me was shot not far from here in Scripps Ranch at the now famous School W. Tony Hawk came out that day and, needless to

say, I was stoked to skate street with him! I remember sitting back, because I wanted to watch him skate, watch him feast. He ended up 5-0 grinding the handrail. I remember it pretty well, as that was the day he asked me to ride for Powell-Peralta skateboards as an amateur. That definitely stands out to me, being at the spot, seeing the trick go down, and then seeing it in the magazine. There is some history for you!

Which skateboarders have inspired you the most? Why?
Tony Hawk, because he can and will perform on command no matter what. He's just simply rad to watch skate on the vert. I do miss skating with him on the streets just like when we were filming for *Feasters*. Jeremy Klein, because he's just RAW. Steve Caballero and Christian Hosoi for their finesse. Eric Koston and Guy Mariano for their innovation.

What have been the highlights of your time in skateboarding?
Ultimately, traveling the world for skateboarding is the best.

Who are your current sponsors?
Birdhouse, Tracker, Satori Wheels, Bones Bearings, Paradox grip tape, Arnette and Willy's Workshop.

What do you enjoy doing besides skateboarding?
I enjoy being with my wife, Shalihe, my son,

Willy Santos
I N T E R V I E W

Willy Jr., and my daughter, Phelisha.
Closing comments?
I'm really grateful to be backed by Tracker Trucks. They work, and they do the job, as you can see from my board! I'm just grateful to be a part of skateboarding.

Above: **Willy Santos flicks a no comply in Vancouver, Canada, circa 2006.**
Below: **Willy cracks a kickflip in Kitchener, Ontario, Canada, circa 2007.** Both photos: Daniel Mathieu

By Jake Stewart + GSD

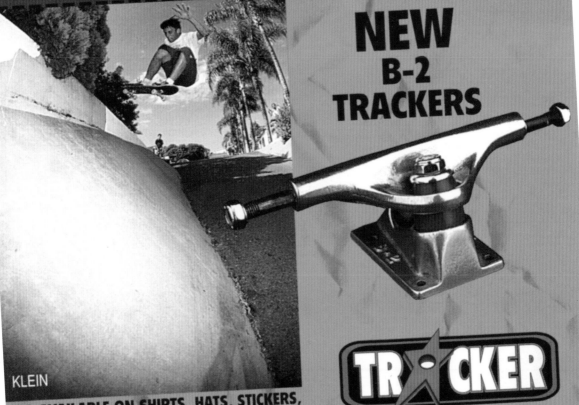

Jeremy Klein, Summer 1996.

TRACKER B2

Out of the Hole (1995)

Four years after suffering a drastic financial crash, we unveiled the Tracker B2, which was our ticket out of the hole. Although the Tracker B2 baseplate looked almost identical to the classic Tracker baseplate, it incorporated an additional five-degree turning angle that originated with the Aggro baseplate. Boasting a normal height, not low like the B52, the Tracker B2 was delivered with a raw finish. The B2 name was borrowed from the B-2 Stealth Bomber, a long-range aircraft first flown in 1989 and still in use today by the US Air Force. The B-2 Stealth Bomber was featured heavily in the news media for years due to the exorbitant cost of its high-tech design. The Tracker B2 came in 129 mm, 139 mm and 149 mm axle hanger widths. Since the trucks were normal height, they could be used with softer cushions and, if set up with space pads or wedge pads, could turn extremely well with large diameter downhill and cruiser wheels.

Over half of the Tracker B2's sales were comprised of the 149 mm width, which were destined for use on Gravity and Sector 9 longboards. The partners at Gravity and Sector 9 enjoyed downhill free riding more than racing, which was really just street skating on a larger scale. Back in 1978, Ed Economy speculated in *Skateboarder* magazine, "Someday, someone will come up with such a hot, functional longboard that everybody will get into it. Even if they ride a little board, they'll want a longboard on the side." Well, by 1995, Ed's dream had come true, as the longboard's time had come. A whole new skateboarding segment was born, and over the next 10 years, longboards of every style and size quietly became the largest selling skateboard equipment ever. This all happened despite the fact that ever since the early '90s, during the ascent of handrail, gap and ledge skating, the main skateboard magazines and videos shunned longboards (as well as downhill, slalom and freestyle), which were all deemed dorky and weird by the newly emerging cool police. Well, we here at Tracker shunned the cool police and embraced longboards from the very start, which was the key to ramping up our production once again. In fact, longboards increased Tracker's B2 truck production to over 20,000 units per month. Of course, Tracker still offered the B-52 Floater with axle locknuts as a low-slung technical street truck. —**LMB**

Opposite page, top: **Tracker B2.**

armando barajas

new B2 trackers

send buck for stickers and info 3210 production ave. #B, oceanside, ca 92054

tracker

Aramando Barajas, August 1996.

Andrew Reynolds, Ron Chatman, June 1995.

Tracker B2s, Summer 1997.

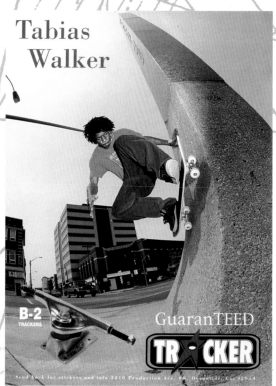

Tabias Walker, December 1996.

john
THE MAN
reeves

new B2 trackers
send buck for stickers and info 3210 production ave. #B, oceanside, ca 92054

tracker

John Reeves, July 1995.

TONY HAWK

TR★CKER

Tony Hawk, November 1996.

TRACKER
HAWK TRUCK
Spreads its Wings (1996)

In 1996, Tracker unveiled yet another first: a pro model truck, which was endorsed by legendary skateboarder Tony Hawk. After toying around with the idea of doing a truck with Tony since the early '90s, we finally made it happen. Make no mistake about it, this was no mere colorway of an existing truck; it was a totally new model designed by Tony and me. During development, Tony requested an all-aluminum truck so it would be as lightweight as possible yet still strong enough for both vert landings and the increasingly intense abuse that '90s street skating was unleashing upon skateboard equipment. The Tracker Hawk truck, which featured the same five-degree increase in turning angle that started with the Aggro baseplate, was much lighter than the Aggro Street Track. Offered in four widths: 129 mm, 139 mm, 149 mm and 159 mm, the Hawk hanger boasted quite a different look for the face of

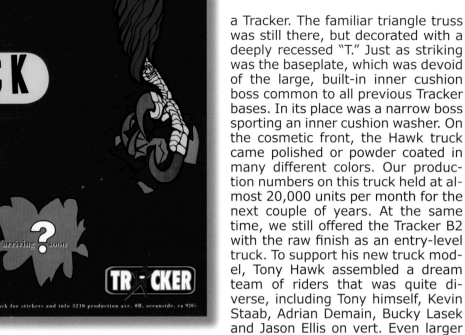

a Tracker. The familiar triangle truss was still there, but decorated with a deeply recessed "T." Just as striking was the baseplate, which was devoid of the large, built-in inner cushion boss common to all previous Tracker bases. In its place was a narrow boss sporting an inner cushion washer. On the cosmetic front, the Hawk truck came polished or powder coated in many different colors. Our production numbers on this truck held at almost 20,000 units per month for the next couple of years. At the same time, we still offered the Tracker B2 with the raw finish as an entry-level truck. To support his new truck model, Tony Hawk assembled a dream team of riders that was quite diverse, including Tony himself, Kevin Staab, Adrian Demain, Bucky Lasek and Jason Ellis on vert. Even larger was the street team, which was composed of icons like Jeremy Klein, Ron Chatman, Laban Pheidias, Andrew Reynolds, John Reeves, Nate McGlone, Cory Federman and Matt Goldsby, who rode the Tracker Hawk to new heights on the streets. By 1999, Blitz Distribution, the home of Tony's skateboard brand Birdhouse, unleashed a new truck brand called Fury. Under pressure to ride for them, Tony eventually relented, leaving the Tracker Hawk truck to fly off into the sunset.—**LMB**

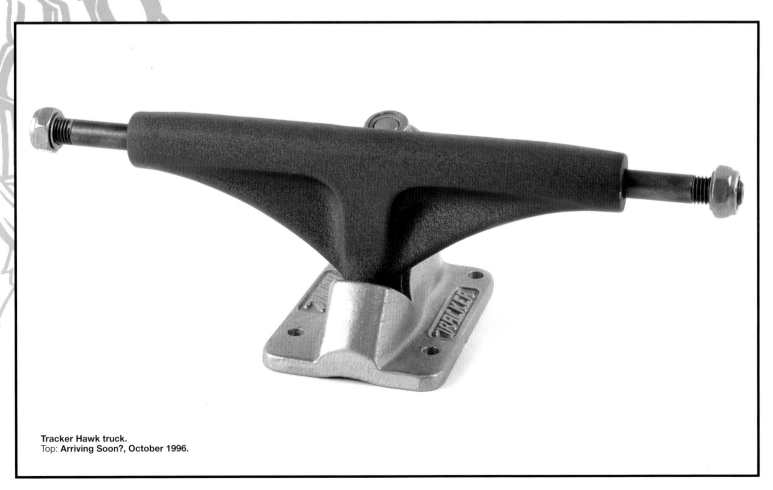

Tracker Hawk truck.
Top: **Arriving Soon?, October 1996.**

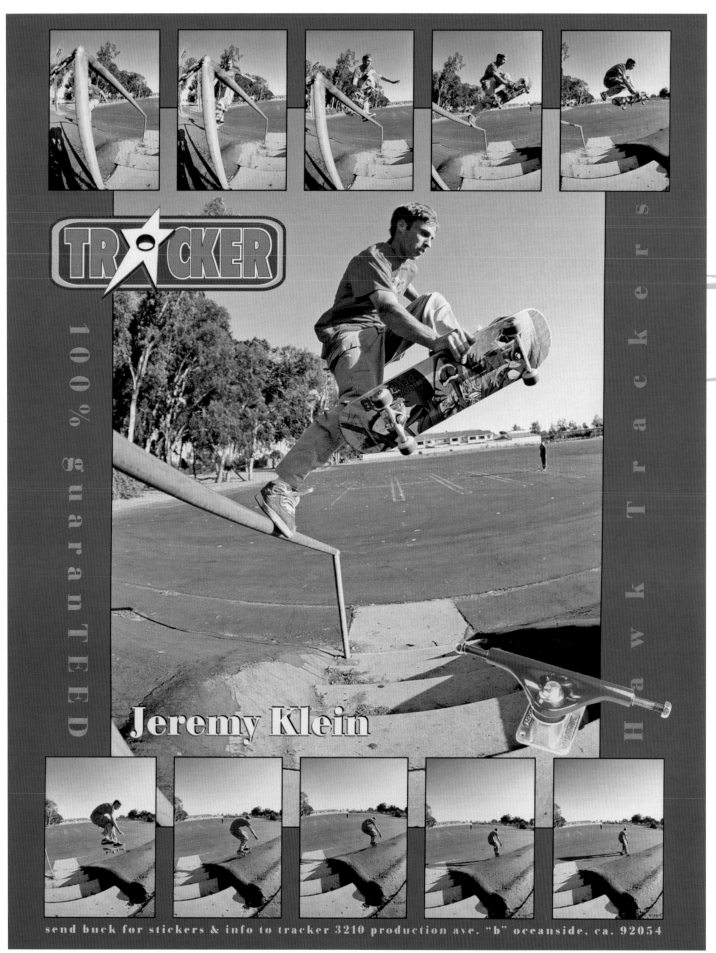

Jeremy Klein, March 1997.

Dan Rogers, September 1997.

Laban Pheidias, December 1996.

Dan Rogers, April 1998.

Jeremy Klein, January 1999.

Laban Pheidias, June 1997.

Jason Ellis, May 1998.

John Reeves, January 1998.

Frank Hirata, December 1998.

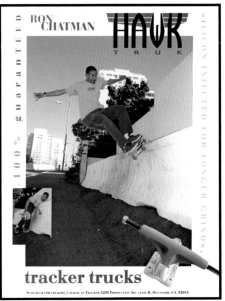

Ron Chatman, August 1997.

After getting gassed at the dentist, Tony Hawk feels a little loopy, so he skates it off at Bob Burnquist's crazy compound in Vista, California, circa 2002. Photo: Dave Swift
Opposite page: **Tony Hawk and Kevin Staab double their fun at the Hawk facility in Vista, California, circa 2009.** Photo: Grant Brittain

274

Simply put, Tony Hawk is the greatest, most famous and successful skateboarder of all time. Back in the 1980s, his ability to execute original groundbreaking technical tricks on command led to a vert contest dominance that is unmatched to this day. In fact, the list of advanced tricks he invented, including the 720 and 900, can and does fill up pages. Tony has appeared on countless TV shows, movies, magazines and products, including the popular *Tony Hawk's Pro Skater* series of video games. Today, when Tony's not skating or being blitzed by the media, he runs the Tony Hawk Foundation, which helps fund public skateparks in low income areas. Originally from Phoenix, Arizona, Kevin Staab has been a So Cal local since the very late '70s, when he logged in plenty of time at spots like Del Mar and Tony Hawk's ramp, inventing tricks like the blunt and the fakie Ollie. Well-known for his pirate-themed decks on Sims, Kevin also headed up a short-lived apparel brand called 90. Still to this day, if you dare to stand up on the coping block of a tall vert ramp or pool, Kevin won't hesitate to float an Ollie over your face.—GSD

Tony Hawk Kevin Staab
INTERVIEW

LMB: When did you get your first Trackers?
KS: Right after the Del Mar park team sponsored me, Lance Smith picked me up and put me on Tracker. So, it was that quick. I remember the day very well at Del Mar.
TH: I think I asked Lance for a pair of trucks at a Reseda ASPO contest in 1979-'80. I was supposed to be sponsored by Indy, but they never gave me anything. I asked for new trucks, and they sent me a baseplate. I really just wanted a new set of trucks and I knew Kevin was riding Tracker, then Lance offered me a set, so I kind of put myself on Tracker.
LMB: Tony, you and your dad came down to Tracker at our new building in Carlsbad one time, and he wanted our opinion on which deck brand you should ride. I think you were riding an Alva deck at the time, and the question was, "Who is this Stacy Peralta guy?"
TH: Oh, I was riding for Dogtown, but they went out of business without telling any of their riders, me specifically. I literally found out from Stacy. He called me and said, "Hey, man, I heard that Dogtown went out of business." At the same time, G&S was asking me about riding for them, and I just wasn't sure what I wanted to do. I was leaning more toward G&S because they were San Diego-based, then my Dad wanted to gauge it, too, and I think he asked your advice because you were the industry expert.
LMB: He didn't know Stacy, and wanted to know what kind of guy he was.
TH: I didn't know what a monumental decision it would be for me. I definitely knew that the Bones Brigade was the most elite team at the time. As much as I liked G&S and their riders, I thought if Stacy's really interested in

what I do, then I should ride for the Bones Brigade, because that's the team.
LMB: Kevin, do you remember when we hopped the fence at Colton skatepark and almost got arrested?
KS: Yes, I do, because those photos have resurfaced a couple of times. I was really afraid being there. I don't know who was more afraid—me or Adrian Demain—because I remember riding the pool for a little bit and riding the medium snake, then the cops came when we got down to the bottom. I was like, "Oh, great. I'm going to get in a lot of trouble for this." You guys kind of played it off, making like it was going to be way worse for us by talking to the cops. "Okay, let's just scare these guys. It's okay, we're going to let you go." Yes, that scared me. Thanks for that (everyone laughs).
LMB: How did it feel to ride skateparks after they were closed down?
KS: It was the best feeling ever. One of my favorite times was when Tony invited me back to Del Mar because they were filming *Thrashin'*. He was like, "Yeah, dude, we can ride the pool." I was super excited. I walked into the pro shop, and all of a sudden, it was like, "Cut! Hold on, who's that guy? What are you doing in here?" I said, "I'm going out back to skate the pool." They asked, "Are you in the movie?" I said, "Yeah." I had no idea, you just said come ride, so it was great. I went out and got to ride for the day, we got to ride the next day, and at the end of the second day, I got a check.
TH: Del Mar was closed at the time, and because the production company had their own insurance, they could open it up and let us skate. So, we got to skate Del Mar one last time and got paid for it.
KS: I was so excited I got to fly back from Arizona and go there. It was insane.
TH: I never got to skate Carlsbad. My dad drove us there and talked to the security guy with the rock salt shotgun. My dad tried to talk him in to letting us skate, but the guy wasn't having it.
KS: That guy was scary. I remember that.
TH: Yeah, that was my one regret. I didn't get to skate there. I didn't get to skate Spring Valley, either, because I wasn't old enough for a membership.
KS: Breaking into High Roller was another good one, because that was my home park in Arizona, and it was one of the last ones left. I remember Todd Joseph and I got to go ride one day. We tried to hop the fence and got pretty far until the cops came. We were lucky that Todd's mom came to pick us up, because she was really cool about it. She was like, "You don't need to punish the boys like this. They're good kids, they just want to skate." She actually talked them out of giving us community service, which is pretty awesome. I was actually more scared riding there because it was Arizona, and it's scary going to jail in that place. But, we got away with it. Then there was the other fun thing about getting busted by the cops and using other peoples

names. I was Mike Smith one time when I got busted street skating. That was fun.
LMB: Why was Tracker so important in the history of skateboarding?
TH: Tracker was important because they were there from day one, obviously, and became a standard. In the later years, they came to represent a certain style and ethic of skating, and also even geography. At some point, Tracker was Southern California—that's where we lived, that was our life. It came to represent so much more than just an original truck. We had a crew.
KS: I wanted to ride for Tracker because of the Bones Brigade guys. Straight up, that was it. Those were the raddest guys.
LMB: Which tricks did you guys invent on Trackers?
KS: (Speaking to Tony) Are you going to run with that? I'll take a break. I'll be back in a few minutes (laughs). I've got the blunt.
TH: Yeah, he invented the blunt on Trackers. That's pretty monumental right there. Fakie Ollie. I did the tricks I'm most proud of—most of my monumental tricks—when I was riding for Tracker: fingerflip air, backside Varial, Madonna, 720 and all of the different 540 variations. There are all of these little tricks that I don't even think about. I'm trying to think of the ones that had longevity, like the stalefish.
LMB: You really pushed the level of skating with the fingerflip, and people thought, "Oh, yeah, that flippy stuff. Whatever." What made you think of doing something like that?
TH: I did fingerflip airs because I was watching Rodney Mullen. He was such a master technician on the flat. I always wanted to figure out how, because he only had a few inches of air time to do a trick, and we got four or five feet of air time. Well, if he was doing it that close to the ground, it was obvious that

By Larry Balma + GSD

Above: **Kevin Staab invented the fakie Ollie and boosted it higher than most. Here, he elevates one out of Colton Skatepark's pink pool in Colton, California just before the cops showed up, circa 1983.**
Left: **Kevin Staab, Matt Goldsby, Corey Federman, Adrian Demain and Bryan Ridgeway on the way to Upland and Colton, circa 1983.**
Opposite page, left to right, top to bottom: **Kevin Staab lifts an Ollie out of the keyhole at Del Mar Skate Ranch in Del Mar, California, circa 1980. Tony Hawk pulls a layback air on the Booney Ramp in Litchfield, Arizona, circa 1984.** Photo: Jim Goodrich
Tony Hawk portrait, circa 1982.
Hawk flaps an invert at Sadlands, circa 1986. Photo: Dan Bourqui
Hawk and Staab frolick together in a shared Tracker ad, circa 1988.
Tony Hawk kicks back with his friend the Tracker logo at Kona Skatepark in Jacksonville, Florida, circa 1983.
All photos: Grant Brittain, except as noted.

we could do it above coping. We just had to figure it out. That was my motivation, for sure. And then it went the other way. I learned Airwalks, and then he started to do Airwalks on the ground, which seems way harder to me, because you have no time.

LMB: Did you try those tricks on the ground first?
TH: No, I was the worst freestyler. I had what I considered vertosis: I did everything when I was skating vert. So, I had to go with my expertise. But, some of the stuff was obviously inspired by what Rodney was doing. All of the flip tricks, shove-its—anything without grabs—was all inspired by freestyle, mostly Rodney.

LMB: You and Christian really put on a show in the '80s. The most memorable was the explosive runoff between you guys at the Vision *Skate Escape*. It was intense. Christian was flying higher than ever, and you were doing back-to-back tricks like there was no tomorrow.
TH: Yeah, it was fun, the whole era when people were pitting me against Christian. We were actually friends, it just became that you were tricky and technical, or all style and air. To be honest, I only had a couple of friends who were into the trick thing—Kevin and Lester—and that was our crew. All we cared about was new tricks. We didn't care how you looked doing them. We just knew the difficulty factor of it. Christian was all style. It was so apples and oranges for judges, and there was always controversy. But, no matter who won, it didn't matter. The *Skate Escape* was the culmination of that, because all I had was tricks, Christian had the airs and the style, and we both pretty much did our best, the epitome of what our styles meant. At that time, it was so subjective. I didn't really care. I was stoked. I wish I had made my last 720. I still think about that sometimes. I kind of made it—I slid off the ramp. But, it was so incredible to be on that kind of stage, because that was the biggest event ever at the time. It was a sold out arena for a skateboard competition, which was unheard of.

I went to South Africa three or four years later, and the *Skate Escape* had such an impact on them, they recreated that ramp for a demo, with the spine, the mini-ramp and the same kind of venue. They flew Ray Barbee and me there and Ray did flatland demos in front of the ramp. I'm not kidding. I think they had a jump ramp for him in front of several thousand people. They were just so excited about the idea of skateboarding and the spectacle of it and that whole scenario, that they recreated the whole *Skate Escape* thing for two dudes. And they did it because they watched the video, and saw how big it was. And to their credit, they had the same size crowd. It was crazy.

GSD: Tony, have you kept all of your contest trophies over the years?
TH: I don't have any trophies.

GSD: Did you just chuck them out or give them away?
TH: I usually gave them away at the event. Part of it was because I didn't want to look back all the time. I just always wanted to keep progressing and looking forward, so I didn't want to rest on these previous accolades. But, there were also these obnoxious BMXers who would pose with a million trophies behind them, because they had a race or two every single weekend, and they placed third and got a trophy. I remember seeing those photos in magazines, and I thought, "I don't ever want to be one of those dudes."

LMB: Did you keep your *TWS* trophies?
TH: I have kept my *TWS* ones. I kept anything that was unique and cool looking. But I got rid of any trophy with the corny skater pose.

LMB: So, you guys rode the Trackers with the nylon baseplates. Did you ride your trucks really loose at the time?
KS: My trucks didn't turn, ever, so it didn't matter what I was using, because I rode super tight trucks all the time. I remember driving six hours from Arizona, getting to Del Mar, be-

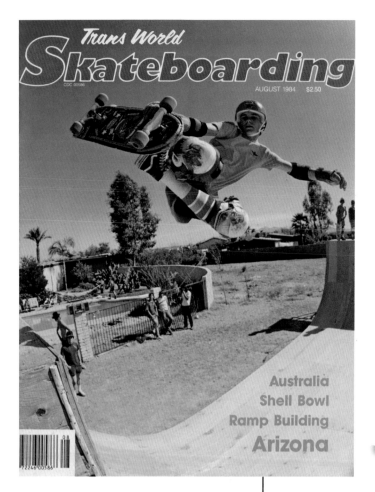

ing totally stoked, bailing on my second air at night, my board going down and watching the baseplates just shatter as soon as it hit the cold. But, in Arizona, it was great, because they just twisted and bent all over the place. I was just so excited to have something so light. I had the magnesium hangers with the plastic baseplates. Then the Copers came out, and came in all of those colors.

TH: Then you balanced out all of that weight loss with all of the plastic accessories, like Nose Bones, rails, Lappers and Copers.

GSD: And Tail Ribs.

TH: No Tail Ribs, that's were I drew the line. The nylon baseplates were the perfect bad storm scenario in that when we'd skate Del Mar at night, the wind would come off the ocean and it would be so cold that those things would get super hard and break. I broke a ton of them at Del Mar. They wouldn't break anywhere else, but I broke a ton at Del Mar. And I'm the same as Kevin; I kept my trucks so tight, because I like to think we're going faster than most people, so we needed that stability. So, I kept my trucks super tight, and when something would go wrong, the baseplate would just break.

GSD: Did you skate Tracker aluminum or magnesium baseplates at any point?

TH: Magnesium, yeah. When we were growing up, magnesium was the holy grail of trucks, because we couldn't afford them. It was like, "Oh, you have magnesiums? That's amazing."

KS: As soon as I got my first pair from you (Larry), I didn't want to scratch them, so I put Copers on them right away.

GSD: Kevin, on the first *TransWorld* cov-

er you got, did you make that tweaked out frontside air?

KS: Yeah, because it was off the extension, so I had to grab early. Grant Brittain asked, "Oh, have you seen the cover of the new mag?" He handed it to me, and I was like (big eyes). "I got the cover. Like, wow!" I was freaking out.

GSD: Some people thought it looked like a bail shot.

KS: No, it wasn't.

TH: If you took a picture of Kevin doing any frontside air, it would be up for debate if he made it.

GSD: How did you come up with that pirate theme for your Sims decks in the late '80s?

KS: Because of all of the characters I liked as a kid, pirates were always one of my favorites. It was kind of like, "After the mad scientist graphics on Sims, what am I going to do next?" I had it in my head that I wanted to do a pirate. The first artist made it look too realistic for me, and I didn't want that. It was almost too evil. I wanted it to follow the cartoon feel of the mad scientist, but I also wanted the pirate to look like the singer of the Cult, so that's where that came, too.

LMB: Tony, you came to Tracker and explored the idea of starting your own board company with Lester and Adrian. When was that?

TH: Yeah, sometime around 1987-'88. Powell thought I was diluting myself by doing all of these sponsorships, so they were frustrated with me. Christian Hosoi had started his own thing, and I was like, "Oh, I could do that." So, you and I were talking about

working together on it. I started taking it pretty seriously. Then at some point, I realized I just wanted to skate. I didn't want to be responsible for a company's direction or make the decisions. I appreciated the opportunity and the fact that you believed in me, but I just wasn't ready for that yet in my skating career. I loved the actual skating way too much, and so I went back to Powell with my tail between my legs. "I'm sorry I even thought about this. I'd rather just skate for Powell." "Well, you've got to drop all of these other sponsors and endorsements that you're doing," which meant fingerboards, backpacks and all of this random shit that I'd signed off on. So, I did and got sued by one for breach of contract. But, it was worth it to me to be more focused, and to be respected more for my abilities instead of being known for my exploits.

LMB: When did you start Birdhouse?

TH: We started Birdhouse in 1992, because I could tell that my career as a skater was fading. Being a vert skater was impossibly hard at the time, plus I wanted to start a company with my own direction. Things were getting weird in the industry. Steve Rocco was dominating, and it was all about talking shit on other brands to make your brands seem cooler. I didn't want any part of that, and Powell got caught up in it. I just wanted to promote a brand through good skating, not through sarcasm. I wanted to do it because it was fun and our guys were good, not because we were good and they sucked. That was my inspiration for starting Birdhouse, and the main skaters on Powell were all doing their own thing anyway. Lance and I left together, and I partnered up with Per Welinder, who had left, as well. So, the timing was right, and little did we know when we actually decided to do this that Stacy had already left. We didn't even know that. He hadn't made it known.

LMB: They're working on a book up at Powell, too.

TH: Yeah, the thing about the Powell book is it ends before what I'm talking about. So did the Bones Brigade doc. It was kind of like, "Yeah, it was fun, then it was over." They don't talk about how things went awry. It's got a little happy bow on the end.

GSD: Did the Powell doc mention the Rocco thing in the end?

TH: A little bit. At the time, Stacy wanted to fund our companies, but George wasn't really into it. When we started Birdhouse—I'm going to get in so much trouble—we had already sourced everything, and we were doing it ourselves. Then George sent us boards with the Birdhouse logo we created—production skateboards. We didn't talk to him at all, he just did it. So, we got these boards and it was like, "What is this?" Per was like, "I guess George made those for us because he wants to manufacture them." "Okay, we're just going to pretend we didn't see those. We'll put them over there and go on our way." He lifted the logo from an ad that I made.

GSD: It was all pixely.

TH: Oh yeah, not that my ads were all high-res or good in any form in the beginning. Yeah, that was weird. We patched up all those things, but at the time, it was strange.

LMB: So, we have the Tony Hawk truck here that Tracker made for a while. You had an amazing team.

Opposite page, left to right: **Kevin Staab pulls a tweaked frontside air on the cover of** *TransWorld Skateboarding*, **August 1984. He made it. Tony Hawk portrait, circa 1989.** Photos: Grant Brittain
Below, left to right: **Staab boosts a Boneless One out of the keyhole at Del Mar Skate Ranch in Del Mar, California, circa 1986.** Photo: Grant Brittain
Hawk lifts a hammer at the Animal Chin Ramp in Oceanside, California, circa 1986. Photo: Dan Bourqui

TH: Yeah, I was really pretty proud of this truck. You know why? Because it still looked like a Tracker truck, but it was iconic, and a lot of people associated that with the T [on the truck's face]. I just thought it was cool that we managed to take advantage of the Tracker design, but altered it enough so it was iconic, but still identifiable as a Tracker. That was fun.

GSD: Did you work hands-on with Larry for the design?

TH: I knew Larry had ideas for new trucks, and putting my name on it was good for changing it up fairly drastically, so I trusted his instincts on that. I was more into the graphical design of it, how this would show up and this would look. I mean just using that lettering was no joke with trying to get this approved by Powell, but we did it. To be honest, when things were pretty rough for me financially in the mid '90s, this truck saved my life in terms of being able to pay a mortgage, eat and raise a family.

LMB: Kevin, tell us about your Tracker Staab truck.

KS: Buddy Carr said, "What do you want? I can wrap a truck for you. What's it going to take for you to ride Trackers again?" I said, "Make me a purple truck." So, he made me one and I rode it. Then he said, "We can do an awesome wrap. What do you want to do?" I told him we either have to use a leopard print or a pinky purple color with pirates on it. I was just stoked when he sent me that sample, and, as far as I know, they sold out pretty much immediately, because I never got a second set. So, I was super stoked.

LMB: I drove down to Buddy's to get that truck because I don't even have one.

KS: Seriously? Collectors and people like that are holding onto things that are coming out again. I think that a lot of them were the ones who ate up those things right away, or the European dudes.

LMB: It was super expensive to do that. I don't know if we could recreate it now.

KS: I think it is super expensive, because I don't see anybody wrapping trucks like that

now. They're usually just printed. I was just honored that it happened. Buddy let me know that it was going to be a little more expensive and Tracker would make a little less, but I just wanted to see it happen.

LMB: Tony, did you ever film any Tracker video parts?

TH: As Powell riders, we weren't allowed to be in other videos. There was a ban on shooting anything for anyone else. But, the loophole that Ridge figured out with Stacy was that if you shoot them at a contest, then it's okay, because it's a public viewing anyway. I always wanted to be in Tracker videos, and I always wanted to have good footage in them. I didn't want it to be a contest run, so in practice for contests, I would purposely get Ridge on the ramp and shoot just tricks. That was my way of following Stacy's orders but actually getting footage for the Tracker videos. So, all of the early footage is of me just skating contest ramps, but I was doing some of my hardest stuff just for that video. It was stuff I wouldn't do in the contest, because it was too hard. So, that was my way of getting new footage. That's what I can remember vividly, because I so badly wanted to be in a Tracker video.

LMB: How about you, Kevin?

KS: It was just that all of my friends were on Tracker. Tony is my best friend, and then it was, like, Lester Kasai, Joe Johnson and Ray Underhill. We were such a close-knit group, and Ridge always had us do everything together. And when you look at all of the ads that were popping up all over the place, I know those are the things going in the book and those are the times I remember. "Hey, we're going to do an ad today." It was always something goofy, and it was always fun to be part of everything that was going on.

TH: And, for the most part, we all lived together. My whole household was Tracker. I lived with Ray and Joe. Kevin would come and stay. That was it. We were the Tracker Del Mar crew.

KS: It was a brotherhood. You wanted to be on the same team all of your friends were on.

Kevin Staab, May 1984.

Kevin Staab, October 1989.

Kevin Staab, February 1988.

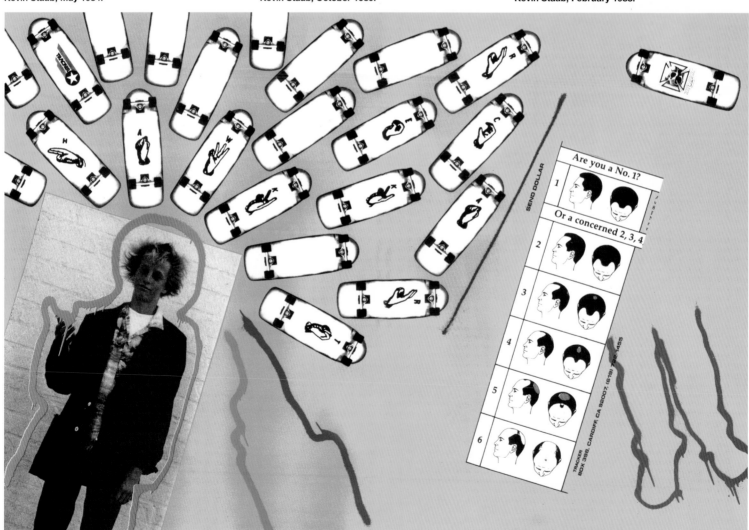

Tony Hawk, April 1985.

Top to bottom: **Tony Hawk, Ray Underhill and Joe Johnson, triples time at Hawk's ramp in Fallbrook, California, circa late 1980s.** Photo: Grant Brittain

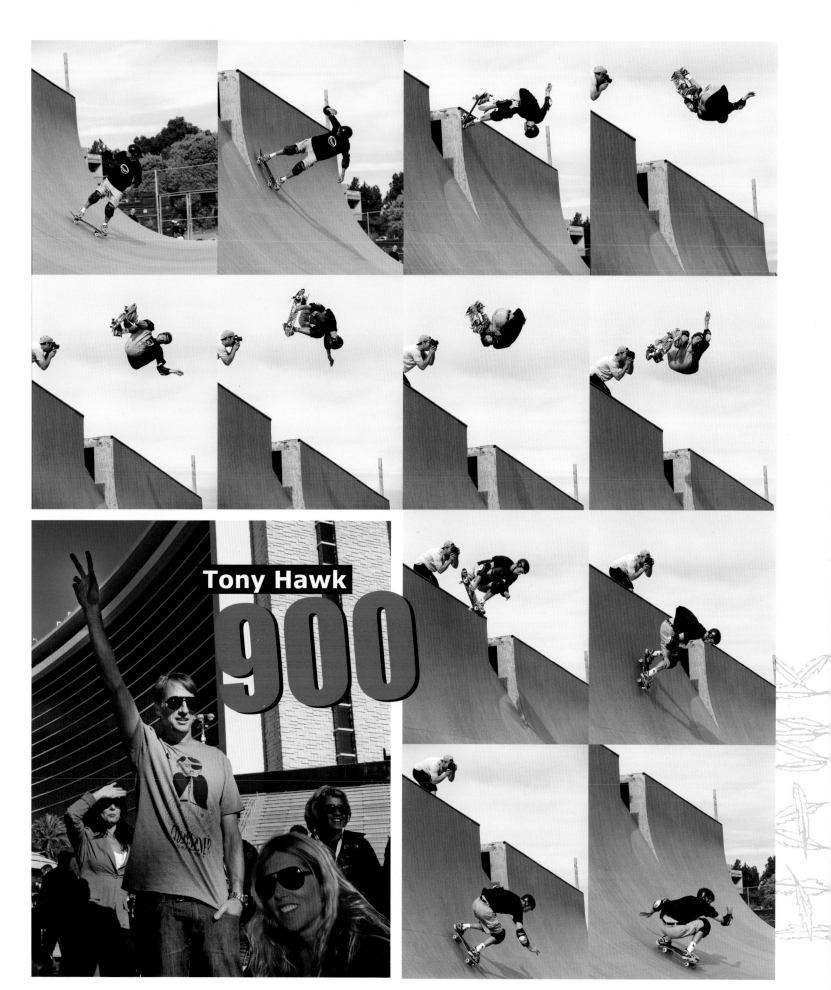

Tony Hawk

900

LMB: Which trucks are you riding now?
TH: I went through a couple of sponsors after Tracker. Fury. That's what happened. I try to erase Fury from my mind. So, basically, after Tracker, none of the guys I knew were on Tracker, and Per Welinder, my partner at Birdhouse, wanted to help start a company, so we started Fury. We actually funded it and it went okay for a little while, but all of the main riders left. Then I got a chance to ride for another new company, Thieve, but that didn't work out at all.

I rode for Thieve mostly because all of the people I knew at Tracker were gone, and I had an opportunity to help a start-up. I was excited with the success of Birdhouse, so I decided to do that with a truck. That ended up not panning out very well, so I went to Indy, because that's were I started. I wasn't looking to get deeply involved with a truck company again. I just wanted to be a rider. I didn't want to have to worry about the promotions and stuff like that, so it's nice to be one of the crowd with Indy. I'm just one of the gang there. My relationship with Tracker was one of my longest sponsorships ever.

LMB: We'd like to have you back.
TH: (Laughs) I'm pretty happy just being low-key.

Above: **Kevin Staab clowns around at the Hawk facility in Vista, California, circa 2011 and clacks a frontside rock at a brand-new skatepark in Encinitas, California, early 2014.**
Opposite page, top: **Tony Hawk demonstrates the easy way to do a 900. Now it's your turn! Mission Valley YMCA in San Diego, California, circa 1999.** For years, the 900 was the ultimate holy grail trick on Tony's wish list. When he finally landed it at the X Games in 1999, it made Tony Hawk a household name in the wider world outside of skateboarding, leading to a major autobiography, *Tony Hawk: Occupation Skateboarder*, not to mention the *Tony Hawk's Pro Skater* series of video games and many other things. The 900 really gave skateboarding the boost it needed to go mainstream.
Opposite page, bottom left: **Tony hails a cab at one of his Stand Up For Skateparks events in Las Vegas, Nevada, circa 2012.** All photos this spread: Grant Brittain

283

Laban Pheidias first earned a living as a juggler before he transformed himself into a pro skateboarder in the early '90s. Not surprisingly, Laban's keen coordination skills gave him a head start on flinging himself down huge gaps, stairs, handrails and school buses back when that kind of skateboarding was just starting to catch on like wildfire. Laban has always moved in a positive direction even when facing a great deal of personal adversity. In addition to becoming a director, actor and breakdancer, Laban is a also lifelong vegetarian who has done promo spots for PETA.—GSD

Laban Pheidias
INTERVIEW

Where were you born?
I was born in a house in Leucadia, California.

Where did you grow up?
My early years were spent in San Diego, my teen years were spent in Maine and Oregon.

Tell us about your circus family.
The whole growing up in a circus thing was completely fabricated. I'm pretty sure Dan Drehobl started that rumor because I used to juggle all the time. When I was a kid, I went to all of the juggling conventions. I also did some street performing and passed the hat.

When did you start skateboarding?
I first stepped on a board in Encinitas, California when I was 10 years old. I used to kickturn and carve little banks. But, I really started skateboarding and got completely obsessed with it in Maine when I was about 14 years old. I used to breakdance and Rob Collinson (owner of Lowcard) walked up to me and said, "Hey, you'd be good at street plants. We should go fucking skate." Basically, from that day on, we skated all the time.

Describe your first good set-up.
My first good set-up was a Santa Cruz Jeff Kendall graffiti graphic deck with Tracker Trucks and OJ wheels. I did a lot of launch ramping with that.

When did you get your first Trackers?
I was probably around 16 years old. I had entered a contest and I wanted to skate in a division I felt that I was good enough for, but I had no sponsors. So, I scrounged up enough money and said I was sponsored. I lied about being sponsored so I could enter against people like Jeremy Klein. I can't remember, maybe it was Donger, maybe it was John Reeves, maybe it was these people who I wanted to enter against. The next level down was kind of pointless. So, that little lie got me a package from Tod Swank from Foundation. I was probably only on flow from Foundation for about a month before I entered another contest. From that contest, I got offers from Tracker, House of Kasai, and I think it was A1 Meats. I'm not sure if that wheel company was around yet, but either way, it was a package deal and I said yes! So, right away, I got sponsored and that's when I got my first box of trucks. Not too long after that, I shot my first ad for Tracker, which was the first ad I ever had.

Did Bryan Ridgeway put you on?
It was Ridge, for sure. When I got that big box, I was so psyched! I was like, "Okay, this is better than one board company. Now I get free trucks and wheels!" I was squatting in an abandoned house at the time and getting product was really hard. It made sense to me to get every product, because it was like this cool package deal. I eventually got on Blockhead skateboards, too. But my first ad was for Tracker. It was a double ad with Duane Pitre. I was doing an Ollie impossible stale fish grab at the old Big Bear bump. At the time, all of those Powell kids like Guy Mariano, Paulo Diaz and Rudy Johnson were spon-

By Jake Stewart

TRANS WORLD
Skateboarding

June 1996
U.S. $3.95 CANADA $4.50
06>
0 74470 01548 2

Reeves • *Caballero* • *Brazil* • *Nor Cal*

sored by Tracker and, for whatever reason, Ridge put us together and we skated and took pictures. That was cool, because I had only seen them in videos. It was rad to skate with those guys, and they ripped. I remember that session pretty well, actually, it was at Eden Gardens in Solana Beach.

When and how did you turn pro?
I was 19 years old. I was sponsored by Blockhead and Dave Bergthold said he had something to tell me. I thought for sure I was getting kicked off the team. Instead he turned me pro.

Do you remember which Tracker truck model you were riding?
I do remember I really liked them, but I don't remember which kind they were. Were Ultralights around at the time?

Did you invent any tricks?
I don't think I have my signature on any trick. Skateboarding was evolving so fast back then and we were all just learning new tricks. It seemed like everything was new at that point in time. If you learned something on a ledge, it was time to do it on handrails early on. I was never good at lipslides, but for some reason I could Ollie impossible to lip slide, so I had weird things like that with my skating. But, I definitely don't claim any tricks. I just had fun learning most of them, and the ones I didn't, I would force myself to do it once and leave it behind. I always liked to jump off of things, like big gaps. I used to enjoy that. I used to not mind taking a slam for a good wake-up call to get the session going.

In your opinion, who were some of the best guys on Tracker?
During my time, I would say Mark Gonzales and Tony Hawk for sure, because he was always an amazing skateboarder. As far as street, it was people like Paulo Diaz during that time, because I really liked his style. I liked the way he skated and the way he did nollies. I remember skating with Armando Barajas. Those were some fun times.

Do you have any special memories of the

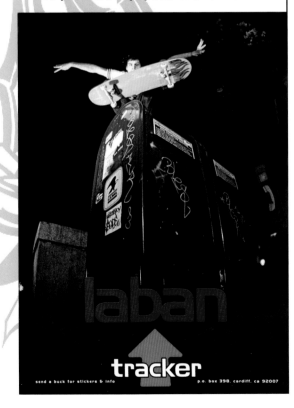

original Tracker factory? Tracker was pretty much the first company to build a skatepark for their guys, and I know you skated there.
I used to skate it all the time. We had so many sessions there! We even had a rainbow rail. We would set that up over the hip and they had that halfpipe with a bowl. There were so many sessions there. I remember Simon Woodstock coming there a couple of times and killing it. He was always rad to skate with. I don't think he rode for Tracker.

He does now. He loves them and buys trucks every month. He's got all kinds of projects making 20-wheel boards.
Oh, does he? Nice. We had plenty of sessions at that training facility. That hip was always awesome. We'd skate there all the time.

Why was Tracker so important in the history of skateboarding?
Tracker is one of the originals. It's been around forever, and it's always supported skateboarding 100%. For me, Tracker was my first real truck sponsor and gave me the coverage and the advertisements; and putting me out there was a real honor. I think it's important to my life and it probably is to a lot of other people. On the whole, it just adds up. If you look at the team list, it adds up, so of course it's a very important part of skateboarding.

Which Tracker ad is your favorite?
There were so many Tracker ads. I was in so many Tracker videos and ads. At the time, everything was happening so fast in skateboarding, whether it was new tricks or video parts. There were so many video parts and so many ads, it all becomes a blur to me. Those were crazy times back then. Tracker got me through many grinds and manuals and hill bombs and slappies and handrails and gaps. It got me through a lot of what I needed to get through and I needed to do all of that. Tracker helped me do it, so I appreciate that.

Tell us a couple of crazy stories from road trips.
One time, Wee Man and I set off a bunch of fireworks inside the van while driving down

the freeway. Another time, I was doing a demo in Baltimore and a psycho cop tackled me and took me to jail, and from there, I got taken to prison. That sucked. Another time, I got dosed right before I had to do a huge demo. I was tripping so hard I could barely see straight. Somehow, I managed to go out there and make some tricks.

Which skate spots are your favorites?
Right now, my favorite skate spots are ditches and curbs. I never get sick of slappies.

Which skateboarders have inspired you the most? Why?
Rob Collinson, because he goes for it, takes slams, gets back up and hangs on. Dave Bergthold, because he still skates harder than anyone I know. My brother, Eric Amadeus Von Preising, because he never ceases to amaze.

What have been the highlights of your time in skateboarding?
Some of my skateboarding highlights would have been getting a gatefold cover of *TransWorld*, making the *Caught Clean* (juggling/skateboarding) videos, also my 411 Profile, because people still come up and quote it. Traveling the world, starting a board company called Invisible with Dave Bergthold, and basically learning how to run a business and do video production. Skateboarding was my film school.

Who are your current sponsors?
I don't skate for sponsorship or money anymore.

What do you enjoy doing besides skateboarding?
Besides skateboarding, I enjoy directing music videos and films, playing accordion, growing gardens, vegan cauldrons in the backyard, expanding the mind with psychedelics, Taichi, meditation, and aligning myself with the Tao.

Above: **Laban Pheidias closes a junkyard gap, circa late 1990s.** Photo: Grant Brittain
Left: **Tracker, Laban, April 1994.**
Opposite page: **On Super Bowl Sunday 1996, Laban finger-flips a fountain gap for fun in Carlsbad, California, as his friends Ted, Ako, Heather, Sefra and Mike look on.** Photos: Grant Brittain

Born on December 3, 1972 in Baltimore, Maryland, Bucky's real name is Charles. Starting skateboarding in 1984, he has listed his occupation as pro skateboarder (vertical) since 1990 whenever he fills out a form. Bucky's biggest trophies include 12 X Games medals, six of which are gold. He usually places in the top five at any contest he enters, making him one of the top contenders in Tony Hawk's post-competitive era. Speaking of the Bird, Bucky was also a character in the *Tony Hawk's Pro Skater* series of video games. In addition to skateboarding, Bucky also enjoys racing rally cars professionally. Above all of this, his proudest achievement is being a dedicated husband and father.—GSD

Bucky Lasek
INTERVIEW

When did you start skateboarding?
I was 12 years old. I was at a mall near my aunt's house, and while I was inside, someone stole my bike. I figured if I could take my transportation with me inside, that was most logical. So, I asked for a skateboard for Christmas, and my friend Charlie got a Lester. All we did was street skate and do slappies on curbs and Boneless Ones off of driveway bumps. After about a month, we met other skaters and ended up skating hours and hours a day.

Describe your first good skateboard.
It was a Steve Caballero complete with Trackers and maybe a Lapper.

When did you get your first Trackers?

I went to a Powell-Peralta demo in Baltimore, where Tony Hawk and Mike McGill saw me skating and asked if I'd like to skate for Powell one day. Stacy Peralta spoke with me, too, and said I had to quit Skull Skates before they could send me anything. I did and they did. That same week, I got a box of trucks from the Tracker team manager, Bryan Ridgeway. I was 14 years old at the time.

How did you get on the Tracker team?
I heard Stacy, Hawk and McGill all spoke to Ridge, and that was good enough. I think I got the Tracker trucks before the Powell stuff, actually. I can't be sure. It was fast, though.

Which Tracker models did you ride?
Sixtracks, Quicktracks, B52s and Hawks.

Name your favorite Tracker ads.
I spent a lot of time with Tony, so I always liked anything with him skating. I liked the ads with a series of comments about why we rode Trackers. They were funny and pretty true, actually.

During your time on Trackers, What stood out about their performance?
They were so stable, and any adjustment I made remained, so I knew what I would get run after run. They were strong. I could ride the same pair forever, but I gave my old ones to my friends who couldn't afford new gear. I hated new cushions, though, because they took a long time to wear in just right.

Tell us about a couple of memorable times with the Tracker team.
I just remember traveling to contests and seeing someone from Tracker every time. As a little teenager, it really meant a lot to have someone looking out for you when you went to new locations. Everyone who ever showed up was just the coolest. Ridge, Chris Carter and Keith Lenharr all were just cool! Maybe we connected more since they were from the East, too. I just knew support meant a lot then, and looking back, I'm glad I realized it then. I had great times filming videos, because they would come film back East instead of me having to go to California.

Tell us a couple of crazy stories from road trips.
I was staying at Ridge's place with Dom Kekich and his brother from Australia, and we were driving back from McGill's skatepark in the dark. A spider went up Dom's brother's leg, and he screamed, "Spider up mmmmmeeeeeeee leg! Spider up mmmmmmeeeeeeee leg!" He was going crazy in the back seat. :-) At an NSA district qualifier in Virginia Beach one year, I was on the deck with Ridge talking through my line. He said how funny would it be, despite all of the crazy tricks I had, to fall while dropping in, which was something that had never happened in a contest. We both laughed hard

at the prospect of the silliness. I dropped into my run, made it three quarters of the way through, and then bailed on a trick. I ran back to the top of the deck to finish, then dropped in and fell! I looked up at the deck to see Ridge with his mouth wide open. Neither of us could believe it! We laughed for days.

I think I got dead last. At another contest, Omar Hassan and I got locked out of our rooms and no one would let us come into theirs. They kept opening doors, but by the time we got to any open door, they shut them on us.

Why was Tracker so important in the history of skateboarding?
I can just speak about how it was important to me to have the support and the product, and to know all I had to do was skate. They cared about how I did, they cared about my mom, and they took the time to come to Baltimore and spend time with me on my turf. They also had a lot of my favorite skateboarders on the same team, so they had that history. The older I get, the more I realize who came before me, and tons of them had connections to Tracker, as well—product, riders and support over years and years.

Which skaters inspired you the most?
Tony Hawk the most. The way he was always coming up with something new and fresh gave me so much reason to want to learn new stuff. Staying with him helped me a bunch, too. That's mostly where I stayed in California. There are plenty of others, but he had the biggest impact on me. When I won my first contest, I'll never forget him saying, "What took you so long?" Danny Way pushed me, too. We were on the same team, Powell, when we were little, so we pushed each other.

What have been the highlights of your time in skateboarding?
Seeing the world while doing the thing I love. My three kids and beautiful wife being in my life. X Games giving vert another shot in the arm. All of the people I've met, skated with and worked with over the years. Being in Hawk's video games and doing my best in events over the years. I had a rough go for a while with injuries and a lack of sponsors believing in me, but I always believed in myself. At age 40 last year, I won all of the major events. I always got a text from Ridge before and after events, through thick and thin, even though neither of us are with Tracker. That says something right there.

What are you up to today?
I have a bowl at my house that I skate and have charity events at. I drive a rally car and am sponsored by Puma and Subaru. I alternate races with skateboard contests series. I help raise my three daughters.

Closing comments?
Thanks to Tracker for all of the support, meals, couches, trucks and, in general, great times during the best of years. You never forget the ones who stood behind you in the beginning.

Above: **Tracker, Bucky Lasek, circa early 1990s.**
Left: **Lasek, January 1989.**

By Bryan Ridgeway

286

Bucky Lasek hangs a table top Gunnair high above the Fallbrook Ramp in Fallbrook, California, circa 1989. Photo: Grant Brittain

ellis
B-2
HAWK

THE BEST QUALITY TRUCKS
GUARANTEED FOR LIFE

TRACKER TRUCKS

Jason Ellis, February 1999.

Born in 1971 in Melbourne, Australia, Jason Ellis started skating in 1987, and went on to spend the decade of the 1990s and early 2000s as one of the top vert pros and Mega Ramp masters. Jason now lives in Hollywood, California, where he divides his time between truck racing, motocross riding and hosting *The Jason Ellis Show* on Sirius XM Radio. As if all of that weren't enough, he even published his own book called *The Awesome Guide to Life*. Oh, Jason's also into mixed martial arts big-time, so you definitely don't want to piss him off!—GSD

HAWK
T R U

JASON
ELLIS

TRACKER TRUCKS
S I L I C O N   I N J E C T E D
SEND BUCK FOR STICKERS/CATALOG TO TRACKER 3210 PRODUCTION AVE. SUITE B, OCEANSIDE, CA. 92054

Which tricks were invented on Trackers? Thinking back, two things you did stick out in my mind. 1. The fact that you were the second person ever to skate the Mega Ramp (on Trackers, no less!) 2. You invented the ape hanger (air to hang in the rafters to bomb drop back in) before anybody else.
Well, I know exactly why I did that. I remember it like it was yesterday. You know, there was a time there when I skateboarded every day and all I cared about was skateboarding. Then there was a time when I was really good at skateboarding and got kind of famous. Let's just say I sort of lost concentration around that point. I was still good every now and then, but I spent a lot of time being hung over. I remember being on the gigantic Tony Hawk tour and it was a big fucking deal. It was on TV! So, at that point, let's just face it, I was so washed-up, it hurt. But, I took the tour as a really big deal. I remember at the first demo, Tony dropped in and did a 540 and I said to myself, "He's just going to do that at every demo, and this is going to go on

for three months. Every time he drops in, he is just going to smoke me!" I couldn't let that happen, so I needed a plan. Simple! I would just jump out of the rafters! The first time I actually hung from the rafters was at the DC ramp in Vista, California during the one contest Colin McKay and Danny Way ever held there. I hadn't slept the night before, because I was at some crazy party all night. When I arrived at the ramp feeling like shit, a "friend" kindly offered me some cocaine. So, basically, I did some cocaine and invented the ape hanger. Fuck! Stay in school, kids.

You also flipped your board into it, as well, if memory serves me right!
Not straight off the bat, but that's how it escalated. First I did a lien air into it, and people thought that was cool. Then on the Tony Hawk tour, I really started hanging on to them. I did a slob one, then I learned heelflip slob airs, so it was only a matter of time to do the heelflip slob air ape hanger. Oh, and also Madonna ape hangers. Oh, wait! I also did a tail grab ape hanger. When I did that, I figured that maybe I needed to calm down on grabbing onto shit, because it was too much of a clusterfuck to hold on to the rafters and the tail of the board at the same time. I remember seeing a photo of it and thinking, "Okay, dude. You have officially grabbed onto too many things."

Were you not also the second person in the world to drop into the now famous Mega Ramp?
As far as I know, I was the second person to jump down it, because Colin McKay didn't want to do it. He can say that he was hurt, but he was fucking scared! Straight up! Don't get me wrong, he is a better skater than me, but he also has a bigger vagina than me. That was one of the things I knew I could get to work for me. I wasn't very good, but I could go straight well and I'm not scared to go fast or big. So, when Danny built that thing, it was so up my alley. Go straight and big, land, then go straight and big again. No turning all over the place, just go!

I remember the first time being on the deck of that thing, with nobody there. It was Danny and I. He had already jumped it a couple of times doing backside 360s, which was mind-blowing, and I was tripping! It was the first set-up at Point X, and the run-up was different than it is on the newer ramps. It was mellower. On my first go, I was wearing a DC basketball jersey, Lycra shorts, no elbow pads, no socks and my little Tracker Axis 149 mm trucks. It was, basically, my Super Ramp set-up. (The Super Ramp was the halfpipe that Danny used to jump out of the helicopter and was, at the time, the largest ramp ever skated.) I remember going to roll in for the first time and as I started to go, he started to tell me something, but I couldn't hear him. That put the fear of God into me as I wondered if I missed some life-saving info. Luckily, I cleared the gap without my board. Then I politely told him, "Don't fucking talk to me when I'm going down the roll in. What the fuck was that?"

So, on the second go, I cleared the

gap and landed, looking at this giant fucking quarterpipe I had to deal with. I believe my words were simply, "FUCK!" As soon as I said that, my legs whipped out from under me, my helmet bonked off the coping, and I came back into the ramp the same way: upside down. Long story short, I got masonite burns all over my body—literally everywhere! This tattoo (pointing to left bicep) is still burnt. It straight melted me. So, I got an Oxycontin from Danny and had a beer to chase it down. I remember how badly burned I was. My whole chest was scabbing over, and if I turned at all, it would tear open. But, after a few minutes, my thoughts changed to, "Man, I feel great! That pill is amazing!" Then I woke up stuck to my sheets. Lesson learned. The Mega Ramp gave me a new love for skateboarding, to put it plainly. I didn't even care if anyone filmed or shot photos of me. It was just that fun and offered a second or third wind to my skateboarding career, if you can call it that. I felt like a little kid again.

You broke the world record for bomb dropping into a ramp. How did that manifest itself?
Danny got a call from the guys at the *Guinness Book of World Records* and they offered him 10 grand to break his world record, and Danny, being himself, laughed at them and said, "I know a guy who will do it for 10 grand but, it isn't me." So, he offered it to me, and at the time, 10 grand was a pretty big chunk of change. Something you have to understand is that when Danny sets out to do something, he thinks it through and makes a decision based on its plausibility. I, on the other hand, do not. So, when it came time to build the ramp, I simply told a crew of non-skateboarders to build a quarterpipe. When they asked how big, I said, "I don't know, a normal ramp has 12 foot transitions, so how about 16?" It was a complete guess! To make it even more laughable, they added two feet of vert to it. Looking back now, I laugh, thinking how I was trying to break a record, but I added two feet of vert to the ramp, knowing it would be impossible to land on the vert! So, basically, I just cut two feet off my fucking world record. Genius! In the end, I think I ended up jumping 14 feet.

Closing arguments?
Honestly, the best I ever skated was on Tracker trucks. Around the time when I was on XYZ clothing, I might not have been very consistent, because I liked to party. But, to

Jason Ellis
I N T E R V I E W

me, what I did, how much I practiced and the way I did it, I just liked the way I skated, you know? Sometimes, I could do an eight-foot tail grab 540 and sometimes I would fall off on an axle stall. Looking back on it, I kind of thought that was cool. At the time, I was pissed I couldn't be "that" guy. That's carried over to what I'm doing now, because I'm not getting last in this, I'm winning it!

Read the full-length interview at trackertrucks.com

Above left: **Jason Ellis, October 1997.**

By Jake Stewart

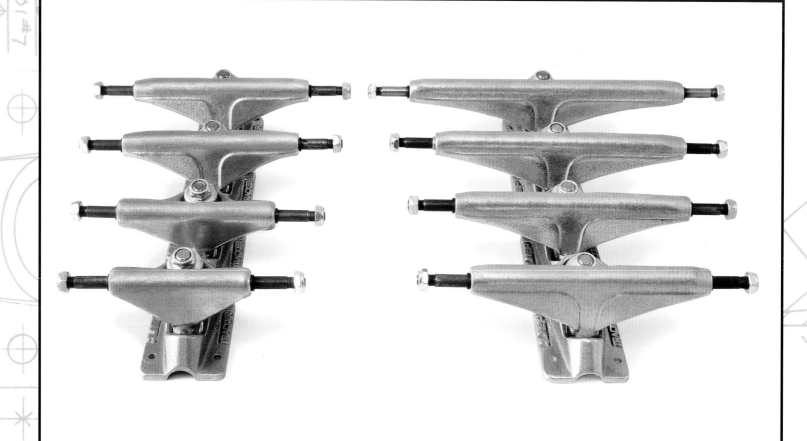

TRACKER DART

An Evolution of the B2 (1999)

Closing out the 20th century with its debut in 1999, the Tracker Dart was an evolution of the B2, which made it an all-terrain truck. Street? Vert? Downhill? Longboards? The Dart covered it all. Sporting the same geometry as the B2, the Dart's baseplate incorporated a wider blocked-out nose and cushion boss that helped with blunt, tail and nose slides. The first hanger we used with the Dart baseplate was actually the Hawk hanger, which we shipped for a couple of months while our production tooling for the new Dart hanger came on line. The second-generation Dart hanger featured a new look on the Tracker truss, which contained a slight design hint of the Hawk and sported the same geometry.

Released in an expanded range of widths, including 5 1/8" (129 mm), 5 1/2" (139 mm), 6" (149 mm), 6 3/8" (161 mm), 7 1/4" (184 mm), and 8 1/2" (219 mm), the Dart was produced with a polished or powder coated finish in many color combinations over the years. During the Dart's early reign, we continued to offer the Tracker B2 in a raw finish as an entry-level truck. Some of our customers who sold completes were slow to change over to the Dart, even though it had the exact same geometry as the B2. To this day, we continue to produce the Tracker Dart, which offers a stable ride reminiscent of the classic Gnarly Trackers, but with a slightly quicker turning action.—**LMB**

Brad Edwards slashes a classic layback at Alex Road Skatepark in Oceanside, California, 2014. Photo: Lance Smith
Opposite page, top: **A Tracker Dart first production run truck.**
Opposite page, bottom, left row front to back: **Tracker Dart Midtrack, Dart Fultrack, Darts 129 mm and 139 mm.** Right row front to back: **Darts 149 mm, 161 mm, 184 mm and 219 mm.**

Tracker Dart
Kevin Staab Colorway

I saw Buddy Carr a few years ago, and he asked, "What's it going to take for you to ride Trackers again?" I said, "Make me a purple truck." So, he made me one and I rode it. Then he said, "We can do an awesome wrap. What do you want to do?" I told him we either have to use a leopard print or a pinky purple color with pirates on it. I was just stoked when he sent me the first samples and, as far as I know, they sold out pretty much immediately, because I never got a second set. So, I was super stoked. Collectors are holding onto things that are coming out again. I think that a lot of them were the ones who ate up the Dart Staab right away, or the European dudes. I think it's super expensive, because I don't see anybody wrapping trucks like that now. They're usually just printed. I was honored that it happened. Buddy let me know that it was going to be a little more expensive and Tracker would make a little less, but I just wanted to see it happen.—**Kevin Staab**

Kevin Staab, December 2008.

Longtime Tracker rider Jimmy Leaphart shreds a lay-back grind at the Clover Bowl in Northglenn, Colorado, August 15, 2013. Photo: Craig "Hector" Ogata

292

Rocking a pair of the Tracker Dart 184 mm, Adam Taylor blasts off from Woodward Skate Camp in Tehachapi, California to launch a 540 toward the Sun, circa 2013. Photo: Dan Bourqui

Tracker Lester Kasai Reissue Decks Available Now
Trucks You Can Trust Since 1975 / trackertrucks.com

Lester Kasai, 2006.

Jean Postec - Kickflip Backside Lipslide - Photo: Fick
Tracker Trucks · Since 1975 / Guaranteed For Life / trackertrucks.com

Jean Postec, Holiday 2005.

Steve Revord
Mctwist
Tracker Trucks
Guaranteed for life
www.trackertrucks.com

Steve Revord, Spring 2004.

294

Tracker Trucks - Since 1975 / Guaranteed For Life / www.trackertrucks.com
Darin "Cookiehead" Jenkins / Fingerflip Lien To Tail

Darin Jenkins, Fall 2005.

Daniel Lebron, April 1999.

Jesus Fernandez, May 1999.

Born in Huntington, West Virginia, John Reeves grew up in San Diego, California, where he started skateboarding in Mira Mesa in the mid '80s. Already pro for Life Skateboards, a subdivision of H-Street, by 1991, John dove headfirst into the street skating explosion of the '90s. Currently sponsored by Bodega, Tracker, Iron Horse grip tape, Nike SB and Bones Bearings, John, like all lifers, still rips it up today.—GSD

John Reeves
INTERVIEW

How did you start skateboarding?
In the mid '80s, in my neighborhood, Mira Mesa, skateboarding was just part of the culture. It was one of the things that all of the kids did or tried to do along with BMX and break dancing. Eventually, my best friend and I got good boards and his dad built us a quarterpipe on his driveway. I've been hooked on skateboarding ever since.

Describe your first good set-up.
It was a raw Blockhead Sam Cunningham shape from the Uncle Wiggley factory with the first generation Tracker Ultralite trucks, OJ II wheels and NMB bearings. The deck didn't have a graphic, so my older sister Vanessa painted one on it for me: a silhouette of Rob Roskopp doing a backside air with something written in the Thrasher font. It was purple, funny and totally '80s. I will never forget that board.

When did you get your first Trackers?
In the late '80s, probably 1987-'88

Who gave them to you?
The first ones I remember getting were given to me by the great Primo Desiderio!

Which model did you mostly ride? Tracker Ultralites with the thicker reinforced baseplates. I'm not sure what size the hangers were, but they weren't freestyle trucks. Ha! They must have been 129 or 139 mm.

When and how did you turn pro?
After I got sponsored by H-Street and started filming with Mike Ternasky in 1989 or 1990, I entered the major amateur contest circuit, which was called the National Skateboard Association, and I did pretty well. I think that's right around when Ternasky first started thinking about turning me pro. But, it was really not until after the Life Skateboards video dropped in 1991 when Ternasky, Ron Allen, and T-Mag decided to turn me pro and give me my first pro model on Life Skateboards, which was born out of H-Street.

Tell us a couple of crazy stories from road trips.
Oh man, where do I begin? Ha! Should I tell you about the Montreal assault / arrest story when the Invisible team manager, Joe Piccolo, had to call all of the jails in Quebec to find me so he could bail me out? Should I tell you about Neal Heddings fearlessly walking around naked in an Australian airport yelling,

"Rock out with your cock out!"? Or should I tell you about the time when the Australian Outback got so incredibly hot that I took a cold VB beer shower inside of a convenience store? That shower was very convenient!

Why was Tracker so important in the history of skateboarding?
Tracker was the original skateboard truck geared for going fast, bombing hills, performing high-impact tricks, and grinding pool coping.

During your time on Trackers, what stood out about their importance?
For me personally, being from San Diego, in the late '80s Trackers were the top-of-the-line trucks to have, and the first real pro skateboard trucks that I ever even heard of. Every kid wanted Trackers at that time. See, I grew up in Mira Mesa right near the Gordon and Smith and Uncle Wiggley factories, and most of the older skaters I saw who were riding those boards were riding Trackers, too. In fact, one of my first real boards was a Blockhead Sam Cunningham shape from the Uncle Wiggley factory.

Which Tracker riders influenced you? Who were the guys you looked up to?
Neil Blender, Jim Gray, GSD, Lester Kasai, Adrian Demain, Billy Ruff, and all of the guys on the Bones Brigade who rode Trackers, like Tony Hawk, Mike McGill, Steve Caballero. It seems like everyone on Powell-Peralta and the Bones Brigade rode Trackers at one time or another. And it was their videos that I grew up on—The Bones Brigade Video Show, Future Primitive and The Search For Animal Chin—where I first started seeing and knowing about Tracker and their logos.

Tell us about some memorable times with the Tracker team.
One thing that I remember is how stoked I was when I first got on the pro team around

1993, visiting the Tracker warehouse, how nice everyone was and how awesome it was to work with Bryan Ridgeway and Linda Prettyman. After that, I really felt at home every time I visited Tracker.

Which skateboarders in general inspired you the most?
In the beginning, it was Dogtown and Z-Boys, The Bones Brigade, team Alva, Santa Cruz, Vision and all of the '80s stuff inspired me the most. In fact, that stuff still inspires me, because it's what I grew up on. Now, I am inspired by people who genuinely love skateboarding.

Which are your favorite skate spots?
Usually, I like to skate anything that has never been skated before, I like to bring spots to life. But, now I love skating a well-designed park with street and vert elements.

What have been the highlights of your time in skateboarding?
I guess I had a pretty good 1996. Ha! I had one of the first-ever 12-page Pro Spotlight interviews in the June issue of TransWorld Skateboarding. I qualified first in one of the world's biggest contests of the time, Slam City Jam in Vancouver. That said, there have been a lot of highlights in my time of skateboarding, and there will be many more.

What do you enjoy doing besides skateboarding?
I like to make music, sing, play guitar, write poetry and lyrics, draw, paint and cook. I like to get creative.

Closing comments?
I just want to say thanks for all of the magazine ads over the years, especially the ones on the inside cover of TransWorld Skateboarding! I also want to say that I hope Tracker lasts another 40 years!

Below: **John Reeves, April 1999.**

By Max Dufour + GSD

John Reeves takes a shortcut over the gate, 1990s. Photo: Grant Brittain

Bill Danforth stretches a classic DP layback in Bathurst, New Brunswick, Canada, 2009. Both photos this page: Daniel Mathieu

To say Bill Danforth is a living legend is an understatement. He got his first skateboard in 1972 and has never slowed down. Bill turned pro in 1986 for Madrid, then Alva, and created a cult-like following as the American Nomad. His legend lives on today with the likes of the Barrier Cult and Skull Skates. When asked recently why he still skates, Bill replied simply, "I didn't start skateboarding to quit, so I never will! I might get a little older, but the memories will always be there. Not riding my skateboard would be like forgetting to breathe!"

Bill Danforth
INTERVIEW

When did you get your first Trackers?
I purchased my first set of Trackers in 1978 from the local shop with paper route money.

How did you get involved with the Tracker family?
Basically, when the Sixtrack came out, it was the truck that best fit the board I rode. But, even up until then, I always rode Trackers. In 1981, Madrid had sponsored me and it was then that Stacy Peralta wanted me on the Tracker team. I got the actual phone call that put me on the team from Neil Blender. So, we're going back a long way! I still have the actual letter from Stacy saying, "I'm going to help you out however I can to get you on Tracker." It's surreal to look at now, a letter signed by Stacy. Wow!

I had always thought that you were on Tracker during your entire time in skateboarding, but there was a brief period when you went to try something new.
I quit Tracker for a brief moment to help G&S design a new truck. I showed Larry Balma my contract, and he said, "Look, we are not going to re-design the Tracker Truck. I know you've always wanted to design a truck, so go for it. But, as soon as your G&S contract is up, you're back on the Tracker team." It was a family thing. It's funny looking back, because I was given the opportunity to design a truck from scratch, but when I sat down and put pen to paper, I just knocked off the exact design of a Tracker (laughs).

Why was Tracker such an important part of skateboard history?
Because of its history and the people who rode for and supported the company. A lot of people jumped ship, but the fact of the matter is Tracker has always been there, and been a consistent product. I like to think back to the 1980s during the Tracker vs. Indy war. It was great not being the guy who rode for Indy. It was punk to ride for Tracker. Keep in mind that a lot of the guys riding for Indy at that time started at Tracker, not at Indy. Steve Olson, Salba. You guys have the sponsor me letter Salba sent to Larry, right? (See page 104.)

It seems like you were a good person to test out products based on the way you skated, which was aggressive and hard.
Well, personally, I wasn't the guy doing

lots of airs. I liked the lip tricks. I street skated the old-fashioned way, on loading docks, etc. Being from the Midwest, we skated in colder climates and I saw a lot of trucks break, but Trackers always held up. I did help out after the launch of the Ultralite baseplates, because those did crack in the cold temps, but because I passed on the info, they were able to fix the problem quickly.

Who are the greatest riders in the history of Tracker?
Anybody who still rides Trackers. I'm not going to name one person. Seriously, anybody who has stayed true through the years is my hero!

Which Tracker ad stands out to you?

Yes, I had a favorite ad, for sure. It's me with this big, busted-up face. I hung up on a rail in Arizona, took a full header to the concrete, and my face was all fucked up. That one made me popular with the chicks, because I looked all tough.

Do you recall any memorable times with the Tracker team?
I remember a great trip we did with Tom Groholski, Dan Wilkes and Jeff Phillips, when we did all sorts of demos and shop appearances up and down the East Coast. The best part was the

day we didn't have anything scheduled. We rode this old abandoned skatepark in Redding, Pennsylvania and just went off. No video cameras, no photos, just a bunch of boneheads getting out of a van and having fun. The footage would be monumental today, but the best part was that it was never shot, so it's only in our memories! I remember it feeling like we were all 15 years old again. We had the whole skatepark to ourselves.

Closing comments?
Ride Tracker, fuck Indy. Anything made in the USA is better, and the best thing made in the USA is Tracker Trucks.

Above: **Tracker Dart Bill Danforth colorway.**
Below left: **Bill Danforth, all busted up after a contest in Tempe, Arizona, circa mid 1980s.** Photo: Grant Brittain
Below right: **Bill Danforth grabs a Texas plant in St. Louis, Missouri, circa mid 1980s.** Photo: Grant Brittain

By Jake Stewart

THE
BARRIER
KULT.
THE
DANFORTH
TRACKER
SIXTRACK.

KNIFE RITUAL

Top left: **Tracker / Barrier Kult / Danforth ad, 2010.**
Above: **Depth Leviathan Dweller and the Nomad Bill Danforth, 2011.** Photo: Jeff Cole
Left: **Deer Man of Dark Woods conducts a knife ritual prior to engaging in a second knifing ritual upon a set of holy Jersey barriers in British Columbia, Canada, 2010.** Photo: Depth Leviathan Dweller
Below: **Tracker Dart Skull Skates blackened colorway.**

BARRIER KULT
and Tracker Trucks

FOR A FEW YEARS IN THE EARLY 2010s, THE BARRIER KULT EXPRESSLY RODE THE TRACKER SIXTRACK DANFORTH. BOTH ENTITIES DIRECTLY RELATED TO SKULL SKATES, THE BA. KU. AND THE NOMAD DANFORTH. THE BARRIER KULT INEVITABLY RODE THE BLACKENED HANGER SIXTRACK.

THE CHARACTER LINEAGE THAT THE BA. KU. EMBRACED WAS PALPABLE: DAN WILKES, GSD, THE NOMAD DANFORTH, NEIL BLENDER, JINX, JOHN A. GRIGLEY, STEVE GODOY, DAVID HACKETT, ALLEN LOSI.

THE LINEAGE OF ACTION WAS INFLUENTIAL:
• CHRIS RAY'S SIXTRACK HANGER GRINDING "THE NAMELESS QUARTERPIPE DITCH IN DEL MAR."
• THE TRACKER EXTRACK - GSD BONELESS ONES AT THE GEMCO BANK.

• THE NEIL BLENDER SIXTRACK GRIND MOTIONS THROUGH THE TRANSITIONS OF SADLANDS.
• THE DEL MAR SIXTRACK SMITH GRINDS OF ALLEN LOSI.

THE FANATICAL TIGHT TRANSITION WORSHIP OF THE BARRIER KULT - THE FASCINATION WITH THE TRUCK HANGER AGAINST THE SHARP CONCRETE LIP. THE HIGHWAY BARRIER - TIGHT TRANSITION ALTAR TO THE SHALLOW END OF A POOL, THE ELLIPTICAL TRANSITION OF AN EARLY '80s HALFPIPE. ALL OF THE ABOVE OBSESSIONS WERE CONGRUENT TO THE ACTIONS AND RITUALS OF THE BARRIER KULT.

DEPTH LEVIATHAN DWELLER
THE BARRIER KULT
KNIFING RITUALS

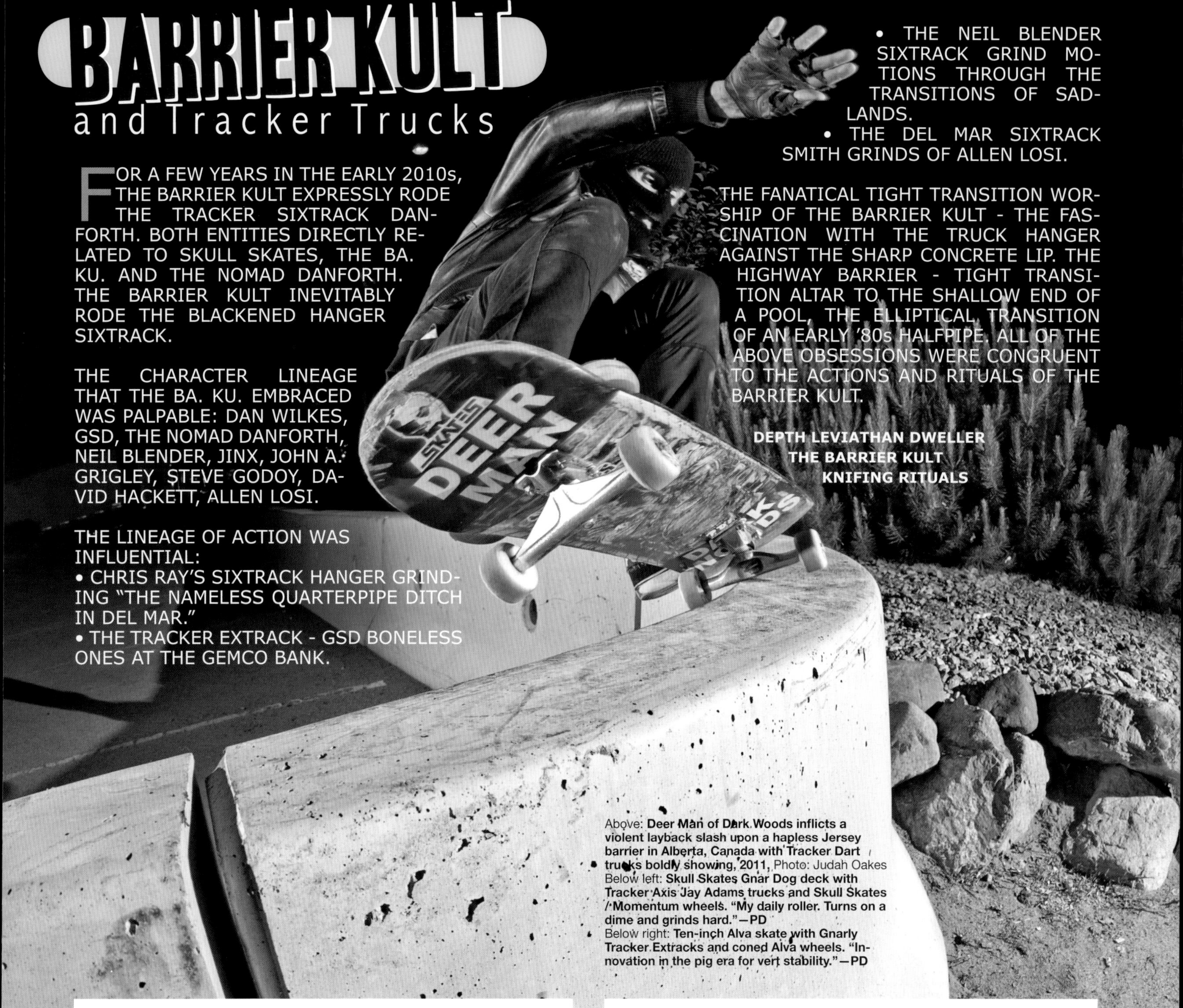

Above: **Deer Man of Dark Woods** inflicts a violent layback slash upon a hapless Jersey barrier in Alberta, Canada with Tracker Dart trucks boldly showing, 2011, Photo: Judah Oakes
Below left: **Skull Skates Gnar Dog deck** with Tracker Axis Jay Adams trucks and Skull Skates / Momentum wheels. "My daily roller. Turns on a dime and grinds hard."—PD
Below right: Ten-inch Alva skate with Gnarly Tracker Extracks and coned Alva wheels. "Innovation in the pig era for vert stability."—PD

301

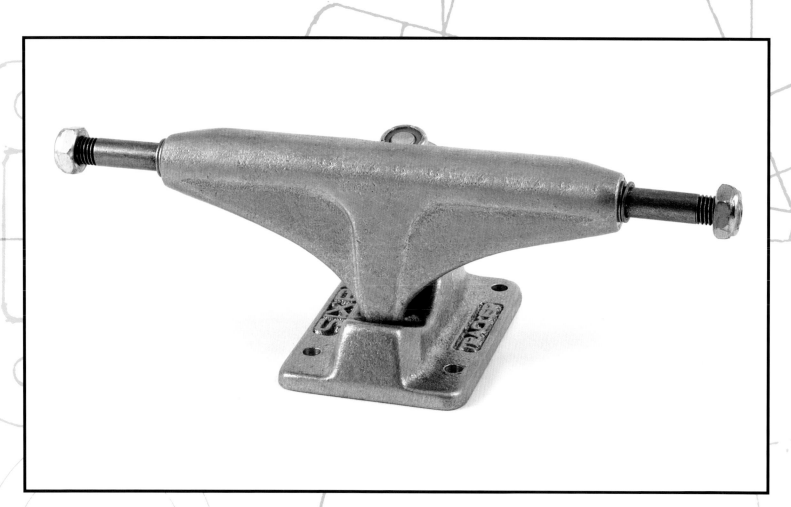

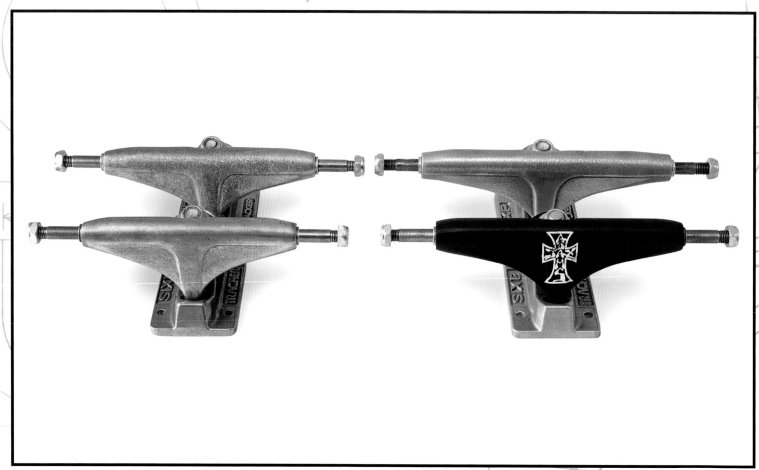

TRACKER AXIS PIVOT BUSHING
POLYURETHANE 80+DURO

43.5°

Willy Santos nose grinds his way to freedom, 2014. Photo: Adam Small
Opposite page, top: Tracker Axis.
Opposite page, bottom, left row, front to back: Tracker Axis 129 mm and 139 mm.
Right row, front to back: Axis 149 mm (Jay Adams colorway) and 161 mm.

TRACKER AXIS
A Quicker Geometry (1999)

By the time Windansea, California surfer Peter Parkin bolted together the first 2" x 4" skateboard in 1947, Chicago had been producing their double-action roller skate truck for 25 years. In the '50s, surfers immediately adopted skateboarding as a way to travel to the beach while enjoying the freedom of gliding just like riding their surfboard. This was a time when kids built homemade skateboards out of 2" x 4" planks and cheap, discarded metal wheel roller skates. Although toy companies produced skateboards on and off over the years, by the early '60s, surfboard manufacturers were making higher quality skateboards using their brand names, which resulted in the first popular explosion of skateboarding. At the time, Chicago was the most widely available truck and was thus used on many of the better skateboards of the day. Suddenly, by 1965, skateboarding was declared too dangerous and the fad quickly died off.

During the early '70s, a second skateboarding boom was underway, ignited by the Cadillac urethane wheels. In 1975, the Bennett Hijacker debuted with the same geometry as the Chicago, but with a raised axle, which resulted in a very high roll center combined with a lot of trail and an extreme caster angle. Although the Bennett Hijacker felt quick, it was also tippy and prone to the dreaded speed wobbles. In contrast, we here at Tracker based our original Fultrack geometry after the Sure Grip roller skate truck, which was smooth and stable. As the head honcho at skateboard manufacturer and distributor, NHS, Rich Novak began selling both Tracker and Bennett trucks in 1975. Around 1977, he gave a Tracker and a Bennett to Fausto Vitello and Eric Swenson—from a foundry called Ermico—and Santa Cruz / Tracker pro Rick Blackhart and told them to combine the two into a new truck that he could sell. This partnership resulted in the Independent truck, which was released in late 1978. Independent chose to use the Chicago roller skate truck geometry that Bennett had started with before he raised the axle. Although Independent lowered the axle somewhat to remove as much caster as they could, the truck still had a high roll center. But, the tippy feel, strong logo design and hardcore image won Independent a very loyal fan base that has endured to this day.

By 1999, we decided to produce a truck with a steering angle and roll center comparable to Independent. Dubbed the Axis, it was the first Tracker to utilize the Chicago roller skate truck geometry, which Bennett and Independent had copied. Up until this time, all Tracker hangers and baseplates could be interchanged, but this was not the case with the Axis, which was incompatible. Lightweight with a slightly higher roll center than other Trackers, the feel of the Axis was quicker turning, but not as stable as the Dart or the classic Trackers. (However, the actual turning angle was exactly the same as the Dart.) Tracker Axis hangers were produced in 4 3/4" (119 mm), 5 1/8" (129 mm), 5 1/2" (139 mm), 5 7/8" (149 mm) and eventually in 6 3/8" (161 mm). As of 2014, we offer the Axis in all sizes except the 119 mm. Because the Racetrack X also features the Axis geometry, skaters now have a choice of truck geometry dialed in to the feel that they expect from their skateboard, combined with Tracker's legendary strength and quality.—**LMB**

Sky Siljeg blasts a layback air at the Bondi Bowl in Sydney, Australia, circa 2008. Photo: Dean Tirkot
Opposite page: **Matt Pennington drops a bio Ollie to wall ride in Denver, Colorado, 2014.** Photos: Joel Freeman

TRACKER AXIS PIVOT BUSHING
POLYURETHANE 80+DURO

43.5°

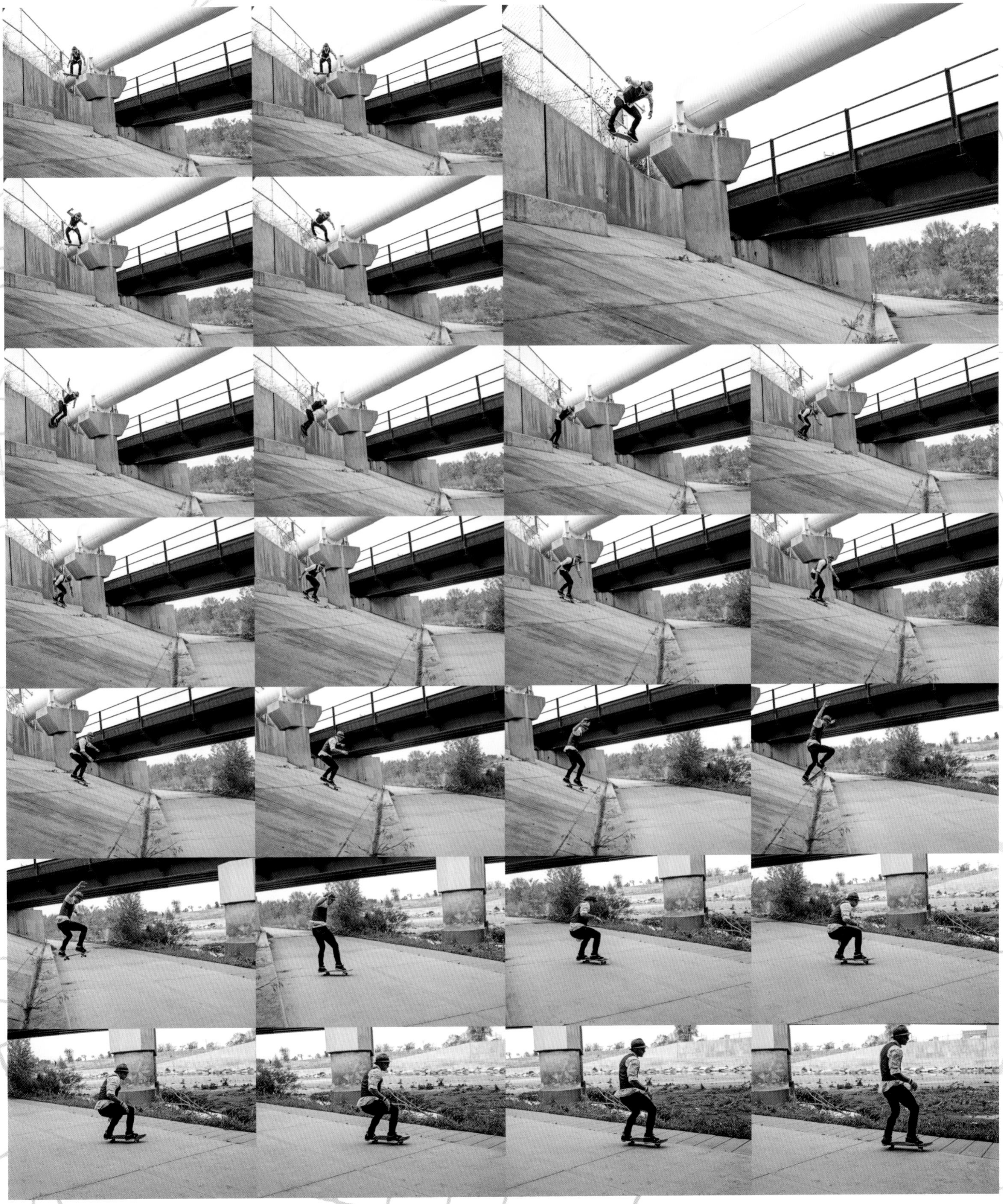

TRACKER TRUCKS / FFWD

LIGHTWEIGHT + FASTEST TURNING RADIUS + UNMATCHED STRENGTH + NON SLIP AXLE + GUARANTEED QUALITY

KRISTIAN SVITAK

TRACKER TRUCKS_3210 PRODUCTION AVE SUITE B OCEANSIDE, CA 92054 TRACKER-TRUCKS.COM

Kristian Svitak, March 2000.
306

TRACKER AXIS PIVOT BUSHING
POLYURETHANE 80+DURO

43.5°

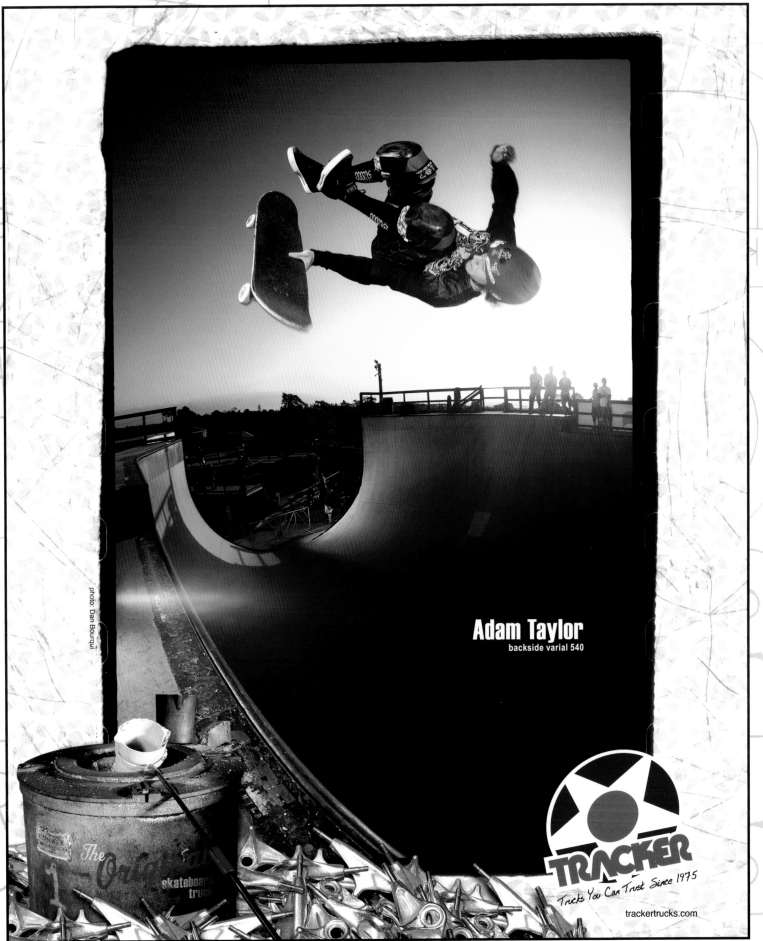

photo: Dan Bourqui

Adam Taylor
backside varial 540

TRACKER
Trucks You Can Trust Since 1975

trackertrucks.com

Adam Taylor, Winter 2010. Photo: Dan Bourqui

Blind Test

From day one, the Tracker R&D team tested all brands of skateboard trucks in blind tests using several identical non-branded slalom and pool skateboard decks. I set up each deck with an identical wheelbase, not just the same truck hole spacing in the deck, but the same distance from the front axle to the rear axle. (The center of the axle in relation to the base mounting holes varies from truck to truck.) I used the same kind of wheels and bearings on each board and added spacers so that the truck widths were the same. I also used the same cushions and made sure that the ride height matched. I placed a number on the top of each deck so I could keep track of the feedback on my clipboard. The skaters would ride one board and then another without turning them over to see the trucks. This way, they had no preconceived notions of how the truck worked and their feedback was pure. Stepping from one identical deck set-up to another, the skater was able to "feel" the geometry of each truck. Skater height, weight and riding styles varied along with the skate terrain. This process helped us develop protoypes during the research and design phase of each Tracker truck model. —**LMB**

Geometry 101:
How a Skateboard Truck Works

Some skateboarders say that the pivot angle dictates how a truck turns. Others think it's the kingpin angle. On every truck design, except for a reverse kingpin, the actual steering angle is impossible for a layperson to measure. Even then, what does that number really mean? There is no magic number that represents the geometry of a skateboard truck. As simple and basic as a skateboard truck may look, there are a lot of factors at play that, when combined, equal its "geometry." Turning angle, kingpin angle, built-in bind, caster or trail, roll center and center of gravity are all variables of skateboard truck geometry. Working at Tracker for 40 years, I have

experimented with many truck designs. All I have to do is look at a truck and I'll have a general idea of how it will work. A hardcore skater knows the feel of a truck and can tell after a couple of runs which one he likes better. He may also say that one truck turns more than another. I've heard many skaters say that Independents turn more than Trackers. In fact, the turning angles between the two truck brands are the same.

The Independent truck has a higher roll center than the classic Trackers or Dart. The higher roll center causes the deck to rock farther side to side. As it flops to the side, leverage is increased, which requires less pressure to turn. The board feels tippy and appears to turn sharper. Tracker has a very low roll center that allows the skater to push into his turns harder, and with more commitment. Trackers feel more stable and less tippy, even with the same turning angle. A Tracker rider may land a trick smoothly and make it look easy, while an Independent rider may land the same trick sketchy and make it look more difficult. Of course, there are other factors at work. The amount of built-in bind on the cushions greatly affects the ride, not to mention the cushion material, memory and hardness. How much caster is built into the truck? Caster can both help stability on the front truck and cause speed wobbles on the rear truck.

Most skateboards are designed to be ridden in both directions so the front and rear trucks are the same. Slalom and downhill skateboards can take advantage of having different geometry on the front and rear trucks for maximum speed, stability and turning response. You can increase or decrease your steering angle by inserting a wedge-shaped space pad between your baseplate and deck. Raising the rear of the baseplate will increase the steering angle for quicker turns. Raising the front of the baseplate will decrease the steering angle and decrease the caster for less chance of speed wobbles. Tracker offers wedge pads with a five-degree angle for this purpose (see page 336).—**LMB**

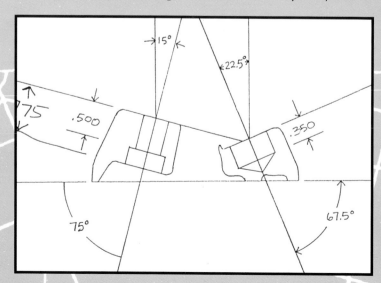

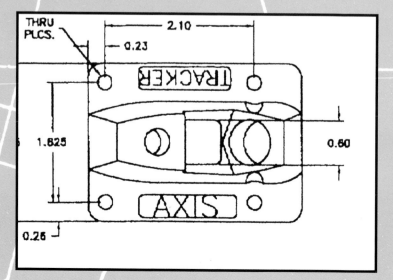

The Big Five

Skateboard manufacturers have always formed associations over the years, including the PSA, ISA, NSA and now IASC. Enormous associations are like a democratic government: too bureaucratic and cumbersome to be able to make timely decisions for the good of the whole group. If you were sponsored or worked in the skateboard industry in the 1980s, you probably heard of the Big Five: Brad Dorfman of Vision, George Powell and Stacy Peralta of Powell-Peralta, Rich Novak of NHS, Fausto Vitello of Independent and *Thrasher*, and yours truly, Larry Balma, of Tracker and *TransWorld Skateboarding*. The Big Five was formed as an informal group of major industry players who met, discussed and directed skateboarding in order to promote and grow the entire sport. By the mid '80s, we were all seasoned businessmen who understood profit margin and cash flow, which meant we were able to fund our pro skaters, contests and promotions. At the time, there were no huge corporate sponsors or cable TV networks with their checkbooks out. So, the Big Five did what it had to do: We each pulled $10,000 out of our budgets on a monthly basis to give our pros contest exposure on a public stage. We held bi-monthly meetings inside a restaurant in the LAX Theme building, bringing input from our pro skaters and product managers. At times, our meetings could become a little intense—remember, we were all very passionate about our sport and our product lines. In the end, we would all go back home and lead the skateboard industry forward with the decisions that we agreed upon.

One of the guys from the Big Five that I was the closest to was my friend, Fausto Vitello. That's right, he was my friend, God rest his soul. Legendary artist, writer and photographer CR Stecyk III knew both of us, as we were both clients of his, and it was he who was instrumental in pulling Fausto and I together. Since Fausto ran Independent and *Thrasher*, and I ran Tracker and *TransWorld Skateboarding*, most people viewed us as fierce enemies. Yes, we were huge competitors in the skateboard marketplace, each striving for the success of our brands, but we were also partners working together to promote and grow skateboarding. We both understood that the bigger skateboarding

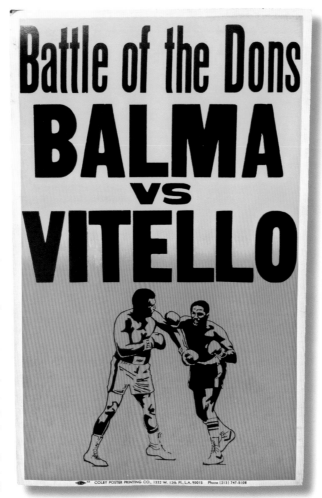

became, the larger our pieces of the pie would become. Fausto and I had a lot of things in common. We both shared an Italian heritage, not to mention ownership of major truck, deck and wheel brands, and, of course, the magazines. With no one in the world the wiser, Fausto would occasionally fly to Orange County—and sometimes I would fly to San Francisco—for private meetings between just the two of us. We shared our ideas about the skateboard industry and discussed our personal lives. I'll always treasure my time spent with Fausto, who was one of the biggest movers and shakers in skateboard history.

In the early '90s, many of the new, upcoming street skateboard brands, which preferred to remain small and nimble, regarded the Big Five as old, lumbering dinosaurs. As the months and years went by, we realized it was time to pass the baton to the newcomers. Luckily, at the same time, a bunch of huge non-endemic sponsors were finally ready to come on board and flow the big bucks necessary to support rapidly growing pro contest circuits like the X Games and others, which helped promote skateboarding to millions. The small hard goods brands of the mid to late '90s were all more focused on their own success and survival than working as a group to promote and grow the entire sport of skateboarding. As a result, prices were cut and profit margins dissolved until it became very difficult to run a hard goods business. Ultimately, by the time the 2000s rolled around, many of these brands finally came together and backed IASC, who lobbied to the California Congress to declare skateboarding a hazardous activity. This removed the threat of lawsuits from municipalities, which allowed the construction of public skateparks to begin all over California and eventually across the United States and even abroad. Today, the Tony Hawk Foundation carries the torch by helping fund public skateparks in low-income areas. This is the legacy of the Big Five's durable influence: a skatepark in every town and a skateboard in every house.—**LMB**

Above: **A poster advertising a non-existent boxing match between Larry Balma and Fausto Vitello at the Action Sports Retailer trade show, circa late 1980s.** Left: F**austo and Larry mug it up at a skateboard contest, circa late 1980s.** Photo: Louise Balma

Four years after he arrived kicking and screaming into this world in 1961, Jay Adams started skateboarding and surfing. A white-hot fireball of explosive spontaneity and aggression, Jay has been described as nothing less than "the archetype of modern-day skateboarding." Getting upside down when everyone else was right side up, Jay attempted the first handplants on vertical in 1976, and often contorted his body into unique positions that no else has before or since. As the prototype Z-Boy, Jay was featured prominently in the films *Dogtown and Z-Boys* and *Lords of Dogtown*. Who can forget the famous photo of him on the former's promo poster, crouched down low, turning around a cone with his fist in the air and a pissed look on his face? No one, that's who, because it's the all-time classic skateboarding photo, the one that should be sent up on the next Voyager spacecraft to let aliens know what our "sport" is all

Jay Adams
INTERVIEW

about! Having done some hard time in prison over the decades on assault and drug charges, Jay lived a life that was impossible to sugarcoat. News flash: Sugar is bad for you anyway. In recent times, Jay bucked the odds and turned around his life. Just before he passed away on August 14, 2014, Jay was holding down a job at Hurley, mentoring youth so they could avoid the mistakes he made, and spending lots of quality time with his wife, Tracy, daughter, Venice, and son, Seven. Needless to say, Jay

Adams shredded the concrete and waves until the day he died. Skateboarder for life!—GSD

DH: When did you get your first set of Trackers?
I can't honestly remember the exact date, but it was after the Bennett truck days. I think it went Roller Sport, Bennett, Tracker, to whatever came after. Tracker's have been good for a long time.

DH: So you've been a Tracker rider for how long now?
I don't know, 1975-'76. I can't remember. When did they come out?

DH: They came out in 1975. What was it like when you rode your first set of Trackers? Getting on Trackers after skating on something like Sure Grip or a smaller truck like that, what was the difference?
What I remember about Trackers and what I liked about them was that they were pretty stable. They didn't squirrel out, as opposed to Indys, which had a squirrel to them. The Trackers would turn, they were always a little less squirrely. That's what I liked about them.

DH: In your mind, who were some of the biggest Tracker riders, the guys who really made a difference for the Tracker brand?
Wow, there was a time after Bennett when everybody rode them. There was a time when there was a big Tracker vs. Indy war going on, but I always preferred Tracker.

DH: So, tell us about the Tracker Axis Jay Adams signature colorway? What makes it different?
Simply put, it's like an Indy but it's a Tracker.

DH: Wasn't Indy made like a Bennett, through?
I don't know what Independent was made like.

DH: Indy's geometry copied Bennett.
Fausto was cool. I thought Indys were cool when Fausto was around, because he was a cool guy, but Trackers have been my go-to trucks for a long time. Everybody seems to make good trucks now, and Tracker makes them as good as anybody. You can't say Trackers don't turn anymore, because for a long time people did say that. You know that, right?

DH: Oh yeah, absolutely.
You can't say that anymore, my trucks turn as good as Indys do.

DH: I think better.
If you want to be truthful, there were *Thrasher* guys on Indy, and there were *TransWorld* guys on Trackers. Kind of like the San Diego, *TransWorld*, Tracker dudes and the San Franscico, *Thrasher*, Indy guys.

DH: Would you say that most of the tricks in skateboarding were done first on Trackers because Indys didn't even exist?
Well, of course. There was a whole time period before Indy when a lot of people rode Trackers. Guys like

Henry Hester, he was a full Tracker guy. A lot of guys rode Trackers before Indy, and a lot of guys have gone back to Tracker now since Fausto isn't around. Who owns Indy now? I don't even know. I don't even read *Thrasher* anymore. I looked at an issue in the supermarket and it was just guys flying down stairs every picture.

DH: What's it been like skateboarding your whole life?
Well, I've seen a lot of people come and go, and there's been a lot of guys who have stuck with it for a long time. Tracker's been there a long time, too. Surfing and skateboarding are things that I've always done, and I still like them today as much as I did when I was a kid.

TM: There are not a lot of people who do something their entire life and are still stoked on it!
Skateboarding is so fun! You get to enjoy the sun and all of the kids around. It's good family fun now, not some a criminal activity like it used to be in the '70s when we were sneaking into people's pools. I like the skateparks.

TM: What do you think about all of the new skateparks? There's so much good concrete.
I think its great. It's just good family fun, because everybody can enjoy it: little kids, girls and dads are doing it. Even grandpas are doing it. Some guys have been skaters their whole lives, like me (laughs). It's just as fun now as it was a long time ago. It's funner now, actually.

DH: Do you think we skateboard better now than when we were kids?
Well it's hard to say. When you're younger, you're lighter on your feet and you've got more spring in your step. But, the progression has gone so far that you might be doing more stuff than when you were younger. I know I have just as much fun now, probably more.

Jay Adams grabs a classic backside off the lip at the Dogbowl in Santa Monica, California, 1977. Photo: Glen E. Friedman
Opposite page, top: **A Z-Boy's work is never done. Jay emanates a vicious intensity at Venice skatepark in Venice Beach, California, 2014.** Photo: Chris Hooten
Opposite page, bottom: **Jay Adams, David Hackett, 2013.**

311

Straight outta Montreal, Canada, Max Dufour is a member of that rare breed, the vertical skateboarder. Max started skating in the mid '80s and grew up on brands like Invisible and Tracker in the '90s. As the proprietor of Woodchuck Laminates, Pure Distribution, and now Tracker Trucks, it's obvious Max is in it for the long haul. Mr. Dufour has competed in contests like the X Games (in which he won a silver), Vans Triple Crown and the Dew Tour, and still kills it on the perpendicular today, landing plenty of high-tech moves like his signature kickflip tail grab 360 to fakie.—GSD

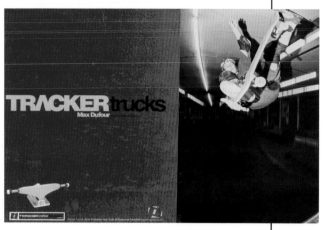

LMB: When did you start skateboarding?
I started skateboarding in 1984-'85 when *Back to the Future* came out. That's what got me into skating. Then I picked up *TransWorld Skateboarding*, read it inside and out, and went to the only skate shop in Montreal called Footloose. That's when I got my first set-up: a Brand-X board with Variflex wheels and Venture trucks.

GSD: Did you skate street or just vert?
I skated street, too, but I really just skated a lot of vert.

GSD: Did you ever do handrails?
Yeah, I did some. But, when I grew up skating, we had six outdoor vert ramps on the south shore of Montreal. The cities were building skateparks and they only knew how to build vert ramps, so it was kind of crazy.

LMB: When did you get your first Trackers?
When I was riding for Invisible, I asked Dave Bergthold and then Ridgeway for some. So, I started riding them in 1997. The Axis first came out a year or two after that. I started riding the Axis 139 trucks and I never changed after that.

LMB: Why was Tracker so important in the history of skateboarding?
For me, Tracker is skateboarding. It's all of the legends. Everyone grew up on Tracker, and everyone who skated was connected to Tracker in some shape or form. Even the guys who never rode Trackers recognized the brand.

LMB: Who were the riders that you looked up to?
Tony Hawk, of course, Jeff Phillips, Neil Blender and Chris Miller. Chris never rode Trackers, but those were the riders who I looked up to a lot, and still do.

LMB: Do you recall a memorable event with the Tracker team?
Yeah, one was with the Invisible team on a tour we took to Arizona in the Commander RV. That was a great time. It was with John

Reeves and Tabias Walker. It was a fun trip. We got to skate this platform that's in the Arizona desert that they use for car ads. It was a big, rotating quarterpipe. I got to skate it on that trip, and that was a highlight of my skating life, for sure. I think it was featured in a Santa Cruz movie a long time ago. I'm not sure if it was Corey O'Brien or someone like that. Dave Bergthold knew roughly where it was, but it was like a wild search party before we finally found it. I actually got a photo in *TransWorld* skating there.

LMB: Did you climb up on that thing and drop into it?
No, you couldn't drop into it, because it was too high. It's got a massive amount of vert with a tight transition. But, it's just so rad, and it's in the middle of the desert. You could rotate the whole platform to get the lighting you wanted. You could hit it from side to side. It's still there. I saw it in a Volcom movie not too long ago.

GSD: Name some tricks that have given you the most difficulty to learn on vert.
The 540 took a while. I learned it pretty late. Another trick that was really hard was the fakie 540.

LMB: Did you invent any tricks yourself?
Yeah, a trick that I've never seen anyone do is a Sal flip 360 to fakie. I've done four.

GSD: What's a Sal flip?
It's like a hand flip, but you kind of flip it sideways. I would go up the ramp, do a 360 to fakie and at the same time do a Sal flip. It was named after Sal Barbier. It's kind of an exaggerated finger flip. I did it at a best trick contest at the Slam City Jam in Vancouver in 2001. That was a trick that I was really happy about. I also did a kickflip tail grab 360 to fakie sequence, and a double kickflip to Indy fakie that I haven't seen else anyone do yet.

Louise Balma: How do skaters today deal with their sponsors? What's important to them and what's not?
Skateboarding has progressed a lot, and it's still progressing. That's the fun part of it—it hasn't stagnated. There are always tricks being created or added, and I think that's what keeps it fun, so that's great. In terms of trying to make a career out of skateboarding, it's pretty difficult—especially for vert skating. If you're a vert skater and you want to make a career out of it, you really need to branch out with corporate sponsors like an energy drink and stuff like that. I guess board companies are still important, but they don't have the financial support they used to. There's less and less money in skateboard brands, because it's really watered down now; it's over-saturated. From the late '80s to mid '90s, there was more money to support the skateboarding professional, but nowadays, it's really difficult. If you're a professional skateboarder and you want to make a living off of it, you have to use different outlets than the regular hardgoods companies.

GSD: Are there many vert ramps left?
Yeah, they're all in San Diego, which is a really good place to skate vert, but outside of that...

GSD: How many are there?
There's Tony Hawk's ramp, you've got the monster DC ramp, Elliot Sloan just built a

vert ramp in Vista, there's another local vert ramp in Vista not far form there, Bob Burnquist's vert ramp, which turned into a bowl, Encinitas skatepark, and also Mission.

GSD: What about other areas of the country? Are there any left?
There are some on the East Coast. There was one in Atlanta that just closed. There are several vert ramps in Florida, maybe one in Jersey and that's it. There are not many, that's for sure. There are less and less of them. In Canada, there are no vert ramps left.

LMB: There are skateparks that have vert pools.
Yeah, there are pools, and that is definitely helping vert skating come back. The growth in skateboarding is more in transition, like parks, small bowls and snake runs.

LMB: You've taken over Tracker and Tracker production now.
I've always had a heart for Tracker, like when I was riding for Invisible. I like the production part of the business. In 1996, I started a wood factory called Woodchuck. I made boards with my own hands, and I've always liked the manufacturing part of skateboarding. I remember when I rode for Tracker and Invisible, I would check out how things were done. I thought that was unique and great. I always kept in touch with Linda Prettyman at Tracker, and in 2008 or so, we talked and saw that there was an opportunity. Then I talked to you and we struck a deal, and I've enjoyed it since then. I just like making products; the manufacturing part has always been interesting. Tracker has a huge history, and it needs to be exposed as much as possible. So, yeah, I took over the production part. We have different projects in the works. One of them is a big 300 mm Fastrack truck. We're doing a project with a company called the Longboard Stroller. They contacted us to do a specific truck for it. They are attaching a baby carriage to a longboard and need a specific truck, so they asked Tracker to design one. So, we came out with an extended version of the Fastrack that Larry created. If you compare it to the Fultrack, it's pretty crazy wide. So, I think Tracker has the biggest truck on the market.

LMB: And Tracker still produces most of the sizes and styles that it ever made. There's still a demand.
Tracker has the biggest line of trucks ever.

Max Dufour
INTERVIEW

It's got the biggest line up of all types of trucks. No one else can even come close to it. We've got trucks for cruising, racing, freestyle, street, vert and bowl. We've got sizes from 85 mm to 106, 129, 139, 149, 161, 184, 219, 230 and now 300.

LMB: Closing comments?
To me, Tracker is part of skateboarding history, and I'm really thankful to be part of it. It's a great story and it will carry on for years and years.

Read the full-length interview at trackertrucks.com

Above: **Max Dufour, Tracker Axis, June 2001.**

Max Dufour flicks himself over the channel, circa early 2000s. Photo: Daniel Mathieu
Sequence: **Max performs his signature trick, the kickflip tailgrab 360 to fakie, at the YMCA in Encinitas, California, 2006.** Photos: Dan Bourqui

TRACKER AXIS PIVOT BUSHING
POLYURETHANE 80+DURO

43.5°

Patrick Melcher floats a rare Ollie to nose / tail slide off a burly bright yellow rail in Los Angeles, California, 2008. Photo: Sean Peterson

TRACKER AXIS PIVOT BUSHING
POLYURETHANE 80+DURO

43.5°

Patrick Melcher
INTERVIEW

By Jake Stewart + GSD

Patrick Melcher is a professional skateboarder who lives in Los Angeles, California. After growing up around Chicago, Illinois and living in the city itself for many years, Patrick's background combines a big city pace with the watchful eye of a constant traveler. He can usually be seen in and around the LA area DJ-ing soul and oldies music to a dancing crowd. Prizing new experiences and an off-the-beaten-path outlook, Patrick views skateboarding as sort of a conduit to a broader spectrum. He found skateboarding in the late '80s and is attributed to having a somewhat unique style in the sport. Seeking out interesting obstacles and new ways of looking at old tricks, Patrick's skateboarding style reflects that of his interests and passions—combining timeless classics with refreshing innovation and high-speed aggression.

When and how did you start skating?
Santa got me a skateboard. I was 11 years old and it was the best thing in the world. I took it everywhere, and it quickly became as much a part of me as the shirt on my back.

Describe your first good set-up.
1988. Vision Mark Gonzales, a set of blue Trackers with plastic baseplates and a Lapper, because Tony Hawk had one. I didn't even know what a Lapper was, I just knew I wanted one. I remember that I really wanted T-Bones, too, but the day I went to the shop, they were gone. All they had left were the smaller versions called G-Bones, which turned out to be better for me.

How did you turn pro?
John Lucero called me up one day and said, "Hey, I've heard that you're interested in skating for Black Label. I'm going to send you a box of stuff and see if we can't make this thing work." The next day, he called back and said, "Okay, I'm just going to put you on the team full-on." It was fucking rad. Then a year or so later, I was working at a photo studio when John called and said, "Congratulations, you're pro now. Start thinking of what you want on your first graphic. Oh yeah, you should think about quitting your job at the photo studio."

Who are your current sponsors?
Death Skateboards, Purveyor Wheels and Tracker Trucks.

Why was Tracker so important in the history of skateboarding?
What stands out to me was all of that old footage of the pool contests, like Del Mar and stuff. There was always a Tracker logo or banner up in the mix. For me, Tracker has been there from the very beginning of what I came to know skateboarding to be.

Which Tracker riders influenced
you? Who did you look up to?
Tony Hawk. He was the best representative Tracker could've ever hoped for.

Tell us a couple of crazy stories from road trips.
The best things that stick out in my head about the many years of traveling are actually not skating. Being ready to accept adventure and just go with it brings on the best times. One time, I was in a van full of dudes and we were traveling through the Redwood forest. It's so beautiful out there—the trees and wildlife—it's so grand. We pulled off the trail and onto this pebble beach determined to swim in the clear mountain stream that was flowing through the forest. There wasn't another soul around for miles, so I pulled the tour van right up to the edge of a stream and we all jumped out and submerged ourselves in it. The quiet, clear day was shining down on us like heaven. We were looking up and downstream marveling at nature when I spotted a bear catching fish. The bear was quite a ways away from us, but close enough for us to see that he was just a massive beast. He started slowly making his way toward us. We quickly dried off and got back in the van. As I tried to pull the van out, it became stuck in the gravel. The rear wheels were spinning and shooting up rocks all over the place. While I tried rocking the van back and forth, I could tell that it was getting worse. As it became more and more entrenched in its own wheel ruts, the bear had now taken an interest in us. We were making a bunch of noise and freaking out as the bear was making its way to us with purpose. The van wasn't moving at all. There was just enough time for a couple of dudes to get out and try to wedge their skateboards under the tires to act as a solid surface for the tires to get a grip on. The van broke loose and the skaters jumped in as the bear was standing no less than 50 feet away from us, dumbfounded. We could have easily been lunch for that grizzly had it not been for the adventurous spirit and agility of a few skateboarders.

Name your favorite skate spots.
Say what you will, but I'm a sucker for some smooth, hard surface. The way the concrete is laid makes a big difference. The kind of pavement that feels like you're riding on marble—that's my jam.

Which skateboarders in general have inspired you the most?
Matt Hensley and Danny Way: true hero status. But nothing will compare to the passion and gnarlitude that John Cardiel has brought to skateboarding.

What have been the highlights of your time in skateboarding?
There are a few times, when you attempt to film a trick, when security guards or cops are moving in fast and you know it's the last try. Pulling your trick after a battle, when you've bargained for "one more try" with the cops, that's a damned good feeling.

Below: **Patrick Melcher unleashes a backside Smith, circa 2014.** Photo: Marfa Capadanno

315

2000s-2010s
Skateboarding Timeline

2000 · Amidst the corporate chaos infiltrating skateboarding, some top pros hire managers and agents.

· In contrast to decades past, when contest series were the main thing pros concentrated on, team tours overseas become the next big thing.

· With the rise of e-commerce and B2B, skateboarding companies go online en masse.

· A new generation of skatepark designers / builders arises, including Wally Holldyday's California Skateparks, Purkiss Rose, Team Pain and Dave Duncan Designs.

· As big as two football fields, the new Millenium Skatepark in Calgary, Canada becomes the largest free skatepark in the world.

· Rob Dyrdek opens the first proper team training facility.

· éS Footwear debuts its first video, *Menikmati*.

· The staff of *Big Brother* conceives of the TV show *Jackass*, which features people performing various dangerous, crude, self-injuring stunts and pranks.

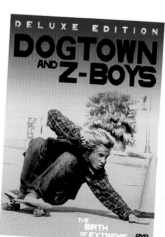

· Andy Macdonald makes the *Guinness Book of World Records* with a long jump measuring in at 52' 10" on a precursor to the Mega Ramp.

· Upcoming talent includes Colt Cannon, Chris Cole, Aaron Suski, Rodrigo Tx, Tosh Townend, Tony Trujillo and Brian Wenning.

2001 · Stacy Peralta directs the *Dogtown and Z-Boys* documentary, which busts wide open the old school skateboarding phenomenon / nostalgia market.

· A mint Dogtown Bob Biniak Bullet model from 1978 sells for $3,550 on eBay.

· The first Old School Skate Jam, a family reunion of skateboarders from previous decades, goes down at the Skatelab skatepark and museum.

· Pool skating enjoys a sharp resurgence, even among young street skaters. Slalom racing also makes a comeback.

· Tony Hawk publishes the first pro skater autobiography, *Hawk Occupation: Skateboarder*, which becomes a *New York Times* bestseller.

· Chico State University sponsors the first skateboard PE class, resulting in an overwhelming response from students.

· Street skaters throw increasingly difficult tricks down huge rails like El Toro, Hollywood 16, Wilshire.

· A loop at the Skatepark of Tampa sends Peter

Hewitt and Brian Schaeffer to the hospital. Of course, Bob Burnquist effortlessly pulls it switch.

· Upcoming talent includes Caswell Berry, Corey Duffel, Patrick Melcher, Paul Rodriguez, Jose Rojo, Austin Stephens and Mikey Taylor.

2002 · Tony Hawk launches the Tony Hawk Foundation, a charity that helps build free, public skateparks across the United States.

· Danny Way designs and skates the first Mega Ramp at Point X Camp. DC Shoes releases *The DC Video*, in which Way sets two world's records in the same run: longest jump (75') and highest air (23' 5").

· Louisville, Kentucky opens a massive free public skatepark complete with a full pipe, 24-hour lights and a circus-like atmosphere.

· Published in *TransWorld Skateboarding*, Lance Mountain's wide-ranging collection of skateboarding memorabilia inspires the "new old stock" collecting craze.

· A rare near-mint Powell-Peralta Tony Hawk model from 1982 sells for $6,000 on eBay.

· Stevie Williams launches DGK (Dirty Ghetto Kids) skateboards, which was the name of his skate crew growing up in Philadelphia.

· Nike launches its first pro skateboard shoe program called Nike SB. 88 Footwear starts up with Neil Blender on board.

· Ollie Pop bubble gum debuts. It's official: skateboarding is mainstream.

· As the skateboard business booms, magazines get ultra huge, with the thickest ever issue of *TransWorld Skateboarding* weighing in at 424 pages.

· *Concrete Wave* magazine launches to cover all forms of skateboarding, contrary to other mags, which mostly feature street and a little tranny.

· Tony Alva wins the Legend title at the TransWorld Awards. Even street skaters get ads skating backyard pools.

· Relatively unknown PJ Ladd from Boston, Massachusetts startles the skateboarding world with his advanced technical street skating in *PJ Ladd's Wonderful Horrible Life* video.

· *Stoked: the Rise and Fall of Gator*, a documentary detailing the life of 1980s pro skater Mark "Gator" Rogowski, who was convicted of murder, debuts.

· The first show of its kind, *Tony Hawk's Boom Boom Huck Jam* features the best skateboarders, BMXers and freestyle moto-x maniacs in a choreographed extravaganza with bands.

· Bob Burnquist airs over an upside-down gap that opens up in the roof of his loop.

· Upcoming talent includes Josh Harmony, Bryan Herman, PJ Ladd, Johnny Layton, Greg Lutzka,

Billy Marks, Tony Silva and Justin Strubing.

2003 · Inspired by simple and harsh skateboarding of the early '80s, the Barrier Kult forms in Vancouver, Canada. Avoiding Ollies and handrails and wearing all black, the BA. KU. skates only Jersey barriers and other tight transitions.

· Another legendary street spot, LOVE Park in Philadelphia, Pennsylvania, is rendered permanently unskatable.

· Woodward skate camp opens its second facility, Woodward West, in Tehachapi, California.

· Numerous skateboard brands begin to boycott decks made in China.

· *Viva La Bam*, a reality show about the exploits of pro skateboarder Bam Margera plus his friends and family, debuts and runs for five seasons on MTV.

· Large corporations like Boost Mobile, Mountain Dew, NBC, Red Bull and T-Mobile offer big bucks for sponsorships and prize money at contests.

· éS Footwear debuts Eric Koston's Game of SKATE, the first flat ground street contest series.

· Attempting to realize a dream many have had, Bob Burnquist nearly completes a loop at the Mt. Baldy pipe, but slams coming down the other side.

· The Agenda trade show launches as an alternative to Action Sports Retailer.

· Upcoming talent includes Matt Allen, Dennis Busenitz, Justin Eldridge, Kevin Long, Cale Nuske, Collin Provost, Dylan Rieder, Jereme Rogers, Leo Romero, Ryan Sheckler, Braydon Szafranski and Darrell Stanton.

2004 · The word Ollie enters the *Oxford English Dictionary*.

· George Powell and Stacy Peralta reunite for the first time since 1991 to reissue vintage '80s Powell-Peralta skateboard decks and DVDs.

· After producing a special Tony Hawk issue of *TransWorld Skateboarding*, most of the main staff leaves to start *The Skateboard Mag*.

· Larry Flynt Publications pulls the plug on *Big Brother* magazine.

· Skateboard coffee table books proliferate with Independent's *Built to Grind*, the *Surf Skate and Rock Art of Jim Phillips*, and *Disposable*, the first extensive survey of skateboard deck graphics.

· Rodney Mullen pens his autobiography, *The Mutt*.

· Aaron Rose launches *Beautiful Losers*, a huge art show, book and film featuring skateboarder / artists Ed Templeton and Chris Johanson, etc.

· Skateboard videos slowly migrate from VHS to DVD. Likewise, still photographers switch from film to digital.

· IASC launches the first annual Go Skateboarding Day on June 21, which celebrates and promotes skateboarding on the first day of summer. A few skaters refuse to participate, claiming "every day is Go Skateboarding Day."

· Inspired by Critical Mass bicycle rides, Emerica launches Wild in the Streets, an annual mass skate session through city streets and spots.

· Danny Way introduces the Mega Ramp to the X Games and wins his first gold medal on it.

· Bastien Salabanzi takes the etnies Goofy vs. Regular contest by storm with a mind-blowing show of flawless technical street skating.

· Upcoming talent includes Tyler Bledsoe, Devine Calloway, Shane Cross, Antwuan Dixon, Garrett Hill, Lizard King, Mike Rusczyk, Anthony Shetler and Brandon Westgate.

2005 · As skateboard brands begin social network marketing on MySpace, e-commerce grows.

· Rob Dyrdek designs the DC Skate Plaza in Kettering, Ohio, the first entirely street-based skatepark with no tranny. The world's largest skatepark opens in Shanghai, China, boasting 40,000 square feet of

gnarly terrain.
• Powell-Peralta mounts a museum-like timeline display of their skateboards and related materials at the ASR trade show.
• One of the 1990s' most beloved brands, Plan B, re-launches.
• Skateboard shoes begin to trend toward simple designs, in addition to high-tech models.
• Sole Technology opens skateboarding's first on-site biomechanics facility called the STI Lab to test footwear designs and high tech materials.
• The scripted movie *Lords of Dogtown* is released, based on the true story of the infamous Z-Boys skateboard team of the 1970s.
• YouTube launches, soon to be filled with skate footage of every stripe: original, bootleg, unauthorized, etc. Due to the deluge of free moving images, complimentary promo DVDs from skateboard brands become common.
• The Dew Tour debuts as the first season-long action sports tour.
• The first big pool contest in 20 years, the inaugural Pro-Tec Pool Party, goes down in the Vans combi pool. Chris Miller wins the Masters division.
• Using the biggest Mega Ramp ever created, Danny Way pulls a backside 360 air over the Great Wall of China with a broken ankle.
• Bob Burnquist completes an upside down air across an open top corkscrew.
• Upcoming talent includes Anthony Acosta, Silas Baxter-Neal, Kenny Hoyle, Torey Pudwill, Eli Reed and Bobby Worrest.

2006 • At the Bodyworlds exhibition of real human cadavers, one is displayed doing an invert on a skateboard.
• Popular vintage skateboard decks—especially from the '80s—get reissued left and right.
• Lance Mountain pulls the plug on The Firm, while Andrew Reynolds launches Altamont Apparel backed by Sole Technology; and Erik Ellington, Tom Penny and Antwuan Dixon debut Supra footwear.
• This year's coffee table books include Andy Howell's *Art Skateboarding and Life*, and *Concrete to Canvas: Skateboarders' Art*.
• The reality TV series *Rob and Big* debuts on MTV, following the lives of Rob Dyrdek and his best friend and bodyguard, Christopher "Big Black" Boykin.
• Tony Hawk and friends conduct surprise sessions with fans across the United States in *Tony Hawk's Secret Skatepark Tour*. Likewise, Heath Kirchart and friends embark on Heath's Harley Tour, the first skateboard / motorcycle tour.
• Bob Burnquist skates down a 40-foot-tall ramp, up onto a metal rail hanging over the rim of the Grand Canyon and launches straight into a BASE (parachute) jump 1,600 feet to the canyon floor below.
• Danny Way bomb drops 82 feet from the top of a gigantic neon sign shaped like a guitar into a huge ramp outside the Hard Rock Hotel and Casino in Las Vegas, Nevada.
• Upcoming talent includes Lyn-Z Adams Hawkins, Chima Ferguson, David Gonzales, David Loy, Sean Malto, Dyson Ramones and Nick Trapasso.

2007 • 1990s street skating hero Guy Mariano makes a comeback in Girl's *Fully Flared* video and a Pro Spotlight in *TransWorld Skateboarding*.
• Steve Berra and Eric Koston open a privately-owned, indoor skatepark called the Berrics, plus a hugely popular website of the same name containing content filmed in the park and other skateboard-related media.
• Australian Oliver Percovich opens Skateistan skatepark / school in war-torn Kabul, Afghanistan.
• Tracker unveils its first reverse kingpin truck, the Fastrack.
• Grant Hicks of Perth, Australia builds the world's

biggest skateboard, measuring in at 2' 9" tall x 4' 9" wide x 20' 1" long for the *Guinness Book*.
• A documentary called *The Man Who Souled the World* debuts, covering the profound effect Steve Rocco and World Industries had upon skateboarding in the 1990s.
• The world's first smartphone, the Apple iPhone, debuts and goes on to change the way skateboarding media is consumed.
• During the high air event on the X Games Mega Ramp, Jake Brown falls vertically 45 feet, slamming into the bottom of the transition with such force that both of his shoes blow off his feet. Jake's injuries include a fractured vertebrae, bruised liver and lung, ruptured spleen, fractured wrist and a concussion.
• During a street contest at the Vans Downtown Showdown, Omar Hassan gets scalped by the

sharp edge of a tunnel under a ramp.
• Upcoming talent includes Willy Akers, Mike Mo Capaldi, Sierra Fellers, David Gravette, Jimmy McDonald, David Reyes and Kevin Romar.

2008 • Topping out at four stories tall, Tony Hawk's Halfpipe water slide opens at Six Flags America.
• A severe economic recession rapidly unfolds and remains for years to come. Many skateboard companies go under or downsize, reducing staff and team riders.
• Snowboard company Burton purchases DNA Distribution / Alien Workshop.
• *Slap* magazine stops publishing their print magazine, but maintains a web site and a much loved / hated message board.
• With a few exceptions, the web renders full-length

Tracker team rider **Adam Taylor launches a mega high air on the Mega Ramp at the X Games in Los Angeles, California, 2010.** Photo: Dan Bourqui
Opposite page, left to rght: **Dogtown and Z-Boys, 2001.** The first issue of **Concrete Wave, Summer 2002.** Photo: Attila Aszodi.
The Skateboard Mag, 2004.

skate team videos, which become too expensive and take years to produce, obsolete. Instead brands post online tour videos.
• Paul Rodriguez snags a cool $100,000 first place prize money and a custom $10,000 Nixon watch in the first Maloof Money Cup, the most widely respected street contest in ages.
• *TransWorld Skateboarding* hosts its first annual Skate and Create contest, in which they stick four teams in a warehouse for nine days each, building artistic skatable sets for photo and video shoots. DVS wins.
• One of the friendliest people anywhere, Theotis Beasley comes up big-time, collecting more sponsors than anyone, ever. Other upcoming talent includes Curren Caples, Marisa Dal Santo, Chris Pfanner, Jamie Tancowny and Willow.

2009 • In the social media realm, everyone gradually migrates from MySpace to Facebook and Twitter.
• Rob Dyrdek builds the world's largest skateboard, measuring in at 36' long, and debuts a new reality TV show called *Rob Dyrdek's Fantasy Factory*.
• Many skateboard magazines start to offer digital versions of their print editions.
• Sean Cliver publishes *The Disposable Skateboard Bible*, an illustrated coffee table book charting the history of skateboard decks, which is a follow-up to his original 2004 book. Also on the bookshelf are a history of skateboard shoes called *Made For Skate*, *Vans Off the Wall* and *Blabac Photo: The Art of Skateboarding Photography*.
• Corey Adams premieres *Machotaildrop*, a highly visual and fantastical movie about an amateur skateboarder, Walter Rhum, who realizes his dream of turning pro and riding for the world's greatest skateboard company.
• IASC and Skatelab inaugurates the Skateboarding Hall of Fame.
• Leo Romero scores the cover of *Skateboarder* with the first grind up a legit handrail on a staircase.
• Upcoming talent includes Mike Anderson, Ryan Decenzo, Dan Plunkett and Ben Raemers.

2010 • Due to a declining market and the continuing recession, the Action Sports Retailer trade show calls it quits after three decades, leaving Agenda and regional and local trade shows to fill the void.

• Alien Workshop releases a series of skateboard decks with artwork officially licensed from the estate of Andy Warhol, in contrast to the usual skateboard industry practice of simply ripping off graphics.
• Several deck brands begin using Pro 2 Technology, which consists of six-ply maple with one ply of Kevlar for durability and pop.
• Adio continues to make skateboard shoes, but drops its team.
• Alex Corporan publishes a book called *Full Bleed: New York City Skateboard Photography*.
• Emerica premieres its long-awaited *Stay Gold* video to rave reviews. Many videos now debut as paid downloads in addition to DVD.
• Dylan Rieder releases *Dylan*, the first full-length, stand-alone official video part on the web, making

official web footy legit overnight.
• Skateboarding iPhone apps become popular.
• Rob Dyrdek launches the first professional league for street skating, Street League Skateboarding (SLS), an international contest series featuring 24 pros competing for the largest prize money in history.
• Bob Burnquist lands a fakie 900, proceeding into and out of the trick backward.
• Upcoming talent includes Elijah Berle, Nick Garcia, Felipe Gustavo, Riley Hawk, Boo Johnson, Mark Suciu and Ishod Wair.

2011 • Incredibly, '70s-inspired small plastic skateboards make a comeback as hip retro novelty cruisers. Nobody sees that one coming!
• *Thrasher* celebrates its 30th anniversary.
• Ben Marcus publishes *The Skateboard*, a coffee table book on the history of skateboarding. GSD publishes *The Best of Skate Fate* book, a 30th anniversary celebration of the first homemade skate zine.
• At the Maloof High Ollie Challenge, Aldrin Garcia performs the world's highest Ollie at 3' 9".
• Upcoming talent includes Joey Guevara, Emmanuel Guzman, Daniel Lutheran, Tom Remillard, Auby Taylor, Kevin Terpening, Sebo Walker and Neen Williams.

2012 • As the recession rages on, more brand and team cutbacks go down in the skateboard industry.
• Rob Dyrdek buys DNA Distribution / Alien Workshop from snowboard company Burton.
• Young upstarts are popping Ollies higher and longer than ever up stairs, handrails, etc.
• Legendary street skating spot the Carlsbad gap gets destroyed during renovations to the property.
• Alien Workshop releases a series of Keith Haring decks and a cut-your-own-shape rectangular skateboard complete with stencils.
• Sole Technology lays off the entire staff and team of éS Footwear, then puts the brand on hiatus.
• *TransWorld Skateboarding* celebrates its 30th anniversary…a year early. D'oh! In a special issue, TWS names Mark Gonzales the most influential skateboarder of all time.
• Jack Smith launches *The Skateboarder's Journal*.
• Christian Hosoi publishes his memoirs, *Hosoi: My Life as a Skateboarder Junkie Inmate Pastor*.
• Jim Fitzpatrick edits a book on the Skateistan skatepark and school in Kabul, Afghanistan.
• Stacy Peralta directs *Bones Brigade: An Autobiography*, a documentary on the most influential skateboarding team of the 1980s.
• DC releases *Waiting for Lightning*, a documentary on Mega Ramp pioneer Danny Way.
• Rob Dyrdek produces an animated series called *Wild Grinders* on Nickelodeon, based on his crew growing up.
• Due to smart phones' ease of use, sponsor me footage increases tenfold. On the social networking front, the photo sharing app Instagram becomes popular.
• Upcoming talent includes Daryl Angel, Trevor Colden, John Fitzgerald, Wes Kremer, Josh Murphy, Stevie Perez, Ryan Reyes, Na-Kel Smith, Kyle Walker and Rowan Zorilla.

2013 • NHS / Santa Cruz celebrates their 40th anniversary by opening their very own museum.
• Rob Dyrdek sells DNA Distribution / Alien Work-

shop to Pacific Vector Holdings, a "premier action sports retail and consumer brands company."
• As if it were 1976, Alien Workshop releases a solid oak wedge tail deck.
• Amidst a crowded market, a strained economy and competition from the web, *Skateboarder* magazine ceases publication, making this the third time the storied title has gone under. Except for *Thrasher*, the surviving mags are down to double-digit page counts.
• Nyjah Huston bags a sweet $100,000 at the Kimberly Diamond Cup in South Africa, and pulls a 270 kickflip lipslide down a handrail, to boot.
• Jake Brown lands the first 720 Ollie over a Mega Ramp gap at the 2013 X Games in Foz Do Iguacu, Brazil.
• Wes Kremer dark slides a handrail.
• Upcoming talent includes Curt Daley, Daniel Dubois, Matt Gottwig, Jared Huss, Cyril Jackson, Braxton Powers, Xavier Walker and Chase Webb.

2014 • Red Bull funds the first public sculpture specifically made for skateboarding and art lovers, the Red Bull Skate Space in Seattle.
• Citing financial difficulties, Pacific Vector Holdings shuts down DNA Distribution / Alien Workshop, a move which stuns the world of skateboarding. Rob Dyrdek promptly buys DNA / AWS again with plans to re-launch them on a smaller scale.
• Blockhead owner Dave Bergthold markets Skate Crate, incredibly the world's first commercially produced crate skateboard—a modern tribute to the originals hand-built in the early to mid 20th century.
• Canadian skateboarding magazine *Color* folds.
• The Berrics buys *The Skateboard Mag*.
• Craig Snyder publishes *A Secret History of the Ollie*, a huge 912-page skateboarding history book.
• Sebastien Carayol authors the book *Agents Provocateurs: 100 Subversive Skateboard Graphics*.
• Back to the past? Tony Hawk appears in a hoverboard hoax video.
• A full 15 years after Tony Hawk lands the first 900, 12-year-old Tom Schaar lands the first 1080 on a Mega Ramp quarterpipe at Woodward West in Tehachapi, California.
• Upcoming talent includes Kevin Bradley, Blake Carpenter, Julian Davidson, Clive Dixon, Grayson Fletcher, Cyril Jackson, Willis Kimbel, Jeremy Leabres, Oscar Meza, Tristen Moss, Donovan Piscopo, Jon Sciano, Dakota Servold and Miles Silvas.

2015 • Tracker is honored to celebrate its 40th anniversary with an Icon Award from IASC and the Skateboarding Hall of Fame.

The Future • Skateboarding keeps on rolling forward. What will you do to make history?

Sources and contributors for entire timeline 1900s-2010s: *Action Now*, *Big Brother*, *Concrete Wave*, *Juice*, *Skateboarder*, *Skull Skates*, *The Skateboard Mag*, *Thrasher*, *TransWorld Business*, *TransWorld Skateboarding*, Larry Balma, Steve Cathey, GSD, Peter Ducommun, Mackenzie Eisenhour, Bob Feigel, Jim Fitzpatrick, Dan Gesmer, Larry Gordon, Keith Hamm, Jonathan Harms, Mike Horelick, Russ Howell, Gordy Lienemann, Monty Little, Ben Marcus, Dave McIntyre, Jim O'Mahoney, Jon O'Malley, Stacy Peralta, Dale Smith, Jack Smith, Craig Snyder, CR Stecyk III, Dave Swift, Miki Vuckovich, Mike Williams, Woody Woodward.

Matt Pennington cracks a big Ollie in Denver, Colorado, 2010. Photo: Joel Freeman
Opposite page, top to bottom: Skate Crate and Penny skateboard.

319

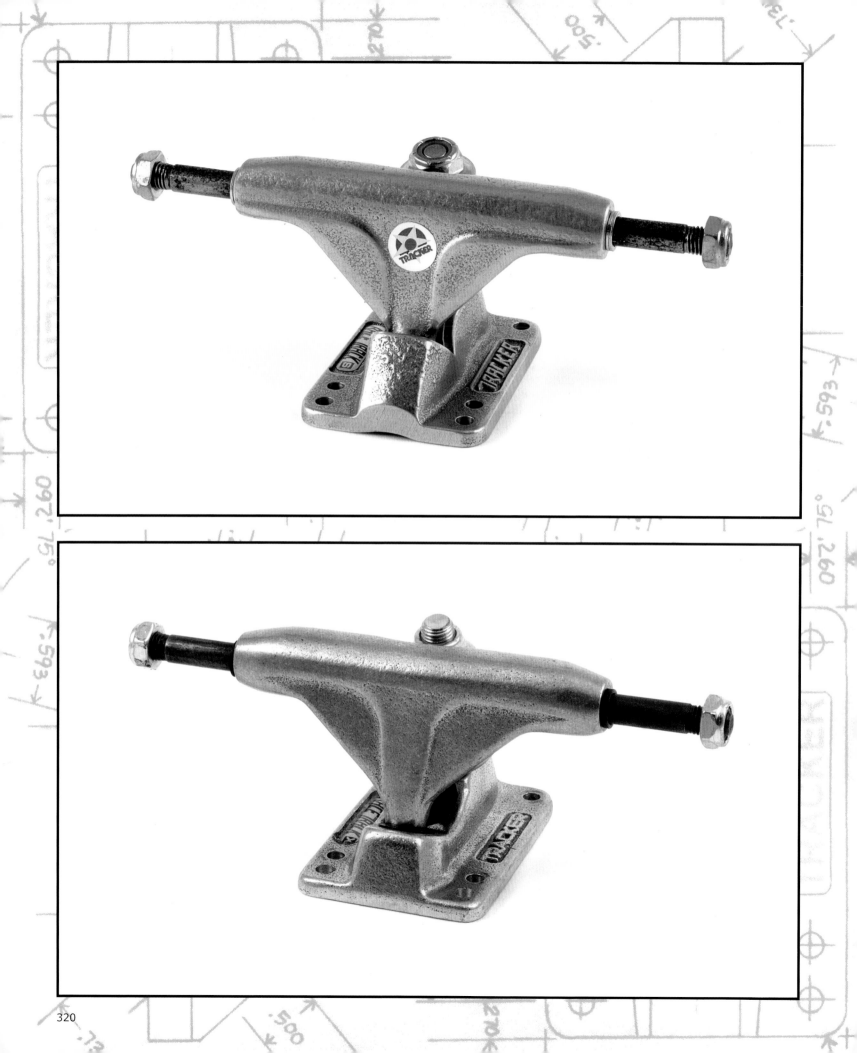

TRACKER
RACETRACK
Entry Level Slalom Truck (2002)

In 2002, Tracker brought to market production Racetrack trucks reminiscent of the hand-built slalom trucks that I had crafted for slalom racers in 1976. If you read page 85, you may recall that some of our slalom racers liked the action of the Haftrack but still preferred the width of the Fultrack. So, I machined a batch of spacers and welded them to some Haftrack hangers, increasing the width to 4 1/4" and inserted the Fultrack axles. These hand-crafted custom trucks were affectionately called Racetracks.

Although slalom racing mostly died out when vert ramps and street skating came into vogue, dedicated racers living in mountain communities all over the world stayed true to slalom. Many slalom skaters were snow skiers who were trying to keep fit in the off-season. Tracker supplied these skaters with trucks and an occasional promotional package for contest prizes. By 2000, some of the original slalom racers from the '70s in California began to organize meets up and down the coast. Tracker took notice and attended these events. Our goal was to produce slalom-specific trucks that would perform well at a reasonable retail price so that beginners or part-timers could afford to participate. The billet-machined trucks with custom adjustable geometry favored by top slalom pros cost hundreds of dollars and thus have never beeen conducive to the growth of slalom.

The Tracker Racetrack S is based on the original classic Tracker Haftrack geometry with an additional five degrees built in for a quicker turn. Many racers prefer to use the Racetrack S as the rear truck on their downhill or slalom deck, because it offers more stability at speed. Using a wedge pad to relax the turning angle on the rear truck also reduces the caster, which results in less chance of experiencing speed wobbles. Some slalom skaters choose to use the Racetrack S baseplate combined with the Dart hanger on both wider and longer decks. You can special order Racetrack baseplates with Dart hangers in the following widths: 106 mm, 129 mm, 139 mm, 149 mm, 161 mm, 184 mm and 219 mm.

The Tracker Racetrack X is based on the Axis truck geometry. Many racers choose to use the Racetrack X as the front truck on their downhill or slalom deck because of its slightly higher roll center, which results in a quicker turning feel. Experienced and aggressive racers use wedge pads to increase the turning angle of the front truck even more for quicker turning action around the cones. Skaters riding wider and longer decks can special order the Racetrack X baseplates with Axis hangers in the following widths: 106 mm, 129 mm, 139 mm, 149 mm and 161 mm.

Jay Shuirman of NHS originally designed a slalom skateboard truck with an offset axle that was meant to flex in the manner of automotive independent suspension in order to help keep the wheels from sliding out during hard turns. John Hutson rode these trucks in 1978 and won some races on them, but after a few runs, the metal axles would lose their spring temper. Although these trucks never made it into production, their name, Independent, stuck. The one thing slalom racers learned is that using an offset axle for the rear truck helped cancel the caster effect and eliminate the dreaded speed wobbles.

Tracker also offers both the Racetrack S and the Racetrack X with an offset hanger. These trucks work great when they're used on the back of your slalom deck. The axles have spacers that allow you to adjust the width of your wheels from 90 mm to 116 mm. Choosing between the Racetrack X or S geometries and adding wedges allows you to fine tune your board to get the feel that suits you the best—depending on your size, the riding surface and the angle of the hill.—**LMB**

Above: **Elijah Goodman cruises down the hills of Cardiff, California on Tracker Ractracks, 2014.** Photo: Steven Levas
Opposite page, top to bottom: **Shown here in the 106 mm hanger width, the Tracker Racetrack S and Racetrack X are also available in widths up to 219 mm.**

One of the original inspirations for the Tracker Race-track, Tommy Ryan, draws a stylish line through the cones, circa 1976. Photo: Unknown

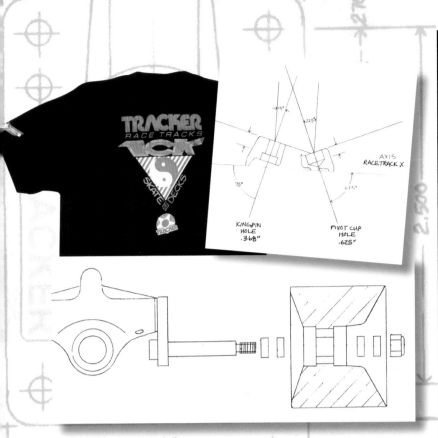

RACETRACK-OFFSET-X

ADJUSTABLE FROM 88MM TO 112MM

- ADJUSTABLE WIDTH OFFSET GS/SLALOM TRUCK
- OFFSET AXLES ALIGNED WITH KINGPIN
- HOURGLASS BOTTOM CUSHIONS, TALLER TOP CUSHIONS
- SLIGHTLY LONGER KINGPIN FOR MORE FINE TUNINGS
- GREATER STABILITY AND INCREASED RIDER CONTROL
- QUICKER TURNS

TRACKER
Trucks You Can Trust Since 1975
trackertrucks.com

Above: **Tracker Racetrack t-shirt and concept drawings, circa 2002.** Drawings: Balma
Right: **Tracker Racetrack Offset X ad, 2004.**
Below, clockwise from top left: **Tracker Midtrack offset prototype truck made for Beau Brown, circa 1977. Tracker Racetrack S offset. Tracker Racetrack S offset. Tracker Racetrack X offset.**

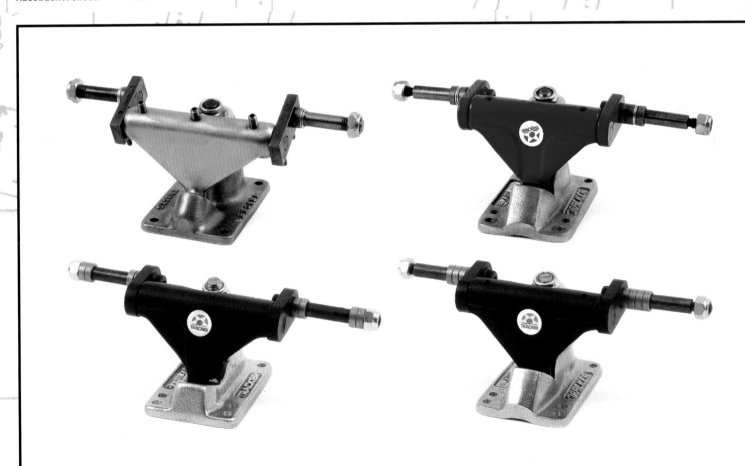

By Larry Balma

A first generation Badlander, Steve Evans grew up in Upland, California, sessioning spots like Mt. Baldy, L-Pool and the Pipeline Skatepark. With his sidekick Charlie Ransom, Steve was better known as a formidable competitor on the slalom circuit of the late 1970s and '80s. They even scored a duo interview together in *Skateboarder* magazine's January 1979 issue. Continue reading for the details and a little catch-up.—GSD

Where did you grow up?
I grew up in the Badlands—Upland, California—next to Magnolia Elementary School, which become the first skate spot in the Badlands, pre-urethane. We just surf-skated during the day until we could get to the beach. It was our wave and ski slope. We practiced the surf moves we saw in the movies and skate mags, and emulated the ski slalom racers we watched on TV. The Badlands is also the home of the Mt. Baldy Pipe, the Pipeline Skatepark and Ick Sticks slalom racing decks created by Rick "Ick" Howell.

When and how did you start skating?

Steve Evans
INTERVIEW

I started skating on a Roller Derby Deluxe 20 with clay wheels when I was around 10, 11, 12 years old. At the time, I didn't do anything other than just ride around. When I started high school, there were some surfer cats who started riding (surfing) at the school next to my house. That was their wave. This got me into a whole new adventure in skateboarding and changed my life. This was still pre-urethane. I still can't believe the turns we did on those clay wheels. I was still riding Roller Derby trucks, the single bushing style. I remember the day we got a hold of those first urethane Metaflex roller skate wheels. They didn't slide! The grip was amazing!

When did you get your first Trackers?
My first set of Trackers was a set of Haftracks I got in the '70s. We had a bro, Buddy Allred, who somehow got a set of Fultracks, which were prototypes, because no one had trucks that huge at the time.

Which Tracker model did you ride most of the time?
Haftracks were my first, but I rode Mids, Fuls and Extracks, too. I also ended up working on the design of the Tracker Racetrack series. We were designing Tracker slalom trucks in the '70s and '80s with Dave Dominy, putting Midtrack axles in Haftrack hangers and Fultrack axles in Midtracks. We were always working on trying to get a faster steering truck for the front. In the more modern years of slalom, I helped work on the offset series of racing trucks.

Why was Tracker so important in the history of skateboarding?
Trackers changed my life. They helped me become the slalom racer I always knew I was. Tracker worked with me to develop a better racing truck, which is simply amazing for a racer and I will be forever grateful.

During your time on Trackers, what stood out about their importance?
They were the trucks all of my idols were using and shredding on. They were made by skater/surfers, which in my world is a HUGE bonus point! They also wanted to work with the riders to develop a better product.

Which Tracker riders influenced you? Who were the guys you looked up to?
All of the La Costa racers, most notably my friend and racer Bobby Piercy. His style was and still is something I am in awe of. He was simply beautiful to watch, fast as Hell on a race coarse, and an awesome guy!

Do you recall any memorable times with the Tracker team?
I kind of had my own personal Tracker team with Charlie Ransom. We were out of the typical team loop, but every time we met up with our Tracker brothers, it was instant bonding! The whole summer in Colorado racing the ARA (Another Roadside Attraction) circuit with Charlie, Curt Kimbel and Harvey Hawks, put on by Peter Camann. There are too many stories. It was just one big, fantastic, summer memory.

Share some crazy road trip stories.
One of the best times that I can still remember (too many party years) was driving up to the first Capitola Classic downhill race in the early '80s with Dave Dominy and Lance Smith. I lived in Huntington Beach at the time, and a sizable south swell was just starting to appear that morning. They picked me up and we stopped at County Line for an evening surf on the way up. The swell slowly started showing. Damn! Our next stop was Jalama campground to surf and spend the night. The surf started building again, so every five minutes it got cleaner

and bigger. "Oh, wait. It's time to get on the road again. Damn!" We finally reached Capitola, and went out for an evening surf. Once again, the surf was small but starting to build. "Damn! We've got to go race tomorrow!" My mom created a Lycra speed suit for me; racers were only using leathers at the time. The racers were freaking, going to their cars and putting on their wetsuits for a better aerodynamic advantage. I ended up third or fourth that weekend. The trip was as fun as the race!

What have been the highlights of your time in skateboarding?
Winning two major races at La Costa both in my early and later days. Coming in second twice behind my Badland brother Charlie Ransom (Tracker Boy) at the Runway Banked Slalom. Coming in second place overall at Another Roadside Attraction summer races put on by Peter Camann against the best racers in the world at the time. The most important thing I treasure is all of the fantastic friends I've made from skateboarding, the crazy times and stories, the loves and failures, all wonderful!

Who are your current sponsors?
I got vertigo in 2005, so no more skating for me right now. It's very sad, since I was almost back in racing form again at the time it

happened. So, do I still have my sponsors?

What do you enjoy doing besides skateboarding?
Hiking to stay in shape and I still do a little surfing, but the vertigo makes it a little tough. I love photography and art, and I started a graphics/fine art company creating art on ceramic and metal tiles.

Closing comments?
Tracker took me under their wings and helped me both financially and especially in the R&D department. I can't thank them enough for believing in me and for being great friends. Thanks to Dave, Lance, Larry and Buddy.

Read the full-length interview at trackertrucks.com

Above left: **Steve Evans, Fall 1977.** Photo: Warren Bolster
Above right: **Steve Evans, January 1984.**

If you skated in the 1970s, numerous images probably run through your head whenever you hear the name Carrasco Brothers, such as a Pepsi ramp demo or maybe a Tasmanian Devil-like figure twirling a blur of 360s for the *Guinness Book of World Records*. Read on to hear a bit of Richy and Rene's long and colorful history in skateboarding. Unfortunately, their brother David was not present.—GSD

Carrasco Bros
INTERVIEW

LMB: Where did you guys grow up?
Rene: Garden Grove, California in the OC.
Richy: Our house was located two blocks from the original Fruit Bowl and a half block from where Vans shoes were first made.
Rene: That's a story in itself. Vans was at the end of this little dirt road next to our house. This was in the late '60s and, every day after lunchtime, they would let out steam and the whole neighborhood smelled like Vans shoes for three hours. So, their rubber is in our DNA.

GSD: Tell us some Fruit Bowl stories.
Rene: I remember one. After I raced at La Costa during the day, I was tired from driving back to Orange County, so I took a long power nap. At 3:00 am, I woke up, went to Jack in the Box, grabbed a burger, pulled into the Fruit Bowl's parking lot, through the woods and right up to the pool. I turned on the lights, and all of a sudden, a bunch of people popped up, came alive and started skating, just waiting for a car to light up the pool.
Richy: They were skateboard zombies. The Fruit Bowl was located at a sanitarium called Greenbriar, and we used to run around there with my buddies when people were actually being housed and recuperated there. It was an asylum and also a rehab place for alcoholics and drug addicts. People from Hollywood would come to Greenbriar to get away from everyone in Hollywood.

LMB: When did you guys start skating?
Rene: My brother Ray started skateboarding before me. I started in 1959. Larry Miller and Billy King were riding and I joined them. We hack-sawed steel shoe skates in half and attached them to a 2" x 4" board with nails. It was so fun. Before that, of course, were the soapbox scooters. In high school, I rode a little bitty board that would fit with my books so I could take it inside class. Back then, if you skated, you were a hoodlum. I told everyone, "Someday, they're going to pay me to skate," but nobody believed me. I was at the Fruit Bowl and I would put an RC Cola logo on the bottom of my board, because those were my initials. After the session, everybody was sitting around talking, and I remember looking at my board and saying, "Someday, a cola company will probably sponsor skateboarding and we'll make money." Everybody laughed at me. A year later, I was sponsored by Pepsi and made a living skateboarding for the next five years. Don't give up on your dreams. Go for it.

GSD: Talk about those really narrow wheels you used for spinning 360s.
Richy: Well, there was an evolution of those. It all started with the Power Paw 50-50

wheels splitting in half. [Half of the wheel was urethane, half was rubber.] Guys were spinning on the leftover urethane half, and said it was easier to spin on a skinnier wheel. Then the whole 360 thing just went crazy. Everybody who was serious about 360s was cutting down their wheels narrower. Back then, doing 360s was a whole different thing. I can't even explain to kids now about how popular and important it was.

GSD: I remember in the '70s it was, "How many 360s can you do?" and by the '90s it turned into, "How high can you Ollie?"
Richy: That's right. The best thing that ever happened to me was going with Rene to the Hang Ten International, when I could do four 360s. Then I saw Bob Jarvis spinning, and that was the greatest thing I ever saw. He was doing 13 one-foot tail 360s, and I just watched him and watched him. That day, I decided I wanted to be the 360 king. I really started practicing and practicing. A year later, I was beating all of the best guys in the world.
Rene: They had the first *Guinness Book of World Records* 360 contest. Richy was only 14 and he won it.

GSD: Which year was that?
Richy: 1977-'78. They said I hit 35 ½ on asphalt. Some of my friends who were there said I hit 41, but I think they wanted to smooth it over because the champ, Russ Howell, was there. I can't believe to this day that I hit that many on asphalt. It's all about speed when you're spinning and slick concrete is the most desirable surface. For me to hit 35 ½ on asphalt, I can't believe how strong I was.
Rene: Later that year in Oceanside, he won it again with 47 ½. All of the top guys were there and my brother beat them all.
Richy: That was probably the biggest 360 showdown of all time.

GSD: That was in the late '70s?
Richy: Yeah, 1978 still. There was Dan Yule from Santa Cruz, Russ Howell had a guy on his team called Chris Larsen, and even Andre Walton. Anybody could have won.

GSD: So, what is the world's record for 360s now?
Richy: The record now is officially 142 in the *Guinness Book*, set by me. By the grace of God, and hard work and my wife Maria, I started training again in the late '90s. I told Maria one thing I want to do again is to get my 360s back. Well, all of that work and training got me to 142 in 2000. I can't explain the feeling of 360s on steel wheels, the sound and speed! When you're spinning, they roar and they're so fast, it's a really exciting thing.

GSD: Do you pull in your arms slow?
Richy: It all depends on what I'm trying to do. I did a demo at Slam City Jam in Canada, and I told those guys, "You need to clean out this area if I'm going to do 360s." When I went out there to perform, it was full of dirt and wood chips, and I said, "Dear Lord, help me to not fall in front of all of these kids." So, I threw my arms out, and once I started going, I found my center. Then I just pulled them in as hard as I could and held on. I think I did almost 90. The kids were going

crazy. It was like a UFO had landed. They gave me a standing ovation when I was only half way done.

LMB: Who do you look up to?
Rene: Early in our career, we saw a demo that made an impact on my life. I have to publically thank Tom Padaca (RIP), the surfing legend. He was doing a skate demo at Toy City in Westminster by our house. I remember Tom saying, "You can do what I'm doing. All you guys have to do is practice and get on a team." I just thought, "That's what I want to do." So, you go for your dream, practice and work on it, and it becomes reality.
Richy: There was a Pepsi team tryout and they actually had different teams from different areas. Not to be a fat head or anything, but we had an audition in front of the Pepsi corporation big wigs and we won.
Rene: There were 10 teams, five guys per team, including all of the top guys from Los Angeles to the Badlands to San Diego. We took it seriously. We had taped music, Pepsi posters and skateboards, etc. We really knew how to present it. All of the other skaters were chasing each other, pinching each other's butts and acting stupid, but our Carrasco team was professional. Halfway through our demo, the Pepsi executives said, "Stop right there. We've been watching all of you kids wasting our time by playing around and not taking it seriously, so the Carrasco Brothers are going to be the main Pepsi team." We said, "Yes! Thank you, Lord." We had to earn it, but we did our homework.
Richy: But, that's they way we were. As the Carrasco Brothers, we had to prove ourselves everywhere we went. We were hungry. Everything we got—any accolades, magazine coverage or anything—we worked for it.

Nothing was handed to us. For some Mexican kids from Garden Grove, we did okay.

LMB: Closing comments?
Rene: The Carrasco brothers give all of the glory to God for blessing us with good health and opportunities. When we started skateboarding, we were just having fun. It's 2014, and racing and 360s are still going for us. We thank God for all of this, and thanks to you, Larry, for all of the Trackers over the years.

Read the full-length interview at trackertrucks.com

Above: **The Carrasco Brothers—Rene, David and Richy—flow a nose wheelie trio in Carlsbad, California, circa mid 1970s.** Photo: Unknown

By Larry Balma + GSD

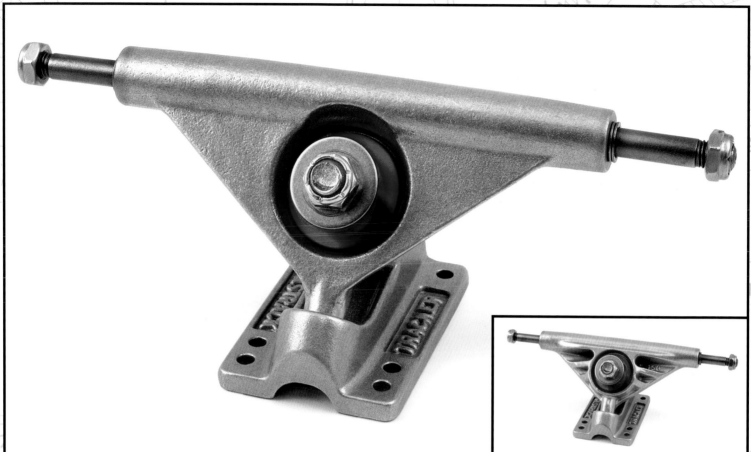

TRACKER FASTRACK

Our First Reverse Kingpin (2007)

The first reverse kingpin trucks appeared on scooters with steering handles in the 1930s and '40s. Released in 1975, Speed Springs were the first reverse kingpin trucks designed for skateboards. The first version of Speed Springs, true to their name, employed actual springs, which, because they were unstable, were abandoned in 1976 for urethane cushions that worked quite well. Not surprisingly, all trucks today use urethane cushions. Although Speed Spring trucks were lightweight, they never were quite strong enough to survive the abuse that skateboarding dished out. Despite the fact that Speed Springs were not around for very long, their geometry went on to be copied by many other truck brands over the decades, including Gullwing, Variflex, Radikal and Randall. To this day, many downhill trucks employ the reverse kingpin design first established by the scooters and Speed Springs.

In 1976, slalom racer Mike Williams worked with HPG to release their version of the reverse kingpin truck called Gullwing. Although some slalom racers preferred the Gullwing, most freestyle and bowl skaters preferred conventional double-action trucks like Tracker. As slalom waned in the '80s, Gullwing caved in to market pressure and released a conventional truck, ultimately discontinuing their reverse kingpin design until they launched the Gullwing Alpine in 2005 to a new generation of longboarders. Variflex was the next to build a reverse kingpin truck, which they called the Connection. Oddly enough, it was marketed to vert skaters. Although Randall first produced a truck in the late '70s, slalom was declining in popularity at the time, so sales never took off. By the mid '90s, longboards were back in vogue for both cruising and downhill, prompting Randall to bring reverse kingpin trucks to the longboard market, which, at the time, was owned by the Tracker B2 Fultrack.

By 2007, due to an inconsistent supply of Randall trucks, we decided to produce our own version. We actually started working on it before brands like Bear, Paris and a few others put reverse kingpin trucks on the market. Working with skateboarder and photographer Dan Sturt and Don Tashman of Loaded Longboards to develop the Tracker Fastrack, the first thing we did was design the hanger. It boasted the familiar

Tracker triangle truss in front with Art Deco-inspired ribs on the back to make it lighter and stronger. The hanger could actually be flipped, which changed the caster and trail geometry. Some downhill skaters flipped the hanger on their rear truck for more stability. (Because the increased leverage of the reverse kingpin design combined with the width of the truck benefited from the use of larger diameter cushions, we increased the cushion size, but skaters could use conventional cushions, as well.) We also added internal webbing on the baseplate for strength, which allowed for an easy drop-through deck mounting option. The Tracker Fastrack is available in the following widths: 6" (150 mm), 7 1/4" (180 mm), 8 5/8" (219 mm), 9" (230 mm) and 11 3/4" (300 mm).—**LMB**

Opposite page, top: **Tracker Fastrack 150, front and back view.**
Opposite page, bottom: **The Tracker Fastrack 180, the new ultra-wide Tracker Fastrack 300 and the narrower Fastrack 230.** "Skaters were asking us about a wider hanger for the Fastrack and I was making some drawings when the Longboard Stroller Company came along and wanted to go really big. For those of you with babies, the Longboard Stroller will teach your child the feeling of freedom on a skateboard at an early age while keeping you in shape. Of course, there is a brake to avoid accidents, or in case you have to step off."—Larry Balma

JIMMY RIHA

Fastracks
Available in sizes
150 mm & 180 mm
polished or black

TRACKER
Trucks You Can Trust Since 1975
trackertrucks.com

Jimmy Riha, Spring 2010.

Busted!

Back in 1976, Tracker graphic artist Chuck Edwall drove up to the offices of *Skateboarder* magazine to drop off our latest ad on a tight deadline when he saw the layout of an upcoming G&S ad. This ad featured young Tracker team rider Steve Sherman holding a G&S Fibreflex slalom board equipped with Gullwing trucks. Seems that Dave "Fibrefats" McIntyre, who was running the skate team for G&S, had for some reason set up the shoot to showcase the new Gullwings. When I heard about that, I went to the G&S office to have a little talk with him.

Before long, the conversation built up to a standoff. I said, "Why are you featuring Gullwings in your ads? Those trucks are weak. I could break one with my bare hands!" I only said that because I had previously watched Mike Williams perform R&D on Gullwings on the Black Hill at La Costa and noticed a design flaw. McIntyre buzzed Larry Wilson back in the shop and told him to bring in a Gullwing truck. Then McIntyre called Walt Tiedge at Gullwing and told him what I said. McIntyre leaned back in his chair with his feet up on his desk and chuckled with

Walt. I was sitting quietly, waiting. By the time they brought in the complete skateboard, my adrenalin levels were peaking. Despite the fact I had never seen a Gullwing truck break, I turned the board upside down on the floor, placed my foot on the center of the deck, grabbed one wheel and yanked as hard as I could. The kingpin promptly snapped the baseplate.

After I tossed the hanger in the air, it bounced on the desk and landed right in McIntyre's lap. Almost falling over backward, he yelled into the phone, "Larry broke it! He broke it with his bare hands!" McIntyre agreed then and there that they could not sell Gullwings. We agreed to have Chuck Edwall reshoot the G&S ad photo and deliver it to *Skateboarder* magazine that day. But first, Chuck had to call Steve Sherman's father so we could pull Steve out of school to re-shoot the photo. Finally, after all of that went down, we rebuilt the G&S ad and submitted it to the mag. Because of that little episode, Gullwing redesigned their kingpin and even added in a steel support plate for it that bolted under the baseplate with the mounting hardware so the baseplate wouldn't break and they could continue making more trucks. Despite that, Steve Sherman continued to race on Trackers.—**LMB**

Eijah Goodman, 2014. Photo: Steven Levas
Above: Who's your Sugar Daddy? D. David Morin, Dave "Fibrefats" McIntyre and Stacy Peralta clown around, circa 1978. Photo: Jim Goodrich

DOWNHILL
A Need For Speed

Ever since the invention of the wheel, humans have enjoyed the adrenaline rush that is brought on by riding down steep hills. Today, more than ever, we continue to seek the euphoric feeling of speed. The skateboard is the perfect vehicle to experience an intense downhill speed run—no engine required! Although early skateboards brandished primitive steel or clay roller skate wheels and tiny, weak trucks that were almost impossible to control at speeds over 15 mph, the early '70s brought polyurethane wheels with precision bearings and strong, wide skateboard trucks that changed all of that. The urethane wheels rolled easily over rough pavement, the sealed precision bearings offered speed, and the wide skateboard trucks added stability. This was the magical combination that made downhill speed runs on skateboards possible.

In May 1975, , Jim O'Mahoney, who promoted skateboard contests from Santa Barbara, California south to San Diego, held the first Skateboarding World Championships at Jack Murphy Stadium. Shortly after that event, he was approached by *The Guinness Book of World Records* show on ABC to hold competitions that would establish world records. For downhill speed, Jim formed a stand-up class, and ultimately a modified prone or kneeling class that included aerodynamic fairings. Remembering his youth growing up in Long Beach, Jim chose Hill Street on Signal Hill for the competition. The steep 30-degree Signal Hill was a test not only for the riders, but for skateboard equipment. The races, held from 1975 to '78, led to inno-

Roger Hickey rockets downhill on his own custom luge, circa mid 1990s. Photo: Ed Hickey

vations in equipment that helped advance the sport of skateboarding in all disciplines.

Longshoreman Sam Puccio conceived, built and tested the first-ever luge skateboard using Tracker Fultracks with small pivots. When Sam showed up at the Signal Hill race in 1976 with his steel toe logger boots and strange craft, everyone asked, "Who is this guy?" Well, as it turned out, Sam was the man who won the race that year, clocking in at 54 mph and taking home the money! John Hughes came in second and Tommy Ryan claimed third—both on prototype Gnarly Tracker Fultracks. Mike Goldman won the stand-up race at Signal Hill on Tracker Fultracks in 1977, followed by John Hutson, who won the stand-up race using the new Independent trucks in 1978. Hutson's victory set off a series of downhill challenges with his arch rival, Tracker rider Roger Hickey. Hickey beat Hutson for the first time at Laguna Seca in 1981, then he named his deck "Lucille" after BB King's guitar, and went on to ride 321 stand-up races on her. Oh, by the way, he won 314 of those races.

A 10-mile stretch of road with 123 corners—including two with signs that say, "Slow to 20 mph," which the luge skaters would take at about 50 mph—Glendora Mountain Road was the premier spot for downhill skateboarding in the 1980s and '90s. More than just downhill, it was a road race. Riders drafted each other just like racecars, and positions could change many times during the race. Ten miles in nine minutes, you do the math. That's hauling tail in my book. During weekend races, Roger Hickey skated five stand-up races and 10 luge races each day, which added up to 150 miles on a skateboard per day! Try to imagine squatting in a speed tuck for 12 minutes, only changing position slightly to catch some air and slow for the corner. Then realize that your average speed has to be about 50 mph to be competitive in stand-up. Okay!

One day while chasing Roger Hickey, Tracker rider Beau Brown fell at the first slow corner. When Beau stopped sliding, he got back on his board and continued, even though Roger was gone. Then Roger crashed at the second slow corner and got back on his board, crossing the finish line just one foot ahead of Beau. This is only one among many stories from the legend of Roger Hickey. Here's another one:

Skateboarding is not a crime, unless you break the

speed limit. In 1993, Roger Hickey was returning to his hotel room in Las Vegas with his brother after a long day of filming for a GTE Super Bowl commercial. It was almost midnight with a full moon as they crested the final hill on I-15 East that drops about 10 miles into the Las Vegas valley below. There was absolutely no traffic on the highway, so Roger could not resist. He just had to do a speed run! After suiting up in leathers for the run, Roger told his brother to hang back, because he was worried that the headlights from behind could interfere with his night vision. Half way down the hill, Roger noticed a couple of black and whites off on the side of the road, no doubt relaxing with their coffee and donuts on just another boring weeknight. All of a sudden, their radar guns began beeping faster and louder, a car was approaching at 87 mph! Then, "Whoosh!" a mysterious

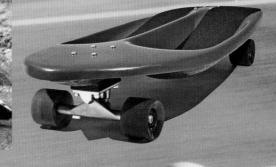

black object low to the ground rushed by in the blink of an eye. A shot of pure adrenaline raced through the officers as they pulled out in their patrol cars with lights and sirens blaring. The chase was on! Of course, since his luge had no brakes, Roger could not slow down, much less stop. He couldn't use his shoes, either, as they would have worn through before he could even slow down. Likewise, he couldn't pull off onto the dirt shoulder, or he would have crashed.

So, Roger had to continue his run into the valley until the road leveled out and he could finally slow down. Once he coasted to a stop, the cops couldn't believe their eyes. They thought Roger was some kind of space alien piloting a UFO. So, they drew their guns. After a few tense moments, Roger explained the situation and actually made friends with the officers. A while later, they sent him the photo above taken from their dashboard camera. With downhill and slalom racing in our roots, Tracker is proud to make trucks of all widths and several different geometries to satisfy any skater's need for speed.—LMB

Like a sunbaked alligator on speed, Don Baumea dons green leathers for a speed run on his luge, circa 1990s. Photo: Unknown
Above left: **Roger Hickey's Genesis street luge board with 5" diameter wheels was featured in the** *Guinness Book of World Records*, **clocking in at 78.496 mph in 1990, beating all comers by 10 mph, a record that still stands. Off the record, Hickey has gone as fast as 87.80 mph on this evil-looking rocket!** Photo: Unknown
Top right: **Outlaw meets Johnny Law.** Photo: Johnny Law
Above right: **Downhill kneeboard designed by Larry Balma, circa 1977.**
Opposite page, top left: **John Hughes relaxes in layback luge style at 65 mph using a pillow on his Turner kneeboard on the Black Hill at La Costa, California, circa 1978.** Photo: Lance Smith
Opposite page, top right: **With his aerodynamically ground Tracker Sixtracks, Roger Hickey grabs first place in front of John Hutson at the 1981 Laguna Seca Classic.** Photo: Waggoner
Opposite page, bottom right: **Roger Hickey in the lead, followed by Beau Brown, skating downhill trials in the Pyrenees mountains that form the border between France and Spain. The International Olympic Committee hosted these trials to determine if downhill skateboarding should be allowed into the Summer 1992 Olympics. Although skateboarding ultimately didn't make the cut, Roger Hickey took home the gold medal on this day! After John Hutson's downhill champion reign in the late '70s, Hickey beat Hutson for the first time at Laguna Seca in 1981 and went on to become the man who couldn't be beat in downhill races throughout the '80s and '90s.** Photo: Unknown

1

2

3-A　**3-B**

6

7-A

7-B

7-C

9-B

9-C

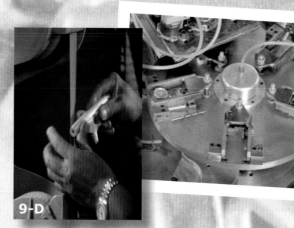

9-D　**10**

11-C

13

23-A

23-B

4

5

8

9-A

How to Make a TRACKER T R U C K

Have you ever wanted to build your very own Tracker Trucks? Just follow these easy steps!

1. Envision a truck design and build a model of it in your prototype shop. **2.** Build a master pattern for a baseplate and each hanger width, and / or create a 3-D CAD file. **3.** Use the master pattern to make a match plate or a permanent mold. **4.** Build a core box for axle holes for each hanger width for sand casting. **5.** Take the match plate or mold and the core box to the aluminum foundry. Make sand cast molds or pre-heat steel molds. **6.** Place the axle cores or axles, if cast in, in the molds. **7.** Melt ingots of A356 aluminum alloy to 1525 degrees in a crucible and pour it into the mold. **8.** Cut away the truck castings from the mold rack and heat treat them to T6 hardness for strength. **9.** Grind off all molding lines (seams) and any bumps until smooth. **10.** Build four drilling jig fixtures for baseplate machining and one for axle reaming or squaring. An air-driven machine drills all baseplate holes as they turn around on a Geneva wheel. **11.** Polish the castings to a bright silver finish in a tumble polish machine (11-A) or a tumble raw machine (11-B). Option: Send the polished parts to receive a painted, powder coated or anodized finish (11-C). **12.*** Order raw material from the steel mill for axles and kingpins. **13.** Send the steel to the screw machine factory with your axle and kingpin parts drawings and specs. **14.*** Heat treat the axles and kingpins for strength. **15.*** Press in the axles and kingpins using a specially constructed hydraulic press and jig fixtures. **16.*** Make two steel dies to form the cupped washers for cushions. **17.*** Order aircraft locknuts and axle washers. **18.*** Make two molds for the inner and outer cushions. **19.*** Cast and heat treat polyurethane cushions in desired durometer and rebound. **20.*** Make a mold for the pivot cup and cast in the desired urethane. **21.*** Quality control: Inspect and test every part when it's received to be sure it meets spec. **22.*** Order custom built cardboard boxes with Tracker logos and dividers for 50 trucks. **23.** Gather all of the Tracker truck parts in a production line setting. Assemble and tighten them with air-powered tools. **24.** Place 50 Tracker trucks per size and style in a box to ship to a distributor.—**LMB**

* These steps do not have photos.

Go to trackertrucks.com/video and click on Truck Manufacturing Process to watch a video about how Tracker Trucks are made.

11-A

11-B

24-A

24-B

LESTER
KASAI DESIGNS

SKATERS:
LESTER DECKS
ALL COLORS
AVAILABLE NOW
ASK YOUR
LOCAL SKATE SHOP

SKATESHOPS:
TRACKER DECKS
AVAILABLE FROM...
ATLANTIC SKATES
AWH SALES
GULF COAST SKATEBOARD
NATIONAL SKATE
RAX WORKS
SMOOTHILL SKATES
ULTIMATE SKATEBOARDS
VISION SPORTS
WALKER SKATEBOARDS

SEND BUCK
TRACKER
BOX 398
CARDIFF, CA.
92007

GNARLY TRACKER HARDWARE

Lester Kasai, February 1987.

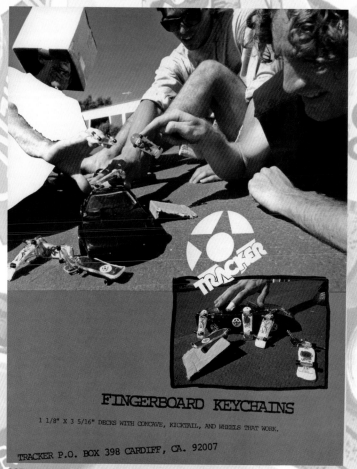

FINGERBOARD KEYCHAINS

1 1/8" X 3 5/16" DECKS WITH CONCAVE, KICKTAIL, AND WHEELS THAT WORK.

TRACKER P.O. BOX 398 CARDIFF, CA. 92007

GSD, Lester Kasai, Dan Wilkes, December 1987.

Tracker Stimulator Cushion

Peter Kiss from Czechoslovakia sketched out the original design of the Tracker Stimulator, which was only available as an inner cushion. As your truck turned harder, the Stimulator bulged out, offering increased compression. The Stimulator debuted on the Tracker Aggro Quicktrack in 1990 and continued on with the Street Track. After that, we offered it only as an accessory. The Stimulator was molded out of a costly, high-grade, extremely resilient urethane compound, and it was tricky to mold without air bubbles, which made the cost even higher. It was cast in three durometers, color coded blue, yellow and green. The Stimulator remains one of the most sought after cushions today; a diehard Stimulator fan will gladly fork out $10 for each one!—**LMB**

Lester Kasai, Tony Hawk, February 1990.

334

Gnarly Accessories, February 1987.

TRACKER
ACCESSORIES
Fingerboards, Keychains, Watches

As part of the Tracker System (see page 176), we've offered many accessories over the years, including cushions in a variety of hardnesses so skateboarders could tune their trucks to their height, weight and riding style; skate wrenches for truck adjustment and mounting hardware; as well as promo items like t-shirts, hats, keychains and fingerboards. By the mid '80s, the Tracker brand was so hot, we could sell anything with our name on it. Swatch watches were all the rage, so Jim Gray set up a watch program for Tracker that went over big time (pun intended). At one point, we even offered Tracker five-pocket denim jeans. Later, focusing on our performance roots, we expanded our parts line to include high quality Tracker Racetrack bearings.—**LMB**

Tracker Watch Fiasco

In the mid '80s, I worked in the mortgage banking business and made decent money. I honestly thought the skateboarding business was pretty rinky-dink. I assumed I was going to be a real estate mogul. I had gotten my real estate license when I was 18, but I got bored with the people in that industry. Then I ruptured my spleen skateboarding. When I was off healing, I just didn't want to put on a suit and tie and go back into that friggin' office and underwrite loans. So, I did independent real estate appraisals. I remember going down to Tracker and talking to Larry Balma. My spiel was, "Hey, I would love to help you do some stuff, but I'm not going to be some kid you give 10 bucks an hour to work in the warehouse. That's not who I am. I want a piece of something."

I could see, just from knowing Larry as a sponsor, that he had so much stuff going on. He owned Tracker and TransWorld, and needed people who could help him do things. But, I didn't want to be just another employee, so I threw that out there. He responded, "We'll set up this separate company," and I had no idea what we were doing. That's how Brainstorm started. We worked on a couple of projects for Tracker, then it was like, "What else can I help you with?" Brainstorm was fun, but the Tracker watch deal didn't work out. I learned something new every day. Like, "How many should we buy?" You said, "Let's make 1,000 of them." I still remember the first phone call you made to a distributor, who said, "I'll take all of them." "What the hell? Shit! We need more of these things!" Those were different times.

The first Tracker watches were really good, but the broker for the watch factory in Hong Kong changed them from Swiss jewel movements that run forever to Hong Kong movements that wear out fast. The batteries wore out quickly, too. I think about that to this day. I tell people stories when they talk about manufacturing in China. I leaned my first lesson in 1986. We ordered 1,000 Tracker watches, and in my first sales phone call, they were gone. So, Larry ordered 10,000 more. Then Brad Dorfman got wind of it and said, "I want some watches." So, another 10,000 watches were coming, and were probably all sold, too. Then Tracker stepped up for another 20,000 watches and Brad ordered 33,000 more. So, I had one order for 53,000 watches coming and that's when all of the movements were changed. To this day, I tell people that crooked broker probably made 25 cents more off of each of those 53,000 watches by putting the cheaper movement in there. He ended up getting himself in a lawsuit, which screwed us all up and killed the Brainstorm business we started. He had to write us a check for somewhere around $100,000 to $150,000. The whole thing was a mess, all so the guy could make an extra $10,000 by changing a part.—**Jim Gray**

Kevin Staab, August 1986.

Adrian Demain, February 1988.

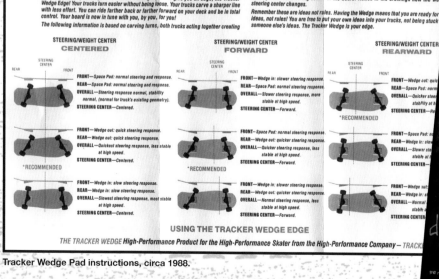

GRAB AN EDGE, TRACKER WEDGE

Congratulations on your purchase of the Tracker Wedge Pads. We at Tracker believe that skaters should have options and again, we have done something about it.

The Tracker Wedge allows you to tune in the turning radius, tracking ability, and overall response of your trucks. Until now, you were limited with your truck's stock steering geometry. With the Tracker Wedge, you can custom tune that geometry to response that fits your own height, weight and radical skating style. We give you an edge; the Tracker Wedge Edge! Your trucks turn easier without being loose. Your trucks carve a sharper line with less effort. You can ride farther back or farther forward on your deck and be in total control. Your board is now in tune with you, by you, for you!

The following information is based on carving turns, both trucks acting together creating the overall response you want. Kick turns and slides are affected as well when you use the Tracker Wedges. These Wedge combinations are only a guide. For all around skating, try the *RECOMMENDED ways first. When testing the new tune of your board, start off with carving turns. This will allow you to feel the change and find your new weight/steering center. Look at how you stand on your board. While carving, your weight center should be directly over the steering center of the board. Notice in the drawings how the weight steering center changes.

Remember these are ideas not rules. Having the Wedge means that you are ready for new ideas, not rules! You are free to put your own ideas into your trucks, not being stuck with someone else's ideas. The Tracker Wedge is your edge.

STEERING/WEIGHT CENTER CENTERED

FRONT—Space Pad: normal steering and response.
REAR—Space Pad: normal steering and response.
OVERALL—Steering response normal, stability normal, (normal for truck's existing geometry).
STEERING CENTER—Centered.

FRONT—Wedge out: quick steering response.
REAR—Wedge out: quick steering response.
OVERALL—Quickest steering response, less stable at high speed.
STEERING CENTER—Centered.

*RECOMMENDED

FRONT—Wedge in: slow steering response.
REAR—Wedge in: slow steering response.
OVERALL—Slowest steering response, most stable at high speed.
STEERING CENTER—Centered.

STEERING/WEIGHT CENTER FORWARD

FRONT—Wedge in: slower steering response.
REAR—Space Pad: normal steering response.
OVERALL—Slower steering response, more stable at high speed.
STEERING CENTER—Forward.

FRONT—Space Pad: normal steering response.
REAR—Wedge out: quicker steering response.
OVERALL—Quicker steering response, less stable at high speed.
STEERING CENTER—Forward.

*RECOMMENDED

FRONT—Wedge in: slower steering response.
REAR—Wedge out: quicker steering response.
OVERALL—Normal steering response, less stable at high speed.
STEERING CENTER—Forward.

STEERING/WEIGHT CENTER REARWARD

FRONT—Wedge out: quic...
REAR—Space Pad: norma...
OVERALL—Quicker steer...
stability at h...
STEERING CENTER—R...

*RECOMMENDED

FRONT—Space Pad: n...
REAR—Wedge out: slo...
OVERALL—Slower ste...
stable at h...
STEERING CENTER—...

FRONT—Wedge out...
REAR—Wedge in: s...
OVERALL—Normal...
stable a...
STEERING CENTER...

USING THE TRACKER WEDGE EDGE

THE TRACKER WEDGE **High-Performance Product for the High-Performance Skater from the High-Performance Company** – TRACK...

Tracker Wedge Pad instructions, circa 1988.

GRAB AN EDGE

tracker WEDGE
do it

THE TRACKER WEDGE – high performance products for high performance skaters from the high performance company... TRACKER

Grab an Edge, Tracker Wedge, June 1988.

TRACKER SPACE PADS

Wedge Your Bets! (1978)

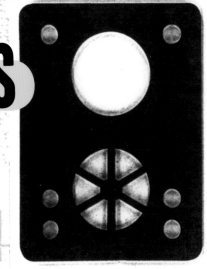
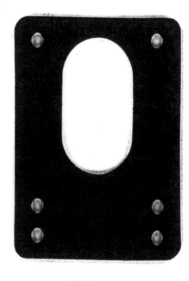

In 1975, original Tracker Fultracks were sold including a 1/2" Finnish Birch wood space pad dyed black. A year later, Tracker Haftracks included a 5/16" wood pad. The Tracker truck retained the low center of gravity mounting option, but if you had large diameter wheels and no wheel wells, you could use the space pads for clearance. In 1977, lightweight rigid space pads injection-molded with high-density polyethylene were introduced by Tracker in a variety of colors. We made one major upgrade by adding more ribs to better hold the Space Pad's shape. They came in two thicknesses, 5/16" and 9/16", and also in a 9/16" wedge pad with a five-degree angle built in similar to Rad Pads, which initially introduced the wedge pad in heavy solid rubber. If you angle the truck toward the ends of the skateboard by raising the back of the truck, it will increase the steering angle, resulting in a tighter turning radius. Downhillers often raise the front of their rear truck to reduce the turning angle and decrease the caster effect, which helps eliminate the high speed wobbles. Tracker also produces 1/8" rubber pads that act as a gasket to keep your trucks mounted tight to your deck.—**LMB**

TRACKER RISER PADS
INJECTION MOLDED HDPE
SCALE 1:1 = INCHES — DO NOT SCALE
TRACKER STAR ART = RAISED LOGO
.095 WALL THICKNESS + DRAFT
HOLES .200 + DRAFT
3-25-09 BALMA

WEDGEPAD 5°
5/16 SPACEPAD
9/16 SPACEPAD

Top right: **Tracker rubber shock pads.**
Above: **Tracker Base Grip, February 1990.**
Right: **A meticulously randomized assortment of Tracker space pads.**

TRACKER TEAM
SCRAPBOOK
The Biggest Team in Skateboarding History

Even more important than our groundbreaking skateboard trucks are the team riders who have become part of the Tracker family. Back in 1975, the very first people Tracker sponsored were slalom and downhill skateboarders, followed by pool and bank riders and freestylers. As Tracker sales grew, mostly through skateboard deck manufacturers, Tracker would flow a box of trucks to their team riders, who would also carry extras to give to other hot skaters they met in their travels to contests and demos around the globe. Using this method, the Tracker team began its rise to become the largest skateboard team in history. At first, Tracker team riders were just flowed trucks. As time went on, Tracker shared contest entry fees and travel costs with the deck manufacturers. In late 1978, Tracker began paying salaries to the cream of the crop of our team. The following list of Tracker team riders is compiled from our vast archives in loose alphabetical order, using the first letter of the last name only. The list is as complete as we could make it, including photos of everyone we could find. Our most sincere apology goes out to any Tracker team rider who has been overlooked. Riders not pictured are listed on page 381. Unfortunately, a few of our team riders, designated with RIP, have departed too soon to shred that great skate spot in the sky. We here at Tracker are honored to have been a part of their lives. —LMB

Left to right: **Rodd Saunders, Dave Dominy, Kim Cespedes, Jeff Tatum (helmet), Rodney Jesse, Lance Smith (yellow hat), Gunnar Haugo, Gregg Ayres, Curtis Hesselgrave, Brian "Pushead" Schroeder, Tom Stewart, Chris Strople and Stacy Peralta** relax after a session on the Tracker ramp at the glider port in La Jolla, San Diego, California, circa 1979. Photo: James Cassimus
Opposite page, top: **Keith Lenharr, Ray Underhill (RIP), Marty Jimenez, Lester Kasai, Tony Hawk, Adrian Demain and Joe Johnson** clown around, circa 1990. Photo: Unknown
Opposite page, bottom: **Kevin Staab, Mike McGill, Stacy Peralta and Tony Hawk** check out a freestyle event in the reservoir during a contest at Del Mar Skate Ranch in Del Mar, California, circa 1982. Photo: Unknown

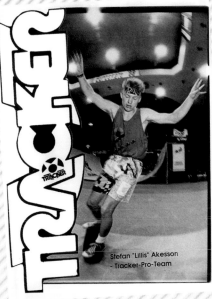

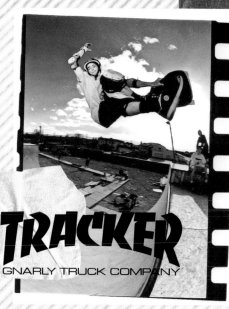

Stefan "Lillis" Akesson, circa 1980s.

Soren Aaby, circa 1980s. Photo: Unknown

Tim Adams. Photo: Shapiro

Dennis "Polar Bear" Agnew (RIP), 1979.
Photo: Unknown

Starr Adams. Photo: Swansen

Darren Allred, 1978. Photo: Lance Smith

Mikael "Slappo" Adolfsson,
1980s. Photo: Grant Brittain

Jimmy Akins, circa 1977.
Photo: Jim Goodrich

Fabian Alomar, September 1999.

Davey "Pappy" Andrews, 1976.
Photo: Lance Smith

Jim Alesi, circa 2000s. Photo: Unknown

Jimmy Astleford. Photo: Joe Picciolo

Sal Barbier, October 1989.
Photo: O

Gregg Ayres, 1976.
Photo: Gary Medeiros

Chad Bartie, 2000s.
Photo: Unknown

Dylan Baker, circa 1980s. Photo: Peder Draxton

> "Trackers were the strongest trucks, by far. They were the first trucks that really worked and gave me that professional quality I needed to take it to the next level." —Tony Alva

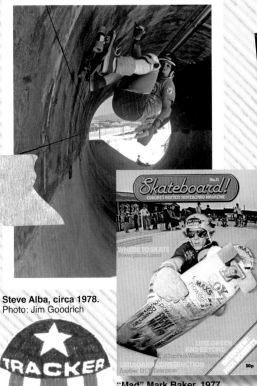
Steve Alba, circa 1978.
Photo: Jim Goodrich

"Mad" Mark Baker, 1977.
Photo: Robert Vente

TRACKER USA

Steve Bacon, 1990s.

TRACKERtrucks
Steve Bacon

Professional skaters need equipment that works and equipment that they can depend on. That's why professional skater Steve Bacon's choice is with Tracker.

TRACKERtrucks "trucks you can trust!"

TRACKER

Waldo Autry (RIP), 1976. Photo: Gary Medeiros

Jay Adams, circa 1977. Photo: Unknown

BURBANK DOWNHILL INVITATIONAL

> "The fastest I've ever gone was on Tracker Trucks. —Don Baumea

Tony Alva, circa 1979. Photo: Lance Smith

(nollie nose grind)

tracker

Send buck for stickers & information. P.O. Box 398, Cardiff, CA 92007

Armando Barajas, January 1995.

David Andrecht, circa 1978. Photo: Chuck Saccio

341

Jim Bates, 2001. Photo: Matt Mecaro

Steve Beaudoin, mid 1980s.
Photo: Davo Scheich

Above: Dave Bedore, 1983. Photo: Brittain

Left: Chris "Rude Boy" Baucom, 1980s.
Photo: Bruce Hitchcock

STEVE BERRA

Dayne Brummet, 2014. Photo: Kimathi Smith

Dave Bergthold, 1989.
Photo: Grant Brittain

Steve Berra, September 1992.

Bill Billing, 2000s. Photo: Lance Smith

Fred Blood, early 1980s.
Photo: Goldman

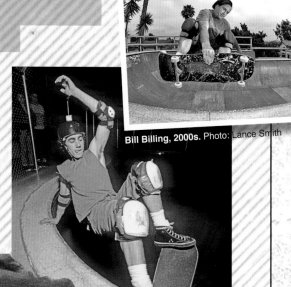

AXIS 139MM
AVAIL: 129MM•139MM•149MM

RIDER: JASON BARR

LOW AND QUICK – STEEPENED PIVOT ANGLE
FOR BETTER TRICK RESPONSE
SILICONE POWDER COAT

TRACKER

Frank Blood, 1978.
Photo: James Cassimus

342 Marty Beaudoin, 1980s. Photo: Davo Scheich

Jason Barr, 2000s. Photo: Kimathi Smith

Warren Bolster (RIP), 1970s.
Photo: Ralph Starkweather

"Trackers turn, they don't flop.—Beau Brown**"**

Bobby Boyden, 1977.
Photo: Warren Bolster

Above: **Larry Bertlemann, 1976.** Photo: Steve Wilkings
Left: **Joe Bowers, mid 1980s.** Photo: Grant Brittain

Florian Bohm, mid 1980s. Photo: Thomas Kalak

Kevin Bergthold, 1989. Photo: Unknown

SKATEBOARD WORLD
A PRO GETS THE BUSINESS
CANADIAN RACES
MAY 1978 • $1.25 UK55p
JIM MUIR: RESTLESS DOGTOWN NATIVE
FRENCH SKATING: SURF & TURF
DOUBLE YOUR PLEASURE: THE EIGHT-WHEEL ADVENTURE

Brad Bowman, May 1978. Photo: Stan Sharp

Neil Blender, 1980. Photo: Lance Smith

Billy Beauregard, early 1980s.

Reggie Barnes, 1978.
Photo: Bob Ballou

Ellen Berryman, late 1970s.
Photo: Battipaglia

Beau Brown, late 1980s. Photo: Chip Morton

343

"Tracker is like a Crescent wrench—something that's going to work. It's the rad tool.—Neil Blender"

"With Neil Blender, GSD and Tony Hawk, the '80s Tracker roster had some of the most creative people in skateboarding.—Miki Vuckovich"

David Carrasco, 1977. Photo: Glenn Miyoda

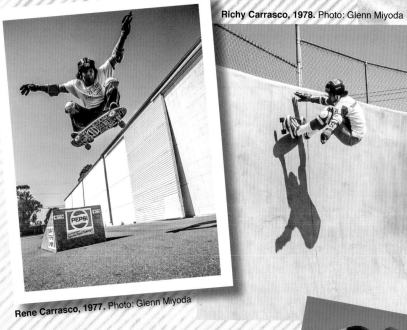

Rene Carrasco, 1977. Photo: Glenn Miyoda

Richy Carrasco, 1978. Photo: Glenn Miyoda

ACTION NOW

SUBSCRIBE & SAVE!

GET IT CHEAPER
Save $9 off the Cover Price

GET IT SOONER
Weeks before the Newsstands

GET IT AT HOME
Every month in your Mailbox

Send $15 (foreign, $21; foreign airmail $45) to
ActionCentral, P.O. Box 1028, Dana Point, CA 92629
or use the handy sub envelope. Get it now.

Steve Caballero, 1981. Photo: Ted Terrebonne

Ron Cameron, early 1990s. Photo: Unknown

Keith Butterfield. Photo: Unknown

TRACKERtrucks
Quim Cardona

AUTHORIZED DEALER
PERFORMANCE PROVEN

Quim Cardona, May 2001.

Alan Burr, late 1980s.
Photo: Paul Sunman

Mark Buncy, mid 1980s.
Photo: Bryan Ridgeway

Tony Campen, 1978. Photo: Lance Smith

Tommy Budjanek, early 1990s.
Photo: Unknown

Al Brunelle. Photo: Unknown

INTENSE DOGTOWN INNOVATION

Logan Earth Ski Team member and Dogtown Park and Pool Master, Bob Biniak grinds it at the new Vista Pool. Bob, like most professionals, chose his trucks carefully, after trying lots of different combinations, he rides Trackers exclusively, the trucks you can trust! At Tracker we are skateboarders, designing and producing products for skateboarders. When we sell you a set of trucks, it's like we are going along for the ride!

Send 50 cents for a sticker, brochure and order form to: Tracker Trucks. P. O. Box 398, Cardiff-by-the-Sea, California 92007. Dealers call 1-714-451-9551.

Bob Biniak (RIP), August 1978.

Buddy Carr, late 1980s. Photo: O

Kim Cespedes, circa 1978. Photo: Lance Smith

> **Tracker is the blueprint for the modern truck.**—Buddy Carr

Tate Clair, 1980s. Photo: Unknown

Jon Jon Bryan, late 1980s. Photo: O

Jason Catalano, mid 1980s. Photo: Grant Brittain

Chris Carter, 2000s. Photo: Steve Buddendeck

Tim Cline, 1982. Photo: Bryan Ridgeway

Steve Cathey, 1977. Photo: Lance Smith

Tony Chiala, late 1980s. Photo: O

Chet Childress, early 1990s. Photo: Mark Waters

MIKE CHU

Mike Chu, September 1989.

347

Eric Chang Eddie Chang
Oasis Skatepark

Eddie Chang, Eric Chang, 1978. Photos: Lance Smith

Brad Coleman • FS Channel Hop • Tracker Trucks - Since 1975 / Guaranteed For Life / www.trackertrucks.com

Brad Coleman, 2004. Photo: Dan Sturt

SEND BUCK FOR STICKERS AND INFO   P.O. BOX 398 CARDIFF, CA. 92007

Ron Chatman, July 1995.

Jon Comer, January 2001.

Gary "King Fish" Coccaro, 1977. Photo: L. Smith

Chris Chaput, 1977. Photo: Unknown

Cleo Coney, early 1980s. Photo: John Grigley

Baby Paul Cullen (RIP), 1977. Photo: Unknown

Sam Cunningham, early 1990s.
Photo: Tobin Yelland

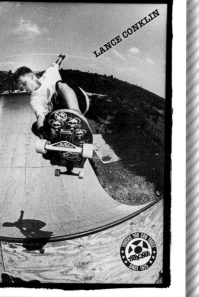

LANCE CONKLIN

TRUCKS YOU CAN TRUST SINCE 1975 TRACKER

Lance Conklin, early 1990s.

Lynn Cooper, 1980s. Photo: Swank

Jason Carney, early 1990s.
Photo: Mark Waters

Bill Danforth, mid 1980s. Photo: Miki Vuckovich

Sean Coons, 1980s. Photo: Swank

Paulo Diaz, November 1993. Photo: Chris Ortiz

Adrian Demain, 1987. Photo: Grant Brittain

Doug de Montmorency, 1978. Photo: Jim Goodrich

Michael Cottrell, 2013. Photo: Bill Billing

Paul Constantineau, 1979. Photo: Goodrich

Primo Desiderio, 1984. Photo: Unknown

Diane Desiderio, 1984. Photo: Unknown

Curt Cortum, 1978. Photo: Hazelton

Julio de la Cruz

Julio de la Cruz grew up on the tough streets of Bell in the South Central area of Los Angeles. Despite the rough environment, he took up skating at a young age, which helped him stay away from the heavy gang influence. Even though he occasionally saw people get shot, Julio concentrated on his skating and worked with youth groups to show kids that there was another path to take. He even got the city of Bell to build a skatepark! Julio took over as team manager for Neighborhood when Armando Barajas fell deeply in love and was forced to slack off on skating. Down with the entire LA skate scene, Julio put many Neighborhood skaters on Tracker, using the Pirelli Tire logo for inspiration for a new Tracker logo. Tracker team manager Bryan Ridgeway let Julio run with the Tracker street team for a few years in the '90s. Although Julio came up with an idea for Tracker to advertise on bus benches, it turned out to be too expensive. Julio was even tight with the Mayor of Bell, who funded Julio's youth programs until the Mayor was caught for embezzlement. At least the Mayor was funneling *some* of the dollars in the right direction!—**LMB**

Dave Crabb, 2000s. Photo: Unknown

Julio de la Cruz, 1990s. Photo: Unknown

347

ROBERT DOUGLAS

Robert Douglas, January 1996.
Photo: Miki Vuckovich

Chris Dobstaff, 1990s. Photo:Ed Dominick

PETE DOSSETT

TEAM

TRACKER

Pete Dossett, 1988.

GNARLY

NO SKATING

Chuck Dinkins, June 1989.

Rob Dyrdek, early 1990s. Photo: Mark Waters

FUN

Brenda Devine, 1980. Photo: Cassimus

Mike Early, 2006. Photo: Lance Smith

348

Dave Dominy, 1975.
Photo: Larry Balma

Mike Dahre, late 1980s.
Photo: Steve Sherman

GSD

GSD, 1985. Photo: Neil Blender

Dale Dobson. Photo: Lance Smith

Kevin Dickmann, 1980s.
Photo: Rogers

Lance Smith

INTERVIEW

So, now we're interviewing Lance Smith, the Tracker team manager and photographer since day one.

Day one, baby! That's right, they threw me in Dave Dominy's garage, and, like a peasant, I worked my fingers to the bone making trucks. I put races with loose ball bearings on Fultracks, and I was happy to do it, because I was into skateboarding big-time, and Trackers were just unbelievable.

Where did you first see Tracker Trucks?

I first saw Tracker Trucks when I had a surf shop called Surf Lines in Cardiff that went out of business, and I was selling my stuff at the flea market over at the North end of Leucadia. There were these twins, Chuck and Bill, and I could never tell them apart, because they were identical. I think it was Chuck who saw that I had old skateboard decks and old wheels, so he showed me the Tracker Fultracks. I looked at those Trackers and said, "Oh, my God! What planet are those from? They're insane! I want some." So, he arranged for me to meet Dave Dominy over at 7-11. The surf shop I was working at, Leucadia Surf Shop, was selling Cadillac wheels before the Trackers came out. So, naturally, we threw those things on some Trackers and I ended up out at La Costa. Eventually, I started skating out there with the Logans. I met Dave Dominy again out there. We started running cones, and it all took off from there. It just went crazy. Everybody started showing up. Then we got into the Sunday races and the Black Hill was in full bore.

That was a pretty cool group of guys.

Chris Yandall, Danny Bearer, Mike Williams, Bob Skoldberg and Henry Hester—the La Costa boys—were formed, and started racing out there. It was a revolution, man. It was great. I can't tell you how many people we had out there on a Sunday—two or three hundred, I'll guarantee you that.

At Tracker, you started out doing grunt work, then we moved to Sorrento Valley.

Right, we got big-time when we moved there. I still worked in the trenches, but Dave and I had been hanging out and skating everywhere, so we started getting our riders to hang out with us, and, eventually, I became the public relations guy for Tracker. That morphed into the team manager, even though we really never had an official team. We started to, but it wasn't like the Sims or

G&S teams. We just provided all of those guys with trucks. But, we'd pick up guys once in a while, like the Rockit Man, Russ Gosnell, and Gunnar Haugo, Murray Estes and Jeff Tatum. We started trying to win contests with everybody on Tracker Trucks.

You were the team manager, the guy to score some trucks off of.

I was the man with the goodies, and I said, "Here are some stickers and trucks." I wouldn't just give them away to anybody. I looked for guys with style. And if my team members were behaving themselves, if they were doing well, then I would set them up and take care of them. Eventually, we started paying their way into contests. Then Stacy Peralta hooked us up with guys from Florida, like Alan Gelfand and Mike McGill. The next thing you know, I was constantly sending them trucks, sending them checks, making them custom trucks. It got pretty big-time. It was a lot of fun.

Who were your all-time favorite Tracker team riders?

The down South boys were always my homies who I hung out with and skated with. I was the team manager, I skated with them and gave them trucks, so I really got to be tight bros with Gunnar Haugo, Murray Estes, David Paul, Jeff Tatum, Sonny Miller and all of those guys. I also hung out with the Dogtown guys when we went up to Marina for contests, and got to be tight with the Badlands guys, who were some of the best skateboarders I've ever seen in my life. They kicked ass on everybody at first. All of those guys are my favorite skaters, but as far as hands-down pure style, Tony Alva can't be beat. Chris Strople and Tom "Wally" Inouye were really right up there, as well. I just loved those guys.

What was your favorite terrain to ride?

Well, I started off racing slalom, and it's always been my first love, but that really morphed into vertical. I really liked riding in places that weren't designed for skateboarding.

Read the full-length interview at trackertrucks.com

Below: **Lance Smith gets his slalom on at La Costa, California, circa 1975.** Photo: Chuck Edwall

By Larry Balma

Lance Smith was born in Santa Monica, California in 1950 and moved down to North County, San Diego in 1972. A surfer, skater and entrepreneur, he opened a shop called Surf Lines Skate and Surfboards. By 1974, Lance began skating at La Costa and got a job in the shop at Tracker, eventually becoming our first team manager and photographer. When the skateboard market crashed for the second time in 1980, Lance turned to construction work. Ultimately, he was able to pursue his passion as a freelance photographer. Lance has taken thousands of photos for Tracker, many even in recent times. Much of his work is shown on the pages of this book.—LMB

Max Dufour. Photo: Grant Brittain

Scott Dunlap, 1977. Photo: Jim Goodrich

Eddie Elguera, March 1978. Photo: Unknown

Brad Edwards, 2013. Photo: Dan Bourqui

Eric Dressen, 1977. Photo: Unknown

ED ECONOMY, FULTRACK skater from the SIMS PURE JUICE team, photo: FreeLance Smith
Send 50¢ for brochure, order form and sticker to: Tracker Trucks, P.O. Box 398, Cardiff-by-the-Sea, California 92007.

Ed Economy, September 1978.
Photo: Lance Smith

John Duff, early 1990s.
Photo: Grant Brittain

Raul Escobedo, 1981. Photo: Unknown

Chris Farrell, late 1980s.
Photo: Grant Brittain

" Honestly, the best I ever skated was on Tracker Trucks. "
—Jason Ellis

Jason Ellis, April 2001.

350

Murray Estes. Photo: Lance Smith

Steve Evans, 1977. Photo: Unknown

SkateBoarder
A SURFER PUBLICATION

VOL. 5, NO. 4 NOVEMBER 1978 $1.50

GETTING DOWN ON THE PIGS
A revolution in skateboards

EUROPEAN SKATE EXPOSÉ
'Don't give up on us yet!'
ROLLER RAGING
The rollerskate resurgence
QUIVERS — PART I

Mike Folmer, November 1978. Photo: James Cassimus

Alfonso Fernandez, December 1999.

Tom Fain, 1977. Photo: Fineman

JUMP ON IT!

Chris Fisher, 1977.
Photo: Jon Malvino

Jesus Fernandez, 1999.
Photo: Unknown

Skip Frye, 1975. Photo: Larry Balma

Ray Flores, 1977. Photo: Rudy Manheim

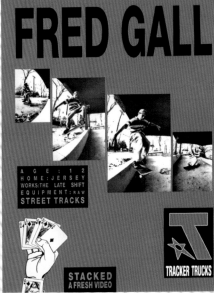

FRED GALL

A G E : 1 2
H O M E : J E R S E Y
WORKS:THE LATE SHIFT
E Q U I P M E N T : R A W
STREET TRACKS

STACKED
A FRESH VIDEO

TRACKER TRUCKS

Fred Gall, March 1992.

Pete Finlan, 1983.
Photo: Unknown

Greg Fountain / Tracker Trucks · Trucks You Can Trust Since 1975 / trackertrucks.com

Greg Fountain, Holiday 2007.

Scott Foss, 1979. Photo: Lance Smith

Bobby Fraas, 1977. Photo: Jim Goodrich

TRACKERS ONLY

Rod Fukimoto, 1978. Photo: Jim Goodrich

John Fudala, 1980s. Photo: Grant Brittain

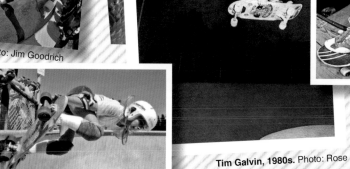

Ruben Garcia, 2001. Photo: Ed Dominick

Denise Flemings, 1978. Photo: Ed Economy

Tim Galvin, 1980s. Photo: Rose

Al Gibson, 1980s. Photo: Unknown

Jimmy Gaunder, 1977. Photo: Lance Smith

John "Tex" Gibson, April 1989.

Sean Goff, 1989. Photo: Paulo Duffy

Jami Godfrey, 1979. Photo: Glen Friedman

Benji Galloway • FS Disaster • Tracker Trucks - Since 1975 / Guaranteed For Life / www.trackertrucks.c

Benji Galloway, 2004.

352

Alan Gelfand, 1980. Photo: Unknown

"Basically, Tracker Trucks revolutionized skateboarding."
—Russ Gosnell

Mark Gonzales, 1985. Photo: Larry Balma

Steve Godoy + Art Godoy, June 1986.

Matt Goldsby, 1988. Photo: Unknown

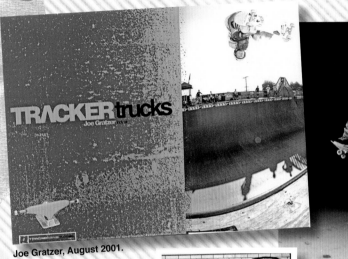

TRACKERtrucks
Joe Gratzer

Joe Gratzer, August 2001.

Claus Grabke, mid 1980s. Photo: Uli Niewohner

Shorty Gonzalez, 1990s. Photo: Seu Trinh

Chuck Gillette. Photo: Unknown

Hans Gothberg, 1980s.
Photo: Unknown

Rockit
SKATEBOARDS

BURBANK DOWNHILL INVITATIONAL

GNARLY

TRUCKS YOU CAN TRUST
TRACKER
SINCE 1975

GROHOLSKI

Peter Gifford, 1978. Photo: James Cassimus

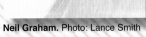

Neil Graham. Photo: Lance Smith

Russ "Rockit Man" Gosnell, 1976.
Photo: Bruce Cooley

Tom Groholski, January 1989.

353

Matt Goodman. Photo: Unknown

Donny Griffin, 1980s.
Photo: Brans

Mike Goldman, 1977. Photo: Gary Medeiros

Elijah Goodman. Photo: Unknown

Tracker was the first true quality skate-board truck. Tracker stepped out of the roller skate era with a truck designed for skateboarding.—Jim Gray

You have to be from that '80s generation to understand how intense the whole Tracker vs. Indy thing was.—Omar Hassan

Jim Greco, 1990s.
Photo: Unknown

Scott Hostert. Photo: Craig Fineman

NICKY GUERRERO

Nicky Guerrero, September 1989.

Guy Grundy, 1977. Photo: Larry Balma

Jim Gray, 1980s. Photo: Tod Swank

TRACKER
USA

Henry Gutierrez, 1980s. Photo: Unknown

David Hackett + Paul Hackett (RIP), 1977. Photo: Jim Goodrich

Get Bio
Get **Tracker**

John Grigley, April 1984.

Kevin Harris, late 1980s. Photo: Grant Brittain

Jay Henry, 1987. Photo: William Pickett

Omar Hassan, 1990. Photo: Steve Sherman

> **When things were pretty rough for me financially in the mid '90s, the Tracker Hawk truck saved my life in terms of being able to pay a mortgage, eat and raise a family.** —Tony Hawk

Yoshi Hayasaka, late 1980s. Photo: Nisi (RIP)

Jamie Hart. Photo: Neil Britt

Stephen Harnish, 1980s. Photo: Unknown

Tony Hawk, mid 1980s. Photo: Grant Brittain

> **Changing to Trackers increased our speed by 20%. That's how revolutionary the trucks were at the time [1970s] for slalom.** —Henry Hester

Jeff Hart, 1990s. Photo: Joe Picciolo

FASTRACK 180MM

Kevin Harris, 2000s. Photo: Spencer Johnson

Harvey Hawks, 1977. Photo: James Cassimus

Henry Hester, 1977. Photo: Lance Smith

Lucian Hendricks, 1980s. Photo: Brider

Louie Hayward, 1985.
Photo: Grant Brittain

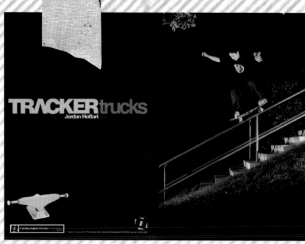

TRACKERtrucks
Jordan Hoffart

Jordan Hoffart, September 2001.

Garrison Hitchcock, 1970s.
Photo: Unknown

I was blessed to have Tracker support me at 10 years old when my first photo appeared in Skateboarder.—Christian Hosoi

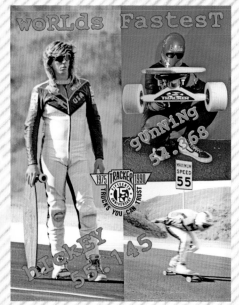

Roger Hickey, December 1990.

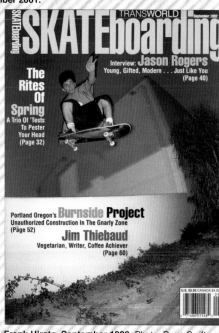

Frank Hirata, September 1992. Photo: Dave Swift

Skitch Hitchcock (RIP), 1978.
Photo: Glenn Miyoda

If you drew a skateboarding family tree containing every famous pro, eight out of 10 of them started on Tracker.—Di Dootson

TRACKER

Shane Hidalgo. Photo: Unknown

Gunnar Haugo, 1977. Photo: Lance Smith

Mike Hill, 1980s. Photo: Unknown

Frankie Hill, 1989.
Photo: Scott Starr

April Hoffman, mid 1980s.
Photo: Grant Brittain

Jeff Ho, 2010. Photo: Lucia Griggi

Christian Hosoi, 1981. Photo: Rusty Harris

Paul Hoffman, April 1978. Photo: Cassimus

Marc Hostetter, 1988. Photo: Grant Brittain

> **Some say Trackers don't turn. I think they're crazy. I turn circles around most other skaters. I love my Trackers.**
> —Tom "Wally" Inouye

Tom "Wally" Inouye, 1979. Photo: Lance Smith

Curtis Hesselgrave, 1977.
Photo: James Cassimus

Per Holknekt, 1980s.
Photo: Unknown

Mark Huebert, late 1980s. Photo: Dave Swift

Marc Hollander, 1978. Photo: Craig Fineman

Darren Ho, 1977. Photo: Kris White

Puttis

Watch out for TRACKER

Hans "Puttis" Jacobssen, 1980s. Photo: Unknown

Bela Horvath, 1978.
Photo: James Cassimus

Tay Hunt, 1977.
Photo: James Cassimus

> **Some of the funnest, funniest memories came from my years traveling with Ridge, Sarge and the Tracker team. Those friendships influenced my character and how I'm wired today.** —Marc Hostetter

Hailing from Huntington, West Virginia, Bryan Ridgeway started skateboarding in 1976 and became Tracker's team manager in September 1983, a post he held all the way until 1997. Since then, his deep involvement in the skateboard industry has included various executive management positions at Blitz, Black Box, CreateaSkate.org, DSM-Dwindle/Globe and Juggernaut, as well as consultation for Quiksilver (Hawk Clothing) and the National Scholastic Skateboard League. He also volunteers his global strategy expertise to Skateistan.org and The Stronghold Society.—GSD

By Larry Balma

Talk about when you first came to work at Tracker answering kid mail.
When I first started working a Tracker, there was a front office and basically a warehouse / manufacturing area. So, in the daytime, I would split my time between writing letters and working in the shop building trucks. I handled any mail that came in from kids, which was the same thing that originally created my relationship with Tracker: I sent letters to Tracker for stickers and somebody wrote back to me. At first, it was Jan Cleveland, then Peggy Cozens after that. Jan was an office manager for Tracker who handled fan mail before I arrived. Any letters or zines that I sent to Tracker went through her until she left the company in late 1983. She wrote back and even took a few calls from me.

Eventually, I rented a room at Jan's pad in Encinitas after I officially moved out to California. She lived with a few other people who also worked at Tracker. I stayed there three months before getting a place with Grant Brittain in Solana Beach. So, back to the mail, it was just like a scene from *M.A.S.H.* I saw that mail truck come in, and I was just like, "I got a hundred letters today. Oh, man." But, I knew how it felt to get a reply, so that's what I did. I not only made sure kids got stickers, I would look to see where they were from and say something cool. At night, we would go skate Del Mar, then come back and work on *TransWorld* magazine. Back then it

was bi-monthly, so we had a little time to spread it out a bit. But, it seems like it was always last-minute. Tracker was a cool place. Neil Blender and Lance Mountain would come down and we'd work on the magazine. Marty Jimenez, GSD and myself stayed there all the time. We slept on the floor for months.

Favorite Tracker riders?
I like all of the Tracker riders. I basically had relationships with every rider, in one shape or form—that's the cool thing. I wanted to have pro and am riders from all over the US and world who represented scenes and all cultures when possible. I definitely went for diversity, because that's how all-inclusive I thought skateboarding could be.

When I was homeless living on a trampoline at Del Mar, I would get fresh pillow cases from Steve and Art Godoy from Pennsylvania screened with their scarecrow graphic just to look out for me. Then there was Dan Wilkes, who we helped get a legit hearse that he could drive to events—no casket included. He also had a pet black scorpion, which I thought was just as spooky. I would hang with his dad in Dallas and learn more and more about jazz music. Everyone was so cool. Allen Losi was great to have on, too. I had a blast with all of them, but I thought it was cool when we got John "Tex" Gibson, from the old Caster days, back on Tracker. When Marty Jimenez and I were moving out to California in 1983, we stayed at Gibson's house. That guy was exactly like I thought he would be: super cool, humble and down to Earth. If you took the word pro away from him, that dude was just a bro. I loved his style, and everybody loved the guy. I think the title on his business card was "Friend." Getting him back on Tracker was one of the best things, which also made Jeff Phillips want to be part of the deal after he saw how cool and supportive we were of Tex. Neil Blender was really close with Jeff. I liked Phillips, because we would talk even when he was on Gullwing. I wasn't trying to steal any of their guys, but I started rapping to Phillips and connected a little bit more.

During the 1986 World's Fair in Vancouver, I was judging the contest, and playing team manager for Tracker. Of course, I drove other team riders, who didn't have a real team manager, to the events and back to their hotels, too. That's just the way I rolled for Indy or Gullwing. I hooked up anyone who needed it. Anyway, I went to the hospital with Jeff Phillips, who had a seven-inch splinter in his foot, because nobody else could go with him. The dude was in a lot of pain. I was sitting there with him in his room. It had nothing to do with Tracker. I just wanted to hang with him and give him some support. There was another time when he said he needed more [sponsor] support. I said, "I'll send you some trucks, but you've got to quit Gullwing first. Just make sure that's what you want to do." He replied, "No, man, I want to hang out with you guys," and that's what he did. From that point on, I had to deal with him eating 20 bags of candy at every contest, and missing contests because he had tooth problems galore. He missed, like, three contests, because he had to have oral surgeries. I miss the guy to death. I just remember talking to him, hanging out with him, and how he told me he didn't care what anybody else was able to do; he just wanted to be great in skateboarding. I think he was

great at skateboarding. He can be proud of that. His mom can be proud of that.

Obviously, Tony Hawk, Lester Kasai, Adrian Demain, Sam Cunningham, Omar Hassan, Dan Rogers, Ron Chatman, Jeremy Klein and all of the people I travelled with on some crazy trips. All of those guys were really good to work with. During new eras, when Tracker got a new cycle of riders, I never lost touch with the guys I had great memories with, that I built relationships with and supported all of those years. They did just as much for the company, too, with their skating, innovations, progression, and just representing. Even if they left to ride other trucks, the only thing that changed was the shape of a truck, because those guys are my bros for life. There were a lot of things I worked on with people, like videos, and Bucky Lasek coming up. It was really cool seeing this little kid from Baltimore finally get to the point where he was going to be one of the leaders of the future, and he's still killing it today. Omar Hassan. Everyone who's ridden Trackers—even those who have come and gone—still has that little bond from the time that they spent with Tracker. They know they were part of something really special, too—a really great team with a history.

The list goes on for a long time, because there are a lot of guys, like John Grigley. I could just keep going. I liked working with the guys who came from other areas, like Ray Underhill, East Coast guys getting some attention. Mike McGill was back in Florida most the time, until he moved out to California. It was really easy for me to relate to all of the people from different areas in the US, and then around the world—all of the vert guys and freestyle guys. Tracker wanted to have the best guys all around the world, and people wanted to be on Tracker, they wanted to be affiliated with it. They felt like if you were on Tracker, you rode for the top company in skateboarding.

Do you have any closing comments?
When you talk about the history of Tracker over time, it's really hard to name any other brand that's as tried, tested and true. Tracker is right there at the top of skateboarding history. Tracker has contributed much more than just a truck to skateboarding. To all of the riders who have come and gone from Tracker, it's been a place to go for support and gain camaraderie. It's also been a hub for a lot of different things besides skateboarding. Some people who worked there have moved on to contribute more to skateboarding.

The Ridge
INTERVIEW

"From the deep hollers of Huntington west of Virginia, across the paved prairie and out past to the mountains of majestic concrete, Ridge rolled supreme, always advancing the sport."—**CR Stecyk III** (skateboard industry analyst / historian / documentarian / participant / visionary)

Read the full-length interview at trackertrucks.com

Above: **The Ridge on the fridge. Bryan Ridgeway slaps a rock on a chilly extension at Sargepark in Oceanside, California, circa 1988.** Photo: Steve Sherman

Tony Jetton, 1979. Photo: Jim Goodrich

Lester Kasai, 1988. Photo: Grant Brittain

Tony Jansson, mid 1980s. Photo: Grant Brittain

NOLAN JOHNSON

Trucks You Can Trust Since 1975 / trackertrucks.com

Nolan Johnson, Winter 2007. Photo: George Medino

"The best trucks I've ever ridden are Trackers. They improved my vertical skating 100%. Super smooth, steady lines, no wobbles.—Tony Jetton

Kyle Jensen, 1979. Photo: Lance Smith

"The people at Tracker took care of me like family. They taught me, they cared for me, they supported me.—Lester Kasai

Marty Jimenez, 1987. Photo: Unknown

Torger Johnson (RIP), 1975. Photo: Lance Smith

John Hughes, 1976.
Photo: Larry Balma

Ron Hudgins, 1977. Photo: Jim Goodrich

Roy Jamieson, 1977.
Photo: Unknown

Rick Howell, 1976. Photo: Di Dootson

Joe Johnson, late 1980s.
Photo: Sean Sullivan

359

klein

Jeremy Klein, February 1994.

Jeff Kendall, 1983. Photo: Bob Pribble

kuhns
tracker
send a buck for stickers & info   p.o. box 398, cardiff, ca 92007

Bobby Kuhns, May 1994.

John Hutson, 1976. P: Unknown

Rodney Jesse (RIP).
Photo: Lance Smith

Eddie Katz, 1975.
Photo: Larry Balma

Mike Jesiolowski, 1978. Photo: Suzie Palmer

Derek Krasauskas, 2000s. Photo: Unknown

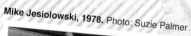

" **Tracker is the real deal.**—Hunter Joslin "

Jeff Jones.
Photo: Steve Sherman

Steve Lis, 1975.
Photo: Larry Balma

Shogo Kubo (RIP), 1977.
Photo: Boyd Harnell

Bert Lamar, 1979. Photo: Lance Smith

360

Bucky Lasek, late 1980s. Photo: Grant Brittain

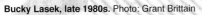

Daniel Lebron, August 1999.

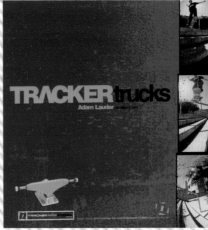

Jim Korten. Photo: Di Dootson

Curt Lindgren, 1977. Photo: Jim Goodrich

Steve Lippman, 1979. Photo: Lance Smith

Adam Lauder, July 2001.

Kurt Kimbell, 1978.
Photo: Jim Goodrich

Jeff King, 1990s.
Photo: Grant Brittain

Arthur Lake, 1976.
Photo: CR Stecyk III

Fabian Kravetz, 1980s.
Photo: Grant Brittain

Dominic Kekich, late 1980s.
Photo: Ed Dominick

Peter Kiss, 1980s.
Photo: Grant Brittain

I used to skate. Now I just hang around.

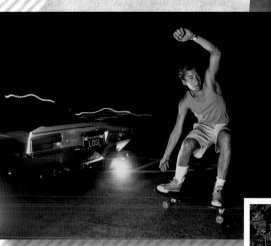

Mitch Long, 1979.
Photo: James Cassimus

Allen Losi, 1986. Photo: Grant Brittain

Keith Lenharr, late 1980s.
Photo: Doug Pensinger

Chris Livingston, 1980s.
Photo: Lloyd

Hans "Hazze" Lindgren, 1980s.
Photo: Grant Brittain

Brian Logan, 1976.

Brad Logan, 1975.
Photo: Chuck Edwall

Robin Logan, 1977.
Photo: Tim Bee

Bruce Logan, 1978. Photo: Lance Smith

Chris May, 1983. Photo: Unknown

362

Tony Magnusson, 1987. Photo: Grant Brittain

Ralph Morris, 1978. Photo: Hazleton

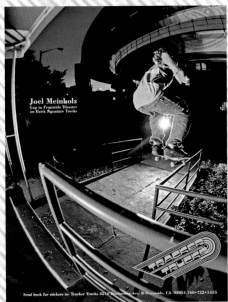

Joel Meinholz
Gap to Frontside Disaster
on Hawk Signature Trucks

Send back for stickers to: Tracker Trucks 3210 Production Ave, B Oceanside, CA. 92054 760•722•1455

Joel Meinholz, August 1998.

luke mckirdy

TRACKER

new hawk trackers

TR CKER

Kym Milburn, 1978. Photo: Lance Smith

Luke McKirdy, January 1997.

PT Martinez

PT Martinez, March 1995.

Frank Messman, 1980s.
Photo: Lance Mountain

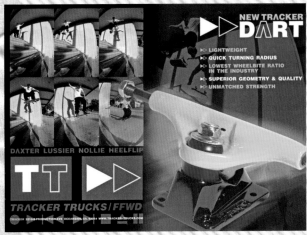

NEW TRACKER
DART

▸▸ LIGHTWEIGHT
▸▸ QUICK TURNING RADIUS
▸▸ LOWEST WHEELBITE RATIO IN THE INDUSTRY
▸▸ SUPERIOR GEOMETRY & QUALITY
▸▸ UNMATCHED STRENGTH

DAXTER LUSSIER NOLLIE HEELFLIP

TT ▸▸

TRACKER TRUCKS / FFWD

trac

John Lucero, 1982. Photo: Unknown

Brian Martin, early 1980s.
Photo: Grant Brittain

Daxter Lussier, March 1999.

Dennis Martinez, 1978.
Photo: Unknown

Cameron Martin, 1980s.
Photo: Unknown

Jim McCall, 1980s.
Photo: Unknown

Chuy Madrigal, 1976. Photo: Larry Balma

Colin McKay, late 1980s. Photo: Grant Brittain

Leslie Anne Miller, 1983. Photo: Per Holknekt

Darrell Miller, 1977. Photo: Glenn Miyoda

Sonny Miller (RIP), 1980. Photo: Grant Brittain

Patrick Melcher, 2014.
Photo: Marfa Capadanno

Bob Mohr, 1976. Photo: Unknown

Conrad Miyoshi (RIP), 1976.
Photo: Larry Balma

Glenn Miyoda, 1978. Photo: Unknown

Nate McGlone, 1990s.
Photo: Jesse De Martino

Trackers – Building Trucks Not Trends Since 1975
The infamous Belconnen Bowl in Canberra, Australia / www.trackertrucks.com

John McGaughey, 1978.
Photo: Unknown

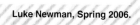

Luke Newman, Spring 2006.

Mike McGill, 1980s.
Photo: Britt Parrott

Every great, legendary skater came up on Trackers.—Sonny Miller

Sean Miller (RIP), 1980s.
Photo: Dave Swift

Allen Midgett, 1980s.
Photo: Tod Swank

Ellen Oneal, 1976. Photo: Warren Bolster

DART 149MM

Mick Mulhall, 2000s. Photo: David Pang

Donny Myhre, 1987. Photo: Grant Brittain

Layne Oaks, 1977. Photo: Lance Smith

Tuan Nguyen, late 1980s. Photo: Jay Bridges

Art "Rat" Mingeaud, 1977. Photo: L. Smith

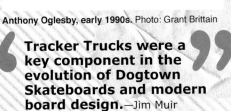

Anthony Oglesby, early 1990s. Photo: Grant Brittain

> **Tracker Trucks were a key component in the evolution of Dogtown Skateboards and modern board design.** —Jim Muir

Chris OP Moore, early 1980s.
Photo: Davo Scheich

Jim Muir, 1976.
Photo: CR Stecyk III

Andrew "Morri" Morrison, 1980s.
Photo: Dave Swift

365

Rodney Mullen, 1983. Photo: Larry Balma

Bryan Pennington, 1987. Photo: Grant Brittain

Britt Parrott, late 1980s. Photo: Grant Brittain

David Paul, 1977. Photo: Jim Goodrich

Günter Mokulys, 1980s. Photo: Uli Niewohner

George Orton, 1977. Photo: James Cassimus

Stacy Peralta, 1977. Photo: Glenn Miyoda

David Nielson, late 1980s. Photo: Grant Brittain

Jeff Newton, 1982. Photo: Unknown

Moses Padilla, 1977. Photo: Bruce Hazelton

Don Nelson, late 1980s. Photo: Marshall Denton

Geoff Ortlip, 1980s. Photo: Bill Minadio

> " My only truck sponsor from the beginning 'til the end.—Bruno Peeters "

> " The invention of the Tracker Truck was one of those pivotal moments in skateboarding when we could suddenly see that there was going to be a future for us as skateboarders.—Stacy Peralta "

Bernie O'Dowd, late 1980s.
Photo: Grant Brittain

Monty Nolder, 1979.
Photo: Jim Goodrich

Tom Padaca, 1976.
Photo: Unknown

Mark Partain, late 1980s.
Photo: Grant Brittain

Jeff Phillips (RIP), late 1980s. Photo: Grant Brittain

John Pryor, early 1990s.
Photo: Steve Sherman

Don Pollard, mid 1980s. Photo: Grant Brittain

Bobby Piercy (RIP), 1977. Photo: Goodrich

Matt Pennington, 2014. Photo: Unknown

TODD PRINCE

Todd Prince, May 1989.

Jon Nixon, 2015.
Photo: Unknown

Ty Page, 1976. Photo: Erik Gross

> As far as I'm concerned, the Tracker logo is iconic. I felt like I was part of something rad! —Bryan Pennington

367

By Larry Balma

Buddy Carr grew up in a little farm town called Springboro, just outside of Dayton, Ohio. In 1985, he moved out to Oceanside, California to work in the shop at Tracker and live the California dream. Starting out as an accomplished grinder of truck castings, Buddy eventually graduated to become Tracker's shipping manager, shop manager, product manager and, after Bryan Ridgeway left, team manager. Part of the Alva posse, he was well-known for sending his long dreadlocks flying during frontside Smith grinds on the coping of many a backyard pool. After 25 years at Tracker, Buddy departed in 2010 to start Tail Tap, an online skateboard shop, and run marathons when he's not busy slashing up some local vert.—GSD

DEC. 1, 1988

SKATEBOARDING IS NOT A CRIME

When did you start skateboarding?
I don't even know what year it was. I must have been about 12 or 13. I remember my first board: it was this blue, plastic thing with hard urethane wheels and trucks that didn't turn. But, I was so amped to get it.

When did you get your first Trackers?
It must have been in the early '80s, when I got a bigger skateboard and needed wider trucks—probably 1980 or '81. I tried a bunch of different trucks. You know, when you're coming up in skateboarding and you try this truck and that truck? I always liked Trackers because of the Copers, the way they bolted onto the sides. It was cool.

Tell us about moving to the West Coast.
I knew that I wanted to come to the West Coast, because that's where the two remaining skateparks were—Upland and Del Mar. I knew that Del Mar was the place I really

wanted to be. I was going to ride my bicycle to California if I couldn't afford an airline ticket. I was gong to get here one way or the other. I ended up getting a one-way ticket to Los Angeles for only $99. Eventually, within a week, I had made my way down to the Del Mar area. It was quite a journey to find a place to live. But, I was at the skatepark, so nothing else really mattered.

How did you end up working at Tracker?
Through Bill Danforth, I had an open door to Tracker, because he was a Tracker rider. Back in '83 and '84, we didn't have cell phones or Internet, so you got a zine in the mail from somebody on the West Coast, or you knew someone who was traveling back and forth. Bill Danforth would make these journeys in his Ford Escort back and forth from the Midwest to the West Coast all the time. So, he was the connection; he opened the door for me at Tracker. Bill said, "Go apply for a job at Tracker when you get there." So, long story short, I did just that. [Tracker Peggy's mom] Sam Mullen gave me the job application. I filled it out and used Bill Danforth as a reference. I'm sure he nudged Tracker Larry or Peggy, because I somehow managed to get a job there within a week of arriving on the West Coast. And that job lasted 25 years! So, I owe a lot to Bill Danforth. He opened the door for me, and I'm thankful for that.

What jobs did you do at Tracker?
My very first job there was pressing kingpins. My arm was so sore after a day of pressing hundreds of kingpins. I went from there to packaging Lappers and Copers. I remember pressing Lappers. I put them in the toaster oven, then in a press for 10 minutes, followed by a garbage can full of water to cool 'em down. I was amazed, like, "This is how they're made?" I thought some big, technical machine made them, but it was just a skateboarder putting plastic in a toaster oven. We also used that toaster oven at lunchtime to cook our lunch (laughs). Eventually, I started grinding trucks, which was cool, because I could earn extra money—a penny per part. So, if I ground a thousand trucks, I could earn an extra 10 bucks per day. That was my goal every day—to get an extra 10 bucks, which would feed me for a couple of days. At the time, I was making $3.35 per hour, so an extra $10 per day was a lot of money. If you think back on it, you wonder, "How could I survive on that?" But, you're skateboarding, living at the skatepark, and nothing else matters.

Well, look at how slim you are. You probably didn't eat that much anyway! Tell us about skating pro for Alva.
I don't know that I was ever officially pro. I didn't have my name on an Alva skateboard. I was just part of that whole '80s posse, which was rad, because it wasn't like I was trying to join something. I just got accepted. I remember Dave Duncan saying, "Hey, we want you to ride this board." It was one of those, "Wow, really?" things. Before, I always bought Alva boards, because I was into it. It was the anti-Powell. It was "over there," and that's where I always played. I was nev-

er in the popular crowd. I wanted to be on the fringe. So, being given one by the team manager was amazing. Then being invited to these sessions with Tony Alva at Gonzales pool in LA was crazy. It was like, "Pinch myself, is this really happening?"

As the Tracker team manager, who was your favorite skater?
There are so many good skateboarders, I don't know if I have a favorite. All of the Tracker riders stand out. But, as for who really broke ground and made things change, of course, Tony Hawk did with his innovation. But, I think the guy who really stands out would be Mark Gonzales, for taking a Rodney Mullen stationary Ollie and clearing a three-foot gap. It was amazing. So he's the one who really stands out in my mind, not as a favorite, but the one who rode Trackers who really opened up a whole new era in skateboarding—Ollieing up things and over things.

I remember at an ASR trade show up in Long Beach, I followed him out in front of the convention center and he Ollied up onto a handrail and slid down it. I was completely blown away.
We had a picnic table at Tracker, and it was part of the pro street course [at a contest in San Diego], with the U-curb. I remember seeing Mark Ollie up to a pivot and just being blown away. We wondered, "How does he Ollie up to the seat?" Then, after the contest, we put it back in the factory, and we tried it for weeks and weeks, but there was no way

Buddy Carr
INTERVIEW

we could make it. It was amazing. You look back and realize it was groundbreaking.

Do you have a favorite Tracker ad?
You're talking hundreds and hundreds of ads. I don't know which one would stand out. The early ones in *Skateboarder* magazine, when Alan Gelfand started doing Ollies. I think Steve Caballero was on Trackers then, too, and I remember seeing pictures of him and Christian Hosoi. The pictures of those guys in the parks stand out. I think it was the colors and the whole mystique, because, at the time, we didn't really have skateparks where I grew up. It was just this West Coast thing.

Did you ever sleep at Tracker?
I slept outside [behind the Tracker building] in a little hut that I made out of pallets and cardboard. That was crazy. You had a guard dog named Kahn, and I'd have to save a little bit of my dinner and throw it into the far corner, then the dog would go chase the food so I could hop over the fence and get into my little pallet shack.

Why was Tracker Trucks so important to the history of skateboarding?
It's the blueprint for the modern truck. Every truck now looks back to Tracker. You can change the look, you can change the angles to make it turn more or less, but Tracker's the blueprint, what you work off of.

Read the full-length interview at trackertrucks.com

Above: **Buddy Carr slashes a frontside Smith grind at the Pala pool in Oceanside, California for this Tracker "Rasta Trucks" ad, January 1989.**

Rhino Team: Teddy Emrich, 1978. Photo: Lance Smith

Rhino Team, 1977. Photo: Lance Smith

Rhino Team: Rick Wynne + Mitch Mitchell, 1976. Photo: Warren Bolster

Bruno Peeters, late 1980s. Photo: Grant Brittain

John Reeves, May 1995.

Joe Perez, 1980s. Photo: Grant Brittain

Bobby Reeves, circa 1986. Photo: Jim Goodrich

Andrew Reynolds, 1990s. Photo: Unknown

Davy Philip, 1980s. Photo: Unknown

Bryan Ridgeway, 1980s. Photo: Brittain

Laban Pheidias, 1990s. Photo: Mike Ballard

Steve Revord, Spring 2004. Photo: Dan Sturt

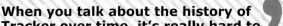

> **When you talk about the history of Tracker over time, it's really hard to name any other brand that's as tried, tested and true.** —Bryan Ridgeway

369

Collin Ruloff, late 1980s. Photo: Mike Blake

Dan Rogers, February 1997.

Jordan Richter, early 1990s. Photo: Steve Sherman

Shreddi Repas, 1978. Photo: Jim Goodrich

Ray "Bones" Rodriguez, 1981. Photo: CR Stecyk III

Toby Russell, late 1970s. Photo: Dobie Campbell

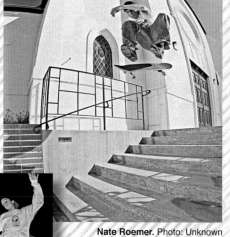

Charlie Ransom, 1977. Photo: Lance Smith

Chris Robison (RIP), early 1980s.
Photo: Unknown

Nate Roemer. Photo: Unknown

"Then and now, Tracker Trucks have always impressed me with how they've kept their finger on the pulse of skateboard evolution." —Shreddi Repas

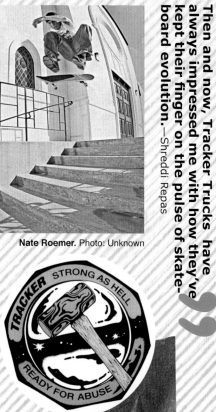

Sam Puccio, 1976.
Photo: Larry Balma

Jimmy Plumer, April / May 1979.
Photo: Wynn Miller

Duane Pitre, early 1990s.
Photo: Steve Sherman

Steve Schisler, 1975. Photo: Larry Balma

Rory Russell, 1977. Photo: Lance Smith

Steve Rocco, mid 1980s. Photo: Grant Brittain

Duke Rennie, 2014. Photo: Lance Smith

Eric Sanderson, November 1989.

Doug "Pineapple" Saladino, 1977. Photo: Jim Goodrich

Everett Rosecrans (right). Photo: Grant Brittain

Kelly Rosecrans, early 1980s. Photo: Unknown

Jason Richardson, 1980s. Photo: Xeno

Fred Reeves, early 1990s. Photo: Sutherland Boswell

Marty Ramos, early 1980s. Photo: Unknown

Wentzle Ruml, 2000s. Photo: Patrick Malpass

" I currently ride Midtrack Ultralights with Copers. I've been riding the same plates and trucks for 33 years. How's that for a quality product? —Duke Rennie

Brian "Pushead" Schroeder, 1982.
Photo: Mike Baltes

SkateBoarder
A SURFER PUBLICATION
VOL 5, NO. 10 MAY 1979 $1.50

GIANT PIPES
Outback Odyssey

SHOGO KUBO
From DT to Cherry Hill

WIPEOUTS
On the Verge of Disaster

BONGO
A Most Unforgettable Character

PLUS
International Competition
Free Skatepark Passes

Doug Schneider, May 1979. Photo: James Cassimus

Actual Saiz

Steve Saiz (not shown actual size)

Steve Saiz, August 1988.

TRACKER

Mark "Schmiddy" Schmid, 2000s.

"Tracker 'til I die...four
wheels or eight!—Jimi Scott

SkateBoarder
A SURFER PUBLICATION
VOL 5, NO. 12 JULY 1979 $1.50

STEVE OLSON
Skateboarder of the Year
Exclusive Interview

MAJOR PRO/AM
COMPETITION
Florida and California

TURNINGPOINT
RAMP
Getting Higher
Through Technology

PLUS
Freestyle 79
Mellow Cat vs. the Nerds
Free Skatepark Passes

Jimi Scott, 1987.

Tim Scroggs, July 1979. Photo: James Cassimus

Denny Riorden, 1980s.
Photo: David Barranco

Bill Robertson.
Photo: Unknown

"Another thing about the Ultralite
that was appealing was the light
weight, which allowed me to get
that extra pop I wanted!—Willy Santos

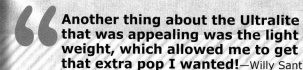

Kent Senatore on
TRACKER HAFTRACK TRUCKS
Just one of the radical
VAL SURF boys Trucks
You Can Trust

TRACKER TRUCKS
P.O. Box 217
Cardiff-by-the-Sea, CA 92007 Photo: Chuck Edwall

Kent Senatore, 1977.
Photo: Stan Sharp

Joe Roper, 1975.
Photo: Larry Balma

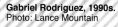

Gabriel Rodriguez, 1990s.
Photo: Lance Mountain

Tommy Ryan, 1976.
Photo: Chuck Edwall

Rodd Saunders, 1977.
Photo: James Cassimus

Joachim "Yo-Yo" Schulz, 2010s.
Photo: Matt Pingel

John Schultes, late 1980s.
Photo: Mark Zemnick

Christian Seewaldt, 1980s.

TRACKER TRUCK CO.

Marty Schaub, 1977. Photo: Warren Bolster

Paul Schmitt, 1980s. Photo: Unknown

SkateBoarder

INTERVIEW:
John Hutson,
The Racer Of The Year.
"...You only lose if you quit."

THE RAMP RAGE

AN EAST COAST RAP

PLUS
SKATEBOARD MADNESS:
THE FIRST IN A SERIES
OF TRAVEL ADVENTURES:
IN FLORIDA
AND HEADING SOUTH

Scott Senatore, March 1978. Photo: Guy Motil

Willy Santos, 1992. Photo: Grant Brittain

Pierre André Senizergues, August 1988.

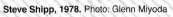

Gary Sanderson, late 1980s.
Photo: Grant Brittain

Steve Shipp, 1978. Photo: Glenn Miyoda

Kyle Jensen + Steve Sherman, 1979. Photo: Jim Goodrich

Tracker Trucks ~ Since 1975 ~ Quality Never Goes Out Of Style
Elliot Sloan / photo Brian Fick / www.trackertrucks.com

Elliot Sloan, Summer 2006. Photo: Brian Fick

Lance Smith, 1976. Photo: Art Brewer

Reese Simpson, mid 1980s. Photo: Grant Brittain

Tom Sims (RIP), 1977. Photo: Unknown

Jim Sigurdson, 1978.
Photo: Lance Smith

Danny Smith, 1977. Photo: Unknown

Jack Smith, 1980s.
Photo: Grant Brittain

Mark Sinclair, 1977. Photo: Robert Vente

Sky Siljeg, 2000s.
Photo: Unknown

Bob Skoldberg, 1976.
Photo: Unknown

Dale Smith, 1970s.
Photo: Lance Smith

374

Denis Shufeldt, 2000s.
Photo: Unknown

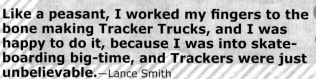

> " Like a peasant, I worked my fingers to the bone making Tracker Trucks, and I was happy to do it, because I was into skateboarding big-time, and Trackers were just unbelievable. "—Lance Smith

Randy Stahlecker, 1979. Photo: Lance Smith

Lee Smith, 1990s. Photo: Shelby Woods

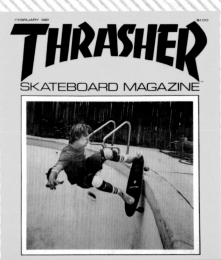

FEBRUARY 1981 $1.00

THRASHER
SKATEBOARD MAGAZINE™

LAKEWOOD HALF-PIPE PRO/AM

COMMUNITY SKATEPARKS

EASTERN FRONT   INTERVIEW, SHAWN PEDDIE

Chris Strople, February 1981. Photo: Kevin Thatcher

Mike Stelmasky, 2000s. Photo: Unknown

Marty Smith, 1977. Photo: Unknown

Dan Sturt, mid 1980s. Photo: Mark Waters

Marc Smith, 1977. Photo: James Cassimus

Mike Speranza, 1987. Photo: Tod Swank

TRACKER TRUCKS

Kevin Staab, 1980. Photo: Grant Brittain

Steve Steadham, 1983. Photo: Grant Brittain

Kenny Stelmasky, 2000s. Photo: Lance Smith

Tom Stewart, 1977. Photo: Lance Smith

Anders Pulpanek Tellen, 1989.

Kristian Svitak, 1990s. Photo: Joe Picciolo

Adam Taylor / Tracker Trucks - Trucks You Can Trust Since 1975 / trackertrucks.co

Adam Taylor, Summer 2008.

Kevin Thatcher, 1978. Photo: Glenn Miyoda

Jeff Taylor, July 1995. Photo: Dave Swift

TRACKERtrucks

Joey Suriel

Joey Suriel, November 2001.

Chet Thomas, late 1980s.
Photo: Grant Brittain

CR Stecyk III, 1976. Photo: Warren Bolster

Jeremy Stoetzel, 1990s.
Photo: Seu Trinh

Jeff Tatum, 1979.
Photo: Lance Smith

Kirk Talbot, 1978.
Photo: James Cassimus

Peter Tholl, 1976.

376

Geno Tocci, 1980. Photo: Lance Smith

Laura Thornhill, 1976. Photo: Warren Bolster

Vince Turner, 1975.
Photo: Larry Balma

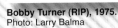

Bobby Turner (RIP), 1975.
Photo: Larry Balma

Danny Trailer, 1977.
Photo: Chris Yandall

Desiree Von Essen, 1977.
Photo: Unknown

Massimo Van Der Plas, 1985.
Photo: Grant Brittain

Martin Van Doren, 1980s.
Photo: Uli Niewohner

Lonnie Toft, May 1978. Photo: Boyd Harnell

John Tuisl, Summer 2003. Photo: John Yunker

Mike Vallely, mid 1980s.
Photo: Grant Brittain

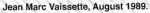

Jean Marc Vaissette, August 1989.

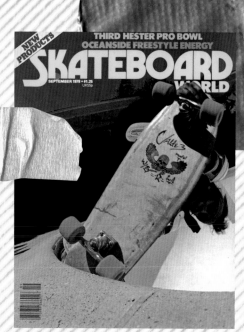

Jerry Valdez, September 1978. Photo: Stan Sharp

Ray Underhill, late 1980s. Photo: Grant Brittain

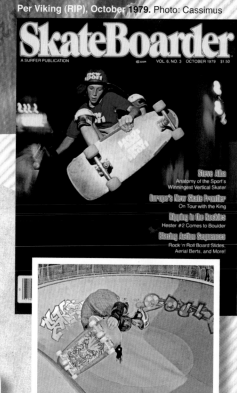

Per Viking (RIP), October 1979. Photo: Cassimus

Jay Vonesh, 2009. Photo: Harold Osborne

Vicky Vickers, 1978. Photo: Glenn Miyoda

Tim Von Werne, 2000s. Photo: Kuda

Morris Wainwright, late 1980s.
Photo: Pete Diantoni

Chuck Wampler, late 1980s.
Photo: Dave Swift

Miki Vuckovich, 1984.
Photo: GSD

Bruce Walker.
Photo: Steve Gaidini

Brian Wainwright, 1987.
Photo: Tod Swank

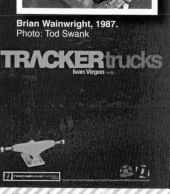

> **With their rounded and wider axle design, Trackers got on and off the coping with more control, which was great to take my skating to another level of radical.** —Jerry Valdez

Ivan Virgen, October 2001.

Charlie Watson, 1975.
Photo: Larry Balma

Gail Webb, 1977.
Photo: Unknown

Mike Williams, 1975.
Photo: Larry Balma

Jack Waterman, June 1978.
Photo: Boyd Harnell

Per Welinder, mid 1980s. Photo: Grant Brittain

Danny Webster, late 1980s. Photo: Grant Brittain

Tabias Walker, December 1994.

Robby Williams, 1978. Photo: Chuck Saccio

Robbie Weir, early 1980s. Photo: Unknown

Cindy Whitehead, 1980. Photo: Unknown

Mike Weed (RIP), 1978. Photo: Glenn Miyoda

Gregg Weaver, 1976. Photo: Lance Smith

You can count on Tracker, the most dependable truck I've seen. —Gregg Weaver

Chris Yandall (RIP), 1976. Photo: Lance Smith

Matt Wood, 1980s.
Photo: Dan Estabrook

Dan Wilkes, 1987. Photo: Jeff Newton

John Winchester, 1978. Photo: Lance Smith

Barry Zaritsky, 1980s.

Simon Woodstock, 2014. Photo: Bryce Kanights

John Woodstock, 1978.
Photo: Glen E. Friedman

Alan Young • Tracker Trucks - Since 1975 / Guaranteed For Life / www.trackertrucks.com

Alan Young, Summer 2005. Photo: Dan Sturt

Scott Williams, 1978. Photo: Lance Smith

Billy Yeron, 1978. Photo: Unknown

Tiger Williams, 2000s. Photo: Unknown

Danny Yarbrough, 1978. Photo: Lance Smith

'Tracker Trucks are reliable, trustworthy and perform well.'—Chris Yandall

'Tracker laid the groundwork everyone followed. Their designs still hold up today—that is what makes history.'—Dan Wilkes

380

Kevin "The Worm" Anderson
Kyle Anderson
Steve Anderson
Ryan Aningalan
Scott Armstrong
Don Baumea (page 331)
Teddy "Boy" Bennett
Terry Bixler
Rick Blackhart (page 105)
Gorm Boberg
Robert Boerleider
Peter Boronski
Richard Brand
Andy Brayman
Jamie Budge
John Bull
Morgan Burgess
Francisco Burgos
Dean Calvert
Paul Campbell
Dave Carroll
Marty Carter
Craig Casselberry
Luis Castillo
Pat Channita
Chris Chaput
Scott Clemens
Marshall Coben
Ian Cocking
Judith Cohen
Cliff Coleman
Sean Collins
Wrex Cook
Jade Corn
Jeremie Daclin
Rick Denton
Dave Dilberg
Dan Dominy
Will Dootson
Charlie Dubois
Greg Ducolon (RIP)
Sam Durik
Adam Effertz
Jeff Emrich - Rhino Team
Skip Engblom (page 80)
Mischo Erban
Mark Erikson
Ray Fennessey
Steve Ferris
David Ferry

Perry Fisser
Gene Foresi
Ray Gardea
Jules Gayton
Dean Godfrey
Steve Gratton
Jackie Grayson
Eric Grease
Chris Griffiths
Marty Grimes
Eric Grisham
Kadir Guirey
John Haas
Dodie Hackamack
Keith Hagan
Kevin Hagan
Peter Haglund
Mark Hamilton
Tony Harnell
Stanford Harris
Mark Hazziza
Dan Hessler
Eric Hilton
Lonnie Hiramoto (page 115)
Mike Hirsch
Steve Hobbie
Herb Hoehn
Don Hoffman
Russ Howell
Bill Hubbard
Paul Hugasian
Wes Humpston
David Hupp
Jamie Ide
Bo Ikeda
Bernt Jahael
Darin "Cookiehead"
   Jenkins (page 294)
Mike Johnson
Rodney Johnson
Rudy Johnson (page 156)
Chris Jones
David Jones
Mark Jones
Gary Keating (RIP)
Mike Kinney
Thomas Kundinger
Stefan Larance
Jimmy Leaphart (page 292)
Steve Leistikow

Ron Lemen
Pat Love
Joerg Ludewig
Chris "Wez" Lundry
Joe Lynch
Sean Mailey
Brian Mank
Guy Mariano (page 156)
Doug Marker
Killian Martin
Matt Matlock
Casey McCrystal
Jodi McDonald
John McGuire
David Mock
Paul Molina
Chip Morton (page 171)
Jamie Mosberg
Pat Ngoho
Dana Nicholson
Steve Noble
Tosiyuki Noda
Steve Olson (page 105)
James O'Mahoney
Manuel Palacious
Steve Park
Leigh Parkin
Paul Patala
Les Pearlman
Dave Perry
Joe Picciolo
Steve Piccolo
Casper Plass
Will Power
Jean Postec (page 294)
Nathan Pratt (page 81)
Bob Pribble
Tommy Redcay
Fran Richards
Mark Richards
Scott Ricks
Jimmy Riha (page 327)
Leslie Ritzma
Jesse Roach
Dan Roberts
Andrew "Andy" Rogers
Billy Rohan
Tom Rohrback
Phil Rouchard
Shane Rouse

Craig Rowe
Tim Runningen
John Sabloski
Richard Salazar
Bob Schmeltzer
Mitch Schmidt
Terrill Schmidt
Carl Schultz
Sean Scott
Anthony Sedilla
Clyde Semmoh
Steve Shelton
Rasmus Skousen
Jay Smith
Sue Smith
Christian Smithers
Go Go Spreiter
Keith Stephenson
Kurt Stevenson
Brad Strandlund
Matt Strople
Martin Sweeney
Steve Szabados
Don Szabo
Mort Taber
Ozzie Taylor
Dee Dee Thunders
Tion Torrence
Mark "Tank" Toycen
John Trimble
Tom Trozera
Patrick Truitt
Billy Valdes (page 258)
Steve Villarreal
Jeff "Mogul Man" Voegeli
Eric Von Preising
Jan Waage
Chuck Walstead
Andre "Andy" Walton
John Warneke
Dwayne Waxer
Frank Wheeler
Jonas Wikstrom
Willy Woo
Matt Wood
Woody Woodward
Terrence Yoshizawa
David Zakrzewski
Doug Zyskowski (RIP)

Mark Ghio, 1970s.
Photo: Larry Balma

Steve Angus and his wife Sal, 1980s.
Photo: Unknown

Joe Bowers, late 1980s. Photo: Unknown

Tracker crew, circa 1977. Photo: Lance Smith

Jamie Briggs, late 1980s.
Photo: Peggy Cozens

Betty Moore, Sam Mullen, 1980s.
Photo: Louise Balma

Dave Uecker, Ottis Tavlin, late 1980s.
Photo: Louise Balma

Chuck Edwall, 1970s. Photo: Unknown

382

TRACKER
STAFF

I always tried to run Tracker as a family unit that started with our staff and ultimately extended to our entire team. Families have some spats from time to time and cousins may move on, but we all had good times growing up together. The next few pages is our family photo album. Note that all of Tracker's key people were skateboarders and possibly surfers, as well. Many were also designers and entrepreneurs who went on to form successful companies of their own.—**LMB**

Dawn Dominy, 1977. Photo: Unknown

"Dave Dominy conceived and ordered four of these fish-shaped surfboards with skateboard graphics for himself, Keith Hagen and me. This one was 6' 8" long and shaped by Topper in Point Loma, San Diego, California. This was my favorite surfboard in the late '70s."—Larry Balma

Joe D'Elia, 1970s. Photo: Michelle D'Elia

Di Dootson and Lance Smith, circa late 1970s. Photo: Unknown

Laurie Balma, 1980s. Photo: Olan Mills

Kevin Bergthold, 1980s. Photo: Louise Balma

Brian Selstrom, 1989. Photo: Unknown

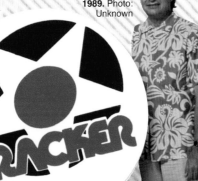

TRACKER

Laurie Balma, 1975. Photo: Larry Balma

Keith Hagen, 1978. Photo: Unknown

Tracker factory team, 1990. Back row, left to right: **Buddy Carr, Marc Hostetter, Beau Brown (seated), Luis Castillo.** Middle row, left to right: **Terrill Schmidt, Keith Lenharr, Bryan Ridgeway.** Front row, left to right: **Dylan Baker, Joe Bowers, Steve Sherman.** Photo: Unknown

Tom Karre, 1980s.
Photo: Louise Balma

Bryan Ridgeway, 1980s.
Photo: Louise Balma

John Wright, 1980s.
Photo: Louise Balma

Britt Parrott, late 1980s. Photo: Unknown

John Sepich, Andy Sepich, Wes Jackson, 1990s. Photo: Louise Balma

Evan Shoman, 1980s.
Photo: Unknown

Chris Carter, Dana Ward, 1980s.
Photo: Louise Balma

Marc Hostetter, late 1980s. Photo: Unknown

"Working at Tracker wasn't a job, it was an environment in which people were friends."—Tom Karre

Phil Cilities. Photo: Unknown

Larry Balma's dad, Maurice Balma, and his wife, Sally, circa late 1980s. Photo: Louise Balma

Jim Gray and his wife, Michelle, 1980s (obviously). Photo: Louise Balma

Tracker crew, late 1980s. Photo: Unknown

Linda Prettyman, 1980s. Photo: Louise Balma

Rudy Zamora, Craig Hansen, 1990s. Photo: Larry Balma

Bruce Goose, mid 1980s. Photo: Larry Balma

"Tracker gave back a lot to the skateboarding industry. Tracker has soul."—Linda Prettyman

CR Stecyk III, 1980s. Photo: Louise Balma

Joe Piciollo, 1990s. Photo: Louise Balma

Dave Bergthold, 1990s. Photo: Unknown

Louise Balma, 1980s. Photo: Peggy Cozens

Mark Adair (RIP), 1990s. Photo: Louise Balma

Tracker crew, late 1990s. Photo: Unknown

Julio de la Cruz, 1990s. Photo: Unknown

Richard Vaughan, 2009. Photo: Unknown

Julie Chandler, Linda Prettyman, Rodney Johnson, Jeff Dunn, Stacey Hostetter, Lolita Arredondo 1990s. Photo: L. Balma

Tracker Dan Santovin

Hailing from Cleveland, Ohio, Dan Santovin was asked by his friend Ohio Dave to come and join us in 2002. Ohio Dave was our shipper and also helped Kevin Bergthold run the Tracker team. Dan worked in production and then sales, and ultimately took over team manager duties, acquiring the nickname Tracker Dan, which he still uses to this day. Eventually, Dan moved on to Vans and then Adio shoes, where he worked with teams and marketing. Today, Dan creates a merchandising environment for the Tony Hawk Inc. offices annually, and with the Anasazi Foundation, he works with at-risk teens and young adults walking the trails of the Arizona wild.—**LMB**

Dan Santovin. Photo: Unknown

Tracker Peggy Cozens, Jamie Briggs, late 1980s. Photo: Louise Balma

> **At Tracker, we had a healthy way of nurturing our team. We had real pride in them and respect for their talents and accomplishments.**—Tracker Peggy Cozens

Tracker crew 2014, left to right: **Josephina Hernandez, Jake Stewart, Francisco Velarde, Max Dufour, Alejandro Pantoja.** Photo: Louise Balma

Ohio Dave, 1990s. Photo: Unknown

Russ Calahan, 1990s. Photo: Unknown

Larry Balma, 1980s. Photo: Louise Balma

TRACK

TIME BUBBLE
and the Master of the Universe

The origin of the book you're holding in your hands, *TRACKER - Forty Years of Skateboard History*, extends back to the year 2000, when Miki Vuckovich researched and wrote an article on the history of the brand called "Skateboarding's First Modern Truck" for *TransWorld Skateboarding Business*. Inspired by that 25th anniversary celebration, some "Being There" columns in the same publication penned by Larry Balma starting in 1990 about his own personal history, plus his vast Tracker archives, the idea of a Tracker book began to swirl in Larry's head. Other early instigators included pro skateboarder Darin "Cookie Head" Jenkins, and a while later, fellow pro David Hackett, who also lit a fire under Larry's ass. In 2004, when Independent's *Built to Grind: 25 Years of Hardcore Skateboarding* hit the shelves, a chorus of voices emanating from all corners of the skateboarding community demanded a Tracker book. But, without any concrete motivation, the idea went dormant.

Fast-forward a half-decade. During one of Tracker's moves in 2009, Larry's wife Louise dug out the Tracker collection, which consists of actual trucks plus decks, wheels, apparel, accessories, photos, magazines and much more, and moved it from the Tracker warehouse to a huge barn at their home in the avocado groves of rural Northeast Oceanside, near Fallbrook. Over the next three years, Louise sifted through the collection

and organized it into boxes, complete with Excel spreadsheets to keep track of it all. In 2011, Michael Brooke from *Concrete Wave* magazine showed an interest in the Tracker book and offered to work on it for a few weeks and help get it published. But, Larry realized it would take much more time, and that the book Michael envisioned was far smaller and simpler than the 388-page monster it would eventually become.

By summer 2012, David Hackett re-entered the picture, pushing his concept of a Tracker book to the brand's new owner, pro skateboarder Max Dufour. In February 2013, David and Max had a series of meetings with Larry, Louise, pro skateboarder Tony Mag and former Tracker team manager and photographer Lance Smith in which they devised a business plan for the book and wrote up a budget. Finally, concrete work on the Tracker book began in earnest, as Larry drafted a rough outline and wrote some of the early chapters, and Louise spent months scanning every photo and ad featuring a Tracker rider that she could find. They also emailed out questionnaires to many of Tracker's past team riders for interviews and quotes in the book. Although David was named the creative director of the project early on, he soon figured out that he didn't have time to take on the role in addition to all of his other freelance work. Then

the book went on the back burner yet again.

By late October 2013, it had been six months since I, Garry Davis, a former Tracker team rider, had submitted my answers to the team interview questions when I emailed Larry to check how far along work on the book had progressed. He invited me out to his home to talk shop. When I arrived the next day, Larry explained all of the production hiccups to date, which had made him feel disenchanted with the whole process. I was surprised to learn that David didn't have time to be the art director and that production on the book had stalled. When I asked Larry and Louise if they had anyone else in mind to be the art director, they said no. I replied, "Well, what about me?" They were flabbergasted. They thought I still had a full-time job working at skate shoe company Sole Technology, when in fact I got laid off in a downsizing move four years before and had been freelancing ever since. The fact that I had once been the art director of their magazine *TransWorld Skateboarding* was a huge plus.

After Larry and Louise got the green light from Max, Tony, David and Lance, I was officially brought onboard as the art director and editor of the Tracker book. To meet the deadline of Holiday 2014, it was decided I would need to work on site directly with Larry and Louise in their barn or the thing would never get done. So, I parked my little truck with a camper shell right outside while Louise set up a mini fridge, a microwave oven, and a plastic table for my laptop. I spent the first couple of weeks sifting through and organizing the thousands of images Louise had scanned over the past year. Then Larry, Lance and I chose the cream of the crop, and I spent four months Photoshopping them. Lance also came over every two or three weeks to do long, grueling product photo shoots. Keep in mind I was in a sheet metal barn all winter with no insulation or drywall. It was so freezing cold at night, I had to bundle up in layers and cover up with a sleeping bag as I banged away on my laptop with my exposed face stinging. Finally, around April, I started to actually design the pages of the book while editing and re-writing Larry's main story and all of the team rider interviews. Oh, and I Photoshopped even more photos.

With the sound of barking dogs, howling coyotes, birds scratching around in the metal rafters and bombs from Camp Pendleton rattling the windows, we trudged on. Month after tedious month, it felt like production on the book would never ever end; like I was trapped in some kind of torturous time bubble that Larry Balma, the Master of the Universe, would never let me out of as he laughed maniacally. But, as it turned out, it was precisely this special circumstance—myself working on site seven days per week, taking on three people's jobs: art director, Photoshop artist and editor—that allowed two years' worth of work to be completed in one year to meet the deadline for the book to be printed in time for Tracker's 40th anniversary in 2015. After all of our hard work, Tracker's legacy as the birth of the modern skateboard truck is now set in stone.—**GSD, December 4, 2014**

Patrick Melcher gets totally tucked into this switch wall ride frontside 50-50 in Los Angeles, California, 2008. Photo: Sean Peterson

Back in 1975, Chris Yandall (RIP), was among the first skateboarders to test ride our prototype Tracker Trucks. After cruising around on Dave Dominy's cosmic Corvette skateboard, Chris was quite impressed, but not so much by the board as by the wide Trackers. In fact, he asked Dave if he could remove the trucks and keep them! Chris became Tracker's first sponsored rider and worked at our factory as our shipper and delivery man. He actually took our first phone order from a skate shop in May 1975. Sadly, we lost Chris on the morning of Easter Sunday 2014. He is shown here during his first ride on Trackers in 1975, barefoot on the glassy smooth pavement of La Costa, riding off into the "sunset." Chris Yandall and Tracker Trucks roll forever.